AF327002

Reconstituting the State in Africa

Reconstituting the State in Africa

Edited by
Pita Ogaba Agbese and George Klay Kieh, Jr.

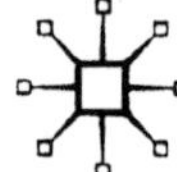

RECONSTITUTING THE STATE IN AFRICA
© Pita Ogaba Agbese and George Klay Kieh, Jr., 2007.

First published in 2007 by
PALGRAVE MACMILLAN™
175 Fifth Avenue, New York, N.Y. 10010 and
Houndmills, Basingstoke, Hampshire, England RG21 6XS
Companies and representatives throughout the world.

PALGRAVE MACMILLAN is the global academic imprint of the Palgrave Macmillan division of St. Martin's Press, LLC and of Palgrave Macmillan Ltd. Macmillan® is a registered trademark in the United States, United Kingdom and other countries. Palgrave is a registered trademark in the European Union and other countries.

ISBN-13: 978–1–4039–7313–9
ISBN-10: 1–4039–7313–X

Library of Congress Cataloging-in-Publication Data

Reconstituting the state in Africa / edited by Pita Ogaba Agbese and George Klay Kieh, Jr.
p. cm.
Papers presented at an international conference.
Includes bibliographical references and index.
ISBN 1–4039–7313–X (alk. paper)
1. Africa—Politics and government—Congresses. 2. Africa—Economic conditions—Congresses. 3. State, The—Congresses. I. Agbese, Pita Ogaba, 1954– II. Kieh, George Klay, 1956–

JQ1875.R425 2007
320.96—dc22   2006040610

A catalogue record for this book is available from the British Library.

Design by Newgen Imaging Systems (P) Ltd., Chennai, India.

First edition: February 2007

10 9 8 7 6 5 4 3 2 1

Printed in the United States of America.

Contents

List of Tables   vii

About the Contributors   ix

Preface   xi

Part I   Background

Chapter 1   Introduction: Democratizing States and State
Reconstitution in Africa   3
Pita Ogaba Agbese and George Klay Kieh, Jr.

Part II   Case Studies

Chapter 2   Statecraft in Botswana: Renegotiating
Development, Legitimacy, and Authority   33
Onalenna Doo Selolwane

Chapter 3   The State in Cote d'Ivoire: Evolution and Constraints   75
Boubacar N'Diaye

Chapter 4   Reinventing and Rebuilding the Ghanaian State:
Toward a New Triumphalism?   105
Emmanuel Kwesi-Aning

Chapter 5   Reflections on the Postcolonial State
in Kenya   127
Anne Nangulu-Ayuku

Chapter 6   Reconfiguring and Reinventing State-Society
Relations in Mauritius   181
Sheila Bunwaree

Chapter 7   The Imperative of Reconstructing the State
in Nigeria: The Politics of Power, Welfare, and
Imperialism in the New Millennium   205
Sylvester Alubo

Chapter 8   The Postapartheid State in South Africa   233
Victoria Maloka

Part III   Prospects for the Future

Chapter 9   State Renewal in Africa: The Lessons   279
Pita Ogaba Agbese and George Klay Kieh, Jr.

Index   295

List of Tables

1.1   UN Peacekeeping operations in Africa as of
      December 2004   5
1.2   Reported privatization activity in Africa:
      Top Eight countries, 1996–2000   15
1.3   Reported privatization transactions in Africa,
      1979–1999   16
1.4   Job losses in selected African countries due to
      privatization, 1988–1996   17
4.1   Trends in Cedi/Dollar exchange rate, 1996–2002   117
4.2   Inflation Trends calculated from the end of
      year, CPI, 1996–2000   118

About the Contributors

Pita Ogaba Agbese is Professor of Political Science and Director of the Center for International Peace and Security Studies at the University of Northern Iowa, Cedar Falls, United States of America. He is also a Senior Research Fellow at the Program in Ethnic and Federal Studies at the University of Ibadan, Nigeria. Previously, he served as Acting Chair of the Department of Political Science at the University of Northern Iowa. His research interests are in the areas of civil-military relations, democratization, political economy, Nigerian politics, and security studies. He has published extensively in these areas. His most recent publication is a coedited volume with George Klay Kieh, Jr., *The Military and Politics in Africa: From Engagement to Democratic Control*, Ashgate, UK, 2004.

Sylvester Alubo is Professor of Health and Social Development, Department of Sociology, University of Jos, Nigeria, and Director of Research at the prestigious National Institute of Policy and Strategic Studies (NIPSS), Nigeria. His research interests and publications are in the areas of democratization, power and privilege in medical care, the state, violence, human rights, and militarism.

Sheila Bunwaree is Associate Professor of Sociology, University of Mauritius. She previously served as Head of the Gender Bureau, Ministry of Women's Affairs, Government of Mauritius and Director of Research and Documentation at the Council for the Advancement of Social Science Research in Africa (CODESRIA), Dakar, Senegal. Her research interests are in the areas of gender and development studies.

George Klay Kieh, Jr. is Professor of Political Science and African Studies at Grand Valley State University, Michigan, USA and Senior Research Fellow, Program in Ethnic and Federal Studies at the University of Ibadan, Nigeria. Previously, he served as Dean of International Affairs, Grand Valley State University and Chair and Professor of

Political Science at Morehouse College, Atlanta, Georgia, USA. Professor Kieh was a presidential candidate of the New Democratic Alternative for Liberia Movement during the October, 2005 presidential election. His research interests are in the areas of conflict and peace studies, security studies, political economy, international cooperation, American Foreign Policy and African Politics. He has published extensively in these areas. His most recent publication is a volume coedited with Pita Ogaba Agbese, *The Military and Politics in Africa: From Engagement to Democratic and Constitutional Control, Ashgate*, UK 2004.

Emmanuel Kwesi-Aning is Expect on Counterterrorism and Common African Defense and Security Policy, Department of Peace and Security, The African Union Commission. His research interests are in the areas of terrorism and terrorist threats in Africa, security and the war on terror, transnational organized crime in West Africa and security sector reform in Ghana. He has published various articles on security issues in Africa.

Anne Nangulu-Ayuku is Chair and Senior Lecturer of History at Moi University, Kenya. She received her doctorate in history from the University of West Virginia, USA. She has published numerous articles in various scholarly journals on the political and economic history of Africa, food security, education, politics, and urbanization.

Boubacar N'Diaye is Assistant Professor of Political Science and Africana Studies at the College of Wooster, Ohio, USA. He has published widely on military and security issues in Africa. His most recent book is *Not Yet Democracy: West Africa's Slow Farewell to Authoritarianism*, Carolina Academic Press, 2005.

Victoria Maloka is a Research Associate at the Center for Conflict Resolution at the University of Cape Town, South Africa. Her research interest is in conflict resolution.

Onalenna Doo Selolwane is Chair and Senior Lecturer of Sociology and Development Studies at the University of Botswana. Her research interests are in the areas of poverty, democracy, the state, rural and national development policy, and gender studies. She has authored several book chapters and articles in various scholarly journals in the aforementioned research areas.

Preface

There is a general consensus that the postcolonial state in Africa has failed to cater to the needs and aspirations of Africans. Consequently, the state has become irrelevant and distant from its own citizens. In fact, the African masses are so fed up with the failed postcolonial state that they try to avoid, evade and cheat it, whenever possible. The crux of the problem is not with the state as a general political construct, but with the type of state (a neocolonial construct), especially its horrendous performance and the associated crises of underdevelopment that it has generated. In other words, there is no doubt that the state is epicentral to development and democracy in Africa. But, only a democratically reconstituted state that is anchored on a pro-people foundation can promote the twin objectives of development and democracy.

So, while the majority of the states in Africa have been plagued by a crisis of legitimacy and relevance since the dawn of the independence era in the 1960s, the states in Botswana and Mauritius have been undergoing reconstitution. In other words, amidst the epidemic of the crisis of the state in Africa, Botswana and Mauritius have been the minority states that have been trying to reconstruct themselves to face the challenges and legacies of colonial underdevelopment. Interestingly, since the 1990s, with the advent of the "Third Wave of Democratization," countries like Cote d'Ivoire, Ghana, Kenya, Nigeria, and South Africa (after the demise of the apartheid state) have been making efforts to join Botswana and Mauritius in the "club of democratizing states." This is indeed an encouraging development. However, cognizance is taken of the fact that the state reconstitution project is an arduous process, given the perennial history of the crisis of the state in Africa. Therefore, there is no doubt that the newly democratizing states will experience successes as well as setbacks as they make efforts to address the patina of problems created by decades of failure and indifference. Nevertheless, it is critical that the democratizing states be committed to the reconstitution project.

This is important in order to avoid reversals—the shift from democratizing reconstitution to the authoritarian past.

This volume is part of a larger research project on "The State in Africa." The research project was conceived against the backdrop of our firm belief that the state in Africa does not need to retreat but needs to be reconstituted. In other words, we maintain that Africa needs strong, democratic, and pro-people states that would provide the basic needs of the people, respect and defend their fundamental individual and group rights, promote gender equality, champion peaceful coexistence among various ethnic groups and religions, and defend the citizens from the exploitation and other vagaries of international finance capital. This particular volume is designed to take stock of the efforts that have been and are being made by some of the democratizing states in Africa, and to proffer some suggestions for addressing the myriad conundrums that are associated with the state-reconstitution project.

The project and this volume were made possible through a research grant from the Ford Foundation. We would like to thank the Governance and Civil Society Unit at the Ford Foundation for recommending the research project for funding. Particularly, we are very grateful to Professor Julius O. Ihonvbere, former Program Officer in the Governance and Civil Society Unit (currently, Presidential Adviser for Policy and Program Monitoring of the Federal Republic of Nigeria), who worked with us in fine-tuning both the larger research project and this volume. Also, we are appreciative of the unfailing cooperation and assistance of the African Center for Democratic Governance (AFRIGOV), based in Abuja, Nigeria, for managing the grant. We would like to single out Professor Aaron Gana, the Executive Director of AFRIGOV, for his usual kind assistance. Kudos go to the Foundation for Security and Development in Africa, based in Accra, Ghana, especially the Associate Executive Director, Afi Yakubu, for hosting an international conference in Accra, in which the chapters in this volume were originally presented. Last, but not the least, we thank all of the contributors to this volume, who devoted their time and energy to conducting research on the various case studies, and for exercising patience as their papers, and eventually chapters, underwent scrutiny from the participants at the international conference, other peers, and the editors of this volume.

Pita Ogaba Agbese and George Klay Kieh, Jr.

PART I

Background

CHAPTER 1

Introduction: Democratizing States and State Reconstitution in Africa

Pita Ogaba Agbese and George Klay Kieh, Jr.

In both scholarly works and in the popular press, much has been written on the failure of the state in Africa. Incessant political instability, high crime rates, lack of access to education and healthcare, deteriorating public infrastructure, and environmental degradation are a few of the features that have come to characterize the modern African state. Scholars and lay people use these as concrete indicators of the failure of the African state to perform its fundamental duties as a modern state. The catalogue of failure is quite depressing. As the *New African Initiative* notes,

> 340 million Africans, or half the population lives on less than US $1 per day. The mortality rate of children under five years of age is 140 per 1000, and life expectancy at birth is only 54 years. Only 58 percent of the population has access to safe water. The rate of illiteracy for people over 15 is 41 percent. There are only 18 mainline telephones per 1000 people in Africa, compared with 145 for the world as a whole and 567 for high income countries.[1]

The Economic Commission for Africa (ECA) has noted that Africa entered the twenty-first century as the "poorest, the most technologically backward, the most debt distressed, and the most marginalized region of the world."[2] Despite the fact that Africa makes up only about 12 percent of the total global population, the continent has the highest number of refugees in the world. These refugees, fleeing from ethnic/communal violence, civil wars, state repression, environmental degradation, and other forms of violence and disasters, are found in virtually every part of Africa. Liberians, in hundreds of thousands, are camped as refugees in Ghana, Cote d'Ivoire, Guinea, Nigeria, and other West African countries. Similarly, Sudanese, in large numbers, are scattered as refugees in neighboring countries such as Chad and Uganda. Many Rwandans eke out existence as unwelcome guests in several countries such as Tanzania and the Democratic Republic of the Congo. Violence and other forms of insecurity have forced hundreds of thousands of Chadians and Sierra Leoneans to flee to other countries. The irony is that conditions in Chad's and Sierra Leone's neighboring states were so bad that despite the horrible situation in the two countries, they have provided refuge to Africans from the neighboring states. In other words, while citizens of the two states sought shelter elsewhere, at the same time, people from neighboring states were so desperate as to flee to Chad and Sierra Leone in search of safety and security. High incidence of violence and the large number of refugees provide clear evidence of the inability of African states to ensure the safety of their citizens. At the same time, the fact that most of the continent's refugees were victims of state-perpetrated or state-instigated violence constitutes a serious indictment of contemporary African states.

It is also a major indictment of the state of governance in Africa that the continent accounts for large proportion of international peacekeeping operations. Over the past few decades, the United Nations has had to shoulder the responsibility of dispatching soldiers to various parts of the continent for peacekeeping operations (see table 1.1). While UN peacekeeping operations were originally designed to serve as a buffer between two or more nations at war, Africa has the dubious distinction of hosting UN peacekeeping troops as a check against civil wars. As in many of these cases, African governments are part of the warring factions, UN peacekeeping soldiers are in effect sent to the continent to provide security for the African population against their own governments. This alone provides an irrefutable proof that the state in Africa fails to fulfill even the most basic function of state: to provide security for its people. If Africans cannot rely on their own states to discharge the most basic obligation of a state, that is, to safeguard its citizens from harm and insecurity, who can they turn to? What else can they demand of their states? If the state itself becomes the fundamental threat to citizens' well-being and prosperity, what recourse do the citizens have?

The typical African state is noted more as a repressive, brutal, corrupt, and inefficient entity than as a mechanism for the promotion of the collective well-being of its citizens. Consequently, the modern African state remains largely irrelevant to the needs, interests, and aspirations of the

Table 1.1   UN Peacekeeping operations in Africa
as of December 2004

Country	Number of peacekeepers
Cote d'Ivoire	6,215
Liberia	15,778
Western Sahara	227
Sierra Leone	4,274
Dem. Republic of the Congo	12,642
Burundi	5,454
Ethiopia/Eritrea	3,918

Source: Global Policy Forum, *UN Peacekeeping Operations in Africa as of December 2004* (New York: Global Policy Forum, 2005).

people. A telling evidence of the vote of no confidence in the African state is the fact that even the African leaders who serve as custodians of the state have very little faith in its ability to cater to their well-being. They, themselves, even as the segment of the population that derives the most material benefits from the state, do not repose much confidence in it. They do not place their own welfare and security under the state's umbrella. They would rather send their children and wards to schools in Europe and North America than place them in local educational institutions. When they or other members of their families fall ill, they do not trust local hospitals and doctors to treat them. Instead, they quickly fly abroad for medical care. Similarly, they do not believe that their money is safe in banks in their own countries. Instead, they lodge their monetary wealth in Swiss and other bank accounts in Europe and North America. Their little faith in their own countries is tellingly registered by their craze to fly their pregnant wives overseas for child-delivery to ensure that they children automatically acquire other countries' citizenship by birth.

African leaders' proclivities to use the state as an instrument of terror and private enrichment has created a wide gulf between states and citizens. The scope of alienation between the two in Africa is marked by widespread insurgency, banditry, tax evasion, smuggling, and other forms of illegal activities. Just as the people do not trust their leaders and devise all manner of tactics to evade and cheat the state that is illegitimate in their eyes, the leaders fear, loathe, and despise the people. Citizens have no faith in their leaders and they entertain no illusion that the state would address their concerns and material well-being. On their part, the political leaders can sense the wide gulf that their inability and unwillingness to govern in the interest of the people has created. They can vividly see the anger and resentment harbored by the people against them. They isolate themselves from the people in order to protect themselves against their anger and their wrath. This mutual distrust between the leaders and the people has persisted for such a long time that a vicious circle has now been created. The more the political leaders isolate and insulate themselves from their citizens, the less trust the people repose in the leadership. As the level of trust in the leadership among the people further declines, so does the sense of fear and insecurity rise in the leaders. They therefore utilize repressive tactics to keep the people at bay or they barricade themselves in impregnable fortresses. Thus, while palatial state houses are supposedly public buildings, most Africans dare not go near them for fear of harming the presidents and other heads of states ensconced in them. As President Julius Nyerere has lamented,

> It is much more difficult to enter the State House grounds now than it was under colonial rule. There have been several occasions when I have wanted passers-by to be allowed into the grounds to enjoy *ngoma* that was going on there. But it has proved impossible for me or anybody else to get the gate opened. Presumably this could only be authorized by means of a cabinet directive! I, myself, cannot leave the State House grounds without the guard at the gate being called out to announce to the city—by fanfare of trumpets—that the president is going out! Hitherto, whenever I have questioned the value of all this very undemocratic pomposity, I have been assured that "the people like it." But this is highly doubtful. Do the people really like being refused permission to join in the *ngoma* which they can see going on the other side of the State House barriers? Do they really love being shouted at to get off the road because the president, or a minister, or a regional commissioner, is taking an afternoon drive? Do they really feel a surge of pride and patriotism every time they are expected to stop what they are doing and stand to attention just because some newly appointed official, whom they may not even have seen before, is being "serenaded" by his friends with the national anthem?[3]

Political leaders' penchant to isolate themselves from their citizens in order to insulate themselves from their wrath implies that more often than not, the relationship between leaders and citizens is mediated by state violence against the people. Thus, human rights violations in Africa do not just measure the scope and intensity of state brutality but they also hint at the underlying mutual distrust between the two groups. In other words, statistics on human rights violations in Africa can serve as a barometer for the degree of distrust and alienation that exists in the continent.

Human Rights Watch and similar organizations that serve as a watchdogs on governments' observance of human rights laws compile annual statistics on human rights conditions in Africa. While the latest report by Human Rights Watch indicates a measure of improvement in the human rights record of some African countries, quite a significant number of them continue to exhibit very poor record. For instance, on civil and political rights, the 2005 report on the Democratic Republic of the Congo notes as follows:

> Local and national officials continue to harass, arbitrarily arrest, or beat journalists, civil society activists, and ordinary citizens. Combatants of armed groups, including those officially integrated into the national army, continue to prey upon civilian populations, collecting illegal "taxes" and extorting money through illegal detention and torture.[4]

The same Human Rights Watch's report on Cote d'Ivoire was even more depressing with respect to the government's complicity in human rights violations. In a very chilling passage that captures the poor record of the Ivorian government's adherence to its human rights obligations, the report noted as follows:

> State Security Forces continue to act with impunity while the Ivorian government demonstrates little political will to hold accountable perpetrators within the government or security forces. From March 25–27, 2004, pro-government forces participated in a deadly crackdown against opposition groups who had planned to protest the lack of progress in implementing the Linas-Marcoussis Agreement. During the violence, members of the Ivorian security forces, including pro-government militias and Front Populaire Ivoirein party militants responded aggressively by using unnecessary and deadly means that were disproportionate to the supposed threat the march posed. Instead of dispersing demonstrators with non-lethal means as they assembled, the security forces shot at and detained them in their communities as they prepared to gather, fired upon them as they attempted to flee, and executed many after being detained. During the violence at least 105 civilians were killed, 290 were wounded, and some twenty individuals "disappeared" after being taken into custody by members of the Ivorian security forces and pro-government militias, many on the basis of their nationality, ethnicity, or religion.[5]

There is no doubt that most states in Africa have performed very poorly on economics and sociopolitical matters. Many of them are unwilling and/or unable to provide basic welfare services for their citizens. Accordingly, qualitative education, good healthcare facilities, electricity, and passable roads are still out of reach of hundreds of millions of Africans. A vast majority of people in Africa continue to be mired in abject poverty and horrible conditions of existence. On a daily basis, they have to contend with the miseries of underdevelopment and economic marginalization. Despite the fact that the continent lags behind other parts of the world with respect to young people's access to education, many parents have been forced to withdraw their children from schools as a result of their inability to pay school fees.

The poor state of affairs in contemporary Africa has belied the expectations that most Africans had on the eve of independence from European colonial rule. Africans expected that the postcolonial era would usher in freedom, democracy, and economic development. It was precisely the realization that liberty, dignity, or economic progress will never become realities under colonial rule that provided some of the impetus and the zeal for anticolonial struggles. Africans recognized that the colonial states were created by European imperial rulers to facilitate Europe's penetration and exploitation of the continent. Under colonial rule, the states in Africa were not states in the juridical sense of independence and sovereignty. On the contrary, they were established simply as a device for enhancing the ability of Europeans to extract resources from Africa. Of equal importance was the fact that the colonial states had no pretense of being an instrument for promoting the security and welfare of the Africans. The sole objective of the Europeans was to use it as a vehicle for extracting African wealth and then transfer it to Europe. Judged from that perspective, one can say that the colonial state did its work admirably. It enhanced the ability of European imperialists to siphon off the continent's resources to Europe for European development, while leaving Africans and their economies poor and underdeveloped.

At its inception, the logic of the colonial state required a wide gulf between itself and the African population for it could not have fulfilled its objective of transferring African resources to Europe, if it had developed an organic linkage with the African people. The colonial state had to be constantly at war with Africans for the very rationale for its creation necessitated mutual antagonism between itself and its African subjects. The interests of Africans were diametrically opposed to the interests of the colonial state, for the very existence of the colonial state lay with maximum economic exploitation of Africa. On the other hand, it was in the interest of Africans to throw off the colonial yoke as quickly as possible. The failure for an organic linkage to develop between the two stemmed from several reasons. First, the Europeans who had set up the colonial states were not only from another continent, they were a tiny, but powerful minority among a weak African majority. Second, since the primary objective of the colonial state was to subjugate Africans to facilitate their exploitation, it was in the interest of Africans to do all they could resist their dehumanization and exploitation by the colonial state that was an obvious target of resistance. Third, the colonial state could have rendered the meaningless the very essence of its creation, if it had devoted meaningful resources to addressing the material needs of Africans. Any social service that it provided was simply designed to enhance future exploitation. Thus, the lesser the scope of social services that it provided, the more resources would be available for transfer to Europe. Fourth, Africans were fully aware that the restoration of their dignity and freedom required direct challenge and confrontation with the colonial state that had compromised their worth as human beings. Africans recognized that the colonial state that was both an instrument of imperial extraction and a symbol of their humiliation in the hands of European imperialists had to be taken away from them.

The totality of the colonial state's power and the fact that the logic of its existence was at variance with African interests meant that there was very little room for compromise. Europeans had used it to dehumanize, exploit, oppress, and humiliate Africans. An important agenda of the anticolonial movement was to capture the colonial state in its entirety. Both the nationalist leaders and the African masses expected that this instrument of European exploitation would, in the hands of Africans, be transformed into a veritable tool for political freedom and economic development.

While the anticolonial movements were certain that the capture of the colonial state was central to the restoration of African freedom and development, they assumed that the fatal flaw in its composition and functioning was that it catered exclusively to European material interests. Thus, at the heart of the struggle against colonial rule was the expectation that with independence, Africans would seize control of the state and use it to serve African, rather than European interests. It was assumed that once Africans put themselves in charge of the colonial state apparatus, it would no longer serve as a tool of terror, oppression, and exploitation. Many of the anticolonial movements did not pause to ask whether the state that had been constructed to advance imperial interests could, without a fundamental transformation, become an instrument for economic growth, liberation, and the welfare of Africans.

Several decades after independence, it has dawned on most Africans that without a fundamental transformation of the state, simply replacing European colonial officials with Africans as rulers of African states was not a sufficient condition for liberation, sovereignty, and economic development. With independence, Africans did become the managers of the state but its essence, character, and modus operandi remained virtually intact. All its repressive paraphernalia were preserved. The new African leaders, like their European predecessors, were intolerant of opposition. For instance, as Jomo Kenyatta was taking office as prime minister on Kenya's Independence Day in December 1963, he warned the opposition in the following stern words:

> Anyone who wants to weaken this government will be dealt with ruthlessly by the government. We recognize the Opposition, but we cannot allow anyone to belittle this government. This is not the government of Nairobi, or Kakuru, or Kisumu, but the government of Kenya, and the sooner the Opposition recognizes this the better. . . . There are those who keep going around saying "this government has not given us jobs." Some of you are in fact being misled by troublemakers, whose only interest is to see you in difficulties. My government is a government of action, and will not hesitate to deal with these few troublemakers in the country.[6]

Just as in the colonial era, most Africans would consider the postcolonial state as corrupt, illegitimate, and inefficient. It is also alienated from its citizens. While nominally, it is independent, in reality, its ability to initiate meaningful economic or developmental policies is highly circumscribed. Its sovereignty and autonomy have been compromised by its heavy reliance on global financial institutions such as the World Bank and the International Monetary Fund (IMF). Beset by huge dubious external debts, many postcolonial African states are beholden to their external creditors who dictate their budgetary priorities. Economic policies must conform to the wishes of their foreign "development partners" who compel them to adopt ruinous measures. Confronted with a choice of serving their citizens' material interests or acceding to extortionist demands by their foreign creditors, African leaders always choose the latter.

This chapter argues that a key to the emergence of a democratic, efficient, responsive, and accountable state in Africa is the adoption of a new compact on governance. It contends that such a compact can emerge only from widespread popular debates, dialogues, and consultations in each African country. Their purpose will be to establish the parameters for a new state whose primary rationale for its existence is to advance the well-being of citizens. A new state built on popular sovereignty will replace the repressive, exploitative, and insensitive state inherited from European imperialists. But then, after all the struggle and strife, the postcolonial state has shown itself incapable of serving as a beacon for freedom, independence, and economic development.

Mere tinkering at the edges by replacing soldiers with elected civilian politicians is not enough. Neither is it sufficient to posit that if the scope of the state's economic activities is reduced through programs of privatization and commercialization, the African state will become more humane and more efficient. Similarly, reformist measures such as anticorruption crusades and public disclosures of politicians' assets are not likely to mean much if, in the long run, the nature, character, and essence of the state are left intact. The fact that all the above steps have been tried without much measurable success is a clear indication that a comprehensive and fundamental transformation of the postcolonial state is what Africa requires.

The sad relationship that exists between states and citizens shows that as presently constituted, African states cannot advance the material well-being of their people. Africa's depressing statistic on socioeconomic measures are more than indices of failure of the postcolonial state. They equally highlight the reality that a major characteristic of the postcolonial state is that it constitutes a veritable danger to its own citizens. Even when it does not pose a direct danger to its citizens through violence, repression, incompetence, corruption, and inefficiency, it remains irrelevant to the needs of the people. A clear illustration of this is the current situation in Somalia. The judicial contours of Somalia as a state, particularly in terms of international law, remain unchanged even though Somalia has not had a government in over twelve years! Ironically, the pre–civil war Somalian state provided so few welfare services to Somalians that not many people in the country would lament its demise. Most people in the country are not necessarily worse off because the state has collapsed. It is even possible that the termination of the reign of terror that the state represented was greeted with a sigh of relief by ordinary people in the country. It is quite telling that most Somalians have not missed the absence of the state. Interestingly, the situation in Somalia is not an isolated case. If most African states in their current composition and character were to disappear the way Somalia did, many Africans would jubilate at what would be good riddance to stinking rubbish. This suggests how detached and alienated the African state is from its own people.

In scholarly terms, the postcolonial state seems confounding to analysts. Part of the confusion with the scholarly treatment of the state in Africa is the narrow framework in which it is conceptualized. Frequently, scholars apply unidimensional characterizations in describing the contours and essence of the postcolonial state. Africa's postcolonial state is often depicted as a "rentier," "prebendal," "extractive," "personalized," "weak," or "overdeveloped."

These adjectives even as they rightly highlight some of the more observable characteristics of the African state, do not capture its true essence. A more robust understanding of the state can be derived from viewing the typical African state as a composite of several tendencies or characteristics. A particular tendency or characteristic may be in ascendancy but that does not preclude the importance of other tendencies or characteristics. Moreover, the dominance or ascendancy of any particular tendency or characteristic is a function of several conjectural factors. Thus, at particular historical moments, some tendencies or characteristics may be more dominant than others. At other times, while those same tendencies may be obscured by others, they do not disappear completely from the political firmament. The type of challenge the state faces at a given time is also a function of the dominant tendency. Interestingly, how the state responds to such a challenge may itself manifest a particular type of character. In this connection, a state that is generally seen as benevolent may become repressive so as to nip a potential threat in the bud. Since the state is an arena for social struggles, the scope and intensity of such struggles tend to be reflected in the ascendancy or the decline of particular tendencies or characteristics.

Although there are still many areas of disagreement among scholars on the nature and characteristics of the African state, there are certain commonly accepted propositions too. First, there is a general understanding that it was a product of colonialism and imperialism. It is also generally acknowledged that the African state was originally constructed to serve European imperial interests by facilitating the exploitation of African resources and transferring them to Europe. As a governing institution, it was not meant to advance the material well-being of Africans. On the contrary, it was designed to ensure the maximum exploitation of Africans and no action by the state was considered too heinous so long as it enabled Europeans to extract resources from the continent. Political independence did not automatically change the nature or essence of the African state.

Second, there is a virtual unanimous understanding that the African state has failed to fulfill the most basic requirements of a modern state. We have earlier highlighted some of the major failings of the African state in this connection. Some of these failures can be rightly attributed to the colonial origins of the state.

Third, in the postcolonial era, the primary purpose of power and control of the state apparatus has been the private accumulation of wealth. Consequently, the struggle over state power has assumed life and death dimensions. Another casualty of the use of state power as an instrument of private enrichment is accountability. Corruption is rampant in the postcolonial era as a direct result of utilizing state power as a mechanism for private wealth accumulation. Examples from numerous African countries vividly demonstrate how ruling classes have used the state as an instrument for personal, class, and ethnic aggrandizement. While Nigeria's cases of stupendous corruption tend to garner more newspaper headlines, corrupt enrichment is a major feature of the contemporary African political landscape. Nigeria's former head of state, General Sani Abacha, stashed away over $505 million in Swiss banks. The Swiss government recently agreed to repatriate this money to Nigeria and a very grateful Nigerian government official commented as follows:

> We hope that the Swiss example at both the political and judicial level will show the way for other countries where our national resources have been illegally transferred. Switzerland's policy on this issue is a clear sign that crime does not pay. Nigeria is ready to work with other governments to achieve the repatriation of other funds which were siphoned out of the country illegally.[7]

Fourth, it is quite clear that Africa cannot continue to operate its politics and its economies in the same distorted fashion that it has done over the past few decades. The conclusion that a new way of doing things needed to be evolved led to the intensification of democratic struggles in the 1990s. Accordingly, a wave of democratic elections, popularly tagged the "Second Independence Movement or the Third Wave of Democratization," swept through the African continent in the 1990s and early 2000s as a response to the failings of the postcolonial state in Africa. Single political party regimes were replaced with multiparty systems. In some cases, amendments were made to the constitutions to facilitate multiparty systems. For instance, Section 2A of the Kenyan Constitution was amended to permit the formation of parties other than the ruling Kenya African Union (KANU). In the wake of political reforms all over Africa, long-term rulers and military autocrats were shoved out of power.

In the aftermath of the electoral defeat of corrupt autocrats and dictators, a new ray of hope emerged in Africa. Nonetheless, the successor administrations in most countries inherited numerous problems from the rapacious erstwhile dictators. President Mwai Kibaki of Kenya captures the difficulties of the new men in power, when he noted during his inauguration speech in January 2003 as follows:

> I'm inheriting a country which has been badly ravaged by years of misrule and ineptitude There has been a wide disconnect between the people and

government, between people's aspirations and the government's attitude towards them. I believe that governments exist to serve the people, not the people to serve the government. . . . Corruption will now cease to be a way of life in Kenya. And, ladies and gentlemen, by the way you have voted in the last elections, I am calling upon all of you to come out and fight corruption, and agree to support the government in fighting corruption as our first priority. The economy, which you all know has been under-performing since the last decade, is going to be my first priority. . . . My government will embark on policies geared to economic reconstruction, employment creation and immediate rehabilitation of the collapsed infrastructure.[8]

In view of the failure of the contemporary African state to live up to its responsibilities, it is imperative to explore options for fundamental restructuring of its essence, missions, and institutions. Various models of state reconstitution have been suggested, and a few of these are examined below.

The Institutional Reform Model is based on several arguments. First, it advocates the elimination of inefficient state institutions. Second, it posits that the trust between the state and its custodians on one hand, and the society on the other, needs to be rebuilt. Third, it advocates the centrality of an independent judiciary. As Leonce Ndikumana notes, "an independent judiciary can guarantee that each crime is prosecuted, regardless of the identity of the perpetrator or the victims."[9] Fourth, the decision-making and decision-implementation institutions and processes must be accountable and transparent.

Much of the emphasis of the Institutional Reform Model is on reducing the scope and parameters of the state's economic role. Privatization of state-owned enterprises and the drastic reduction of the economic regulatory framework are the key policy instruments advocated by this model. By June 2000, in all 3,400 privatization transactions with a total value of $7.1 billion had been finalized in Africa.[10] Nigeria's vice president, Atiku Abubakar, who also chairs the country's privatization committee, defended the policy in the following words:

If there are still those who question the imperative of privatization, it is pertinent to point out that it is inevitable. It cannot be argued that most of our state-run enterprises, especially the utilities, have become inefficient monopolies. These enterprises are also heavily capital intensive. Over the years it has become more and more difficult for government to provide the financial resources to keep them going.[11]

The Institutional Reform Model, drawing its evidence from the failures of the state in Africa, contends that the state is not a viable engine for economic development. Instead, it is the private sector that should assume the position of the "engine of economic growth." Abubakar put this succinctly when he observed, "Nigeria cannot be an exception to the global economic trend that recognizes that the best framework for the effective and optimal performance of an economy is one that limits the state's involvement."[12]

Privatization is also defended on the grounds that it aims to improve efficiency of economic enterprises. Additionally, advocates of privatization contend that if enterprises are efficiently run, governments would reduce public sector borrowing and would free up resources that can be profitably and more effectively allocated by the invisible hands of the market. It is also contended that privatization reduces the state's intervention in the economy and promotes healthy economic competition and that the new regulatory framework put in place in the aftermath of privatization provides protection for both consumers and investors (see tables 1.2 and 1.3). In the words of Vice President Abubakar,

> Privatization goes hand in hand with the establishment of an effective regulatory system that protects the consumers, first and foremost, and also protects the legitimate interests of the investor. A proper regulatory regime will provide assurance to all stakeholders that sufficient expertise and resources will be made available for the overall improvement of enterprises and the services they provide.[13]

Privatization has failed to deliver on its promises. In many cases, it has been carried out without much transparency and the same people who had used their access to state power to denude state-owned enterprises of their resources ended up buying the privatized enterprises.

Table 1.2 Reported privatization activity in Africa: Top Eight countries, 1996–2000

Countries	Last year for reported data	Number of transactions recorded
Mozambique	1997	579
Angola	1996	331
Tanzania	2000	283
Zambia	2000	268
Ghana	2000	233
Kenya	1998	188
Guinea	1998	117
Cote d'Ivoire	2000	105

Source: *Business in Africa*, December 2000/January 2001, p. 33.

Table 1.3   Reported privatization transactions in Africa, 1979–1999

Years	Number	Sale value ($m)
1979–1984	10	1.0
1985	10	0.7
1986	18	1.8
1987	20	10.2
1988	60	14.5
1989	220	685.1
1990	171	71.3
1991	168	155.5
1992	265	216.1
1993	230	131.7
1994	365	537.6
1995	482	423.3
1996	426	757.9
1997	241	2,248.6
1998	126	1,194.0
1999	82	311.6
2000 (6 months)	33	354.2

Source: Campell White, "Privatization: Facing up to the Issues," *Business in Africa*, December 2000/January 2001, p. 34.

In addition, privatization has led to greater concentration of wealth in the hands of a few. The claim that the program would facilitate mass ownership of enterprises has proved to be a hollow one. For most Africans, neither the immediate nor long-term tangible benefits of privatization have arrived at their doorsteps. Instead, it has resulted in the loss of jobs without any social safety net for those laid off (see table 1.4). In some cases, privatization increased foreign ownership in African economies.

The Power-Sharing Model is anchored in the basic premise that antagonistic primordial groups and interests constitute the basis for state failure and state collapse. Accordingly, the reconstituted state must have as its fulcrum, a new governing structure that is ethnically based. Each of the ethnic groups in the country, according to this model, should be granted a great degree of autonomy in policy matters that affect them. So far, only Ethiopia has put this model into practice with its ethnic-based federal arrangement. Nonetheless, the model appeals to some people in some other African countries. It is the basis of political agitation in Nigeria with the call for the convocation of a sovereign national conference composed of representatives of "ethnic nationalities" where the future of Nigeria would be decided.

Table 1.4 Job losses in selected African countries due to privatization, 1988–1996

Country/Period	No. of firms in the sample	Employment at privatization	Employment, first quarter, 1996	Percentage change in employment
Benin, 1988–1995	8	1,872	1,197	−36.0
Burkina Faso, 1991–1995	10	895	901	0.1
Ghana, 1990–1995	7	5,363	4,431	−17.3
Togo, 1984–1995	19	2,882	2,338	−18.8
Zambia, 1993–1996	10	6,150	5,733	−6.7
Total	54	17,162	14,600	−14.9

Source: Med Chottepanda, "Privatization: Breaking the Fall," *Business in Africa*, December 2000/January 2001, p. 37.

The Constitutional Politics Model has good governance as its centerpiece. That is, it posits that the focus of state reconstitution should be the formulation of a governance multiplex that emphasizes adherence to the rules of the "democratic game." This model appeals to many African countries and the "Third Wave of Democratization" fully embraces it. An important element of the remarkable changes that have taken place in Africa over the past few years is the new reverence for constitutions and constitutionalism. Rather than anchoring governance on decrees and the personal whims and caprices of the rulers, governance is increasingly moored on constitutional precepts. Accordingly, the drawing up of new constitutions has become an important task of contemporary efforts to democratize Africa. Among African states that have used the writing of a constitution as part of their transition from authoritarianism to democracy are South Africa, Ethiopia, Eritrea, Ghana, Uganda, and Malawi. In these and other countries on the continent, a new pride of place has been accorded to constitutions and constitutionalism. Unlike the recent past in which African rulers paid scant attention to the rule of law, the notion that governance must be based on legitimate constitutions seems to have taken a firm hold in many countries. As clearly enunciated in Article 9 of the 1994 Ethiopian Constitution, "the Constitution is the supreme law of the land . . . all citizens, organs of state, political organizations, other associations as well as their officials have the duty to ensure observance of the Constitution and obey it."

The Constitutional Politics Model draws its inspiration from both the failures of the postcolonial state and the constitutional foundations of precolonial African societies. It argues that a major factor responsible for state failure, abuse of power, and lack of accountability in Africa is the weak constitutional basis for exercising power. It notes that while most precolonial societies of Africa did not have written constitutions, they were fully anchored on constitutional precepts. There was a general understanding on how the societies would be governed. Elaborate rules and procedures on succession existed and governance was anchored on consensus. Accountability was guaranteed even if the method sometimes was as harsh as regicide. Various rituals such as drama, puppetry, and dance were used to articulate the people's grievances against their rulers. The basic relationship between state and citizen was clearly enunciated and largely respected. Rulers knew that they were accountable both to the living and their ancestors. Thus religion and other forms of spiritual rituals were used as instruments of accountability. As mentioned earlier, under colonial rule, there was no organic linkage between the state and the African people. Therefore, the treaties were not compacts limiting the powers of the colonial governments nor did they obligate them to advance the material interests of Africans.

Colonial rule in Africa transformed the social contract between rulers and citizens. The imposition of brutal colonial regimes on Africa eliminated the various devices created by Africans against arbitrary use of political power. In effect, under colonial rule, the traditional checks against arbitrary power in African political systems were wiped out. To make matters worse, there was no compact of mutual dependence between the governed and the governors. The so-called treaties of protectorate used as a cover for colonial administration were either fraudulently obtained or procured by force. Governments were constituted not in the interests of the governed but for facilitating the latter's exploitation by alien rulers.

The Constitutional Politics Model suggests the reconstruction of the African state through a new constitutional compact.[14] It argues that both the process by which the compact is reached and the specific contents of the compact are equally important. It suggests a people-led constitutional process that, by its inclusivity, provides widespread and vigorous debates and consultations. In the end, such a process leads to the emergence of a legitimate document that provides a framework for resolving political conflicts and for addressing people's welfare. This model also contends that if the constitution is not structured to defend the people's material and other interests, it simply becomes a pious document that nobody takes very seriously. Therefore, the constitution must empower the people in their daily lives.

Constitutionalism in Africa has created an important opportunity for addressing lingering political problems, ethnic relations, regional autonomy, power sharing, and so on.[15] The constitutional process creates opportunities for mass participation in politics. Since independence, the African masses have been excluded from participating in their own affairs by military regimes. Similarly, the era of one-party regimes limited both the range of issues and the class character of participants in the political process. Constitutionalism enables ordinary people to assert ownership over the state and other political institutions. It tears down the notion that government is the exclusive preserve of a few people. State reconstruction can also be effected through constitutionalism. The consensus that may develop from the process of constitutionalism permits the restructuring of state and society along generally accepted parameters.

Rather than relying on the wisdom of political leaders to tackle all problems, the emphasis today is to use constitutional means for addressing pressing and fundamental sociopolitical issues. For instance, a legitimate constitution is now viewed as an important key to addressing ethnic contradictions and their underlying social problems.

The State Deconstruction Model makes several arguments. Its basic contention is that the neocolonial state and its associated relations of production and distribution must be fundamentally transformed. In other words, the model operates on the premise that the neocolonial state has failed and will continue to fail, and even collapse, if its basic nature and dynamics remain unaltered. First, the *raison d'etre* for the existence of the state must be changed from that of serving the interests of the international capitalist order, especially the owners of finance capital, to that of serving the interests of the African peoples. Second, class inequities must be obliterated and replaced by equity in income and wealth. Third, the agendas of the agents of the global capitalist order, especially multinational corporations, should be subordinated to those of the African peoples. In short, the overarching political economy, its power relations, and modes of expropriation and distribution must be fundamentally transformed, in order to arrest state failure and state collapse, and their debilitating cascading effects. State reconstruction in Africa must be a holistic process that embodies a host of essential factors that capture the multiple dimensions of the crisis of the African state.

Africa: The Dawn of a New Era?

Significant political changes occurred in Africa during the 1990s. Popularly elected governments have replaced military and other forms of dictatorships. In place of the single-party system, a multiparty system has emerged in many countries on the continent.[16] The practice of life presidency has been discredited. Instead, many presidents now govern under specific term limits. Elections have displaced the gun as the primary instrument for acquiring political power.[17] Increasingly, the political process features new entrants such as women and youths. New issues of contestation including environmental, gender, and ethnic minority rights are also significant aspects of the emerging political terrain in Africa.

Decades of misrule cannot be wiped out in a few years. Nonetheless, many of the new governments have not made appreciable headway in their inherited crises. In many cases, they have even backslided. Not only have they failed to satisfy people's expectations, in several instances, they have been a total disappointment. In a way, this is not surprising. The focus of the campaign to change the old order was on the persons who ran the old order. There was little attention paid to the structures of oppression, corruption, and exploitation that had been built up over the decades. The impression was that once the Abachas, the Mobutus, the arap Mois, and other hated dictators and autocrats had been swept out of power, the continent's myriad crises would miraculously disappear. Second, the new men and women of power were not really new. Many of them gained credibility as reformers just because they had fallen out with the previous rulers. Quite a number of them were simply opportunistic politicians who capitalized on the popular yearning for a new style of governance to ditch their erstwhile colleagues and benefactors. Third, the new men and women of power had only a limited understanding of the dimensions of the crises that they had inherited. Nigeria and Kenya tend to typify the hopes that were betrayed by the emergent political leadership.

Mwai Kibaki was elected President of Kenya in December 2002 on a pledge to fight against corruption. There was a lot of excitement in Kenya and in other parts of Africa at the apparent demise of the Kenya African National Union (KANU) that had ruled the country for almost forty years. As part of his commitment to fight against corruption, Kibaki appointed John Githongo as the chief of the anticorruption crusade. Githongo however, resigned in February 2005, on charges that the government was not serious in its anticorruption drive. Tajudeen Abdul-Raheem highlighted the apparent transformation and subsequent disillusionment in Kenya with his observation,

Only 18 months ago, President Mwai Kibaki led the overarching multiparty alliance to an unprecedented victory over KANU. It was a silent revolution that was welcomed and celebrated across Africa, promising people's power and peaceful democratic changes as opposed to violent military ones. Kenya showed itself able and willing to follow the democratic path and we were all thrilled. But in just under two years the illusions are clearing. It was an unrealistic, even if unavoidable, mass expectation that the new government will quickly transform Kenya from the corrupt and authoritarian KANU power structure it inherited.[18]

On several fronts, the Kibaki government has been a disappointment to many Kenyans. As Abdul-Raheem has pointed out,

> Ordinary Kenyans, while giving NARC the benefit of the doubt, had a right to expect some light at the end of the dark tunnel. This was not to be. They are harvesting more pain and misery from their would-be liberators. The uneasy alliance is unraveling and bursting at the altar of ethnoregional politics and unbridled ambition of the coalition. The promised transparency, accountability and clean government have given room to KANU-type corrupt business as usual. Maybe this is not surprising given the solid KANU history of most of the leaders themselves. What can one expect from KANU refugees?[19]

Similarly, Olusegun Obasanjo was elected President of Nigeria in 1999 on an electoral promise to fight vigorously against corruption. To his credit, one of the first bills he sent to the legislature was an anticorruption bill. An Economic and Financial Crimes Commission (EFCC) was also set up to investigate and prosecute Nigerians who engage in corruption and other forms of illegal enrichment. Tafa Balogun, the inspector-general of police, was convicted in 2005 as part of the "war against corruption." Many Nigerians contend that though corruption is still quite rife in the country, only a few people have faced legal prosecution for allegations of corruption. Moreover, there is a popular perception that Obasanjo uses the anti-corruption campaign to go after his political enemies since none of those close to the president who are believed to be neck-deep in corruption has been prosecuted. Despite the establishment of an anti-corruption commission, Nigeria is still ranked among the most corrupt nations of the world. Transparency International's latest survey of global perceptions of corruption ranks Nigeria as the third most corrupt country on earth. Although the federal government disagreed with this ranking, it is clear that corruption is the fulcrum on which the Nigerian state revolves.[20] In its review of the year 2004, *The Guardian* noted thus:

> Corruption in public life did not abate, never mind that on the international scene Nigeria's placing appeared to have "improved" from

the second to the third most corrupt nation in the world. . . . As corruption continued to thrive in 2004 and Nigerians realize that only the stupid and uninitiated get caught, observers began to stake criminal corruption behind political expedience, ethnic identification, political witch-hunting, quota and zonal power-sharing, religious affiliation and executive and legislative immunity: . . . An administration that set out in 1999 with a much publicized commitment to dislodge corruption from the land has displayed abject ineptitude in fulfilling that commitment.[21]

Matthew Hassan Kukah, a very astute observer and analyst of the Nigerian political economy, vividly captures the contradictions of the post-military era with his observation that Nigeria is a nation,

of such enormous landmass, yet citizens are fighting over land, a nation of such incredible wealth, yet it wears poverty like a breastplate; a nation of seemingly deep religion, yet so steeped in much sin; a nation so populated by farmers and farmland, yet hunger stalks the land and the nation cannot feed itself; a nation with so many petrol stations, yet, no fuel. . . . [22]

While Nigeria, Kenya, and many other countries are still floundering, Botswana has shown that with wise investment in infrastructure, basic needs, and a commitment to equitable development and good human rights record, it is possible to build a decent, relatively efficient, and accountable state in Africa.

The major purpose of this volume is twofold. First, the book is intended to examine the progress of the state reconstitution project in a sample of seven democratizing African states—Botswana, Cote d'Ivoire, Ghana, Kenya, Mauritius, Nigeria, and South Africa. Clearly, all the democratizing states that are engaged in state reconstitution cannot be covered in a single volume. Accordingly, we made the determination to use a sample of seven states covering the East, West, and Southern Africa regions, and reflecting varying levels in the state reconstitution and democratization projects. The seven states that constitute the sample for this volume commenced their state reconstitution projects at various periods. Botswana and Mauritius have comparatively longer histories in terms of efforts to reconstitute the state than the other five countries. Both these countries commenced their state reconstitution projects during the immediate postindependence era in the 1960s. South African began its state reconstitution project in 1994, after the collapse of the authoritarian apartheid system. Nigeria, Ghana, and Cote d'Ivoire joined the network of reconstituting African States in 1999 and 2000, respectively. Nigeria commenced its state reconstitution project at the end of military rule and the holding of democratic elections in 1999. Ghana began its reconstitution process in 2000 after the electoral defeat of the incumbent ruling National Democratic Convention (NDC) and the end of the authoritarian rule of soldier turned politician, Jerry Rawlings. Similarly, Cote d'Ivoire commenced its renewal project in 2000 after the defeat of the military rule consolidation project pursued by General Robert Guei. The General, who had come to power in 1999, after a military coup, transformed himself into a "civilian," and contested the presidential elections. Although he lost the election, General Guei tried to use the power of incumbency to impose himself as the new civilian president. However, his self-succession plan was rebuffed and strongly resisted by the Ivorian masses, who forced him out of power. Subsequently, Laurent Gbagbo, the winner of the election, assumed the presidency. First, the state reconstitution project in each of the seven countries covered in this volume is part of the broader effort to democratize these countries.

Second, based on the assessment of the progress being made in the state reconstitution project by the seven countries, the volume seeks to suggest ways in which the various conundrums could be addressed as conditions for the success for the state reconstitution project and the larger democratization enterprise. The prescriptions offered and the lessons learned from the experiences of the seven countries covered in this volume have utility for the state reconstitution project and the broader democratization enterprise taking place in other countries on the African continent.

The Organization of the Book

The book is divided into nine chapters. In chapter 1, the editors of the volume, Pita Ogaba Agbese, and George Klay Kieh, Jr. set the context of the volume. First, they examine the general pantomimes of state failure in Africa—cultural, economic, political, security, and social—as the backdrop of the state reconstitution project. Second, the chapter maps out the broad challenges that attend the state reconstitution project. Third, they discuss some of the major theoretical frameworks that have been offered as compasses for navigating the terrain of state reconstitution—Institutional Reform, Power Sharing, Constitutional Politics, and State Deconstruction Models. Agbese and Kieh then establish some basic thresholds for ensuring successful state reconstitution in Africa: (1) A legitimate constitutional basis of the state; (2) the effective management of national resources; (3) improving the material well-being of the African people; (4) the creation of greater space for political freedom; (5) the equitable distribution of national resources; (6) the reduction of communal tension, and the promotion of ethno-cultural pluralism; and (7) the meaningful participation of women, youth, and other marginalized sections of the society in governance. In essence, the chapter concludes that any reconstituted African state will be judged on the extent to which it creates a better life for all its citizens.

Onalenna Selolwane tackles the state reconstitution problematic in Botswana in chapter 2. She begins with a discussion of the historical processes that have fashioned the Botswana state—its form, context, and character. She then proceeds to examine the dynamics of state reconstitution in Botswana, including the roles played by both state and non-state actors and the interplay of societal and sectional interests. She concludes that the state reconstitution project has scored some major successes because (1) the legitimate authority of the state has been established; and (2) modalities have been developed to help address the socioeconomic challenges. Despite the successes, she observes that Botswana still has to contend with other challenges including the electoral domination by the ruling party since independence.

In chapter 3, Boubacar N'Diaye examines the travails of state building in Cote d'Ivoire. Specifically, he probes the attributes and dynamics of the postcolonial Ivorian state: the performance of the state's nation-building functions; the factors that led to the near disintegration of the state; and the challenges of reconstituting the state. N'Diaye contends that the postcolonial Ivorian state is anchored on what he calls the "Houphouet Phenomenon—a mixture of corruption, repression and patrimonialism." He argues that despite the military intervention in 1999, the basic features of the Ivorian state have remained intact. Similarly, despite the holding of multiparty elections in 2000 and the ascendancy of long-time opposition politician, Laurent Gbagbo, to the Presidency of Cote d'Ivoire, the "Houphouet Phenomenon" continues to dominate. In other words, the state reconstitution process is flawed as evidenced by the continual use of repression and the maintenance of the poisonous segregative concept of "Ivoirite"—a citizenship requirement that discriminates against other Africans, who emigrated to and settled in Cote d'Ivoire. N'Diaye suggests that in order for the state reconstitution process in Cote d'Ivoire to be put on a democratic course, the nature and character of the state must be changed; a new model of governance based on decentralization must be designed; and the discriminatory citizenship requirement must be eliminated.

Emmanuel Kwesi-Aning uses the transition from Rawlings' 20-year rule to the regime of John Kufour as the framework for analyzing the state reconstitution project in Ghana in chapter 4. According to Kwesi-Aning, the 2000 Ghanaian elections constitute the watershed in the state reconstitution project in Africa. He then examines the state of the reconstitution project using three broad regime performance indicators—the security sector, the economy, and foreign policy. Kwesi-Aning posits that while some progress has been made in the security sector, there are still major hurdles to cross. In terms of the economy, he notes that much work still needs to be done to combat corruption, financial mismanagement in the public sector, huge external debt, low wages in the public sector, the increasing worthlessness of the cedi, the national currency, high fuel prices, acute dependence on foreign aid, and overall improvement in the standard of living of ordinary Ghanaians. As for foreign policy, he observes that the Kufour regime's links with the quintessential autocrat, the late Togolese President Eyadema, and one of the architects of subregional destabilization, President Compaore of Burkina Faso, undermines Ghana's march to state renewal. He then outlines some suggestions for making the state reconstitution project successful. These include (1) the importance of the Ghanaian leadership committing itself to the state reconstitution project; (2) the subordination of the military to civilian authority; and (3) addressing the myriad economic and social challenges confronting Ghana.

In chapter 5, Ann Nangulu-Ayuku discusses the dynamics of the state-building process in Kenya. Using the precolonial and colonial eras as historical crucibles, she examines the dynamics of the postcolonial state by using the Kenyatta, Moi, and Kibaki epochs as the foci of the evaluative criteria. She asserts that during the Kenyatta and Moi eras, Kenya was an authoritarian state as evidenced by a poor human rights record and other ills. She notes that the new Kibaki regime has set into motion a reconstitution agenda. However, there have been some major drawbacks. She concludes by arguing that the state reconstitution project under way in Kenya can succeed only if it addresses the major lacunas confronting Kenya: undemocratic governance, political repression, economic and social malaise, gender inequities, and a patronage-based civil service.

Sheila Bunwaree deciphers the state reconstitution project in Mauritius in chapter 6. She begins the chapter by examining the evolution of the Mauritian state, including the legacies of Dutch and French imperialism and British colonialism. She then discusses the efforts to refashion the state, so that it can be relevant to the lives of the majority of the people. She observes that the state reconstitution project has scored some successes in terms of the holding of free, fair, and regular elections; the establishment of a vibrant civic culture; a vibrant press; democratic leadership; and the provision of the basic needs of the people. She also discusses some of the major challenges to the state reconstitution enterprise: ethnic marginalization, especially of people of African descent and women; the electoral system based on the "Best Loser System"; and the socioeconomic problems posed by globalization. To help overcome these challenges, Bunwaree proposes that steps be taken to promote gender and ethnocultural equality, to create jobs, to redistribute wealth, and to reinvigorate the "welfare state."

The "tugs and pulls" of the state-building enterprise in Nigeria are succinctly discussed in chapter 7 by Sylvester Ogoh Alubo. Using the colonial, early postcolonial oil boom and oil bust eras as historical periods, he examines the nature, character, and dynamics of the Nigerian state over the last four decades. He insists that the role of the Nigerian state has remained constant throughout the country's history. According to Alubo, the Nigerian state has been preoccupied with the protection of capital, capitalism, and capitalists at the expense of serving the interests of the Nigerian people. He observes that even in the current era of "democratization," Nigeria has remained an "errand boy" of international finance capital. Alubo argues that the combination of the suzerainty of international finance capital, massive corruption, repression, and socioeconomic malaise remains the major obstacle to the successful reconstitution of the Nigerian State, despite the emergence of the so-called "democratization year" in May 1999. He concludes by proposing some measures for making the state reconstitution project successful; (1) the exigency of holding a national conference among the various stakeholders in the Nigerian polity; (2) the establishment and operation of genuine federalism; (3) the need to address the issue of citizenship in the various constituent states; (4) constitutional restructuring; and (5) tackling the myriad economic and social challenges.

In chapter 8, Victoria Maloka examines the demise of the apartheid state and its replacement by a democratizing polity. Specifically, she discusses the nature, character, and dynamics of the apartheid state; the resistance to apartheid and the eventual collapse of the apartheid state. Maloka then turns her attention to an assessment of the state of the reconstitution project. She observes that progress has been made in several areas such as the establishment of a new democratic constitutional order based on the protection of human rights, free, fair, and regular elections, racial equality, educational reform, and the construction of housing for the poor and disadvantaged. As for tackling challenges, she notes that much work still needs to be done in narrowing the economic disparities between black and white people, obliterating the last vestiges of racism and addressing the plethora of social and health problems, including the HIV/AIDS pandemic.

The volume concludes with Pita Agbese and George Kieh drawing the lessons learned from the state reconstitution experiences of Botswana, Cote d'Ivoire, Ghana, Kenya, Mauritius, Nigeria, and South Africa. They posit that while it is true that progress has been made in varying degrees by the seven democratizing states covered in the volume, there are still some challenges that need to be tackled. Among these are the nature and character of the postcolonial state; the need to gain insights from traditional African political systems; the issue of a developmental state; constitution and constitutionalism; democratic governance; viable political parties; vibrant civil society organizations, and the provision of basic human needs.

Conclusion

The primary objective in seeking alternative options for the African state is to make it responsive, responsible, transparent, and accountable to the African people. Such a task is impossible to accomplish without anchoring the state in a legitimate constitutional basis. In other words, a robust, efficient, effective, and accountable state cannot be created in the absence of a popular constitutional system. Development, peace, and democracy will be impossible to attain in Africa if a radical transformation of the state is not undertaken. Despite the current wave of privatization and the agitation for drastic reductions in the role of the state in the economy, the state is an indispensable tool for development, peace, and democracy. What Africa needs are democratic, accountable, efficient, responsive and effective states, and it is possible to create the framework for such states through a popular constitutional base.

Effective management of resources is imperative to peace and stability. Environmental management in Africa has been complicated by the privatization of resources, which without a strong regulatory role of the state poses grave dangers to the environment. It is also difficult to protect the environment without the foundations of good governance. Proper environmental safeguards are part of the process of accountability and if the government cannot be compelled to defend its stewardship of resources, it is impossible to control the environment. Moreover, agitations for a clean and healthy environment are an essential part of the democratic struggle. It is unwise to separate environmental struggles from democratic struggles and the struggles for regional autonomy and self-determination. Empowering people to control their resources and their environment is the ultimate form of political freedom. In the absence of such control, the concept of self-determination becomes meaningless.

The future of Africa depends on its success in accomplishing three crucial tasks: improving the material well-being of the masses of the African peoples; creating greater space for freedom, and distributing national resources more equitably so as to reduce communal tensions; and creating opportunities for greater participation in governance by women, the youth, and marginalized sections of the society. As President Nelson Mandela of South Africa pointed out in response to the electoral victory of the African National Congress (ANC) in 1994,

> [W]e must together and without delay begin to build a better life for all South Africans. This means creating jobs, building houses, providing education, and bringing peace and security for all. This is going to be the acid test of the government of national unity.[23]

Any reconstituted African state can best be judged on whether it has helped to create a better life for all its citizens. Otherwise, reform or reconstitution merely provides a patina of progress for something that stays the same.

Notes

1. See The African Union, *A New Africa Initiative: Merger of the Millennium Partnership for African Recovery Program* (Pretoria, July 2001), p. 1.
2. Economic Commission for Africa, *Transforming Africa's Economies: Economic Report on Africa 2000* (Addis Ababa: ECA, 2001), p. 20.
3. See Julius Nyerere, "Letter to Government Ministers and Officials, July 3, 1963," reproduced in *Voices of Power*, ed. Henry Bienen (Hopewell, NJ: Ecco Press, 1995), pp. 215–218.
4. Human Rights Watch, *World Report 2005* (New York: Human Rights Watch, 2005).
5. Ibid.
6. See Jomo Kenyatta, "Harambee! Uhuru Independence Day Speech," December 12, 1963, reproduced in *Voices of Power*, ed. Henry Bienen, pp. 211–212.
7. Minister of Finance, Ngozi Okonjo-Iweala, as quoted in *This Day*, February 16, 2005.
8. Inaugural Speech by President Mwai Kibaki, Nairobi, December, 30, 2002.
9. Leonce Ndikumana, "Institutional Failure and Ethnic Conflicts in Burundi," *African Studies Review*, vol. 41, no. 1, 1998, p. 48.

10. Dianna Games, "Sale and Reward," *Business in Africa*, December 2000/ January 2001, p. 5.

11. Atiku Abubakar, text of an Address to the Fourth Pan-African Privatization and Investment Summit, Abuja, Nigeria, November 2000.

12. Ibid.

13. Ibid.

14. See J. Oloka-Onyango, ed., *Constitutionalism in Africa: Creating Opportunities, Facing Challenges* (Kampala: Fountain Publishers, 2001); Segun Jegede, Ayodele Ale, and Eni Akinsola, eds., *Path to People's Constitution* (Lagos: CDHR Publications, 2000); Haroub Othman and Maria Nassali, *Towards Political Liberalization in Uganda* (Kampala: Fountain Publishers, 2002).

15. On constitutionalism in East Africa in particular, see Kivutha Kibwana, Chris Maina Peter, and Nyangabyaki Bazaara, *Constitutionalism in East Africa: Progress, Challenges and Prospects in 1999* (Kampala: Fountain Publishers, 2001).

16. See the collection of essays in *The Transition to Democratic Governance in Africa: The Continuing Struggle*, ed. John Mukum Mbaku and Julius Omozuanvbo Ihonvbere (Westport, CT: Praeger, 2003).

17. Carlene J. Edie, *Politics in Africa: A New Beginning?* (Belmont, CA: Wadsworth, 2003).

18. Tajudeen Abdul-Raheem, "Gluttons Who Vomit on Shoes and the Mental Revolution," *Pambazuka News*, July 27, 2004.

19. Ibid.

20. For a very incisive critique of politics and corruption in the post-military era in Nigeria, see Efeturi Ojakaminor, *Nigeria's Ghana-Must-Go Republic: Happenings* (Iperu-Remo: The Ambassador Publications, n.d.).

21. See "Nigeria In Year 2005: Hoping For Better Days," (Editorial), *The Guardian*, January 1, 2005.

22. Quoted in Ojakaminor, *Nigeria's Ghana-Must-Go Republic*, p. 11.

23. Nelson Mandela, Victory Speech after the May 2, 1994 Election, reproduced in *Voices of Power*, ed. Henry Bienen, pp. 305–307.

PART II

Case Studies

CHAPTER 2

Statecraft in Botswana: Renegotiating Development, Legitimacy, and Authority

Onalenna Doo Selolwane

Introduction

It has become common practice among Africanist scholars either to treat Botswana as an oddity when it does not fit the African stereotype of the incompetent, oppressive, and corrupt state or to deny the significance of its deviance from the stereotype in order to maintain a portrait of Africa as a continent of unmitigated failure with regard to the human social enterprise. Using the Botswana case, this chapter will examine how state power was consolidated to win it legitimacy and authority in the context of the challenges of the colonial legacy, deteriorating conditions in the world economy, and the growth of civil society. In particular, the chapter will focus on two key areas of the governance of the public sector (the economy and the political system) to illustrate the development of the Botswana state and its relationship with non-state agencies.

It is not the intention of this chapter either to flag the exceptionality line or to provide more stereotypical examples of failure. Rather, the chapter will examine some key historical processes that have given the Botswana state its form, content, and character. The starting point of my argument is that those who ascend to positions of state power are part of a larger structure of social agents who interact under particular historical circumstances, and that the character of the state reflects the outcomes of such interaction, the universalism of the state notwithstanding. The thrust of this discussion is on the making of the postcolonial state in terms of the roles of both state and non-state agencies, and the interplay of sectional interests and structural factors in the state-building process. This is a departure from the dominant discourse on the African state that is premised on the assumption that the African state is so dominant in political life that its nature and the weaknesses of non-state agencies can be meaningfully read only from the actions and intentions of those who have occupied state structures and institutions and who are linked to the interests of external hegemonies.

Like all other contemporary African countries, Botswana is a product of European colonial domination in the delineation of its political boundaries and the construction of the institutional structures and procedures on which the modern state was founded. Therefore, to understand the postindependence process of state building, it is important to recognize the colonial processes that created the conditions under which that started. Among the key factors that shaped the character of Botswana's formation were the limited presence of colonial administration and the territory's transformation into a labor reserve economy. The reason for minimal colonial administrative presence was that the territory had little of significant economic value to justify colonial administrative expenditure, but it was of strategic importance for thwarting competing German and Boer claims to territory during the scramble for Africa. Due to lack of exploitable natural resources, Botswana came to be used mainly to supply labor to the growing mining industry of the British colony of South Africa.

The administrative presence of the colonial government in this territory was succinctly captured by the white settlers when they stated in 1935, "From the inception of the Protectorate up to almost present times the history of colonial office rule is a very sad one to relate, especially in regard to this territory. It seems as if once the Territory had been declared a Protectorate, its responsibility ended there and then."[1] With limited direct colonial administration, the Protectorate for most of its colonial history was indirectly ruled through the traditional authorities of the most centralized tribal polities parallel to a minimum of colonial structures and institutions (e.g., the police force). The headquarters of Botswana's colonial administration were in South Africa.

Both politically and economically, the Protectorate was not prepared by the colonial administration for eventual autonomy as it was considered too poor to be viable as an independent entity. Instead, plans were made to incorporate it into the Union of South Africa. But these were later dropped when consideration was given to decolonization after World War II. The story of Botswana's postcolonial state building is a story of how this country was able to overcome the colonial legacy of poverty, skeletal administrative institutions, and a labor reserve economy to become a viable state-nation. Contrary to the general stereotype of failed African states, Botswana did become a viable state to most citizens. The minimal colonial presence was to prove an advantage to state building because there was neither any inherited wealth for the elite to scramble over, nor a crystallized class of modern elite in a dominant position of control. This, therefore, enabled the small fragments of white settlers and educated Africans to negotiate for a common ground of interests imposed on them by the survival imperatives of an exceptionally poor economy. This elite alliance was negotiated at the same time as negotiations were started for independent sovereignty from the departing colonial administration, and these initiatives thus became part of the process of forging a common nationality and a new state.

I will start the account on this state-building enterprise by examining the management of the economy, and the role that it played in consolidating state legitimacy and practical sovereignty. The economy is critical because it provides the resource base required for the state-building enterprise.

State Building and Economic Agency: From Labor Reserve Economy to Cattle Beef Industry

When the Botswana flag was hoisted in 1966, the new government inherited a territorial entity characterized by a migrant labor economy where 40 percent of the male labor force was engaged in South African mines.[2] The years leading to independence had also witnessed a long period of drought that decimated a third of the cattle that were the backbone of the largely rural economy, thus reducing national income to dependence on migrant labor earnings. Independence was actually ushered in on the back of food aid to relieve the precarious situation most of the population was in, as a result of the inability of the subsistence activities to meet basic needs.

The 1960s were an auspicious time for countries coming out of colonial rule. The old order of territorial colonialism was being laid to rest in the rubbles of World War II and the United States of America had ascended to the leadership of the Western industrialized world with a new style of imperialism based on decolonization with development. In this new order, former colonies would be assisted to modernize their economies through infrastructural development and under the aegis of a friendlier capitalist system that respected the right of peoples to self-determination. To realize this new order, Western technology, ideas, and money would be systematically transferred to the nonindustrialized countries to engineer development. International organizations and systems including various agencies of the United Nations System were set up to facilitate that transformative transfer of resources. And thus began the United Nations First Development Decade. This was part of an era that H. Singer and S. Roy have dubbed the "golden years of capitalism" where, following the end of World War II and the reconstruction of Europe with American finance, capitalist economies enjoyed an unbroken record of three decades of sustained growth, peace, and stability.[3]

For newly independent former colonies in Africa, the modernization agenda was generally facilitated both by the availability of capital transfers and very favorable international terms of trade for primary goods, resulting in rapid economic growth and tangible transformations in human capital development. With specific reference to Botswana, the golden years of capitalism and the "winds of change" that they heralded created potential for resource transfer from the West in three critical ways. First, the British colonial administration, in anticipation of relinquishing control over Botswana, had started to release state lands for use by an emergent class of cattle ranching, local white elite that would now be expanded by the inclusion of Africans. This was backed up by an unprecedented level of transfers of grants-in-aid to finance the infrastructural and technological development that would support the commercialization of the cattle-beef industry.

Second, other financial resources became available through aid agencies set up by various Western national governments (including those that had never had colonial territories) and the United Nations System. Botswana's political independence came when the first UN Development Decade was already under way, thus making funds available for the infrastructural and institutional development that W.W. Rostow, in his famous Non-Communist Manifesto, had prescribed as a sure way of engineering modernity in backward economies. Rostow's prescriptions included the construction of banking and financial institutions, postal and communications systems, health and educational institutions, administrative and related state buildings, as well as modern townships in the administrative capital and other centers of modern economic activities.

Third, the infrastructural developments that were made possible through grants-in-aid and soft loans, together with the system of guarantees provided by certain UN agencies, the World Bank, and IMF, attracted private capital into economic areas that promised good returns on investment. Direct capital investment therefore became a very significant source of finance. H. Singer and S. Roy have identified this source of capital as a significant player in the misfortunes that befell many African countries when the golden years of capitalism ended and the terms of trade turned drastically against primary-goods-exporting economies.[4] In the 1960s, however, it came to be seen as a key source for financing economic modernization through industrial development.

The potential availability of such private capital encouraged Botswana to search feverishly for potential economic growth areas, particularly mineral deposits, that would attract such investment. Government also set out to negotiate with multinational corporations for joint ventures in the exploitation of mineral wealth. At independence (1966), though, this area of capital resource represented a dream that was still to be realized rather than an actual reality. Decades of prospecting for minerals during colonial times had failed to yield substantive mineral wealth that had sustainable economic value. So, the future seemed rather bleak; conventional wisdom had it that Botswana would never attain more than modest growth in a limited number of niches that might just about provide an economic base for independent sovereignty.

One of those niches was the cattle-beef industry. With the resources made available by the new order of Western capitalism, Botswana embarked on the modernization of the cattle economy that was quickly transformed into a leading export earner, bringing riches hitherto undreamed of for those who had the means to take advantage of this commercial enterprise. Government pursued a policy of sharing (after deducting running costs) profits accrued from beef export earnings with the farmers who had supplied the beef during the financial year. Further, to minimize the extent to which middle men would take advantage of small cattle holders to buy cheaply from them and then sell to the beef marketing board at a high profit, government established more and more depots to enable the Botswana Meat Commission to reach the small farmers in the regions. It also generated the much needed export earnings for the national economy where agriculture accounted for 40 percent of national wealth.

The manner in which this economic transformation was achieved laid the first firm foundation for the building of the nation and the state in that it brought to educated Africans and white settlers the realization that they had a common destiny that would benefit them materially if they worked together rather than at cross purposes. Neither group had by then much economic clout. They entered into a pact for which the

Africans would negotiate with the colonial administration for a national constitution that would guarantee and protect private ownership of land and other productive resources, and thus enable the emergence of a class of commercial cattle ranchers in which they both had a vested interest. White settlers had seen their future only in a racially divided society that privileged them, while the Africans, who had been denied free access to "white enterprise" through institutionalized racism, sought a future that opened up opportunities on a nonracial basis. These differences were relatively easy to reconcile in forging the common purpose of transforming the economy for their mutual benefit and individual wealth. The successful development of the cattle-beef industry thus cemented these small elite factions into a common unit with a vested interest in a functioning state that could effectively protect their cattle interests. But it was also recognized that for this state to have broad-based legitimacy among the rest of the citizenry, it must deliver and be seen to deliver tangible benefits to them all; hence, the commitment to social justice, unity, rapid, and sustainable growth.

The big leap forward for Botswana's economy came with the discovery of diamonds after independence. This set the country resolutely on a path of rapid and sustained economic growth over a period that was arguably the golden age of economic modernization for the nation. It was also to provide the state with the wherewithal to weld the many different interests into a nation forged out of disparate groups of people.

Rapid Economic Growth and State Consolidation

In common with all other postcolonial African countries, the government of Botswana adopted a development strategy based on interventionist state participation in the economy and the conventional wisdom that industrialization was the key to rapid and sustainable growth.[5] This strategy has many of the features that the World Bank and other observers have come to associate with economic failure in Africa. These features include, among others, a dominant state sector, planned development intervention, limited local government autonomy, and reliance on one or two primary products for international trade.

Critics of the postcolonial African state normally identify these strategic initiatives as the root causes of the stagnation that came to characterize many African national economies after independence, particularly in the 1980s and 1990s at the height of IMF/World Bank Structural Adjustment Programs. Botswana shared all these features as can be seen from the fact that the government directly accounted for 35 percent to

40 percent of formal sector jobs and a third of the gross domestic product (GDP). The government contribution to the economy was even larger when one takes into account the fact the state was the principal client of most private sector businesses through the implementation of public investment programs as well as supply requirements. In spite of the dominance of the government in the economy, Botswana has experienced one of the fastest economic growth rates in the world since it became independent, particularly during the first three decades of independence. How did that happen?

A characteristic that has greatly influenced how Botswana would manage its postindependence economic affairs was the recognition, by its national leaders, of the extremely limited resource base of the country. This, in their view, necessitated very careful husbandry to get the most out of the least; hence the imperative of careful planning. In the transitional year of self-government leading to full sovereignty, for instance, Botswana's leaders spurned the advice of the British Ministry of Overseas Development to "leave industrial development . . . for private investment." Instead, the government pointed out that "as has been proved elsewhere in Africa, industrial development requires governmental efforts to promote investment through loans administered by a development bank, and if necessary through a development corporation."[6] The government then proceeded to set up the National Development Bank and the Botswana Development Corporation to act as catalysts for industrialization, correctly perceiving that the circumstances of Botswana, then one of the world's poorest countries in terms of both national income and natural resources, had very little to attract private investment.

Two factors in particular informed the strategy adopted. First, as already noted, every mining venture that had ever been tried within the territory during colonial times had ended in failure after a brief life of struggle, suggesting that the potential for industrialization was very modest, if there at all. The only two major exports that were sustained during the colonial economy were migrant labor and beef. In fact, in the run-up to independence, migrant labor was a greater export earner due to persistent drought and the reduction in the number of cattle in the early 1960s. And while the export of these two national income earners firmly incorporated the Protectorate into the international capitalist system, it also undermined the productive capacity of the household economies that depended on male labor[7] and the draught power of cattle.

Second, Botswana has a very harsh natural environment and a rather tiny and sparse population. This limited both resource mobilization and effective national demand for goods and services due mainly to the 20–25-year rainfall cycle characterized by drought and then relative wetness. During the drought phase, there are huge losses in cattle accompanied by serious food deficits. When the wet phase returns, it takes some time for the cattle herd to be restocked before another drought phase begins, undermining the gains made previously. This has made resource accumulation in the traditional economy difficult to sustain over time, particularly among farming households. Botswana's leaders recognized that for the foreseeable future, the country would have to rely on external resources to initiate economic modernization and that the state would have to play a leading role in marshaling these resources so that they would bring the greatest amount of benefit as rapidly as possible.

The discovery of diamonds immediately following the country's independence provided an opportunity for the government to negotiate partnership deals with multinational companies that enabled the exploitation of this mineral wealth with some benefits accruing directly to the government as shareholder and tax collector. The government derives 40 percent of its revenues from the diamond industry. Most observers agree that the Botswana government has been very prudent in both the use of national revenues and its fiscal policies. And that this has contributed in no small measure to the country's economic stability and growth. In the 33 years between 1966 and 1999, Botswana's GDP increased seventeenfold in real terms as per capita income rose from approximately P1682.50 at 1993/94 prices to P9365.00.[8] At its peak, economic growth averaged 14 percent per annum. Even into the twenty-first century, Botswana's economic growth rate averages a robust 5 percent to 6 percent per annum.[9]

The manner in which the government utilized diamond revenues in its modernization agenda has greatly enhanced people's confidence in the modern state's developmental role and capacity. A critical selling point of the strategy was its emphasis on the development of both physical and social infrastructure. While the state created capital to enable growth, it was the infrastructural development that was a highly visible and tangible result. Though the thrust of this infrastructural development had an urban bias, the state made a deliberate efforts to take these developments to rural areas where the majority of the voters resided. Against the counsel of economic advisors, the political leadership embarked on an accelerated rural development program as soon as the diamond revenues began to come in. This included the building of schools, roads, provision of health facilities and ammenities such as water, and extension services, to support the agricultural activities of both wealthy cattle owners and the poor. This sent a clear message that independence would bring modernization to all citizens.

Starting with the larger settlements and moving down to smaller ones, the state, in an attempt at even distribution, provided infrastructural facilities across regions where people were still settled largely in terms of traditional ethnopolities. The purpose of the policy of evenhandedness was to ensure that no ethnic group would feel that development favored some groups or regional areas more than it did others. With the exception perhaps, of the indigenous minority San groups, this encouraged people to believe that where development had not yet arrived in their area, this was due to population size and limiting resources rather than the ethnic background of the group. There were also special development programs targeted at the San groups (so-called Bushmen) through the Remote Area Dweller strategy. With the rise in national income, there was a greater emphasis on productive development programs aimed at enhancing the resource base of rural populations to enable them to increase their output in subsistence livelihoods.

Although many of the development programs that targeted rural populations did not in fact significantly improve the productive capacity of most rural people, they were important at least as a form of welfare transfer from the state. Infrastructural development on the other hand, changed the quality of life in rural areas, by ensuring greater access to potable water very close to people's homesteads, increasing access to school and health services, and generally improving roads and communication. Very significantly, this strategy also brought government to the doorsteps of many communities through the construction of various government offices and the provision of extension services.

As already noted, besides high visibility and its redistributive qualities, infrastructural development had the concrete benefit of creating capital formation. The construction industry put considerable wind in the sails of the diamond-led economic growth, creating a wider circle of jobs and increasing the demand for goods and services. For three decades, therefore, Botswana enjoyed the benefits of rapid and sustained growth that enhanced the capacity of the state to exercise practical sovereignty and to deliver modernization in varying degrees to every community in the republic. Even during the bad days of crippling debt burdens and structural adjustment programs for most African countries, the Botswana economy was able to weather these challenges remarkably well, maintaining its debt burden at comfortable levels that allowed economic growth rates to stay ahead of population growth.

Economic Slow Down and Privatization

Globally, the 1980s were supposed to represent the third UN Decade of Development. In many African countries, however, economic stagnation and deterioration were more prominent than development if measured by their growth and the maintenance of the infrastructure created during the 1960s and 1970s. Some critics have thus dubbed this period the "Lost Development Decade." In Botswana, overall growth was maintained, but it became increasingly obvious that the heavy investments in physical and human capital had not raised total productivity factor significantly. The 1993 Bank of Botswana Annual Report noted that the payoff for this investment has been low.[10] This tended to negate efforts for economic diversification and expansion of the employment creation base.

Against the international background of IMF/World Bank-inspired structural adjustment policies, critics began to point out that the direct involvement of the state in economic activity and through policy and administrative regulations was inappropriate because it stifled the private sector and created allocative inefficiencies that distorted domestic markets. Therefore, while the economy had exhibited spectacular overall growth, there was stagnation in those sectors that had potential to create more employment. Botswana was caught in a unique situation of excess liquidity in the banking system due to diamond revenues on one hand and credit-starved enterprises on the other hand, partly due to inefficiencies in resource allocation and partly to limited avenues for investment.

The previous strategy of providing development incentives through infrastructural development and investment grants had clearly failed to enhance people's active participation in the economy despite large capital transfers into agriculture, poverty alleviation programs, and industrial enterprises through grants and subsidies. This had created a worrying phenomenon of dependency on both state handouts and urban-rural transfers. Furthermore, while the economic growth had clearly improved the quality of life of most citizens in terms of health, education, and access to public goods, relative poverty and wide income differentials persisted, leading observers to caption Botswana as a "land of poverty amidst plenty." By the late 1980s, a widening gap was seen between planned growth and diversification on one hand, and the implementation of these plans on the other. The limitations of the government as an economic agent also became more apparent to many people.

This state of affairs encouraged the government to accede to pressure from both the nascent local private sector and international agencies for reduction of the state role and the enlargement of economic space for the private sector. This pressure culminated in a series of annual conferences between private sector representatives and top government officials and politicians (including the president and some key ministers) to review and reformulate policy for meaningful private sector participation. At these forums, it was pointed out that while past policies were intended to facilitate private sector growth and economic participation, bureaucratic control had, in fact, strangulated private sector initiatives and made it difficult for business creativity to develop to its full potential. Specific activities of government agencies that were stifling private business were documented and earmarked for redress. These included overregulation, excessive administration of non-mining economic activities, and a general mistrust and hostility toward private business by government bureaucrats.

The result was a policy shift that has served to further enhance the credibility of the state, particularly among the voting public. As was the case during the era of state-led development, Botswana's privatization strategy has been targeted at the development of both the large entrepreneur and the poor classes of potential small and micro-businesses. In a national consultation program initiated by the president to solicit the views of a wide section of the population in small and large settlements on what they thought should be the vision of the nation in the twenty years ahead, people contributed ideas about what had gone wrong in the past and what changes would be necessary in the future. This has also informed the privatization strategy. Thus, for the lower to medium end of the business sector, the government introduced the following programs of assistance:

1. Establishment of an autonomous Small Business Council made up mainly of private sector representation to advise government on policy regarding Small, Medium, and Micro-Enterprises (SMME)
2. Reduction of the regulatory burdens that the private sector had identified as stifling
3. Establishment of a National Micro-Credit Scheme to provide loans to citizens with low income
4. Establishment of a Credit Guarantee Scheme to be applied to large scale loans where 60 percent of the sum loaned by participating commercial banks would be guaranteed
5. Provision of business orientation education and training to help SMMEs with marketing and technological skills and support.

Other complementary instruments have included macroeconomic policy instruments such as the exchange rate policy, interest rate policy, as well as education and training policy. Botswana maintains an exchange rate policy whereby, the domestic currency is pegged to an external reference (a basket of currencies) to avoid the danger of a Dutch-disease-type real exchange rate appreciation that could negatively affect the tradable goods sectors and employment therein. The large foreign reserves that Botswana maintains give the country a degree of flexibility not otherwise available to similar small economies. Botswana also maintains real interest rates that are comparable with those in major industrialized economies, but lower than those prevailing in neighboring South Africa. This has been done through several means. One is by government withdrawing some of the capital inflows from diamond revenues and depositing them in the Bank of Botswana for use only when future spending needs dictate withdrawal. The other is by introducing foreign currency accounts at local banks, as well as requiring commercial banks to deposit excess liquidity into call accounts at the Bank of Botswana. Finally, the government liberalized capital controls to allow individuals to hold their savings offshore. These measures served to reduce inflationary pressure on the local currency and thus creating a stable environment for business growth.

Overall, therefore, the Botswana state has managed the national economy in a manner that has won it the confidence of ordinary citizens; even where there were glaring failures such as widening income differentials and persistent unemployment coexisting with generous financial resources and reserves, the government has steadfastly resisted pressure to draw on its reserves to finance consumption. However, with increasing privatization, there has also been increasing incidents of corruption and mismanagement of public resources by the political and administrative leadership. These incidents have drawn considerable public scrutiny and criticism that led to the establishment of an anti-corruption agency by the government.

State and Political Agency

Together with the economy, political governance is a key area of social life that can be used to critically assess the performance and development of the postcolonial state. As a former colony, Botswana at independence was a political entity that represented a number of disparate ethnic groups whose only common tie had been an externally based colonial administration. Independence therefore represented the beginning of concerted efforts to forge a single nation out of these semiautonomous polities under a constitution that was markedly different from that of ethnic polities. The new leadership hardly had any established traditional authority, particularly with regard to the entire territory. The demise of colonialism presented an opportunity for building new institutions and processes of legitimizing power that differed from both traditional constitutions and colonial rule. In this section, I will discuss the role played by the postcolonial state and the key agencies of political parties, and electorate on the women's organizations role in developing the constitutional and institutional structures and procedures for these forms of legitimizing power.

The Birth of the Popular Mandate and Multiparty Contestation for Government Power

The Republic of Botswana came into existence through an electoral victory that ended a century of colonial domination and subordinated traditional hereditary rule to begin a popular and competitive legitimation of governmental power. Both the elections and the constitution resulted from negotiations among several competing interests. These included the hereditary rulers of the recognized principal ethnic groups, an emerging class of educated leaders (most of whom did not have any traditional claim to power), a minority of white settlers, and the departing colonial administration.

Among the Africans, the traditional leaders saw themselves as the rightful heirs of the colonial polity and therefore agitated for a transfer of power into their hands as a college of hereditary rulers representing their ethnic polities. They envisaged only limited accommodation for those with no hereditary power base. Throughout colonial times, these hereditary rulers had enjoyed a large measure of their traditional authority under the system of indirect and parallel rule. From that base, they had strengthened both their economic positions (e.g., through tax collection, allowances from private concession companies, etc.)[11] and their political sphere of control over other less centralized ethnic groups. They were therefore vehemently opposed to any constitutional change in which the power to govern would not be based on birthright.

In contrast, the educated elites wanted a constitutional dispensation that would ensure a greater political role for non-chiefs. They feared that both traditional chiefs and white settlers would dominate postcolonial modernist government institutions as they had done during colonial times. Many of these were actively political and were involved in the formation of several short-lived political parties before the advent of the Botswana Democratic Party. They agitated for a system of government where the right to rule would be conferred on the basis of electoral competition and a popular mandate. Some, however, were also clearly interested in a type of government that would protect their cattle-owning interests and enable them to modernize their enterprises. But others[12] tended in rhetoric, to favor a system of government where the state would seize and retain control over the basic means of production (i.e., land, industry, transport, communications, etc.). These groups therefore gravitated toward opposing political camps to form separate parties that were eventually to contest for the mandate to rule.

The white settlers had been agitating for the incorporation of the territory into South Africa where both the country's racial laws and the presence of larger number of whites would ensure the protection of their rights against competition from Africans. For them, the idea of an independent Botswana governed by Africans was initially not a very attractive option. But when independence became inevitable, they realigned themselves with the political camp that guaranteed private ownership of cattle and other wealth-creating commercial enterprises.

The colonial administration, in turn, wanted to transfer power to institutional structures that not only resembled Westminster but also commanded legitimacy from traditional authority, since the final mandate to effect a liberal democratic constitution would come from a voting public used to hereditary rule. As already indicated above, in the run-up to independence, the colonial administration had started preparing the territory for self-rule by transferring capital resources to the country to support economic development.[13] The release of Crown lands to facilitate the expansion of private freehold tenure and to provide a base for enhancement of the productive capacity of commercial farms became a means of bargaining for a suitable heir who would guarantee continued opportunity for expanded Western capitalist investment and profit making.

The traditional leaders as a college were not a suitable heirs as they expected the kind of dispensation that maintained hereditary rule. This was not in keeping with the American-led new order of modernization with decolonization. Instead, the colonial administration found a more suitable heir in the Botswana Democratic Party and the group of local elites who favored modernization based on private ownership of cattle enterprises. This was a political party, greatly encouraged in its formation by colonial administrators and led by an educated man who was also the legitimate hereditary ruler of the most populous of the ethnic polities. Once the realization dawned on the other traditional leaders that the colonial government would transfer power with, or without, their participation, their initial objections to political parties soon turned to acceptance for one that was led by one of their own. They wrongly assumed that being himself a hereditary ruler, the leader of the Botswana Democratic Party would be sympathetic to protecting the interests of hereditary power against the incursions of elected office-holders.

In contrast, the other political parties were led by men who had no traditional power base, and were inclined toward socialist principles and a suspicion of the intentions of the colonial administration. So, in terms of their standing in the eyes of both the colonial government and hereditary leaders, they did not enjoy the support they needed to win the mandate of an electorate that was still tied to chiefly power. Their overt opposition to chiefs and the colonial administration was a strategic error that cost them the confidence of tribal voters whose support they needed to win office. They also lost the confidence of the small educated elite whose critical mass they required to field candidates to contest political constituencies.

Botswana's liberal democratic constitution was thus born from these negotiations. Like similar constitutions in Africa, it promised an electoral system of conferment of government power based on multiparty competitions, a separation of government power to provide checks and balances against concentration of power and its possible abuse, and a conferment of equal rights and freedoms on all citizens to enable them to enjoy unfettered competition for office. Victory in the first round of general elections inevitably went to the Botswana Democratic Party that had been able to canvass for support and field candidates in all constituencies with the blessing of both traditional leaders and the colonial administration.

Since then, Botswana has gone on to have seven more rounds of uninterrupted popular elections that most observers would agree have been reasonably free and fair in terms of the subordination of the electoral process to the rule of law and constitutionally guaranteed rights and freedoms. However, concern has been raised over the tendency for this process to return the same party to power every time. In a continent notorious for single-party dominance, coercive rule, and divisive politics, the failure of Botswana's seemingly multiparty electoral system to produce a change of government over such a long period raises many questions about the quality and substance of its liberal democracy, which need to be addressed.

Single Party Dominance and Intolerance of Dissent: the First Two Decades

The ruling Botswana Democratic Party has been in power since the first electoral victory in 1965, when it won all but three of the elected parliamentary seats. Some critics have explained the staying power of the ruling party by referring to the ethnic structure of Botswana society, which they claim gives a natural advantage to this particular party. J.D. Holm, for instance, has argued that the ruling party is perceived by the dominant ethnic groups in Botswana to represent them and therefore they consistently vote for it.[14]

The empirical basis informing this school of thought is, however, very tenuous as (1) it assumes that tribal polities are ethnically homogenous; and that (2) when opposition parties raise questions on cultural inequalities they necessarily represent ethnic groups other than those supporting the ruling party. In fact, the ethnic structure of party affiliation is similar across all parties, and no party therefore can be assumed to represent any particular ethnic group from such a composition. As noted in the preceding section on economic management, the government of Botswana has meticulously followed an evenhanded distribution of the benefits of national wealth to minimize possible ethnic polarization. The success of this policy is indicated by the fact that in the debates on ethnic inequalities that surfaced in the late 1990s (discussed later), the issues were couched in terms of cultural inequalities rather than disparities in the share of national wealth and economic and educational opportunities. In fact, it is the beneficiaries of this even-handed distribution of resources who are now leading the challenge against government for more recognition of cultural inequalities in language, ethnic identity, and the status of their traditional chiefs.

Most importantly, ethnic politics in the hands of political parties has historically been a loser as a vote catcher. Botswana's opposition parties have flagged the ethnic question by challenging the ruling party for its discriminatory constitution that assigned the status of principal ethnic groups to the ethnic Tswana polities and relegated others to a minority status. But as a vote catcher, this political emphasis on cultural discrimination seemed to pale in significance against the obvious material benefits that were distributed without discrimination among all ethnic constituencies. In particular, the benefits of education that had been very scarce during colonial times were made accessible to all regions, and enabled youths from traditionally discriminated ethnic groups to get into well-paid jobs and thus advance materially to an equal standing with those from the so-called principal ethnic groups.

In an insightful study of the impact of expanding employment and educational opportunities on ethnic Bakgaladi, for instance, J. Solway observed how this enabled them to free themselves from an inferiority complex vis-à-vis ethnic Batswana. She notes,

> With glee I was repeatedly informed of recent Kgalagadi successes in
> secondary schools, university, and the job market. Parents told me in 1990
> "our children are mixing with others now, at work and in schools, and
> doing well. We can see now that we are as good as anyone else." Young
> people, successful in school and the job market, have been doubly critical
> in catalyzing and crystallizing the change in ethnic consciousness amongst
> the western Kweneng Kgalagadi. On the other hand success had its
> limits. . . . They ultimately failed in their attempts at assimilation and had
> to confront the fact that they could not escape the stigma of their ethnic
> origins. . . . Their association with other Kgalagadi in town, at university,
> and in the work places . . . reinforced their indignity over their
> treatment. . . . Their accomplishments, treatment, and struggles outside
> the Kgalagadi region have put into perspective their "difference" and
> contributed to providing a basis for a new ethnic consciousness and
> "imagined community."[15]

While J. Solway notes the limitations of poorer schools in Kgalagadi
and the inferiority label still attached to Kgalagadi ethnicity, she provides ample evidence of increasing acceptance of national identity with
equality of citizenship among ethnic groups, particularly those formerly
discriminated against. She also notes the changing material basis of
social relations and the diversity that makes for a complexity of party
affiliations.

Some observers have sought to explain the unfairness of the electoral
process by referring to the advantage of incumbency. In a review of party
politics in Botswana, L. Picard provides an insightful commentary on
how the ruling Botswana Democratic Party has used incumbency to
thwart political opposition and maintain de facto single party dominance.[16]
He demonstrates the ruling party's intolerance for opposition parties,
and argues that these parties were effectively cast as undemocratic agents
who should not be given the mandate to rule, and who might incur banning if they continued in their perceived subversive activities.[17] Kenneth
Good has also argued that the Botswana government has used legislative
measures to limit the rights and freedoms of interest groups deemed to
threaten the stability of the state, thus undermining the electoral process
whose integrity rests on individual freedoms.[18]

There is indeed ample evidence that once in power, the ruling
Botswana Democratic Party became highly intolerant of any opposition
that it deemed a threat to its sovereignty. Very much in line with other

newly independent African states, the Botswana government tended to see dissent as a threat to its nation-building agenda that had not yet consolidated. This concern can be appreciated within the context where the nation was being built on a base where ethnic polities had existed fairly independently of one another, and with only a skeletal colonial presence providing oversight. Almost overnight, ethnic subjects of different sovereigns were transformed into modern citizens under one sovereign with liberal rights and freedoms they were not even fully aware of nor appreciative of. I shall come back to this point later.

To mold these "subjects" into "citizens" along the lines articulated by Mahmood Mamdani, the government in power used a variety of strategies. Having won the confidence of the hereditary rulers to support a party led by a hereditary ruler, the Botswana Democratic Party government then set about to systematically strip these traditional leaders of substantive power by transferring decision-making power to elected offices. The allocation of land, for instance, was transferred to the Land Boards, with the traditional leaders subordinated to the position of *ex officio* members. Lawmaking and application were transferred respectively to parliament and the courts, leaving only an advisory role for the chiefs through the House of Chiefs. Similarly, tribal courts were left with the responsibility to administer certain aspects of tribal law pertaining to property, marriage, and related disputes. But these courts were subordinate to the civil courts. Altogether, these served to sever the vestiges of traditional power bases, and thus to firmly entrench the legal and practical sovereignty in the new state.

As already mentioned, the government took the lead in capital resource mobilization and actively participated in economic development in direct partnership with private international companies. The accumulated wealth was redistributed in a manner that clearly demonstrated that the modern state had greater capacity than previous leaders had to transform people's material life and engender modernity. This not only weaned people from allegiance to their ethnic leaders, but also created confidence in the capacity of this state to really exercise practical sovereignty among all citizens. The authority of the new state in relation to competing traditional and colonial authority was thus further consolidated.

There is compelling evidence that the state utilized its position as resource distributor and accumulator to deliberately influence votes in favor of the ruling party. For instance, in 1974, government awarded large wage increases to all sectors of the civil service five months before the general elections.[19] In rural areas, infrastructural developments were accelerated so that they could be completed before the elections. Further, in the run-up to the 1979 elections, there was greater emphasis on visible rural development projects in terms of grants for household agriculture and infrastructural development, particularly in constituencies where the opposition seemed to have considerable support. This demonstrates that where less endowed governments would have used naked coercion to suppress divergent political opinions that threatened the ruling party's hold on power, the government of Botswana used the relatively generous resources it commanded to ensure continued support to it and to the ruling party across all regional constituencies. With a large parliamentary majority, the ruling party also conferred extensive constitutional powers on the state and the state president, which have sporadically been used to neutralize dissent.

To limit our analysis of the weaknesses of the electoral process to the capacity of the ruling party to manipulate it does not, however, provide a full understanding of Botswana's political processes and the extent of state power. Given that the country has a constitution that not only confers and guarantees liberal rights and freedoms, but also has been respected by the government, it is important to examine the role of other agencies in upholding these freedoms and limiting the powers of the state. The electorate is one such important agency. To what extent did the voting public in fact use their constitutionally guaranteed freedoms and rights to hold the government to account and to recognize the importance of the rights of other political parties to electoral support?

A large part of the answer to this question lies in the cultural background of the voters, who were transformed into citizens with civic rights that were substantially foreign to their experience. In the ideal typical modern liberal democracy, the populace is supposed to organize itself into various agencies for collective bargaining and protection of sectional interests. The right to vote is also supposed to confer on such citizens the responsibility of holding their elected leaders to account, not only through periodic elections, but also continuously through organizational life, the media, public debate, and so on.

However, the people of Botswana were not aware of their civic responsibility to hold their government to account and thereby question its decisions on any infringements on individual rights and freedoms. For instance, the government often used the prerogative of special elections to reinstate candidates who had lost in regular elections to the opposition; or it simply added more party representatives to nullify the effect of the people's choice. This was a serious violation of the popular mandate as it changed the verdict of the elections. But besides the protests of the other contesting parties, the public did not query this repeated misuse of power in several elections. One of the earliest beneficiaries of this abuse was Ketumile Masire, who was rewarded with a cabinet post for losing the elections to the opposition, and then went on to become an unelected president, when Seretse Khama died in 1980.

Given the historical background of hereditary rulers, who were revered and not questioned, there was a tendency for citizens to acquiesce to state silencing of dissent, as any questioning was deemed as subversive and disrespectful. This point is worth emphasizing because all too often social scientists have tended to judge the quality of democratic development or its lack largely in terms of the repressive activities of the state. Therefore, the failure of the public to play their civic role in accordance with the experience of Western democracy is assumed to be caused by the actions of the state. However, given the historical experience of Botswana's citizenry's reverence for legitimate authority, where those in authority were deemed to be performing their duties to their subjects reasonably well, there was no call to change such leaders or be intolerant of some of their indiscretions.

Arguably, the government of the Botswana Democratic Party passed the test when it demonstrated itself as a better manager and distributor of public resources than the former colonial administration and the hereditary rulers. Considering the level of literacy and the state of information dissemination at the time, very few of these voters had a full grasp of the constitutional changes that had occurred with independence, and the extent of the powers that had been conferred on them. That knowledge was still to develop and become a tool for challenging the state and defining the limits of its power. The past history of colonial administration and hereditary rule had left the vast majority of people in Botswana still essentially as subsistence peasant producers. These conditions did not provide an environment conducive to the development of civic rights and duties associated with modern liberal democracies.

With regard specifically to participation in the electoral process and the seemingly unchanging support for one party, a closer examination of the actual votes cast tells a more nuanced story than might be read from the simple aggregate outcome. In 1965 when the people of Botswana first went to the polls, almost 60 percent of the estimated eligible voters cast their vote in spite of the difficulties of transportation and communication at the time. In the three succeeding rounds of elections when their first president was still in power, most of these voters (i.e., 70 percent) simply did not vote. Given the increased turn out at the elections that followed the death of the first president in 1980, it does not seem far fetched to assume that the voters saw themselves as installing a new chief, and therefore blessed the 1984 occasion with a higher turn out than had been seen since 1965.

By the mid-1980s, following two decades of rapid expansion of educational institutions, urban settlements, and greater access to information, the structure of Botswana's voting public had been radically transformed and voting patterns began to change to reflect diversity as well as an increasing appreciation of civic rights and responsibilities. As already indicated in the section on economic agency, some citizens were beginning to display impatience with the lack of economic opportunity for private gain due to the overwhelming dominance of the state and foreign companies in the modern economy. They began to agitate for the recognition of sectional interests that state bureaucrats had tended to dismiss as selfish and therefore not to be encouraged to compete with the global national interests represented by the state. Similarly, there was increasing impatience over rates of unemployment and poor working conditions in urban areas where the greatest employment opportunities resided. Not surprisingly, therefore, this simmering discontent among potential business people and job seekers was reflected in increasing voter support for opposition parties in urban areas; a pattern that has consolidated over the years and spread to other large settlements with increasing de-agrarianization.

Opposition political parties were another key agency that should have played a critical role in holding government to account and blowing the whistle on undemocratic behavior. But besides legitimizing the state by their mere existence, the opposition parties have been largely ineffectual as contenders for the popular mandate. Their weaknesses cannot, however, be reduced simply to the machinations of the ruling party. Rather, there are certain internal weaknesses within the opposition body politic that have contributed considerably to their sorry state. Many observers have cited the opposition parties' lack of financial resources as a contributing factor in their failure to canvass effectively for electoral support. This is often contrasted with the considerable resources the ruling party had that enabled it to campaign in all constituencies and to field candidates comprehensively. While this is essentially valid, it is equally true that the opposition parties have pursued electoral strategies that have consistently undermined their credibility and made them electorally unattractive.

The Botswana People's Party (BPP), for instance, was the first political party to engage in sustained nationalist politics in the last few years of colonial rule. Its first strategic blunder was to alienate potential voters by making public its intentions to abolish the institution of hereditary rule before winning the electoral mandate from constituencies who understood legitimate authority only in terms of birthright. This provided the traditional leaders with an opportunity to use their considerable authority to thwart the political ambitions of this would-be contender. Its second strategic error was to declare its intentions to abolish private ownership of the means of production among a largely peasant constituency of cattle owners. There was also an emerging class of large cattle owners who aspired to a rich future promised by the commercialization of the cattle-beef industry and the redistribution of land initially held by the colonial administration. The party's ideology struck a discordant note with these aspirations and thus lost it potential candidates to field in the electoral constituencies. The same elite were also required to manage the new administrative structure of an independent sovereignty, but they were repulsed by the BPP's socialist rhetoric and gravitated toward the Botswana Democratic Party. The BPP basically reached to the end of meaningful political existence with the demise of its founder-leader after enduring two decades of bruising splits.

The Botswana National Front (BNF) took over the mantle of official opposition in parliament in the mid-1980s. This party was cut from the same ideological cloth as the Botswana People's Party. But unlike its predecessor, it actively sought to accommodate hereditary rulers and other constituencies of disgruntled citizens who were unhappy with one aspect or the other of the ruling party's monopoly of power and resources. Like many political parties of this genre, the Botswana National Front started off its political life guided more by ideological goals than by any substantive practical issues of governance. For instance, though it saw itself as a party representing workers and as positioned to mobilize the peasants, its campaign messages never actually contained any reference to the plight of the working classes and other economically marginalized people in Botswana until the 1980s (i.e., 20 years after its formation). This party is also prone to factional conflicts and damaging splits that regularly happen just before crucial elections, thus costing them electoral losses that have escalated with the rising political awareness of the voting public.

Since the 1980s, however, the opposition parties have repeatedly structured their electoral campaigns to focus on issues with direct appeal to the voters and their interests, particularly about grievances against the ruling party. This enabled them to make significant inroads into the ruling party's electoral support base as demonstrated by the continued increase in their share of the votes in each successive round of elections held after 1980. I will now examine other contributing factors that facilitated the changing structure of voters' behavior and share of support for the political parties.

The Road to Plural Politics

The substantiveness of Botswana's democratic practices has been questioned by many on account partly of the persistent monopoly of government power by one political party and partly by the apparent weaknesses of civil society. In fact, Kenneth Good dismisses elections as nothing more than a formal process of selecting leaders without much substantive participation by the electorate.[20] But in the early 1990s Botswana women's organizations decided to test the substantiveness of these liberal democratic procedures and the constitutional guarantees of equality by challenging the dominance of men in both the party hierarchies and positions of power in the state structures. This challenge was spearheaded by the Emang Basadi Women's Association that was started in 1986, as a legal reform organization seeking to lobby law-makers to remove laws that discriminated against women and rendered their citizenship unequal to that of male citizens.

Against the background of global concern over the status of women and the United Nations Women's Convention, Botswana women had increasingly begun to raise their voices against discriminatory conventions that were embedded in both customs and conventional law. Until then, women were accorded the status of minors by customary law and were thus required to process their interests through male relatives such as fathers, uncles, husbands, and even adult sons. Civil law, on the other hand, reduced women to minority status when they entered marriage. Marital power conferred upon the husband included, among others, sole and exclusive decision-making about family property, the right to chastise an erring wife, and the control of the affairs that had legal consequences (e.g., financial loans). These legal conventions had negative consequences for the welfare of women and their decision-making capacity. For instance, they were linked to escalating and persistent domestic violence perpetrated by men in the exercise of their right to chastise. They were similarly linked to women's deteriorating economic situation where they contributed to family income but had little control over its disposal. These limitations extended to public life where women's political rights were constrained by their legal minority status and thus subordinated to decisions by significant male guardians.

In the 1980s, when women started raising concerns about these discriminatory conventions, such questioning of tradition and challenge to authority was considered disrespectful to deeply held customary values, and was therefore resisted by both the predominantly male lawmaking establishment and traditionalist women who had bargained with patriarchy over time to exercise power indirectly through their menfolk. The Emang Basadi Women's Association embarked on a social mobilization campaign to educate women about the discriminatory provisions and their negative consequences on their health, and material as well as emotional well-being. When the lobbying met with strong resistance, the leaders of the movement changed their strategy from lobbying to active political campaigns that would put women in the highest citadel of lawmaking.

The new strategy was based on the simple calculation that as the majority of voters, women could use their electoral power to force change in established practices and conventions. They also recognized that a major stumbling block to their aspirations was not only the state and political party apparatus but the inability of the voting public to recognize that in a liberal democracy with guaranteed rights and freedoms and a healthy respect for law, they, in fact, had the power to change the situation by judicious bargaining with their votes. The Women's Association therefore set out on an ambitious campaign of voter education aimed at enhancing women voters' ability to appreciate the link between the vote and the decisions of their elected representatives, which affected their private and public lives. At the same time, they launched a lobby campaign that directly appealed to government and political parties to take women's grievances into account in the context of a heightened political education program that would enable these potential voters to ask awkward questions about the intentions of competing candidates. The first of these political campaigns was timed to commence before political parties organized their campaign materials in preparation for the 1994 elections. It was strategically placed to make the maximum impact on the behavior of parties and to get them to make a commitment to gender equality to which they could be held after the elections.

Critics of nongovernmental organizations and women's associations normally dismiss these either as interest groups that are driven by donor agencies or as mere extensions of the state apparatus. The content of the Emang Basadi program of political mobilization, however, had very far-reaching consequences for the conduct of political life and constitutional development in Botswana, despite the fact that eventually, the resources of this association came from external donors with a token from government. At the start of the campaign, the overtly political agenda of the movement was regarded with considerable caution by many potential donors who were concerned at the possibility of such campaigns undermining the position of the ruling party.

Although the actual impact on voting patterns in the 1994 elections has not been gauged, the campaign's inaugural launch coincided with the first time in Botswana's electoral history when votes for the opposition rose significantly enough to increase their share of elected parliamentary seats to 35 percent. The actual votes cast for the opposition were the highest ever at 45 percent. The impact of the campaign was clearly visible in the behavior of political parties. For instance, the ruling party made a concerted effort to support the candidature of a few women politicians and ensured their safe passage through the rites of primary elections and general elections, which increased the number of women in both the parliament and the cabinet. By the next round of elections in 1999, even more effort was expended in increasing the number of female candidates in the contestation for government power. This led to an increase of women's share of elected office to more than 15 percent in the 1999 elections.

The women's political mobilization campaign profoundly and irrevocably changed the nature and quality of state-citizen relations as well as the nature and quality of representative governance, thus putting paid to traditional reverence to sovereignty. The culture of debate and questioning of government decisions that emerged made people realize that in a liberal democracy, such questioning was not treason, but an essential component of meaningful political participation. Led by an organization that was not seeking to replace established political structures but to reform them, this campaign could not be silenced to the same extent that the state had been able to do with regard to opposition parties that sought to replace the ruling party at the helm. So though it challenged the status quo, the women's campaign was for widening the boundaries of democratic participation in issues of concern, defining who is eligible to participate, the significance of the public-private divide, and territoriality in terms of citizenship, and the relationship between the state and the individual.

To that end, it also brought to the fore an important dimension in state-citizen relationships; that is the fact that the conferment of nationality embodies a basic legal relationship between the individual and the state, and that it is the basis on which rights are defined and guaranteed. The extent to which the individual can enjoy unfettered political participation is therefore predicated on whether that person is recognized to have a full legal personhood and can therefore be trusted to take decisions with legal consequences. As long as the law reduced them to legal minorities, women could not enjoy full citizenship and equal access to freedom and fairness.

It took a court case, however, to force the government of Botswana to change the laws to accord women equal citizenship with men. This landmark case also set a precedent in Botswana, which was later to be followed by other organizations and individuals seeking redress from unfair laws. The act of taking government to court and winning the case, underlined the fact that governments were also required to operate within the law, and were not above it. It also sent a message to other people that it was an acceptable thing to do in a democracy to challenge the constitutionality of acts of governments to make governments accountable and respectful of the law. And finally, it demonstrated that governments did not have the monopoly in interpreting the intentions of constitutional provisions, but on the contrary, it was a shared responsibility between the state and the citizen.

In that climate of debate and questioning, the private media also became much more openly critical and positioned themselves to inform the nation on matters, they deemed, required public scrutiny and debate. For instance, reports on corrupt practices and abuse of public resources by the leaders of the nation began to appear with greater frequency than before. These included (1) irregularities in award of tenders in which high ranking officials stood to gain; (2) illegal land transactions where ministers of state had used their offices for personal gain; (3) mismanagement and corrupt practices in parastatal organizations such as the Botswana Housing Corporation where both the ministers and civil servants had used them for personal advantage; and (4) abuse of the National Development Bank (NDB) by government ministers who accumulated huge loans from the bank but were unwilling to pay them back, thus nearly driving the bank to bankruptcy. The press also commented on the annual reports of the Auditor General which indicated serious mismanagement of public resources by government workers and state departments. There was also critical reporting of and commentary on the annual national budget speech and on the quality of the leadership of the State President.

The private press also took up human rights debates by highlighting instances of human rights violations of minority groups and individuals. In particular, the situation of the minority San groups and their treatment at the hands of government officials and public institutions was brought to public attention as human rights issues, thus encouraging the majority ethnic Tswana and other Bantu groups to appreciate the incongruity of such historical forms of discrimination with liberal democratic institutions set to protect and guarantee equality of rights and freedoms.

The response to this critical view of government was predictably the issuance of threats of sanctions and repressive legislation. However, unlike in the 1970s and earlier periods when the press would have been cowed down by threats from the government, journalists held their ground and justified their actions as public service.[21] This provided clear testimony, even to those with government power, that the state could no longer enjoy the monopoly of determining what was in the best interests of the nation. But under a persistent barrage of criticisms, there was a further attempt by the government to punish the most critical of the newspapers by starving it of advertisement funds on the grounds that government had to reduce costs. Not only was this action ridiculed publicly as a thinly disguised attempt to silence criticism, but the papers concerned sought relief from the courts to reverse the decision. The government was directed by the courts to reinstate its advertising patronage and advised to be more tolerant of criticism.

These actions and reactions have demonstrated that Botswana's state institutions and the separation of powers have laid a foundation that is constantly being tested and redefined to accommodate shared power. The unlimited state about which Kenneth Good (1996, 1997a) had complained earlier as undermining participatory democracy is being redefined and curtailed. In the process, space is being created through these struggles for more individual freedoms and liberties, thus demonstrating the fact that the form and content of democracy are not defined just by the state, but rather are an outcome of an ongoing historical process of negotiation and renegotiations.

In this climate of change and diversified points of power, opposition parties have taken advantage of the opportunity to press home for more electoral support. Despite their organizational and strategic weaknesses, the opposition parties have contributed significantly to the legitimation of the state and its power and authority. By their very persistence, they have helped to maintain the spirit of multiparty competitions, though they never successfully challenged the ruling party significantly enough to effect a change of government. But, they have slowly but certainly eroded the ruling party's monopoly of votes, thus setting Botswana on a course of meaningful plural contestation for the popular mandate.

The proneness of the opposition parties to factional splits, however, constantly undermines their capacity to translate their increasing share of votes into outright victory. Significantly, despite their weaknesses and the government's historical tendency to employ its incumbency to prolong its stay in power, the 1990s saw a greater presence of opposition parties in state structures, particularly at local government level. Furthermore, the glaring disparities between the share of the actual votes cast and the share of seats have raised concern and debate about the efficacy of the current electoral system to reflect the aspirations of the voters. The fact that almost half the voting public cast their votes in favor of the opposition in 1999, but the opposition could get only 18 percent of parliamentary seats has led to a call to rethink the electoral system.

Civil Society Agency and the Separation of Governmental Powers

Since the 1990s, the citizens of Botswana have increasingly sought relief from the courts when they have felt aggrieved by the state or failed to get redress through direct lobbying and negotiation. As indicated earlier, the courts have been used by women activists to reverse discriminatory laws, and by the press to force the executive branch of government to reverse punitive actions aimed at silencing criticism. These and similar actions by individuals and collectives have not only served to test the independence of the Judiciary from the Executive, but also facilitated in enhancing constitutional development and deepening the division between and separation of the various arms of government. Similarly, the public debates and political mobilization campaigns by nongovernmental organizations have not only broadened the boundaries of political participation but also qualitatively enhanced the process of selecting representatives to elected public office. This has, in turn, helped raised the standard of parliamentary debates and enabled that arm of government to play its role of oversight over the executive much more critically. The process has been further facilitated by the increased presence of opposition party representatives in Parliament. This has helped to break the tradition of Parliament being merely a rubberstamp body for decisions taken by the executive branch as it had been during the era of single-party monopoly of votes.

Another area of civil society activism challenging state monopoly of power concerns ethnicity and representation. Toward the end of the twentieth century, Botswana engaged in unprecedented national soul searching and debate concerning ethnic cleavages and inequalities stemming from constitutional provisions for national citizenship. The debate has thrown open questions on what determines who is the indigene and citizen, and whether and to what extent citizens can claim equal rights not only as individuals but also as members of ethnic groups. This has thrown into sharp relief, nationality as a contested identity in the process of modern state building, as various ethnic groups attempt to renegotiate power relations and rights to national resources, particularly about land and political institutions.

At the heart of this national debate has been the issue of how people should be represented politically. On one hand, culturally marginalized groups have sought to negotiate for better, more equitable representation while the dominant ethnic groups have countered by reasserting their identity as representing national unity, thus, dismissing calls for more inclusive group rights as sectarian, divisive, and therefore dangerous to national unity. The immediate catalyst of the debate was the constitutional provision that accorded some groups the status of principal ethnic groups and others a minority status. These discriminatory clauses were not a new amendment, but had been there since independence. So, the significance that can be read into their being questioned openly at this stage, after more than three decades of independence, is that they reveal the extent to which the state was now confident of its legitimacy and the fact of nationhood. It was now willing to accommodate divergent views on what constitutes stability and national unity.

For the indigenous Khoe-speaking San groups (known in Botswana as Basarwa and in certain circles as the Bushmen), the issue of social marginalization has been more pervasive covering as it does economic, political, social, and cultural exclusion. There is mounting evidence that the position they occupy today can be explained largely in terms of their historical subjugation by non-Basarwa. Formal conferment of legal equality has not translated into concrete reality for these nationals. The official view on their situation has historically been that to recognize their ethnicity as a variable in analyzing and explaining their impoverishment would be tantamount to discriminating against Basarwa and setting them on a path of separate, apartheid-like development. The argument was that while they have been largely unable as a group to develop with the rest of the population, Basarwa share their poverty and other indicators of disadvantage with other ethnic groups inhabiting the same geographical localities. And that therefore the only legitimate explanatory factors for their position are (1) the spatial distance from the main centers of development and (2) the harshness of the physical environment they inhabit.

Development has therefore taken on a strategy of assimilation and land resettlement from ancestral lands. This follows more than a century of similar assimilationist tendencies entailing dispossession and impoverishment at the hands of Batswana pastoralists, white farmers, Batswana cattle ranchers, and instruments of the State such as the law and development policies and programs. During the nineteenth century, a large part of the territory the Basarwa inhabited in what has since become the Gantsi District was taken from them and converted into freehold land for exclusive use by white farmers. Further inroads into this territory were made with the expansion of freehold farms in the 1950s. This process of land dispossession was further extended in the postindependence era with the launching of the 1975 Tribal Grazing Land Policy (TGLP) that saw more land being enclosed for exclusive use by non-Basarwa cattle ranchers and effectively turning Basarwa into a legally landless people.

Unlike other nationals of the newly independent Botswana state, Basarwa started off at Botswana's independence with no recognized ethnic territory of their own or individual access to any specific territory. This has had far-reaching consequences for their welfare and their capacity to maintain themselves independent of the benevolence of either the state or other citizens. Despite awareness-raising efforts by district officers, anthropological researchers, and nongovernmental organizations to draw attention to the effect of land enclosure on Basarwa, the government continued to parcel out Basarwa hunting grounds to leasehold ranchers in the 1970s and 1980s. Sadly, this process of dispossession and impoverishment deepened even further with the 1991 Agricultural Development Policy that extended land enclosure to ever more territories.

In reaction to mounting international criticism that such development policies undermined the welfare status and human rights situation of ethnic Basarwa, the government has since opted to resettle these impoverished communities rather than deal with the issue of their land dispossession. This tends to perpetuate an age-old problem as Basarwa continue to suffer resettlement schemes and forced removals from land they consider theirs, but the state does not recognize as such. Lack of recognition of Basarwa land rights continues to be reflected in new development initiatives such as the recent Community Based Natural Resources Management Programs, where they are not allowed to determine how best to utilize these resources, but must adopt preferred government priorities.

At a 1993 conference organized to reflect on the position of these nationals, the Basarwa delegates highlighted the limited and shrinking opportunities for alternative income generation. In particular, they argued that they have no employment opportunities outside the lowly and poorly remunerated work as farm laborers. Blaming this lack of opportunity on blatant discrimination by ethnic Tswana officials, they indicated that their ethnicity is usually used as a basis for their being denied life chances. This is further exacerbated by the extremely high rates of illiteracy among them. For instance, illiteracy rates in their settlements are as high as 86 percent compared with a national average of just 26 percent. Despite Botswana's rapid expansion of schools and the improved rates of access for most children nationally, Basarwa continue to have limited access as a result of (1) the discriminatory practices that hinder progress among these children (2) the migratory lifestyles of Basarwa in a situation where schools are provided only at fixed spatial points; and (3) the inability of the government to reach the remotest rural areas effectively. Poor education and training result in low employment opportunities.

Since the 1990s, the Basarwa have organized themselves into various associations to articulate their interests within Botswana as well as internationally.[22] Like other citizens who have sought relief from the courts, their human rights organizations have taken recourse to the courts to have their rights recognized and interpreted from their point of view. Their demands include not only land, but also the right to political representation in the government structures by one of their own as well as the right to have their language and culture recognized and nurtured.

Other ethnic minorities that have also called for economic and political redress, occupy a significantly different economic status from that of the ethnic Basarwa. For one thing, most of them have benefited considerably from the economic and educational advances the country has achieved since independence. Their demands are therefore more about the indignities of cultural inequalities than about material discrimination. Wayei of Ngamiland, for instance, have argued that they were historically subjugated in the tribal polity of Batawana (an ethnic Tswana group accorded the status of a principal tribe) and that it is therefore discriminatory for a postindependence constitution that espouses equality to continue to accord their colonizers the status of principal tribe with a chief who sits in the House of Chiefs while denying Wayei that status. Through Kamanakao, a cultural organization set up to mobilize Waayei and champion their call for equality of citizenship, the Wayei have used local courts and international agencies such as the United Nations to appeal for their ethnic group to be given the same status of equality as the ethnic Batswana. Both the High Court of Botswana, and the 61st Session of the United Nations Committee on the Elimination of Racial Discrimination have validated the claim of discrimination.

Like the Basarwa, the Wayei also want a paramount chief of their own who would sit in the House of Chiefs on an equal footing with those of the ethnic Tswana groups. They also want their language and culture accorded the same privilege as those of Setswana.

The ethnic Bakalanga, on the other hand, are recognized as the most privileged of the ethnic minorities for their material wealth and education. Their demands for ethnic equality are therefore largely focused on language and cultural equality. With regard to the issue of chieftainship, their call is for broadening of representation so that it is not just limited to the institution of ethnic leadership, but includes other interests that are currently not catered to in the constitution. They maintain, therefore that instead of perpetuating forms of hereditary power, the House of Chiefs should be expanded into a House of Representatives to accommodate a wider range of sectional interests. The demands of this particular ethnic group received the greatest backlash from ethnic Tswana groups who accused the Kalanga of practising discrimination by monopolizing key top civil service jobs and private sector business through nepotistic practices. Their citizenship was called into question, with some individuals even advising that if they did not like the situation, they should "go back to where they came from."

In all, the ethnicity debate saw an upsurge in the formation of cultural associations seeking to promote the interests of the various groups.[23] And seeing some commonalities in their grievances, the associations for the minority groups also created a common front to negotiate with one voice against Botswana's discriminatory laws. In the NGO presentation at the 61st Session of the United Nations Committee on the Elimination of Racial Discrimination, for instance, 11 organizations were represented in the submission from Botswana. Among other things, The UN Committee recommended the following with regard to their submission:

1. That recognition and representation of all tribes in Botswana be ensured on an equal basis in the Constitution, and that the Chieftainship Act and the Tribal Territories Act be amended accordingly.[24]

2. That no decisions directly relating to the rights and interests of members of indigenous peoples be taken without their informed consent. And that negotiations with the Basarwa/San and non-governmental organizations be resumed on this issue, and that a rights-based approach to development be adopted.[25]

3. That the State party should fully recognize and respect the culture, history, languages and way of life of its various ethnic groups as an

enrichment of the State's cultural identity, and adopt measures to protect and support minority languages, in particular within education.[26]

When the ethnic debate erupted into the public arena, there were many observers who expressed fear that this meant that Botswana was all set to go down the road of ethnic strife leading to the dismantlement of the state-nation. The debate among the elite in particular was highly charged and on one or two public occasions, almost resulted in violent confrontations that were highly publicized in the media. The president was forced at one point, to tour the tribal constituencies to address tribesmen and women on the significance of the negotiations and the democratic debate, while appealing to their civic responsibilities in the matter. He himself had come under personal attack, with some people questioning his ethnic identity and therefore allegiance to the state whose stability some of the people seemed to believe could only be guaranteed by its maintaining a national identity that was clearly dominated by ethnic Tswana culture.

Many Western observers do not believe that Botswana had a political culture that guaranteed the maintenance and sustainability of liberal democracy because, they argued, there were no cleavages apart from the ethnic and rural-urban inequalities. But clearly, while ethnic inequalities have assumed political significance in public debates, they are among several other political issues that cut across political party affiliation.

No ethnic group has aligned its cultural grievances with partisan politics, but rather has presented them as national issues that must be negotiated through existing state structures, particularly the courts and the constitution. For the most part, there is a tendency for ethnic issues to be articulated through nongovernmental organizations. In the process, the ethnic question has become one of many issues through which the power of the state has been challenged and redefined to allow broader participation in national decision making and constitutional development. None of these issues is being challenged through unconstitutional means, thus clearly indicating the confidence of Botswana's citizens in institutional structures and in their government's respect for the law.

Conclusion: Rethinking the State

Judged by the extent to which it has established legitimate authority and practical sovereignty, Botswana's postcolonial state-building enterprise has so far been a success. The actions of civic organizations in challenging the state and holding it to account, and the ability of the courts to enable these challenges to happen and succeed have indicated the extent to which there has been an institutionalization of liberal democratic practices. Botswana has been fortunate to have circumstances that enabled state and nation building to happen, and thus transform the legacy of colonialism into a model of successful negotiations of power.

Botswana started off its independence from colonial rule with a legacy of poverty, minimal national institutional structures, virtually nonexistent budgetary resources to run the affairs of the state, a sparse population dispersed over a large territory, an almost nonexistent infrastructural base, a predominantly illiterate population, and many other seriously limiting factors. More than most other African countries, the characteristics that have come to be associated with why the postcolonial state has seemed to fail in Africa were most prominent in this country when it set out on the challenging road to building a unitary state and a single nation out of a plurality of nations and clans. In terms of human, natural, infrastructural, and capital resources, this country was more disadvantaged than most other African countries.

Like other countries emerging out of colonialism, Botswana's main source of investment resources initially derived from its former colonial masters as well as the institutions that had been set up at the end of World War II to facilitate economic and political development as encapsulated by the United Nations First Decade of Development. This was meant to allow for self-determination based on accelerated transfer of Western aid. Coming to independence almost a decade after the first cohort of African countries had attained self-rule, Botswana had much to learn from these path breakers, and indeed incorporated some of the lessons it learnt from others into its own nation/state-building project. These are worth restating here because of the significant contribution they have made to Botswana's success in contrast with the negative connotations they have come to represent in the analytical literature on the role of the state in the 1980s and 1990s.

The first lesson was the acceptance that the state must play a significant economic role in the absence of significant local entrepreneurs or direct investors from outside. Therefore, against the advice of the colonial office, the new government set out to intervene directly in economic activity to stoke (or even create) the engine that would facilitate rapid growth and structural transformation of the economy. In the 1960s, while Europe was undergoing reconstruction following the devastation of the War, the terms of trade were certainly very favorable to primary goods exports, and it therefore made sound economic sense for nonindustrialized countries to pursue economic strategies based on this advantage. It is therefore very simplistic to argue, as some political scientists have done, that African states merely continued the extractive economies that colonialism had started. To do so, implies that there were in fact viable alternatives for the taking and that these countries ought to have been able to predict that the world economy would change in the mid-1970s in a manner that would have adverse effects on primary commodity producers.

The reality was not that convenient or amenable to such futuristic predictions. Actually, African countries pursued strategies that, given the prevailing conditions then, suggested they should first concentrate on economic sectors in which they had comparative advantage in relation to existing trading partners and on terms dictated by the availability of investment capital. African primary commodity producers set out to exploit this advantage while also seeking to develop an industrial capacity that conventional economic theory suggested was the surest way to rapid and sustained growth. This had also been tried with some degree of success in Asian countries and led to substantive transformations of these economies before the impact of oil shocks and its aftermath of negative terms of trade for primary commodities caused a temporary setback.

Botswana has steadfastly pursued this development strategy with spectacular results while the stories of other African countries have been either disastrous or seriously flawed. I would like to argue that the apparent failure of other African countries emanated from the timing of the strategies rather than the strategies per se as demonstrated by the fact some Asian countries that had had a head start in industrializing a decade earlier, enjoyed the full benefits of a long period of European reconstruction and good terms of trade for primary commodities. This enabled them to translate the income thus earned into manufacturing capacity, thus beating the clock before the terms of trade turned against primary commodities and in favor of manufactures in the 1970s. As H. Singer and S. Roy have pointed out, "the African countries came in just after this window of opportunity closed and narrowly missed the chance to industrialize."[27]

Botswana was fortunate that the primary commodity it did discover hidden in the bowels of its territory just happened to be a highly protected product monopolized by a conglomerate that has never allowed its prices to fluctuate at the whims of the free market. Diamond happened to be a commodity whose terms of trade could not therefore be affected by unpredictable market behavior, and therefore brought reliable revenues that have cushioned Botswana against the adverse effects of significant inefficiencies in its economic development experiment. For instance, Botswana's venture into the copper-nickel industry has been an unmitigated disaster that would have led the country down the same path as Zambia, had it been dependent on it to the same extent as Zambia was. The lackluster performance of Botswana's import substitutive industrialization could also have had very negative consequences had it not been for the fact that Botswana could absorb such shocks within a margin of safety provided by income from diamonds exports.

In fact, even the periodic devaluation of the domestic currency done more to protect other exports than anything else, has had some positive results for Botswana. It meant that the diamond dollars translated into more pula value to spend on development. As earlier indicated, Botswana's problem of financial resources has been more one of how to spend national income productively than how to find the money to spend. But the structural weaknesses of this strategy have begun to translate into widening gaps in the capacity of the economy to maintain employment creation at pace with demand, following the peaking of the diamond-led and infrastructure-dominated growth.

The success of government's capacity to redistribute its revenues toward the development of the private sector can be read from the fact that, while the state is still the single largest employer at 35 percent to 40 percent, in fact it is the private sector as a collective that has accounted for most jobs (i.e., 60 percent to 65 percent) in Botswana's formal sector. Nonetheless, private sector growth is largely dependent on the activities of government for its main business. It is also important to point out that contrary to the general stereotype of a predatory African state that squeezes wealth from the meager resources of its citizenry so graphically portrayed by various scholars, the Botswana state has, since attaining budgetary independence in the 1970s, relied primarily on resources from diamond revenues and Bank of Botswana reserves rather than on taxing its citizens. It is unlikely therefore that government could ever relinquish its share of the diamond industry and survive meaningfully on the basis of direct taxes on private individuals. This is the one area of the economy, whose full privatization with the state relinquishing its share, would sound a death knell to the state's capacity to continue playing a meaningful role of resource distribution without the alienating qualities that derive from the need to extract direct taxes from the economy in a population that is very small and where most people do not command much purchasing power anyway.

The privatization of other areas of activity is feasible in principle, though its viability and sustainability will consistently be restrained by the smallness of Botswana's market, particularly for private entrepreneurs who would not have the advantage of drawing directly on diamond revenues to bail them out of adverse changes in market conditions. Here, one has in mind the example of the spectacular collapse of Botswana's first car plant in which the Botswana Development Corporation, one of Botswana's parastatals, had invested in the expectation of competing in the South African market. This car plant collapsed with losses of millions of pula (local currency) after a brief life. Privatization will generally demand entrepreneurial skills that are yet to be developed, but that will be required for survival in a competitive market environment.

A second lesson Botswana also learned from countries that had gone the independence route before it did, was that unequal distribution of wealth that clearly followed regional divisions could, if left unchecked, lead to permanent divisions that could scupper the nation-building project. To that end, there was a deliberate effort on the part of political parties and government to minimize such potential divisions by promoting even regional economic development and to ensure that wealth generated from any part of the country should be seen to benefit all regions as fairly as possible within the limits of that wealth, particularly wealth derived from minerals and other non-traditional sources. Fully aware of the exceptionally limited developmental resources against formidably large needs, the government of Botswana did not set out to take over all existing productive activities, but only nontraditional ones where the investment resources required could not be mobilized by local private citizens.

By and large, there was also no attempt to change existing patterns of economic activity when the alternatives still had to be developed. Thus, for instance, the migrant labor system was not disturbed through any policy interventions as it provided a livelihood to many citizens who could not find gainful employment locally. This system was brought to a dramatic end only by the actions of the South African government when it was trying to cater to the increasing demand for black jobs in that country. Similarly, though the construction of new urban and industrial settlements demanded labor transfers from the impoverished countryside, government invested considerable resources in discouraging large-scale rural-urban migration that would disrupt subsistence economic activities and encourage people to search for jobs that would not satisfy such demand. This point is worth emphasizing because many critics of Botswana's rural development strategy have pronounced it a failure in terms of its impact on rural productivity and income levels. But judged from the point of view of a welfare program and settlement strategy, it succeeded in keeping most of the rural population in rural areas to await development from that base.

These programs were of two types: the infrastructural projects aimed at benefiting the public in general, and production programs for agriculture, rural industries, etc., aimed at assisting individuals in their economic activities. As already noted above, these succeeded mainly in transferring government welfare to rural areas and encouraging rural populations to maintain rather than increase traditional subsistence production. Grossly inadequate in relation to the number of beneficiaries within the targeted populations, these programs were nonetheless evenly spread across the regions where they were highly visible and therefore could be appreciated as being available to all within the practical limits of implementation. This point is also worth emphasizing in light of the fact that critics of the African state normally perceive the distribution of state benefits only in terms of ethnic biases that enhance deep divisions among the citizenry and undermine the authority and legitimacy of the state. Despite the relatively generous revenues that the Botswana government has commanded since the 1970s, the actual sums allocated to the majority of subsistence producers through production subsidies and grants have been much lower than actual demand. But they were spread out across the country to ensure that each region had a certain quota.

Depending on the particular angle that political scientists have wanted to emphasize, the distribution of development funding has been read either as buying votes from opposition strongholds by more generous treatment of such constituencies[28] or punishing voters by hesitating to proceed with rural development programs where the opposition is clear and substantial.[29] The actual empirical base political scientists have used to interpret the distribution of development resources at constituency level seems to be amenable to any interpretation that the individual wants to push, probably because it derives from anecdotal evidence and not from relevant empirical research. But at broad regional level, both in policy commitment and practice, there has been an obvious attempt to maintain some level of evenness in resource allocation and increasing the share of rural constituencies generally when compared with urban advantage. To that end, it would also be simplistic to argue that Botswana is just another case of a patrimonial state. Ironically, the greatest disenchantment with government has so far been most discernable where the benefits of this attempted strategy of even distribution of development have tended to concentrate on the urban settlements and urbanizing rural towns. In fact, the more successful the development strategies pursued by government, the more they have helped to engender diversity of interests and social cleavages.

Another area where Botswana started off on a similar path with other African countries, but highlights nuanced differences that warrant comment is the adoption of a liberal constitution guaranteeing multiparty competition for government power and associated individual rights and freedoms. This constitution has formed the basic legal contract between the state and its citizens and has generally been upheld and respected by both parties. It set out the basic rules of behavior and engagement that have increasingly come to be used by aggrieved citizens to seek relief from the activities of the state as law-maker, policy maker, and resource distributor. Although critics usually focus on those activities of the government that demonstrate use of incumbency and state resources in a manner that favors the party in power, in fact, even as early as the 1980s, the government's respect for the rule of law was demonstrated by an incident where a manual worker discovered ballot boxes that had not been opened for counting during the 1984 elections. This fact was made public and by-elections held that swung the results from the ruling party to the opposition, where they have firmly stayed since then representing the capital city's constituencies. Botswana's experience with the rule of law is not that the state has not frequently erred, but that it has been held to account by others when that has happened and others have been sufficiently aware of such breaches. Since the 1980s, partly as a result of the critical mass of educated citizens generated by postindependence educational developments, and partly because of the influences of global political changes and increasing information sharing, the frequency with which the people of Botswana have challenged their government has increased dramatically. This has served to enhance and entrench the quality of the institutional and constitutional base that was initially set at independence for plural sharing of decision-making and power.

Botswana's experience with constitutional development has been that the state has laid a foundation that has gradually been allowed to grow through a process of maturation by both government and non-state agencies. The security engendered by successful management of the economy arguably gave the government of Botswana increasing confidence to face challenges to its initial monopoly of power and its wariness with oppositional contenders. The dominant characterization of the African state as weak and having limited capacity to perform its functions of effective organization of the public sphere is therefore considerably controverted by Botswana's experience that has shared similar backgrounds with other countries, but has nonetheless been able to win the confidence of its people in state institutions despite wide national income differentials and persistent poverty.

A large part of the failure of social scientists to see the nuanced difference is that most of the time their analysis focuses on the state that is judged using a checklist of markers taken out of historical context. For instance, there is a checklist of what democracy is and how much African states fall short in relation to this marker. There are also checklists for good governance, legitimacy, authoritarianism, and so on that are simply lifted from the current status of these products of the historical experience of Western countries and are now used as universal markers. These tell us little about the experiences of African societies and the significance of these experiences in moderating the political space that modern states and governments occupy. We therefore know very little about how African citizens live their political and economic lives except as props in a script about the strongmen, who occupy weak states that are nonetheless powerful enough to be pervasively oppressive. Botswana's state-building experience suggests that in analyzing this sector of social life, we must try to locate the contributions of non-state actors in shaping political space and in defining who occupies what part of that space over time.

Notes

1. See the Letter from the Resident Commissioner to the High Commissioner, February 16, 1935, Botswana National Archives (BNA), S 337/6.
2. I. Schapera, *Migrant Labor and Tribal Life: A Study of Conditions in the Bechuanaland Protectorate* (London: Oxford University Press, 1947), p. 1933.
3. H. Singer and S. Roy, *Economic Progress and Prospects in the Third World: Lessons of Development Experience Since 1945* (Aldershot, UK: Edward Elgar, 1993).
4. Ibid.
5. Bank of Botswana, *Annual Report* (Gaberone: Bank of Botswana, 2000), p. 91.
6. See Botswana Government, *The Development of the Bechuanaland Economy: Report of the British Ministry of Overseas Economic Development's Survey Mission* (Gaberone: Botswana Government, 1965), foreword.
7. The absence of male labor due to migration to the South African Mines left many families with shortage of male labor that was critical for certain tasks in traditional household agriculture, particularly in the management and use of cattle as draught power. Cattle have traditionally been a male area of responsibility and ownership and control tended to pass through the male line of descent. See Athaliah Malokomme et al., *The Report on A Review of the Laws Affecting Women in Botswana* (Gaberone: Women's Affairs Department, Ministry of Labor and Home Affairs, Botswana Government, 1998).
8. Botswana Government, *Labor Force Survey, 1984–85* (Gaberone: Central Statistics Office, 1985).

9. Bank of Botswana, *Review of Economic Development* (Gaberone: Bank of Botswana, 1988).

10. Bank of Botswana, *Annual Report* (Gaberone: Bank of Botswana, 1993), p. 6.

11. Several of the traditional chiefs had enjoyed incomes from concession companies that the British South African Company took over, when it granted a charter over the Protectorate in the late 1890s. See Onalenna Selolwane, "Colonization By Concession: Capitalist Expansion in the Bechuanaland Protectorate, 1885–1950," *PULA: Botswana Journal of African Studies*, vol. 2, no. 1, 1980, pp. 75–123 and I. Schapera, *Tribal Innovators* (London: Frank Cass, 1965).

12. Mainly those who had been involved in work in the South African mines and had become involved with the politics of the African National Congress and other more radical pan-Africanist organizations.

13. S. Morrison, "Botswana's Formative Late Colonial Experience in *Botswana: The Political Economy of Democratic Development*, ed. Stephen John Stedman (Boulder, CO: Lynne Rienner Publishers, 1992), p. 35.

14. J.D. Holm, "Botswana: A Paternalistic Democracy," in *Democracy in Africa*, ed. Larry Diamond et al.(Boulder, CO: Lynne Rienner Publishers, 1988).

15. J. Solway, "From Shame to Pride: Politicized Ethnicity in the Kalahari, Botswana," *Canadian Journal of African Studies*, vol. 28, no. 2, 1994, pp. 261–262.

16. L. Picard, *The Politics of Development in Botswana: A Model for Success?* (Boulder, CO: Lynne Rienner Publishers, 1987).

17. Ibid.

18. Kenneth Good, *Realizing Democracy in Botswana, Namibia and South Africa* (Pretoria: African Institute of South Africa, 1997).

19. Picard, *The Politics of Development*, p. 161.

20. Good, *Realizing Democracy in Botswana* and Kenneth Good, "Authoritarian Liberalism: A Defining Characteristic of Botswana," *Journal of Contemporary African Studies*, vol. 14, no. 1, 1997, pp. 29–51.

21. For a detailed discussion, see Francis B. Nyamnjoh, "Media, Good Governance and Civil Society in Botswana," paper presented at the OSSREA Workshop on Promoting Good Governance in Eastern and Southern Africa, held in Addis Ababa, Ethiopia, November 6–8, 2000.

22. These include First People of the Kalahari and Kuru Development Trust.

23. The following are some of the associations: Lentswe la Batswapong, Society for the Promotion of the Ikalanga Language, Kamanakao Association, Herero-Mbanderu Youth Association, Chelwa ya Shekgalagari, Cisiyi Nkulu Trust, First People of Kalahari, Babirwa Cultural Group, Teemashane Community Trust, Tsoa Cultural Group, and Qonyathie Crisha.

24. *United Nations Committee on the Elimination of Racial Discrimination, Proceedings Sixty-First Session* (New York: UNCERD, 2002), p. 3.

25. Ibid.

26. Ibid., p. 4.

27. H. Singer and S. Roy, *Economic Progress and Prospects*.
28. J. Wiseman, *Democracy in Black Africa: Survival and Revival* (New York: Paragon House Publishers, 1990), p. 47.
29. J. Holm, "Elections in Botswana: Institutionalization of a New System of Legitimacy," in *Elections in Independent Africa*, ed. Fred Hayward (Boulder, CO: Westview Press, 1987), p. 86.

CHAPTER 3

The State in Cote d'Ivoire: Evolution and Constraints

Boubacar N'Diaye

Introduction

Throughout the 1980s, and singularly in the 1990s, the political, economic, cultural, and social contradictions in the postcolonial state in Africa seemed to reach their apex with more than a third of the African states either collapsing or at the risk of doing so.[1] Even for those not threatened with total breakdown, the toll that the so-called lost decade (the 1980s) took on the economy and society in general was heavy and unavoidable. Most African countries exhibited all the signs of advanced organizational, financial, and political decay. In response to this multitude of crises of which the nature of the state seemed to be the locus of inquiry, scholarly interest in the nature, role, and dynamics of the African state increased.[2] This growing interest in the state generated a copious number of studies that attempted to shed more light on the critical dimension of the African reality.[3] I. William Zartman, in an introduction to his edited volume on the grim phenomenon of state collapse in Africa in the 1990s, identifies the following as one of the scenarios that could lead to state collapse.

[A]fter being in power for a long time [the political order] wears out its ability to satisfy the demands of various groups in society. Resources dry up, either for exogenous reasons or through internal waste and corruption (selective misallocation). Social and ethnic groups feel neglected and alienated, causing an atmosphere of dissatisfaction and opposition, which in turn draws increased repression and use of the police and military to keep order. With nobody to watch the watchmen, the military moves in to take over.[4]

Although there has always been a consensus that the Ivoirian state was not likely to follow the path of, for example, Somalia or Sierra Leone, one cannot help but concede the uncanny resemblance between this scenario and the evolution of Cote d'Ivoire starting in the mid-1980s. In sharp contrast with other West African states with the possible exception of Senegal, Ivory Coast was considered a haven of stability in which an orderly state construction and capacity building were taking place. That it dangerously garnered all the ingredients for, teetered on the brink, and then degenerated into violence, holds a wealth of analytical and normative material in the ongoing debate on the problematic of the state in Africa.

There is indeed much to be learned from a systematic and critical examination of the general evolution of the state in Cote d'Ivoire. Today, such a study cannot escape the necessity of scrutinizing the most defining event of that evolution, the December 24, 1999 military coup, if for no other reason that "coup d'état," literally means a "blow to the state." The Ivorian state and society are still reeling under the impact of that initial blow and its consequences. However, this chapter proposes to conduct a much broader and systematic analysis of the Ivoirian state, focusing on the various phases of its evolution and the dynamics and events that shaped it. Using available data, the study attempts to answer questions such as, what are the major attributes and dynamics of the postcolonial Ivoirian state, how does it perform its putative function of nation building, and political and socioeconomic development, and what led to its near breakdown in recent years? These and other relevant questions will be addressed with an eye toward teasing out judicious recommendations for redefining and reinvigorating the Ivoirian state. In this period of unprecedented turbulence, the lessons, if any, to be drawn for the problematic of the African state will also be sketched out.

A discussion of the postcolonial state in Africa, however thorough it may be, would be incomplete without presenting its precolonial and colonial antecedents. Therefore, a segment of this chapter will present the political formations that preceded the independence of contemporary Ivory Coast. Then, the inception, formative phases, characteristics of the postcolonial state, attempts to consolidate it, the achievements, shortcomings and failures experienced over the last 41 years, will be presented and their reasons explained. First, it is necessary to discuss a pertinent portion of the literature on the challenges and prospects of the African state. The insights that the most perceptive studies offer will guide the analysis and inspire recommendations and suggestions to revitalize and reconfigure the Ivoirian state.

The African State: Some Theoretical Considerations

As already mentioned, starting in the1980s, a number of studies signaled the reawakening of scholarly interest in the state in general. Amid an acute crisis, the African state came to be scrutinized like never before and, as the phrases went, the African state had to be brought "back in" and even taken "seriously." A vast amount of theoretical work as well as empirical case studies have produced diagnoses of and proffered solutions and remedies for the state's predicament. Studies of the African states are too numerous and too diverse to be thoroughly reviewed here. However, some of these are particularly insightful in their attempts to conceptualize the state in Africa, unpack and refine it, and penetrate its problematic. Some of the insights these studies yield will be useful to ponder; indeed, some will influence this investigation of the Ivoirian state. But first, a necessary preliminary task is to provide a working conceptualization of the state, this most central concept of postcolonial Africa. Such a definition must apply most aptly to the independent state in Africa and more importantly, allow a meaningful discussion of the Ivoirian state.

Most scholars have used Max Weber's widely accepted definition of the state as a good starting point. According to Weber, the state refers to a "compulsory political association with continuous organization [whose] administrative staff successfully upholds a claim to the monopoly of legitimate use of force in the enforcement of its order . . . within a given territorial area."[5] This is the conception of the state as instrument of domination. Weber has insisted that there are variations between states with regard to the sort of authority and how that authority is exercised in particular.[6] To the Weberian notion, therefore, must be added other pertinent dimensions to fully capture the complete reality of the state in Africa. While one must be careful to distinguish state from political system, regime, and government, things are not that simple in the African context, where, according to Jean François Médard, as one observes the state, one also observes, at the same time, the process of state formation.[7] In that context, "[t]he state, the regime, the party, and even the individual personalities have been closely intertwined in the vast majority of African countries, and are not easily disentangled."[8] Therein lies the complexity of studying an African state. All these components are germane to its study. The line between institutions, personalities, and policies is all but nonexistent. "Autonomous," "hard" or "soft," "weak" or "strong," and "fictitious" (more specifically for Africa)[9] as generic qualifiers are attached to the state in less developed areas. These are supposed to reflect state building, failure, and reconstruction. Beyond these notions however, any meaningful discussion of the African (and Ivoirian) state must focus on other peculiar and more substantive attributes. Only the most significant and consequential of these will be summoned to complement the basic Weberian conceptualization.

Reflecting on state construction, failure, and rebirth, Njuguma Ng'ethe makes a compelling argument that the role of the markedly African phenomenon of the postindependence "strongman," as proxy for leadership, must be made an integral part of any serious discussion.[10] As the ensuing discussion of the concept of neopatrimonialism[11] recurrently affixed to the African state in general and to the Ivoirian state in particular illustrates, an emphasis on the "strongman" as an integral component of the concept of state is most definitely justified. In this regard, suffice it to remind that until his death, Felix Houphouet-Boigny, for example, assumed a role larger than any state institution or symbol. As one author puts it, "He symbolizes [Ivory Coast]. He is George Washington, Abraham Lincoln, the flag, the Constitution, the national anthem all in one. . . . He is the glue that holds the Ivoirian system together."[12] To neo-Marxists such as Robert Fatton, beyond the strongman, the critical dimension to be added to any correct conceptualization of the African state is that of class. Class, more precisely, the perverse effect of the failure of Africa's ruling classes to achieve hegemony (in the Gramcian sense), has such an incidence on the essence and capabilities of the state as to warrant that class be viewed as a crucial conceptual category to be brought "back in."[13] To Fatton, "[i]n Africa, class power is state power; the two are fused and inseparable."[14]

Another critical dimension of many African states, singularly Cote d'Ivoire, is the unique ties that have been woven with France, the former colonial power. That peculiar relationship with the external world, a mixture of extreme vulnerability, powerlessness, and more or less willing resignation seems to characterize most African states. It is this extraversion that seems to confer the very statehood status and, to some extent, an international as well as domestic semblance of legitimacy.[15] In the case of former French colonies such as Ivory Coast, Donald Cruise O'Brien has argued that the "French connection" constitutes an important feature of the Francophone African states. This often unsavory relationship takes the form of pervasive French political, cultural, monetary, and financial involvement, coupled with military presence, all of which weigh heavily on the nature, functioning, and options of many postcolonial African states.[16] To be sure, there are other important aspects of the African state that can be invoked to enhance our ability to investigate it. In the case of Cote d'Ivoire, the concept of *dialogue* as symbolic state hegemonic/ideological discourse to legitimize the state and its policies could be mentioned. The preceding dimensions, however, are so inherent in the state in Africa, certainly in Cote d'Ivoire's case, as to be organically part of its conceptual and empirical fabric. It would be inconceivable, for example, to study to any meaningful extent, the evolution of the Ivoirian state without making either President Felix Houphouet-Boigny (or Henri Konan Bedié), their political party, or Franco-Ivoirian relations, an integral part of the analysis.

A consensus has developed among the scholars of the state in Africa that it is fair and accurate to describe the state as neo-patrimonial. This characterization derives its soundness from serious theoretical analysis and empirical observation. Variations of this label, "patrimonial,"[17] "patrimonial-bureaucratic,"[18] "prebendal"[19] have also been used. Though some authors have quibbled about some of these labels, and others have introduced nuances and conceptual fine-tunings, they describe fundamentally the same phenomenon. They refer to a personalized, varyingly elaborate, national enterprise of perverted resource extraction and distribution, backed up by institutional force, duplicity or ruse and points out that the main purpose of all these is to perpetuate political power, not to achieve development. In such a polity, political power, the embryonic institutions, capabilities, and singularly economic resources of the state are monopolized for the exclusive benefit of a narrow, ethnic, regional, or class-based groups and used, under the authority of the head of state, to perpetuate near absolute control over a presumed national community. As Zaki Ergas argues, whatever their variations, background and key features, African states "have to a significant extent, a common patrimonial core."[20] Because of this, concluding his study of state-class relations, Fatton notes that "coercion rather than persuasion, dominance rather than leadership, and corruption rather than legitimacy constitute the stuff of African politics."[21] This is what makes for the crass "predatory impulse,"[22] also labeled as "the politics of the belly"[23] of the postindependence African state, a feature very widely put forth and scrutinized. This scrutiny has uniformly drawn on either Max Weber or Karl Marx or both in combination and, more or less explicitly, on the dynamics of ethnicity, to explain the predicament of the African state and its relations with the society it purports to serve. These approaches have enhanced our understanding of the way the state works and its pathological tendencies. Neither Max Weber nor Karl Marx has, however, always pushed analyses to their normative logic: what to do with such a state given the daunting challenges it faces in a fast-changing world.

Over the last two decades of reflection on the predicament of the African state, a few studies in English have distinguished themselves for their keen insight into the make-up, workings, and prospects of the state. These studies have been particularly bold in putting the finger on what ails the state and have, more or less, directly pointed toward what could be a way out of, what I have determined elsewhere to be, the limiting straightjacket of the "Berlin Conference/OAU framework."[24] Among these studies, Basil Davidson's *The Black Man's Burden* and *Africa and the Curse of the Nation-State* and Pierre Englebert's *State Legitimacy and Development in Africa* deserve a special mention. And in calling a special attention to the criticality of the choices that Africa's elite must make in response to an array of challenges, Leonardo Villalon and Phillip Huxtable's edited book, *The African State at a Critical Juncture*, has also contributed to the framing of the debate.

Just as the postcolonial state was under pressure from Western financial institutions about what it can do, and how it was to do it to meet the political and especially economic requirements of a brave new world, Davidson shifted the debate toward the suitability of the nation-state itself in its current configuration. He pointed to the utter economic nonfunctionality, culturally alienating, and politically confining concept of the nation-state that was unquestioningly borrowed from the former colonial master. Davidson argued that while the lack of performance of the African state can be partially traced to ill-will and sabotage by former colonial powers, its inadequacy, stifling top-down strategies drew an ever widening chasm between a rapacious, culturally out-of-touch elite, and all segments of the society. As a consequence, the "postcolonial nation-state [has] become a shackle on progress."[25] Beyond eloquently demonstrating its pathological character—by then established—Davidson's merit is to have introduced the welcome, if subversive notion of an alternative to the postcolonial nation-state altogether. This refreshing perspective is given to the legitimacy and appropriateness of the state to embody the hopes of the African masses. It was soon bolstered by what is arguably the most insightful book on the problematic of the African state in recent years, Pierre Englebert's study[26] on the correlation between state legitimacy and its developmental performance. This is of crucial importance to any discussion of the African state. As Crawford Young, agreeing with Weber, has incisively noted, among the necessary attributes of the state, legitimacy and its pursuit are "at the core of [Weber's] notion of the state; absent this property, the state is in a condition of extreme vulnerability."[27] Englebert convincingly argues that the capacity of a state to tackle effectively its developmental role is in proportion to its historical legitimacy and its actual congruence with the indigenous political and cultural realities. He further establishes that the postcolonial state's "legitimacy deficit" creates conditions that lead to dysfunctional, ineffective policies, and behavior. In other words, this deficit is "at the core of the developmental failure of many African states."[28] Given his findings, the African state is in dire need of a far-reaching overhaul, well beyond the policy-focused crisis-response solution typically proffered.[29] For example, neopatrimonialism and related policies and behaviors that failed Africans and eroded the foundations of nearly every developmental policy ever attempted, are only the consequence of this legitimacy deficit. To address them, the "structures" of the state must be the prime target of any reform and the basic philosophy of bridging the legitimacy and performance gap must be to acknowledge the worth, relevance, and benefit of Africa's traditional political and cultural ways, not to correct presumed flaws intrinsic to Africans. This perspective, the conclusions of the study, and the solid quantitative data on which they rest are indeed a break from the common wisdom that takes the postcolonial state in its current configuration for granted. Davidson's and Englebert's works open the possibility, indeed force on us the imperative of looking beyond the African state "as we know it." To this, Villalon and Huxtable's book[30] contributes by highlighting the responsibility incumbent on the African elite in charge of the state to make fundamental choices that will determine the nature and configuration of the state in the twenty-first century. The editors of the book and the contributors generally analyze the state in the usual framework. However, theirs is a judicious invocation of the apt concept of the "critical juncture" as resulting from a "confluence of [political, economic] pressures that will reconfigure the structure of state-society relations in African states." and necessitate for the "elites to develop resources that enhance their abilities to achieve desired goals."[31] What these elite will ultimately do to meet the present and future challenges of the African state remains to be seen, however, as Englebert perceptively urges, we should not allow our imagination to be constrained by the limited options the burdened legacy of the past seems to impose.[32] These are, briefly sketched and are the conceptual considerations and analytical framework in which the evolution of the Ivoirian state must be examined. While this analysis will concentrate on the postindependence period, as suggested above, it is imperative to briefly present the precolonial and colonial antecedents for valuable insights into the postcolonial state.

The Precolonial and Colonial Periods

The state in Cote d'Ivoire, as currently constituted, is a creation of France. It is the outcome of the tumultuous encounter between imperial France, starting in the eighteenth century, and a portion of the western part of the African continent. The slow but steady encroachment on the territory and its inhabitants, the assertion of control by France's plenipotentiaries culminated in the incorporation of the territories as a full-fledged colony in 1893. After the March 10, 1893 decree, Cote d'Ivoire can be said to have entered the status of "colonial state." While before it was carved out as a colony, there was no centralized authority in control of this vast territory, there existed, scattered within and across its confines, numerous constituted political formations. An oft-cited authority on the history of Cote d'Ivoire labeled some of them "great states."[33] He counted six of these: the Malinke Empire of the Touré in the Odienné Region; the Kingdom of Kong of the Ouattara Dynasty, in the north; in the East, the Agni-Ashanti Kingdoms of Bondoukou, Indenié, and Krindjabo; and in Baoule Country, the already crumbling Sakasso Kingdom founded by the legendary Queen Aura Pokou.[34] It is not necessary to dwell on the organizational structures, dynamics, or flaws of these and less centralized political units in the territory today known as Cote d'Ivoire. In general, as George Ayyiteh[35] and others have established, precolonial political entities were known to exhibit a few basic characteristics. They truly emanated from and were congruent with the local cultural traditions. More democratically minded, they were built on participatory, consultative, and communitarian principles, and therefore, were more responsive to the governed. They also had often elaborate systems for checks on the concentration of power and injustice.[36] While many of the local political formations were alienated from and often at odds with one another, they were, nevertheless, naturally evolving in conditions dictated by their natural sociological and political milieu. That evolution was brutally interrupted by the colonial intrusion.[37] As Paul Atger notes, the colonial imposition, even in its earlier phase (1843–1893), far from contributing to the modernization of the existing political formations, accelerated their destruction. It singularly emasculated the traditional legitimate authorities when it took away their power to enforce order, a crucial function they used to exercise quite naturally.[38] This deliberate attitude toward the existing traditional political order was central to the corrupting and disrupting of the entire colonial era and beyond.

The authority of France was established only after a period of expansion and conquest (so-called penetration), brutal military suppression of the widespread resistance of the various populations (so-called pacification) under the infamous Governor Gabriel Angoulvant, and finally, of subjugation, and direct military, and administrative control, that is, "colonization." Before discussing briefly the evolution and features of the colonial state, it is necessary to say a word about what led to it. An aspect of the colonial adventure that is often underplayed, but of critical importance in understanding the many developments that ensued, is the resistance African populations mounted against formidable odds. Generally, only the armed resistance of leaders such as Samory Touré is known. There is ample evidence however, that in the territory of Cote d'Ivoire for example, resistance to subjugation, the elimination of political and cultural referents, and economic exploitation never abated ever since the true intentions of the first colonial administrators became evident. The relation of domination and duplicity that is essential to the colonial enterprise became patent when even the gratuities and other cheap material enticements for collaboration allocated in a plethora of "treaties" to chiefs and kings were rescinded amid other measures to humiliate and subdue the general population. These culminated in the introduction, in 1900 and thereafter, of the head tax, forced labor, and the *indigenat*. D'Aby chronicled the extent of the resistance (killings of colonial authorities, tax evasions, rebellions, etc.) and the toll ordinary people paid in virtually every corner of Cote d'Ivoire throughout the period of "pacification."[39] This resistance that continued throughout the colonial period and culminated in the attainment of political independence, is the expression of a longstanding rejection of imposed exogenous, nonresponsive forms of political and social organization.[40] A reconstruction of the state will have to take into account this feature of the response of the populations of Cote d'Ivoire to the "colonial state," its structure, and method to which we now briefly turn.

Evidently, as Crawford Young has incisively argued, it is somewhat of a misnomer to present the territories formed under colonial rule as "states" since they lacked the key attributes of statehood, "sovereignty" in its international dimension in particular.[41] Nevertheless, this arrangement that, in the case of Ivory Coast, lasted more than half a century, presents definite characteristics that had a profound impact on its postindependence clone.

When, by virtue of a French decree dated March 10, 1893, Ivory Coast became a colony distinct from Benin and French Guinea to which it had been attached, it became necessary to provide it appropriate instruments of control and effective administration. After the "pacification" was completed, and the terms of the Berlin Conference mandating the "actual" occupation of the claimed territory was nearly achieved, the administration of the territory was organized. In 1895, the colony was made part of the *Afrique Occidentale Française* (Federation of French West Africa). Successive decrees (particularly in the later stages of the French presence) and the actions of successive governors in charge of the administration of the colony gave shape to the colonial and postcolonial state of Cote d'Ivoire.

Similar to other colonies, it was subdivided into *Cercles* (headed by a *commandant de cercle*), *Subdivisions* (headed by a *chef de subdivision*), and *Cantons*, the last being the lowest rung of the colony's highly centralized administrative hierarchical structure. The indigenous chiefs and kings were made agents of the colonial administration as *chef de cantons* and the existing political units were fragmented into separate cantons independently linked to subdivisions, further undermining the political standing and legitimacy of the traditional leaders.[42] It is noteworthy that the governor was assisted in his role as the chief executive officer of the colony by a consultative council elected, in the logic of colonialism, by only the European population residing in the colony. Until the post–World War II period, when a series of decrees gradually afforded them limited participation, there was no meaningful representation of the Ivoirian population in the management of their affairs. Throughout, the imperative of economic exploitation and resource transfer to France was the *raison d'être* of the colonial state and its defining feature. This feature demanded that the colonized population be excluded and marginalized. Just as it misused traditional political structures and managed to enlist the collaboration of some traditional authorities in its early stages, the later stages of the colonial state were marked also by assiduous efforts at coopting and using the educated elite and emerging urban and rural upper classes. Felix Houphouet-Boigny, whose influence in the evolution of Cote d'Ivoire since the mid-1940s was immense, was a product and prime example of both stages.[43] Along with his party, the *Parti Democratic de Cote d'Ivoire-Rassemblement Democratique Africain* (PDCI-RDA), he carved a singular course for the country that both dictated the configuration and evolution of the state until his death in 1993. The crumbling of the French colonial empire in the late 1950s, the profound transformation of the French state itself, and the push for decolonization led to Cote d'Ivoire's accession to international sovereignty after a brief period of autonomy and failed attempts at creating a Franco-African community.

The Postcolonial State

Background

When Cote d'Ivoire became an independent state on August 7, 1960, it nominally acquired all the trappings of full statehood, particularly international sovereignty. As Crawford Young has argued, typical of other postindependence African states, the Ivory Coast inherited the administrative structures, philosophy, and ways of the colonial state.[44] Given the more than amicable manner in which independence came, the features, evolution, orientation, challenges, constraints, and performance of the Ivorian state have been profoundly marked by this legacy. A French Fifth Republic-style constitution and laws were enacted to give the new state a constitutional/legal basis, and the adventure into nation-state building commenced.[45] The early years of this adventure are discussed below. This discussion entails the role Houphouet-Boigny, the head of state for more than thirty years, played as well as the monopolization of the state for the exclusive benefit of an emerging state-centered bourgeois class, and the state's peculiar relations with France. First, as indicated earlier, a meaningful analysis of the attributes, evolution, and challenges of the postindependence state must zoom in on the critical turning point in that evolution: the 1999 military coup. In effect, although the intervention of the military in the affairs of the state, often running it altogether, has been a familiar occurrence in the majority of West African states, this development was not supposed to happen in Ivory Coast.

The "Blow To The State"

When, on Christmas eve 1999, it transpired that a *Comite National de Salut Public* (CNSP) led by late General Robert Guei had been constituted to run the country after forcing President Henri Konan Bedié, Houphouet-Boigny's successor, to flee into exile, most observers of Ivoirian politics were astonished.[46] By this action, however, the Ivoirian military had forced a dose of reality on the postcolonial state and possibly afforded it a window of opportunity for rebirth, and reconfiguration. Even a most cursory look at the state in the aftermath of the coup would reveal that such a rebirth did not occur. On the contrary, as the army mutiny that cost General Guei and hundred others their lives vividly reminded us the opportunity that was missed.

A loosely organized group of noncommissioned officers succeeded in pulling down, quite effortlessly and without bloodshed, one of the longest running civilian administrations on the continent. This was evidence enough that the assumptions about the touted strength and virtues of the state in Cote d'Ivoire in contrast to its West African peers were unwarranted. As I have argued elsewhere, the supposed advanced consolidation of the Ivoirian political system rested on an elaborate but fundamentally flawed strategies implemented since its inception and destined to perpetuate the supremacy of the PDCI regime. The coup constituted a repudiation of these corrosive coup prevention strategies, also arguably, the entire state architecture, given the pronouncements of the military junta leaders on the necessity to "clean house."[47] At the same time, the coup embodied the ultimate failure of a construction of the state based on the monopolization of the public institutions by a coterie organized around an individual, using the political machinery of the state, and in which the legitimation imperative was absent, as will be shown in the following paragraphs.

The coup itself, precipitated by the inept leadership, mismanagement, and crass behavior of President Bedié not just brought to the surface, but in fact exacerbated the serious political and social crises the Ivoirian state has been experiencing after nearly 40 years of independence. When the "state of the state" and its performance prior to the coup are closely examined, the coup that toppled one of the reputedly "strongest" states in Africa will no longer be that aberrant. This "blow to the state" is best understood when put in the context of decades of one of the most dysfunctional states, despite the contrary appearances. The military intermission, supposed to prepare the transition to a truly democratic dispensation, did no such thing because of the singularly deficient leadership of General Robert Guei and his murderous will to cling to power. It only demonstrated that the military is seldom the institution capable of presiding over a needed reconfiguration of state and society interface or to help overcome a long legacy of misuse of the state. The attempt proved an unmitigated disaster. Neither the constitution, nor practice or policy initiatives addressed seriously any of the crises that helped prepare the ground for military intervention. Consequently, the problematic nature of state-society relations and the crises to which this gives rise remained unattended.

Nearly three years after the coup (prior to the mid-September 2002 bloody mutiny/coup), a semblance of normalcy seemed to take hold with the submission to President Laurent Gbagbo of the final report of the "Forum for National Reconciliation." It is now evident that a segment of the national elite that a viciously brutal military interlude and deeply flawed transition to democracy have propelled to the helm of affairs has not questioned, much less, altered in any noticeable way, the approach to the state that has prevailed since independence. Only the political personnel seemed to have changed. To be sure, the *Front Populaire Ivoirien* (PFI), President Gbagbo's party, is not the PDCI; he is neither Houphouet-Boigny nor Bedié. A new constitution was drafted and passed. However, Gbagbo and his party's philosophy, the institutions, norms, as well as the state/society project this latest constitution purports to bring about are indistinguishable from the PDCI and the previous constitutions they had set up. The brutal repression experienced after the inauguration of the FPI regime, the nagging latent political, ethnic, and regional cleavages symbolized by the survival of the poisonous concept of *Ivoirité* are clear indications that the fundamentally dysfunctional character of the state remained the same. Even the sense of crisis and urgency did not wane, as the trial of the January 2001 alleged coup plotters and the ongoing controversy over Alassane Dramane Ouattara's citizenship amply had evidenced even before the mutiny and its aftermath. In other words, despite the traumatic events Cote d'Ivoire experienced since that fateful December 24th, 1999, when it comes to the badly needed rethinking of the state, it has, so far been only "business as usual."

The Houphouet Phenomenon

The extreme alienation of the Ivoirian elite regardless of their political persuasion (whether civilian or military), from the population's aspirations for an effective and responsive political authority, for example, has deep roots. The choices Houphouet-Boigny and the PDCI made on the eve of independence and the policies that they enacted and implemented charted the course of the Ivoirian state. They are responsible for the character it took, its evolution, and performance today. An analysis of the Ivoirian state over the last 40 years suggests that as the coup has verified, the solid reputation that Cote d'Ivoire has always enjoyed as West Africa's "model stable state" has been overrated. According to Amondji, a severe critic of President Houphouet-Boigny and his regime, the nature and orientation of the postcolonial Ivoirian state must be traced to *le repli tactique* (the tactical retreat or withdrawal)[48] Houphouet-Boigny adopted under the guidance of the French colonial authorities in the waning days of their presence in Africa. Amondji argues convincingly that because of the strong popular movement that fueled the anti-colonialist struggle of the late 1940s and 1950s, France, desperate to maintain its interests and influence in the postcolonial era, needed an emblematic figure to moderate and lead the accommodating wing of the movement. They found in Houphouet-Boigny that leader, and they proceeded to back him as he adroitly maneuvered to impose his single-minded will to keep and strengthen Cote d'Ivoire's ties with France. An important part of Houphouet-Boigny's agenda was to eliminate the progressive and populist segment of the anticolonialist movement and its organizations. The silence of his colleagues in the leadership of the party made this possible. When, in the early years of independence, by the time many in the PDCI leadership realized his disconcerting, profound convictions and unyielding subservience to France's interests, he had already acquired so much power that it was too late. Methodically, he went on to install a personalist, clientelist regime that, of necessity, grew more and more distant from the Ivoirian people.

A descendant of Baoule chiefs, Houphouet-Boigny was a *chef de canton*. A cocoa planter, he was trained to become a doctor (*medecin Africain*), and went on to help create, in 1945, the *Syndicat Agricole Africain* (SAA), a union of African Farmers, to defend the interests of African farmers against the discrimination and encroachment by large-scale European planters who were supported by French colonial authorities. His political activities propelled him to the position of one of the most prominent political leaders of French West Africa. After founding the RDA and leading the PDCI, he was elected to the post–World War II French Constituent Assembly, where he distinguished himself as one of the sponsors of a law to ban forced labor in the colonies. The intensification of the anticolonial struggles in the late 1940s soured the relationship between the embryonic African political elite spearheaded by the PDCI and the colonial authorities, with mounting challenges to colonialism everywhere as the backdrop. One of the consequences of the post–World War II political turmoil was the separation, in 1947, of present-day Burkina Faso (former Upper Volta) as a territory distinct from Cote d'Ivoire.

A blind repression against nationalists that was fueled by virulent anticommunist sentiments forced Houphouet to abandon his alliance with French communists and their African allies at both the West African federation and Ivoirian territorial levels, and to strike a very conciliatory tone toward colonialism.[49] In the 1950s, he became a senior minister (*Ministre d'Etat*) in the French government where he wove lasting friendships and alliances with various French political leaders and campaigned for the Franco-African community and against immediate independence. There is no doubt that the character and the evolution of the Ivoirian state owe a great deal to the personality and choices of its first president. A consequential aspect of both was his obstinate refusal of independence from France as a viable option, and his strong belief in the maintenance of strong ties with the former colonial power when independence became unavoidable. Given this, it is ironic that his claim to legitimacy, more than his stature as a traditional ruler, was his credential in the struggle *for* independence. For most of his tenure, Houphouet-Boigny enjoyed an unequaled aura as an African sage (*Le Vieux*), qualified as "virtual deification."[50] This image, often propped up by French (and Western) media, was assiduously cultivated by calculated, often beneficent or magnanimous grand gestures in domestic, subregional or international politics. It was also echoed in the state-controlled media and by a legion of laudatory journalists and writers. A veritable legitimizing myth surrounded him, contributing to sustaining his flattering reputation of wisdom and benevolence even after revelations of several schemes and machinations in the West African subregion in pursuit of questionable and egotistical goals.[51]

Throughout, Houphouet-Boigny deftly used the diffuse concept of "dialogue" as a political leitmotiv, as an instrument of conflict diffusion and dissent neutralization.[52] To be sure, the intra-party dynamics and rivalries that Aristide Zolberg has extensively analyzed,[53] were important in themselves. Though not unique to Cote d'Ivoire, they influenced the evolution of the state because of the role the PDCI, as a party-state has come to play.[54] It is evident, however, that an Ivoirian state resulting from the concocted convergence of the interests and agenda of a political leadership (particularly Houphouet-Boigny) "persuaded" not to rock the postcolonial boat and a French state heavily invested in Cote d'Ivoire were bound to sacrifice the aspirations of the majority of the Ivoirian masses on the altar of French interests.

The "Houphouet State"[55]

Personalization of the state is not a new or peculiar phenomenon. However, even in Africa with its Mobutus, Bourguibas, and Mois, no leader has so dominated the state to the extent that there is such a total symbiosis in the mind of most observers between the state and the head of that state as Houphouet-Boigny. He epitomized the "father of the nation" syndrome in African politics. Until his death in 1993, his dominance over the Ivoirian state was absolute and was questioned only in the last years of his long tenure, when the entire "Houphouet state" was seriously challenged for reasons to be discussed below. Before it came to that, however, throughout the 1960s, 1970s, and 1980s, the imprint of Houphouet and his party on the state, its institutions, orientation, and domestic and foreign policies was momentous.

After negotiating the terms of independence with close cooperation with France in several areas, the task of establishing a viable state while maintaining power awaited the new head of state and his PDCI cadre. After a new constitution and a few plebiscitary elections, the stage was set. Among the first measures taken was what Zolberg called the "institutionalization" of the PDCI party and the "one-man-rule" system, giving birth to a new political reality. As Philippe Yacé, one of the architects of this new reality, put it, "[t]he PDCI is now the governmental party in the Ivory Coast. Government, assembly, and Party therefore share the same single goal. This is why you find at the head of the government, a chief, Houphouet-Boigny; at the head of the elected bodies, a leader, Houphouet-Boigny; at the head of the party, a president, Houphouet-Boigny;"[56] To reflect this new reality, the administrative structures of the state and those of the party were made to parallel each other. Every *sous-prefecture* (the basic administrative unit of the state) coincided with a section of the party. At the same time, building on the colonial territorial administration and to ensure tighter control, the number of *departements* and *prefectures* and *sous-prefectures* was multiplied manifold by the mid-1980s.[57] The dominance of the PDCI also meant that the members of parliament, the members of government, of the economic advisory council, the high level civil servants, and regional and municipal authorities were appointed by the party under the tight control of its undisputed leader, Houphouet-Boigny. The Houphouet state was launched.

In addition to virtually all the functions of the state, the heads of the numerous parastatals were also appointed by the head of state and served at his pleasure. The various agents of the state thus selected, were more or less, tacitly given license to accumulate wealth and they owed their fortunes and loyalty to Houphouet-Boigny personally. This situation was aptly described as follows: "Nearly all members of the elite were creations of the Head of State. He brought them into the system, provided them with all their needs."[58] This coterie essentially constituted the "crew" of the Houphouet state ship. It grew into the most significant and decisive component of what Yves Fauré and Jean-François Médard called the "state bourgeoisie,"[59] membership of which was as rewarding in terms of illicit wealth accumulation as it was precarious indeed.

As happened in 1977 after a speech in which he criticized the mismanagement of the economy, he also warned that the seemingly most prominent members of the ruling state elite could suddenly lose their position.[60] This was done in a bid to reassert his authority and remind everyone of his supremacy. This basic characteristic of Houphouet-Boigny's approach to running the affairs of the state was illustrated in what came to be known as the "1963 events." These constituted indubitably a turning point in the consolidation of the Houphouet state. To eliminate any potential challenge to the personalization of power, Houphouet and his allies in the party and state organs declared in 1963 that a group of leaders conspired to stage a coup against the regime. They took advantage of this situation to purge the party and the state of designated conspirators and to reinforce even further the burgeoning Houphouet state. This could have well been the necessary follow-up to the early 1950s *repli tactique* that marked a sharp departure from a fierce anticolonialist, nationalist/populist stance of the party. Just as Houphouet-Boigny's subsequent moves, it certainly brought to light a state that by its very nature, having failed to forge the legitimizing organic connections to the Ivoirian masses and their aspirations,[61] must compensate by remaining vigilant and, now and then, strike against known and putative enemies as a matter of survival strategy.

According to Dwayne Woods, the interactions and relations of the Houphouet state and the Ivoirian civil society organizations and groups can be essentially characterized as a "quasi-corporatist arrangement."[62] By this Woods means that without setting up a full-blown corporatist state as usually understood, President Houphouet-Boigny's regime made it a critical method and objective of governance to exert at least indirect control over any group or entity that purported to engage with or articulate claims against the state. Elaborate systems of co-optation and sanctions (only when absolutely necessary) were developed to ensure that no serious challenge succeeded or was emulated. Consequently, as Robert Jackson and Carl Rosberg[63] and others have demonstrated, Houphouet-Boigny presided over an elaborate system of corrupt and corrupting resource extraction and distribution using the total control of the state. In the end, what was established was a statewide network of clientelist, neopatrimonial relationships the epicenter of which was the president, and whose aim was to perpetuate a certain vision of social relations and the role of Cote d'Ivoire in Africa and the world. Observers noted (in the mid-1980s) that an outcome—and cause—of this had been the emergence of an interlocking web of a few dozen families that are at the same time dependent on, and exercise control over, the Ivoirian state and economy.[64]

Yet, another closely related feature of the Houphouet state was the manipulation and balancing act with regard to ethnicity. While ensuring a certain ethnic balance in the personnel entrusted with the management of the most significant segments of the Houphouet state, a Machiavellian precaution was taken to ensure that those selected on this basis did not actually have any ethnic base from which they could challenge the state.[65] According to Bakary, this singularly contributed to making the Houphouet state highly "autonomous," insulated from, and nonresponsive to, the Ivoirian society.[66] This nonaccountability and distance from the Ivoirian society can also be seen in the associated widespread mismanagement, corruption, and waste of national resources. Cote d'Ivoire is infamous for the number of multibillion CFA Francs financial scandals that regularly come to the surface. One observer estimated that as many as 130 billion CFA Francs are embezzled and taken out of the country annually.[67] Houphouet-Boigny himself never made any mystery of his vast wealth, most of which was accumulated thanks to his control of the state. The objective cost to the development efforts and to the consolidation of the Ivoirian state of such an orgy of national wealth dilapidation must be staggering indeed. This is also central to the problematic of state reconfiguration in Cote d'Ivoire.

With regard to its international relations, a crucial characteristic of the Houphouet state that had a bearing on its internal character was also its relationship with France. Perhaps one of its most distinguishing features was the truly special relations that tied it to France. Such relations were often criticized as neocolonial in nature and effect.[68] In 1961, Cote d'Ivoire signed a number of special economic, cultural, and military agreements with France. In addition to enabling privileged French position in the economic, educational, and cultural sectors, including advisors at all levels of the armed forces, they also stipulate the stationing of French troops on the Ivoirian territory.[69] Even as of 2002, France continued to maintain a battalion of marines at the naval base of Port Bouet, and until 2002, the country hosted the largest and most influential contingent of French citizens abroad. Decades after independence, French citizens and "Cooperants" were present at all levels of the state apparatus, including as prominent advisors to the head of state. Many of these expatriates continued to enjoy very high standards of living and engaged in lucrative business enterprises, while others were involved in the management of the state and its agencies.[70]

The close relationship with France was even more visible in Cote d'Ivoire's international relations in the West African subregion, in Africa, and in the world in general. Cote d'Ivoire was widely perceived as zealously promoting and protecting French (and Western) interests in Africa.[71] In exchange, France has always committed itself not just to the protection of the Ivoirian state, but also to the survival of the Houphouet-Boigny regime.[72] As I have argued elsewhere, the longevity of the regime owed more to that level of French commitment and to similarly shortsighted strategies consisting in ethnic manipulation and co-optation of the military under Houphouet-Boigny and Bedié than to regime-institutionalizing practices.[73] In addition, in the context of the cold war in which it resolutely chose the Western camp, and in contrast to the extensive meddling by Foccart's destabilizing schemes in the domestic affairs of many other Francophone African states,[74] Ivory Coast was essentially "left alone." It was indeed sheltered and its stability never seriously threatened. Not having to worry about its internal and external security as Ghana and Guinea, for example, did constantly, translated into tangible and intangible economic advantages[75] over many other African states. Therefore, the much-touted stability or low vulnerability of the Ivoirian state, variously attributed to its capacity to resist the demands of society[76] or to its effective management of state assets[77] must be understood in this context. In the mid-1980s, Marcel Amondji put forth convincingly a similar argument. It is not fortuitous that the military coup in Cote d'Ivoire succeeded in part because France had abandoned that commitment to allied African regimes after launching the La Baule Doctrine in the 1990s.

The Unraveling of the Houphouet State

Given its features, it is evident that the Houphouet state was riddled with contradictions, that it was unsustainable, and could not possibly meet adequately the expectations and aspirations of the Ivoirian people. Not surprisingly, it started, as early as in the 1980s, to show unmistakable signs of unraveling under the pressure of a worsening economic situation brought about not only by unfavorable developments in the global economy but mainly by years of corruption, waste, and mismanagement. The days of reckoning for the PDCI regime and the Ivoirian state it had symbolized since independence, it appeared, were not very far, as the state resources used to oil it and keep it going had started to dry up. To postpone this reckoning and at the same time maintain power, Houphouet-Boigny engaged, starting in the 1980s, in a veritable salvaging operation. His successor as president continued the salvaging operation that did not entail any break with past practices or the overhaul of the foundations of the postcolonial state and this was to lead straight to the December 1999 military intervention and the subsequent ongoing woes of the country.

Throughout the 1960s and 1970s, Cote d'Ivoire had recorded some of the highest economic growth rates of any developing state. Its generous investment policies attracted foreign (mainly French) investors and led to the creation of rapidly expanding private and parastatal sectors, allowing the creation of thousands of jobs (and patronage employment). Thanks to a state-directed, purposeful, and sustained funding of the educational sector, Cote d'Ivoire witnessed a phenomenal growth of an urban, cosmopolitan, educated, and high-income earning burgeoning middle class gravitating toward the state and all this in the midst of an apparently ever-strengthening and stable political system, even as other states in the region were caught in endless coups and political instability. This led to extensive discussions in the development literature of the "Ivoirian case." However, even amid more or less cautious laudatory commentaries[78] about what was touted as the Ivoirian "miracle" and "model," many observers had warned against what appeared to be a mirage, at best a case of a highly dependent, "growth without development" state.[79]

By the mid-1980s, the financial predicament became so acute that Cote d'Ivoire was forced to stop payments on its already huge debt. This decision in itself constituted the admission of a major failing of the state. However, the number of people employed in the modern state sector decreased by nearly one-third with a concomitant shrinking of major macroeconomic indicators.[80] What Cruise O'Brien called "the show of the state"[81] in Cote d'Ivoire had to come to an end. Throughout the 1980s, under the pressure of the international financial institutions, Houphouet-Boigny had undertaken a series of belt-tightening fiscal and economic reforms one of the effects of which was to limit even further the Houphouet state's ability to buy its way out of the paralyzing national resources distribution crisis. As Woods has argued, this forced Houphouet-Boigny to strenuously attempt to diffuse the crisis essentially using a combination of tried and shrewd moves, neither of which could prevent, ultimately, unsought transformations of his regime.[82] First, he aggressively sought to assert his control over the one segment of civil society that had constantly challenged his authority and legitimacy, the Ivoirian intelligentsia. He used, to no avail, his usual arsenal of behind-the-scenes undermining and manipulation of the leadership of dissenting groups. He appealed to lofty principles of sacrifice and to the virtues of "dialogue" and when all failed, he unleashed the repressive power of the state.

Second, he reconsidered the resource redistribution patterns, reducing, or cutting state patronage benefits, singularly to recalcitrant sections of increasingly restive professional organizations and civil society as a whole.[83] These measures did little to restore the badly damaged image of the Houphouet state. They did not slow down the wave of protests that spared no segment of the population, including the military, nor did it reduce the intense pressure on an ailing Houphouet-Boigny.[84] In fact, they only irrevocably tolled the death knell for the state as signs of the unraveling multiplied. One of the most ominous of those signs was French President Mitterrand's refusal to accede to Houphouet-Boigny's request for military intervention against mutinying soldiers who had occupied the airport and a radio station in 1990 to demand pay increases.[85] In the end, Cote d'Ivoire could not remain exempt from the multitude of crises that affected African states and political systems in the late 1980s and 1990s. Houphouet-Boigny had no choice but to relinquish the monopoly on power he and his party had secured and retained for decades, thanks to their tight control of the state. He agreed to multiparty politics shortly before his death. When Henry Konan Bedié, in accordance with the constitution, became president in December 1993, he failed to carry out any serious transformation of the Houphouet state. However, the fiscal crisis was brought under control, thanks to Houphouet-Boigny's only prime minister, Alassane Dramane Ouattara, and Ivory Coast started to experience major improvements in its overall macroeconomic picture. Bedié almost defiantly mismanaged these positive economic windfalls as he undertook to consolidate his power through dangerous appeals to ethnic and regional demons. These attempts to revert to the most crude, exclusionary, neopatrimonial, and repressive practices of the pre-1990 era squandered an opportunity to revamp the Ivoirian state.[86] They also precipitated and deepened the crisis that ultimately ended his tenure in disgrace. They also brought about Cote d'Ivoire's current trials and tribulations, highlighted by an armed standoff with mutineers after a bloody event that will scare the country forever. They have already transformed the very image of Ivory Coast in the geopolitical landscape of West Africa, as the country threatens to pull the entire subregion into chaos and instability, and bloodshed worse than the civil wars in Sierra Leone and Liberia combined.

Toward a Reconstitution of the State? The Gbagbo Era

After General Guei's failed "self-succession scheme," reflected in his efforts to hijack the 2000 presidential election, Laurent Gbagbo, the leader of the Popular Front of the Ivory Coast, was declared the winner. With a professed commitment to social democracy, the expectation was that the Gbagbo regime would set into motion the reconstitution of the Ivorian state, especially the elimination of its "Houphouet core."

Unfortunately, the state reconstitution project has been hindered by the Gbagbo regime's failure to set into motion the expunging of the "Houphouet Phenomenon" and the elimination of the poisonous discriminatory citizenship requirement. The latter problem provided the trigger for the outbreak of a civil war in September 2002 involving the Gbagbo regime on one hand, and various insurgency outfits on the other (the insurgents have now established a single outfit called the "New Forces"). The civil war has led to the division of the country between the rebel-held sectors and the areas still controlled by the Ivorian government. Despite several peacemaking and peacekeeping efforts, the civil war continues. It is clear that neither the Gbagbo regime nor the rebel outfit is committed to a peaceful resolution of the civil war. Thus, the exigency of the state reconstitution project has taken a back seat to the prosecution of the war.

Rethinking the Ivoirian State: Some Recommendations

To formulate recommendations for rethinking and reconstructing the state inherited from the European colonial enterprise entails dangers. One runs the risk of either indulging in wishful thinking or expounding on platitudes. So daunting are the challenges. Long showcased as the model postcolonial state, the tribulations of the Ivoirian state, still very much threatened with disintegration, as the September 2002 crisis and the subsequent civil war amply illustrate, are instructive for the current discussions on the crisis of the state in Africa. Evidently, the strategic choices made by Ivorian leaders have been patently flawed, and their misjudgments devastating in their effects. After the heightened tensions of the last several years, the semblance of re-equilibrium that seemed to prevail prior to the latest outbreak of large-scale violence proved to be deceptive. As maneuvers are still under way for the control of the state, there is urgency to fundamentally transform it and its relations with the Ivoirian masses. It is remarkable that, during the epic "national conference" movement spearheaded by the liberal and progressive segments of the elite to open up Francophone Africa's awkward and sclerous political systems, there was no debate on overhauling the state itself. In other words, the fighting was over the state apparatus as an instrument and to what uses to put it, not on its nature and character. In that confined framework, various solutions to the predicament of the Ivoirian state[87] were offered, including a federal government structure by the current head of state when he was in the opposition.

I will not suggest a laundry list of usual remedies; my recommendation does not deal with the uses the state in its current configuration should be put to. Rather, it focuses on the kind of tool with which we should equip African peoples, for it is now obvious that the postcolonial state as it evolved in Cote d'Ivoire and elsewhere was indeed a transplant that just did not take root. Therefore, the first step would be, following Basil Davidson, to start to question the very nature, usefulness, and assumptive premise of the postcolonial nation-state as the only sociopolitical arrangement and option for postcolonial Africa. This will not be an easy first step to take in Cote d'Ivoire. Of course, this approach was never on President Houphouet-Boigny's agenda, given his inclination and role as the architect of the postindependence Ivoirian state. Jeanne Toungara has argued that because of his status as the heir to the chieftaincy of the Baoule, a major subgroup of the Akan and his natural tendencies, Houphouet-Boigny had somehow "Akanized" the Ivoirian state through his policies and leadership style.[88] Clearly, this analysis ignores his and the PDCI's general attitude toward African traditional political systems and their relevance in postcolonial Africa. Zolberg's study of these attitudes unequivocally establishes that the leaders of the PDCI despised the cultural and traditional institutions and mores, found them retrograde and embarrassing, and considered them relics of a past to be rapidly overcome.[89] Furthermore, a distinction must be made between the "instrumentalization" and appeal to the people's attachment to their sociocultural referents that undoubtedly Houphouet-Boigny did, and a genuine attachment to, and belief in tapping these to create a socioculturally relevant and responsive new political reality. Houphouet-Boigny did not do the latter. Almost everything about his political career and modus operandi precluded it. Cote d'Ivoire as well as other African states can help solve the crisis of the postcolonial state by revisiting the notion, itself a legacy of colonialism, that African societies have really nothing to offer to set-up polities that would transcend the colonial adventure and its various debilitating legacies. This is a critical psychological step to take.

A second step will be to take a serious look at indigenous forms and practices of political organizations in order to contrive a new and different approach to meeting the needs and aspirations of the Ivoirian people. This can be done in two directions. First, the forms of political organization that prevailed among various groups of Cote d'Ivoire should be seriously studied to identify traits that can inform a redesign of new polity in Cote d'Ivoire. This must be accompanied by a determination to transcend the inherited postcolonial arrangements and should be accompanied by a real effort to decentralize the Ivorian state, even in its current configuration. A devolution of power and a conscious effort to empower politically and economically the grassroots traditional as well as modern structures in all areas of the country will lessen the impulse for controlling the levers of political power concentrated in the capital that has marred Cote d'Ivoire's recent history.

As I have argued elsewhere,[90] a third approach could be to de-emphasize the preoccupation with nation-state building and to link the current national authority to regional and supranational structures in order to minimize the "national" character of the Ivorian nation-state. The dangerous concept of *Ivoirité* and its manipulation go exactly in the opposite direction and are only liable to exacerbate the crisis of legitimacy of the Ivoirian state. If the logic of the *Ivoirité* is not abandoned, the state will continue to be perceived as no more than as an instrument of exclusion and disenfranchisement, as the current crisis abundantly illustrates. Cote d'Ivoire's demographics, with more than one-third of its inhabitants immigrants from neighboring countries, predisposes it, perhaps more than any other state in the region, to abandon this dangerous and narrowly construed citizenship. The ongoing efforts to establish an ECOWAS passport/citizenship, must be accelerated, and the effective implementation of the decisions regarding the free movement and migration of ECOWAS citizens must be given a priority and expanded. These measures will further de-emphasize citizenship based on the postcolonial state.

Putting the finger on the problems the approaches and methods of the PDCI/Houphouet state were bound to create, as Zolberg foresaw, the emergence of the likes of Laurent Gbagbo, the current head of state, to challenge it.[91] Similarly, if *Ivoirité*, and "business as usual" prevail over applying a new thinking to the bankruptcy of the postcolonial state and its failure to live up to the expectations of the Ivoirians, Cote d'Ivoire is likely to continue to drift toward yet another disaster in postcolonial state building. Even when the current civil war is resolved without altering the Ivorian state in its current configuration, only the symptoms of its predicament would have been addressed. The root causes, that is, the extremely dysfunctional character of Cote d'Ivoire as a continuation in form, logic, practices, and methods of the colonial state in its disregard to the aspirations of the Ivorian people would have been, once more, ignored. Another opportunity to overhaul the postcolonial state would have been, yet again, tragically missed. This would only postpone the next inevitable crisis.

Conclusion

This chapter has critically analyzed the evolution of the state in Cote d'Ivoire. It chronicles the creation of the postcolonial state and its transformation, thanks to the action of Houphouet-Boigny and his political party, into a personalized neopatrimonial state, isolated from its society. The chapter contends that with these attributes, what was dubbed the "Houphouet state," could not escape the crisis of the typical postcolonial African state despite its much-touted early achievements and France's protection. The 1999 coup that if anything, made things worse, must be considered the outcome of this crisis. To better understand this evolution, the Ivorian state was presented as a continuation of its antecedent colonial state, in logic, form, and objectives. The colonial imposition and its destruction of existing political structures, the resistance it inspired were also briefly discussed. This followed an attempt to frame the analysis by briefly reviewing a pertinent sample of the literature on the African state and its singular attributes and burdens. The chapter then examined the performance of the Boigny and Bedie governments and the Guei military regime. The basic result was that all these regimes maintained the authoritarian "Houphouet state" that was created on independence. It was hoped that the Gbagbo regime would have ushered in the process of state reconstitution. Unfortunately, the Gbagbo administration's decision to retain Cote d'Ivoire's discriminatory citizenship regime provided the proximate cause for the outbreak of civil war. Thus, the opportunity to reconstitute the state was squandered.

Finally, the chapter puts forward some recommendations for reconstituting the Ivorian state. At the center of the reconstitution efforts must be the resolution of the undercurrents of the civil war, especially the poisonous concept of Ivoirite. Other important measures must include the decentralization of power, the restoration of the importance of traditional African cultural values, and a commitment to regional integration.

Notes

1. John Nellier, "States in Danger," 1993, mimeo, has identified twenty African states in either "serious" or "maximum" danger of collapse. Cited in I. William Zartman, "Introduction: Posing the Problem of Collapsed States," in *Collapsed States: The Disintegration and Restoration of Legitimate Authority* ed. I. William Zartman (Boulder, CO: Lynne Rienner Publishers, 1995), p. 3.
2. The consensus is that this fashion was launched by studies such as those of Peter Evans, Dietrich Rueschmeyer, and Theda Skopol, *Bringing the State*

Back in (New York: Cambridge University Press, 1985); See also Eric Northlinger, "Taking the State Seriously," in *Understanding Political Development*, ed. Samuel Huntington and Marion Weiner (Boston: Little Brown and Company, 1987), pp. 353–390; Stephen Krasner, "Approaches to the State: Alternative Conceptions and Historical Dynamics," *Comparative Politics*, no. 16, 1984, pp. 223–246.

3. See, for example, Leonardo Villalon and Phillip Huxtable, eds., *The African State at a Critical Juncture: Between Disintegration and Reconfiguration* (Boulder, CO: Lynne Rienner, Publishers, 1997); James Wunch and Dele Olowu, eds., *The Failure of the Centralized State: Institution and Self-Governance in Africa* (Boulder, CO: Westview Press, 1990); Pierre Englebert, *State Legitimacy and Development in Africa* (Boulder, CO: Lynne Rienner, Publishers, 2000), among others.

4. Zartman, "Introduction," *Problem of Collapsed States*, p. 8.

5. Max Weber, *The Theory of Social and Economic Organization* (New York: Free Press, 1947), p. 154.

6. Ibid.

7. Jean-François Médard, "Conclusion," in *Etats d'Afrique Noire: Formation, Mecanismes et Crise*, ed. Jean-François Médard (Paris: Khartala, 1991), p. 357.

8. Leonardo Villalon, "The Africa State at a the End of the Twentieth Century: Parameters of a Critical Juncture," in *The African State at a Critical Juncture, Between Disintegration and Reconfiguration*, ed. Leonardo Villalon and Phillip Huxtable (Boulder, CO: Lynne Rienner Publishers, 1997), p. 9.

9. Richard Sandbrook, *The Politics of Africa's Economic Stagnation* (Cambridge: Cambridge University Press, 1985).

10. Njuguma Ng'ethe, "Strongmen, State Formation, Collapse, and Reconstruction in Africa," in *Collapsed States: The Disintegration and Restoration of Legitimate Authority*, ed. I. William Zartman (Boulder, CO: Lynne Rienner Publishers, 1995), p. 256.

11. See, for example, Jean-François Médard, "L'Etat Neo-Patrimonial en Afrique Noire," in *Etats d'Afrique Noire: Formation, Mecanismes et Crise*, ed. Jean-François Médard (Paris: Khartala, 1991); Zaki Ergas, ed., *The African State in Transition* (New York: St. Martin's Press, 1987); Michael Bratton and Nicholas van de Walle, "Neopatrimonial Regimes and Democratic Transition in Africa," *World Politics*, vol. 46, no. 4, 1994, pp. 453–489.

12. Jerome Vogel, "Culture Politics and National Identity in Cote d'Ivoire," *Social Search*, vol. 58, no. 2, 1991, p. 453.

13. Robert Fatton, Jr., "Bringing the Ruling Class Back in, Class, State, and Hegemony," *Comparative Politics*, vol. 20, no. 3, 1988, p. 253.

14. Fatton, Jr., "Bringing the Ruling Class," p. 254.

15. As argued by Robert Jackson and Carl Rosberg, "The Marginalization of the African State," in *African Independence, the First Twenty-Five Years (1945–70)*, ed. Gwendolen Carter and Patrick O'Meara (Bloomington: Indiana University Press, 1985).

16. Donal B. Cruise O'Brien, "The Show of State in a Neo-Colonial Twilight: Francophone Africa," in *Rethinking Third World Politics*, ed. James Manor (London: Longman, 1991), pp. 145–165.

17. Victor Levin, "African Patrimonial Regimes in Comparative Perspective," *Journal of Modern African Studies*, vol. 28, no. 4, 1980, pp. 657–673.

18. Thomas M. Callaghy, *The State-Society Struggle: Zaire in Comparative Perspective* (New York: Columbia University Press, 1984).

19. Richard Joseph, *Democracy and Prebendal Politics in Nigeria: The Rise and Fall of the Second Republic* (London: Cambridge University Press, 1987).

20. Zaki Ergas, "Introduction," in *The African State in Transition*, ed. Zaki Ergas (New York, Macmillan Press 1987), pp. 2–3.

21. Fatton, Jr., "Bringing the Ruling Class," p. 263.

22. Medard, "L'Etat Neopatrimonial," p. 349. The same theme is developed in the Neo-Marxian mode by Robert Fatton, *Predatory Rule: State and Society in Africa* (Boulder, CO: Lynne Rienner Publishers, 1992).

23. Jean-François Bayart, *The State in Africa: The Politics of the Belly* (New York: Longman, 1993).

24. Boubacar N'Diaye, "Beyond the 'Berlin Conference /OAU framework': A Pan-African Analysis of Africa's Security Crisis," *Journal of African Policy Studies*, vol. 7, no. 1, 2002, pp. 107–129.

25. Basil Davidson, *The Black Man's Burden: Africa and the Curse of the Nation-State* (New York: Times Books, 1992), p. 260.

26. Pierre Englebert, *State Legitimacy and Development in Africa* (Boulder, CO: Lynne Rienner Publishers, 2000).

27. Crawford Young, *The African Colonial State in Comparative Perspective* (New Haven, CT: Yale University Press, 1994), p. 37

28. Englebert, *State Legitimacy*, p. 173.

29. Ibid., pp. 10–11, 173.

30. Leonardo Villalon and Phillip Huxtable, eds., *The African State at a Critical Juncture, Between Disintegration and Reconfiguration* (Boulder, CO: Lynne Rienner Publishers, 1997).

31. Phillip Huxtable, "The African State Toward the Twenty-First Century: Legacies for the Critical Juncture," in *The African State at a Critical Juncture, Between Disintegration and Reconfiguration*, ed. Leonardo Villalon and Phillip Huxtable (Boulder, CO: Lynne Rienner Publishers, 1996), pp. 279–280.

32. Englebert, *State Legitimacy*, p. 192.

33. J.F. Amon d'Aby, *La Cote d'Ivoire dans la Cité Africaine* (Paris: Editions La rose, 1951), p. 14.

34. Ibid.

35. Georges Ayyiteh, *Indigenous African Institutions* (Dobbs Ferry, NY: Transnational Publishers, 1991).

36. Ibid., pp. 231–256.

37. D'Aby, *La Cote d'Ivoire*, p. 32.

38. Paul Atger, *La France en Cote d'Ivoire de 1843–1893, Cinquante Ans d'Hesitations Politiques et Commerciales* (Dakar, Senegal: Publications de la Cite Historique, 1962), pp. 182–183.

39. D'Aby, *La Cote d'Ivoire*, pp. 26–29.

40. Marcel Amondji, *Felix Houphouet la Cote d'Ivoire, L'Envers d'une Legende* (Paris: Khartala, 1984), pp. 27–51.

41. Young, *The African Colonial State*, p. 43.

42. D'Aby, *La Cote d'Ivoire*, pp. 30, 35–36.

43. Amondji, *Felix Houphouet*, pp. 63–89.

44. Young, *The African Colonial State*, pp. 283–287.

45. See Francis Wangah Wodie, *Institutions Politiques et Droit Public en Cote d'Ivoire* (Abidjan: Presses Universitaires de Cote d'Ivoire, 1996), pp. 46–53.

46. In fact, this author had warned against the increased probability of a military intervention. See Boubacar N'Diaye, *The Challenge of Institutionalizing Civilian Control: Botswana, Ivory Coast, and Kenya in Comparative Perspective* (Lanham, MD: Lexington Books, 2001).

47. See General Robert Guei's Coup Statement in *Fraternité Matin*, 10556, December 27, 1999.

48. Amondji, *Felix Houphouet*, p. 168. This discussion of Houphouet-Boigny's role in the immediate pre-independence period draws on Amondji's well-documented account of the events that took place then (pp. 136–217).

49. Amondji, *Felix Houphouet*, 162–165.

50. See Jeanne M. Toungara, "The Apotheosis of Cote d'Ivoire's Nana Houphouet-Boigny," *Journal of Modern African Studies*, vol. 28, no. 1, 1990, pp. 23–54.

51. See Howard French, "Houphouet's Region," *Africa Report*, vol. 31, no. 6, 1986, pp. 9–13.

52. For a discussion of the concept of Dialogue, see Michael Cohen, *Urban Policy and Political Conflict in Africa* (Chicago: University of Chicago Press, 1974).

53. Aristide Zolberg, *One Party-Government in the Ivory Coast* (Princeton: Princeton University Press, 1969).

54. Wodie, *Institutions Politiques*, pp. 377–383.

55. This phrase is particularly apt. I adopt it because it cogently captures the reality of the imprint of Houphouet on Cote d'Ivoire. See, for example, Jean François Medard, "The Historical Trajectories of the Ivoirian and Kenyan States," in *Rethinking Third World Politics*, ed. James Manor, pp. 185–212.

56. Cited in Zolberg, *One Party-Government*, p. 266.

57. Jean-François Medard, "La Regulation Socio-Politique," in *Etat et Bourgeoisie en Cote d'Ivoire*, ed. Yves Fauré and Jean-François Medard (Paris: Khartala, 1991), p. 72.

58. Quoted in Robert Jackson and Carl Rosberg, *Personal Rule in Black Africa: Prince, Autocrat, Prophet, Tyrant* (Berkeley: University of California Press, 1982), p. 148.

59. Yves Fauré and Jean-François Medard, "Classe Dominante ou Classe Dirigeante," in *Etat et Bourgeoisie en Cote d'Ivoire*, ed. Yves Fauré and Jean-François Medard, p. 136.

60. See Robert Mundt, *Historical Dictionary of Cote d'Ivoire*, 2nd ed. (Lanham, MD: The Scarecrow Press, 1996), pp. 117–118, 171.

61. Tessy Bakary argues convincingly that this is indeed the case for the Ivoirian state, pp. 75–78. See Tessy Bakary, "Cote d'Ivoire, l'Etatisation de l'Etat," in *Etat et Bourgeoisie en Cote d'Ivoire*, ed. Yves Fauré and Jean-François Medard, pp. 53–80.

62. Dwayne Woods, "Cote d'Ivoire: The Crisis of Distributive Politics," in *The African State at a Critical Juncture, Between Disintegration and Reconfiguration* ed. Leonardo Villalon and Phillip Huxtable (Boulder, CO: Lynne Rienner Publishers, 1996), pp. 214–215.

63. Jackson and Rosberg, *Personal Rule*, pp. 145–152.

64. Tessilimi, Bakary, "Elite Transformation and Political Succession," in *The Political Economy of the Ivory Coast*, ed. I. William Zartman and Christopher Delgado (New York: Praeger, 1984), pp. 21–55; also Pascal Teya, *Le Roi est Nu* (Paris: Harmattan, 1985).

65. Bakary, "Elite Transformation," pp. 76–77; also Jackson and Rosberg, *Personal Rule*, p. 149.

66. Bakary, "Elite Transformation," pp. 76–79.

67. George Ayyiteh, *Africa Betrayed* (New York: St. Martin's Press, 1992), p. 242.

68. Amondji, *Felix Houphouet*, pp. 219–267.

69. John Chipman, *French Military Policy and African Security* (London: The International Strategic Studies, 1985); Guy Martin, "The Historical Economic, and Political Bases of France's African Policy," *Journal of Modern African Studies*, vol. 23, no. 2, 1985, pp. 189–208.

70. See Richard Crook, "Patrimonialism, Administrative Effectiveness, and Economic Development in Cote d'Ivoire," *Africa Affairs*, vol. 88 , no. 351, 1989, pp. 216–219.

71. For a well-informed discussion of the formative years and substance of these relations see, D. Bach, "L'Insertion dans les Rapports Internationaux," in *Etat et Bourgeoisie en Cote d'Ivoire*, ed. Yves Fauré and Jean-François Medard (Paris: Khartala, 1984), pp. 113–121.

72. De Gaulle stated that Ivory Coast was one the countries in which France "would have to intervene," should it be necessary. See Phillipe Gaillard, *Foccart Parle: Entretiens avec Phillipe Gaillard*, vol. 1 (Paris: Fayard/Jeune Afrique, 1995), p. 288.

73. See N'Diaye, *The Challenge*, pp. 99–121.

74. For a fascinating as well as revealing testimony of Jacques Foccart himself on the extent and implication of his activities, see Gaillard, *Foccart Parle: Entretiens avec Phillipe Gaillard*, vol. 1 (Paris: Fayard/Jeune Afrique, 1995), pp. 288– 290.

75. See N'Diaye, *The Challenge*, p. 107.

76. Bakary, "Elite Transformation," pp. 77–78.

77. Crook, "Patrimonialism," p. 227.

78. See Jon Woronoff, *West African Wager: Houphouet vs. Nkrumah* (Metuchen, NJ: Scarecrow Press, 1972), pp. 201–234. In the more cautious category, see Yves Fauré and Jean-François Medard, "Introduction," in *Etat et Bourgeoisie en Cote d'Ivoire*, ed. Yves Fauré and Jean-François Medard (Paris: Khartala, 1984), pp. 11–18.

79. The formula is Samir Amin's *Le Development du Capitalism en Cote d'Ivoire*, (Paris: Les Editions de Minuit, 1967), p. 281. Other studies concurred. See, for example, Bonnie Campbell, "The Ivory Coast," in *West African States: Failure and Promise*, ed. John Dunn (Cambridge: Cambridge University Press, 1979).

80. Robert Mundt, "Continuity and Change in a Semi-Democracy," in *Political Reform in Francophone Africa*, ed. John Clark (Boulder, CO: Westview Press, 1996), pp. 187–188.

81. Cruise O'Brien, p. 146.

82. Woods, "Cote d'Ivoire," pp. 218–231.

83. Ibid., pp. 218–224.

84. Crook, "Patrimonialism," p. 239.

85. See Kaye Whiteman, "The Gallic Paradox," *Africa Report*, vol. 36, no.1, 1990, pp. 17–19.

86. Mundt, "Continuity and Change," pp. 194–198.

87. See Laurent Gbagbo, *La Cote d'Ivoire: Pour une Alternative Démocratique* (Paris: Harmattan, 1983).

88. Toungara, "The Apotheosis," pp. 32–40.

89. Zolberg, *One Party-Government*, pp. 285–298.

90. N'Diaye, *The Challenge*, p.107.

91. Zolberg, *One Party-Government*, p. 340.

CHAPTER 4

Reinventing and Rebuilding the Ghanaian State: Toward a New Triumphalism?

Emmanuel Kwesi-Aning

Introduction

Ghana, sub-Saharan Africa's first independent country, chalked up a veritable democratic victory on January 7, 2001, when John Agyekum Kufuor, the presidential candidate of the New Patriotic Party (NPP), was inaugurated as the president of the Fourth Republic. While, during the heated period of the 2000 campaign, the NPP had adopted the spiritual song, *ewurade kasa* (Speak O Lord), to reflect its uphill battle in attempting to unseat the monolithic National Democratic Convention (NDC Party), its surprising victory at the polls was captured in the captivating religious song, *Aba mu awie* (it has finally come to pass) that the NPP adopted after its victory.[1] Thus, both songs, though with different messages, aptly captured the national sense of relief and joy. NPP's victory at the polls meant different things to the political party and its presidential candidate. For Kufuor, this was the end of a personal and a professional odyssey, an odyssey that had led to 29 years in a "political wilderness" after the-then Progress Party (PP) government in which he was deputy minister of foreign affairs was overthrown in a coup d'état on February 13, 1972[2] by General Ignatius Kutu Acheampong, who established a National Redemption Council (NRC) regime that lasted until June 1979; an odyssey that had even resulted in Kufuor serving in Jerry Rawlings' Provisional National Defense Council (PNDC) as the minister for local government.[3] For the party faithful, the December 2000 election victory was seen as a just payment for their perseverance and for having kept the faith in their political beliefs. Finally, they interpreted their party's victory as an opportunity to "reap" the benefits of being in power.

By the December 2000 elections, Ghana had gone through a democratic transition and consolidation that, in several ways, reflected the struggles for democratic accountability, transparency, and sustainability with broad support from different sections of the community. These conform to the general democratic developments in the 1980s and 1990s, which suggest that the role of the military in politics is receding. Yet, such developments do not necessarily imply that the military and other antidemocratic forces will automatically obey civilian leaders in the new administration. There is a need to understand how, and under what conditions democratic governance and civilian control over the military can be encouraged as a means of further entrenching the gains of democratic governance. This is particularly apt as the Kufour government attempts to "reconstruct" the economy and hopefully reconcile the nation. Now is an opportune time to rethink the ethos of the Ghanaian state.

This chapter analyzes the impact of the NPP victory in the December 2000 elections in Ghana and its significance for state reconstitution in Ghana. With this in mind, what is seen as the transformation of Ghana is contextualized by providing a short background analysis of the events that led to January 7, 2001. Such an approach will provide a framework within which to position and analyze the actions and activities of the Kufour government as it seeks to "reconstruct" and "reconcile" Ghanaian politics in a manner that improves its image abroad.[4] A few specific cases are examined, in particular, the military, foreign policy, and economic programs. In conclusion, suggestions and ideas are offered on what is needed or expected from the government in the coming years, in the efforts to reconstitute the Ghanaian state.

Background

The immediate background to the NPP victory can be traced to when a young and energetic Flight-Lieutenant Jerry John Rawlings overthrew two governments—first, the oligarchic Supreme Military Council (SMC) II on June 4, 1979, after which he launched his House Cleaning Exercise (HCE),[5] and again on December 31, 1981, when he overthrew the corrupt and directionless People's National Party (PNP) led by Hilla Limann and initiated his "Holy War."[6] Interestingly, both intrusions into national politics were widely supported by different sections of the

Ghanaian populace. However, the antielitist, economic austerity programs and anticorruption platforms that were used to justify these incursions were rapidly shelved. Instead, as the wave of domestic and international demands for democracy took hold and the "velvet revolutions" of Eastern Europe succeeded, with bilateral disbursements from donor countries made contingent upon more inclusive forms of governance, Rawlings had no alternative but to succumb to these demands. A constitution was hurriedly drafted under suspicious circumstances and in a national referendum, Ghanaians overwhelmingly voted in support of a democratic form of government. The Provisional National Defense Council (PNDC) was eventually transformed into a National Democratic Convention (NDC) party, and was forced to return to a governmental process that it had earlier disrupted—an open, democratic system of accountability and transparency.[7]

In December 1992, Ghanaians went to the polls for the first time in 11 years. Accusations of electoral fraud and malpractices marred this event with the main challenger to the NDC party, the NPP, accusing the PNDC of having won an election through "a stolen verdict."[8] Despite the evidence of malfeasance, international electoral observers declared the elections to have been free and fair. In 1996, the NDC won a second four-year mandate. When the campaign for the December 2000 election began, so confident was the NDC—a behemoth of a party with offices and branches in all towns and settlements in Ghana—that there was complacency on the part of the NDC party apparatus. However, by December 2000, the party was mired in its own quicksand of corruption and ethnic favoritism. With different power enclaves within the party hierarchy jostling for power, it increasingly became clear that the party was rotten from within and lacked internal democratic structures.[9]

On December 7, 2000, when presidential and parliamentary elections took place, Ghanaians had lost confidence in themselves as a people and a nation. Ghanaians were confronted with a sluggish economy on the verge of collapse, and an uncaring government led by individuals who spouted the rhetoric of economic growth and well-being while denying people any real access to this wealth. Underscoring this were donor governments and organizations based in Ghana that constantly employed spurious data and analyses to support the NDC government, creating a false impression of a country on the verge of economic takeoff. Therefore, when Kufuor took the oath of allegiance to serve the people of Ghana faithfully and uphold the rule of law, people broke down in tears and the Akan spiritual, *Aba mu awie*, was sung amidst the waving of white handkerchiefs (the traditional Ghanaian sign of victory).

Several overlapping interests converged, but the main emotion was one of bitter-sweet relief.[10] Another message that went out clearly from Ghanaians was that what was wanted and demanded was in fact captured in the slogan of the NPP: *An Agenda for Positive Change*.[11] The clear message that the NPP victory conveyed was this: Never again in the nation's history would one group of people be permitted to rule for so long with so little accountability. However, one thing was to make promises of "positive change" in the Ghanaian body politic and the other was to fulfil those promises.

From Opposition to Governing Party

The multiple and differentiated processes of transforming the NPP from an opposition party to a governing party were long and arduous. The party had been in power only once (from 1969 to 1972), since its establishment in the late 1940s. For the December 2000 elections, the party presented a major campaign manifesto to the Ghanaian population, a document that set out its alternative plans for transforming Ghana. To deal with the multiple challenges facing the new administration, it defined for itself, a set of political-philosophical underpinnings that would guide an NPP administration. These were

- Zero tolerance for corruption
- Golden Age of Business
- Good neighbourliness
- Positive change.

The party promised the people of Ghana—in both the president's first sessional address to parliament and in the party manifesto—that it would seek to "liberate the energies of the people for the growth of a property owning democracy in this land . . . as the principles to which the government and laws of the land should be dedicated in order specifically to enrich life, property and liberty of each and every citizen."[12]

This articulated objective of initiating a process toward "a property-owning democracy" smacks of Lockean dynamics of the past. Assuming that it is possible to establish such a class within the constraints of Ghana's weak position in a globalized world, the extent to which an NPP-led government can transform Ghana in relation to the challenges it faces with respect to the military, the state of the economy, and foreign policy still needs to be analyzed. These areas are considered here in some depth, not because other issue-areas are unimportant, but because the perception is that they can potentially pose the greatest challenges to the state reconstitution enterprise.

The Security and Military Albatross

Discourses about Ghana's internal security issues vis-à-vis the military have shown that these are given very high priority by the NPP government. Security is high on the agenda of the NPP-led government because of the extremely politicized nature of the military and its penchant for intervening in national politics. This fact is underscored by a study that showed that Ghanaians were very reluctant to accept the military playing a role in national politics.[13] But if society, in general, were concerned about the military's role in politics, then getting to grips with the rot within the military establishment is a difficult process for it involves taking the military through the reprofessionalization process necessary to enhance its credibility as an institution. One of the primary issues is that of the military hierarchy. In its 2000 campaign manifesto, the NPP saw the role of the security services as follows:

> Their main concern will be the survival of the state and the protection of its territorial integrity and its democratic system. They will not be part of party apparatus and they must not be party members. Security service personnel will thus be expected to show absolute neutrality in political conflicts and will be guaranteed secure tenure, subject to normal disciplinary measures.[14]

In spite of the manifesto's promise to guarantee secure tenure, the actions of the government have so far alienated several sections of the forces. Two examples demonstrate the increasing sense of frustration within the military. First, there have been significant changes in the security sector, particularly in the police, the intelligence services, and the military, with its hierarchy of seven top generals having been asked to proceed on leave in 2001. Second, the appointees, who replaced the top brass, oversee many more senior officials who now have to subject themselves to men who were previously their juniors. Discussions held with some officers painted a picture of one ethnic group replacing its favorites with another. Suddenly, the politics of ethnicity that characterized the 2000 elections, was perceptible in the way in which security-related appointments and decisions were being made. So serious was the concern that senior military and intelligence officials have had to sound notes of caution under the protection of anonymity.[15] Inversely, the government was forced to explain that there were certain officers from specific ethnic groups who were disproportionately represented in the intelligence services and who thus would be naturally affected if mass reassignments were made.[16] This was an apologist's argument that gave the impression that the critics of the government's mass dismissals and reassignment actions were "creat[ing] a consciousness of a situation that does not exist."[17]

The second problem concerned older soldiers who should be discharged and reintegrated into society.[18] This was another area of military restructuring that can pose difficulties for the government and needs to be handled sensitively. In 2001, it was estimated that there were 2,000 overaged soldiers who had to be discharged. There were serious economic and social implications for such a decision.[19]

The third area of concern was the critical and delicate issue of civil-military relations in Ghana and the even more vexatious question of civilian control over the security sector.[20] While all these issues were important, the focus of attention in this chapter is on civilian control and the transformation of the security sector. For the Kufuor administration, discussing civilian control over the military is critical because transitional democracies have to deal with the fundamental issue of establishing civilian control, as well as of establishing the institutions that augur well for democratic governance under circumstances of political instability and security threats, weak state institutions and a weak institutional capacity of the state amid economic hardships. Civilian control over the military under such circumstances is less than obvious, because the issues at stake transcend the military and encompass the security sector as a whole, the police, the judiciary, and the penal system.

"Security sector" here refers to those bodies that are, or should be responsible for protecting the state and the communities within it. This includes

- Groups with a legal mandate to wield instruments of violence—military, paramilitary, and police forces
- Institutions with a role in managing and monitoring the security sector—civilian ministries, parliaments, and nongovernmental organizations
- Bodies responsible for guaranteeing the rule of law—the judiciary, penal system, and human rights ombudsman, particularly where these institutions are weak
- The intelligence community for which the issue of the military is anything but settled.

There are important issues that need consideration. It is necessary first to define civilian controls with regard to the military in policymaking. The critical issue is to prevent interference in government and policymaking by the military and to ensure the supremacy of civilians in military affairs.

Some questions of a more procedural nature also confronted the Kufour administration. Which policies and structures lead to civilian control? How can civilian control be measured and evaluated? What role can the international community play in strengthening civilian control?

Civilian Control and the Security Sector[21]

Creating democratic, civilian control over the security apparatus requires the involvement of a wide range of actors. However, the security forces are not the only national security actors. Civil authorities have important policy development and oversight functions and responsibilities. Civil and political societies have a role to play in developing policy and monitoring the activities of the security forces, as well as those of the civil authorities. Importantly, the activities of other non-state actors such as informal armed groups and private security firms must also be considered.

All these groups in the "security family" must adhere to certain fundamental principles of good governance in the security sector. The following are among some of the basic criteria for such codes of conduct and behavior:

1. The security sector must be accountable both to the elected civil authorities and to civil society, while acting in a nonpartisan manner. Information about security sector planning and resourcing must be widely available both within the government and to the public. This must be defined by a comprehensive and disciplined approach to the management of the sector. It should be subjected to the same principles of public sector management as other governmental sectors, with relatively small adjustments for appropriate national security-related confidentiality. However, the Minister of Defense, Kwame Addo-Kufuor, was not comfortable with this kind of development. In a statement on civil-military relations, he said categorically, "though the military is subjected to civilian authority, there is a limit to which military spending should be exposed to the public."[22]

2. Relations between the military and civilians must be based on an articulated hierarchy of authority between civil authorities and defense forces, and with civil society based on a respect for human rights.
3. It is also important to improve the capacity of civil authorities, for example, the respective parliamentary committees such as Public Accounts Committee, Finance Committee, and the Defense and Interior Committee. Their capacity to exercise political control over the operations and the resourcing of the security forces must be improved. Such a capacity to perform such oversight functions was not readily available because of Ghana's particular political-historical trajectory that made the discussion of security issues difficult. In the aftermath of the reinstitution of democratic governance, however, several efforts, not least by civil society organizations, have been undertaken to improve parliamentary oversight capacity in the security field:

   a. Civil society must have the capacity to monitor the security forces and provide constructive input into the political debate on security policy.
   b. The political environment must be constituted in such a way that civil society can actively monitor the security sector and can be consulted on a regular basis on security policies, resource allocation, and other relevant issues.
   c. The security forces must be trained to discharge their duties in a professional manner consistent with the requirements of a democratic society.
   d. An environment supportive of regional and subregional peace must be fostered and security must have a high priority for policymakers.
   e. Good governance in the security sector must be reinforced.

Since Ghana has joined the community of democratizing states, it is imperative for its government to make efforts to strengthen good governance in the security sector. Looking at military and security spending as simply "unproductive" is passé. Instead, the focus needs to be on the institutional framework that determines how budgets are established, implemented and monitored.[23] To strengthen security sector governance, particular attention must be paid to the following:

- Professionalizing the security forces
- Improving the capacity and capability of civil authorities

- Placing a high priority on human rights protection
- Enabling and capacitating civil society to engage in research and advocacy
- Promoting transparency
- Promoting regional security.

Regional security will require attention because of the regional security environment within which the country finds itself and to which the government needs to respond. Most Ghanaian governments in the postindependence period have carried out policies that can be broadly characterized as "positive neutrality" within which is situated the country's drive for economic growth and good neighborliness. But to what extent can the security and military interests of the government be achieved if Ghana's volatile regional security situation is not taken into consideration? Can Ghana continue to be an island of peace and stability unto itself when the West African subregion as a whole faces serious security threats?

In *An Agenda for Positive Change*, the NPP in opposition sought to "grant a two-month amnesty for all assault weapons and ammunition currently held by unauthorized persons in private homes and thereby outlaw private possession of AK47 and allied weapons."[24] Despite this campaign promise, the government initiated a weapons-for-reward program, which sought to retrieve excess and unlicensed weapons from society. Launching a joint military and police operation dubbed *Etuo mu ye sum* (the barrel of a gun is dark)[25] to mop up excess unregistered guns in the country, holders of such guns were given a two-week ultimatum to hand in their weapons or face the full might of the law. The government later extended the two-week ultimatum. What is worrying, however, is that no codes of conduct or behavior were established for the police to guide their operations, and apart from a few public examples of seizing arms caches, there was a general uncertainty about how many weapons were actually retrieved.[26]

Foreign Policy Options

What foreign policy options were open to the Kufuor administration, when it first assumed office in 2001? If the utterances in its 2000 campaign manifesto are considered, the major rationale of an NPP-led foreign policy thrust was supposed to consist of "the vigorous promotion . . . of the vital interests of the country and its citizens, with the goal of achieving prosperity and dignity for all Ghanaians and ensuring the nation's security."[27]

Interestingly, in the entire policy document, the national interest was not defined. More often than not, it is impossible to differentiate "regime" interest from "national" interest. To differentiate between the two, the foreign policy actions of the government since its inauguration into office would have to be analyzed and compared to the extent to which the undefined "national" interest was achieved.

An early indication of the kind of foreign policy that would characterize the NPP government was hinted at during the inauguration of the president on January 7, 2001. Among the more interesting heads of states present in Accra were Blaise Compaore of Burkina Faso, Gnassingbe Eyadema (now deceased) of Togo and Olusegun Obasanjo of Nigeria.[28] While the inclusion of Nigeria and its leader as the special guest of honor at the celebrations was understandable (Nigeria is Ghana's major supplier of oil on very favorable credit lines and is also the hegemon in the subregion), the invitation to, and inclusion of the Togolese and Burkinabe presidents at the inauguration generated heated debate and speculation in Ghana.

Using *An Agenda for Positive Change* as the point of departure, the NPP in opposition spouted the standard rhetoric of "peaceful co-existence and very close co-operation with all our neighbors, especially in the West African sub-region."[29] Accepting that good neighborliness is both welcome and acceptable, it is nevertheless a legitimate question whether all neighbors should be welcomed irrespective of their norms and values with respect to what the NPP itself claims to be its rejection of "illegal overthrows of government anywhere in the world . . . [and its wish to] emphasize respect for the rule of law and human rights [in] African and world politics."[30]

It is apparent that there was a contradiction between the rhetoric of foreign policy and the reality of its praxis by the NPP government. Two examples will suffice. Six days after his first inauguration as president, before the cabinet had been formed, President Kufuor accepted an invitation from the Togolese leader, Gnassingbe Eyadema, to pay a state visit on January 13, 2001 and participate in celebrations of the thirty-fourth anniversary of the overthrow of the previous government. During the visit, the Ghanaian President was awarded the highest civilian order of the Togolese.[31] According to an editorial in *The Ghanaian Chronicle*, the

> president received an award from this misanthropist who parades himself as the president of a nation! . . . What is the understanding between Kufuor and Eyadema that made it imperative that the Ghanaian leader had to be physically present in Lomé on that day? What was the award for? Which services have Kufuor rendered to Eyadema that he had to be honored? . . . These questions are begging to be answered.[32]

Despite public criticism, the government steadfastly refused to answer any of these questions. For a Togolese government that has consistently refused to democratize and has put impediments in the way of its National Independent Electoral Commission (NIEC), it was not surprising that the Ghanaians were highly critical of this trip. Several reasons explained the disappointment with President Kufour's first foreign visit during his first term in office. While it can be argued that the NPP administration was grateful to the Togolese for closing the latter's side of the border and thereby preventing the expected influx of NDC supporters from crossing over to vote, an effusive NPP administration also served the interest of the undemocratic Togolese administration by preventing anti-Eyadema activists from using Ghana as a political base.

More importantly, however, were the potentially adverse international implications for the Kufour administration of being too friendly with the Togolese administration that was increasingly seen as a pariah and a rogue state for its support for West African rebels and the late Jonas Savimbi's *União Naçional para a Independência Total de Angola* (UNITA).[33] After the international outcry over its role in mining of and trading conflict in diamonds, UNITA shifted its base and headquarters to Lomé, Togo, where these were headed by Marcelo Moses Dachala and João Katende.[34] Already, there were reports in the international media that "Kufuor . . . is an old ally of Savimbi and that he would probably use his influence to try to restart international negotiations on Angola."[35] It is probable that there were long-standing relations with Savimbi stretching back to the early 1970s, when the Progress Party, of which Kufuor was deputy foreign minister, initiated a policy of dialogue with the apartheid regime in South Africa that was supporting the anti-communist Jonas Savimbi at the time.[36] All these interlinkages and interconnections did not paint a picture of positive change for the Kufour administration. Consorting with Blaise Compaore—his role in the Liberian and Sierra Leonean conflicts, as well as his own links with Savimbi, diamonds, oil, and small arms are well documented—and the Togolese leader did not create the investor confidence and the leading role that Ghana expected to play in the subregion.

The Reality of the Challenge of Ghana's Economy

In *An Agenda for Positive Change*, the NPP focused mostly on the economy by arguing about the fundamental weakness and fragility of the Ghanaian economy that, in the perception of the party, had resulted from the "grim reality . . . that the NDC structural adjustment program had wrought on the country." It accused the former government of failing to transform the export sector into a "value added exporting country" thus Ghana was unable to withstand external shocks.[37]

As a party in opposition, the NPP argued that to "re-launch" economic growth, there was the need for "a fundamental change in content, direction and focus of economic policy. . . . [T]he NPP is committed to a radical and fundamental change in economic policy. Today, change in Ghana is not just desirable; it is an imperative."[38] Several options for dealing with the economy were suggested. Some sought to lower the fiscal deficit, inflation, interest rates, public debts, and maintain stable exchange rates. The party promised the people of Ghana in its campaign manifesto that it would embark on a path of change that would be reflected in a lowering of the "intolerably high cost of living and a reduction in the depressingly high rate of unemployment, a change that will bring jobs and a living wage for the majority of our people."[39]

But what were the real economic challenges that the new government faced, taking into consideration that what was stated in the manifesto was reflective of campaign rhetoric? During President Kufuor's inaugural speech to the people of Ghana on January 7, 2001, he enunciated one of the major political-philosophical underpinnings of his new administration, namely the theme of *Zero Tolerance for Corruption*. While on the surface there were no dissenting voices that a national anticorruption strategy was an essential prerequisite for the success of his other economic philosophy of *Golden Age of Business*, both processes and approaches to reinvigorating the economy must complement some of the earlier and ongoing reforms of public sector financial management.[40] Almost eighteen months after zero tolerance for corruption became a household word in the political jargon of Ghana, no operational mechanism for combating corruption was put in place. Government was yet to translate this catchy phrase from an increasingly ridiculed and empty political phrase into a substantive set of specific implementable policy measures.

Zero tolerance for corruption was increasingly seen as a political tool to target earlier NDC functionaries since so far, beyond launching a series of targeted investigations into the actions and activities of the NDC regime, no concrete measure has been taken against corruption. Despite its endeavors, the haul in terms of actual convictions has been paltry, and there have been only a limited number of prosecutions. In fact, so far, only one substantive minister, Victor Selormey, who served as a deputy minister for finance, has been convicted and imprisoned. But even this minimal and difficult victory against the former government was momentary, as the NPP government's own sports minister,

Mallam Yusuf Issah, was imprisoned for embezzlement. What is obvious now, however, is that it will certainly take a long time before the NPP administration can demonstrate any substantial obligation to zero tolerance for corruption among its own members as opposed to the corruption of its political opponents.[41]

During the president's Sessional Address to Parliament, Kufuor promised to "[lead] the country into an era of the golden age of business."[42] However, for this promise to be fulfilled, the new economic team would have to tackle the critical issues of

- mismanagement of the economy
- mass unemployment
- low wages. In April 2002, the NPP government announced a 30 percent increase in the minimum wage from 500.00 cedis to 7,150.00 and
- a rapidly depreciating currency (see table 4.1).

Ghana also has a huge national debt, comprising both domestic and foreign debt, totalling 41.3 trillion cedis or almost US $7 billion. According to the budget statement presented to parliament by Minister Yaw Osafo-Maafo in 2001, Ghana had to join the highly indebted poor countries (HIPC) initiative because it found itself in a debt trap. According to the minister, Ghana spent a third of its gross domestic product (GDP) in 2000 on debt servicing. In 2001 alone, it budgeted 4.4 trillion cedis on external debt and 2.1 trillion cedis on domestic debt interest payments.

High dependence on foreign aid is also an "Achilles heel" of the Ghanaian economy. Ghana depends on external aid for its development plans. Although there are no consistent figures, almost 45 percent of government recurrent and development expenditure comes from external sources.

Table 4.1   Trends in Cedi/Dollar exchange rate, 1996–2002

Year	1996	1997	1998	1999	2000	2002
Cedi/US$	1,754.39	2,272.73	2,325.56	3,500	7,000	7,800
Percentage rate of depreciation	17.4	22.8	23	33	50	

Sources: International Monetary Fund; Bank of Ghana Quarterly Economic Bulletin; Interbank forex rates in the Ghanaian media.

Other major problems of the national economy include the following:

- Extensive corruption in public life
- A demoralized private sector
- Runaway inflation (see table 4.2)
- The high cost of living.

To improve the lives of Ghanaians and increase the amount of disposable income available to people, the 2002 budget announced a number of tax relief measures and incentives to cushion people from the high cost of living. Retroactive from January 2001, the minimum taxable personal income was raised from 900,000 cedis to 1.2 million cedis. These are the major factors that posed serious challenges to the government's plans of restructuring and resuscitating the Ghanaian economy. Another overlooked, yet crucial indicator that can affect the government's economic success is the economic impact of the high incidence of HIV/AIDS in Ghana that is now one of the country's major health challenges standing at about 4 percent of the total population.

What, then, must the government do if it is to attain its economic objectives? The first problem is the issue of corruption. Undoubtedly, corruption has been a major impediment to the socioeconomic and political advancement of Ghana since independence. Its pervasive influence on public decision-making processes has been both a cause and a consequence of structural and economic decay. A recent diagnostic study of the problem showed a veritable culture of graft and rot in several government institutions. Some of the institutions that rated low in terms of honesty and integrity were the police, government ministers, political parties, the customs, excise and preventive services, the judiciary, the Ministry of Finance, and the Lands Commission.[43] In response to the public outcry that met the publication of this report, Vice-President Alhaji Aliu Mahama promised the establishment of a code of conduct and an office of accountability in the president's office to combat corruption.[44]

Table 4.2 Inflation Trends calculated from the end of year, CPI, 1996–2000 (Percentage)

Year	1996	1997	1998	1999	2000
Inflation rate	34	27.9	14.6	13.8	40.5

Source: International Monetary Fund; Bank of Ghana Quarterly Bulletin; and Ghana Statistical Services.

Compounding the issue of corruption is the fact that the results from the last two decades of structural adjustment programs are mixed, at best. The major exports of the country, cocoa and gold, have seen a steady decline in prices since both the international coffee and cocoa agreements and the gold price collapsed. This means that, while the agricultural sector contributes 70 percent of export income and almost 40 percent of economic activity overall, the government's room for maneuver is tight. Probably worse for the government was the need to increase fuel prices immediately after it came into power. Prices went up by a little over 60 percent because of the unsustainability of the daily $900, 000 deficit support for fuel imports. Coupled with the fact that the national currency has progressively lost almost 73 percent in value since January 2000, it can be argued that the main challenges for economic policy in the coming years would be to do the following:

- Eliminate subsidies for fuel, particularly crude oil estimated at 8.3 percent of the fiscal deficit, and depoliticize fuel price-setting
- Improve the tax regime as a means of eliciting compliance
- Reconstitute the Divestiture Implementation Committee (DIC)
- Tie wages to productivity
- Harmonize fiscal and monetary policies.

Reconstituting the Ghanaian State: Some Suggestions

Whither the way forward for the NPP government's efforts at rebuilding and reconstructing Ghana after two decades of quasi-dictatorial rule? Four years after it first won a resounding victory over the NDC government, the NPP won a re-election in December 2004. The re-election victory was an indication of the support from the people and a new tolerance level that is unique in competitive Ghanaian politics. To this end, most of the foibles of the government have been accepted in good spirit. It is encouraging and worthy of support, but there is a downside to this. An intolerance that views criticism as undermining the government is slowly developing in Ghanaian politics. This notwithstanding, an attempt was made in this chapter to highlight areas of concern where the government must tread carefully. These are particularly issues dealing with the military and the need for security sector reform to enable the military to accept civilian control. It is important that such a process is historically based within the Ghanaian context of civilian control as had occurred before in the first republic. More importantly, since Ghana has become a beggar nation par excellence, it is imperative that security sector reform demanded by international partners is acceded to with consideration of the following:

1. The national political leadership should be committed to a significant transformation and reform process. The principles, policies, laws, and structures developed during the reform process must be rooted in Ghana's history, culture, legal framework, and institutions.

2. The process must be consultative both within government and between government and political society. The discussion on foreign policy has demonstrated the need for a more nuanced approach to the concept of "good neighborliness." This must be situated firmly within a clear differentiation between party and national interests. Such an approach would enable the inclusion of more sensitive variables and a deeper analysis of issues before decisions are taken.

3. The economy is the most critical and sensitive problem for the government. Although fuel price increases have been accepted with magnanimity, it is imperative that the economy improves markedly and offers benefits to the public if such tolerance is to be sustained.

In spite of the difficulties confronting the government, all stakeholders appear willing to go an extra mile to make the democratic transitional process a success, because of the belief that this is the last chance for Ghana. This was supported by the very approach to the division of seats in parliament. No party won an absolute majority of seats in the December 2000 election. While the NPP as the majority party had 100 seats (a gain of 36 seats compared with the previous parliament), the NDC had 92 (a loss of 42), the Convention Peoples' Party (CPP) had one, the Peoples' National Convention (PNC) had four, and there were four independent parliamentarians. The message from the results was twofold: there was a need for consensus and coalition building in parliament, and that discussions should be issue-based and should not be divided along partisan party lines.

Conclusion

This chapter has examined the efforts of the Kufour regime to reconstitute the Ghanaian state. Specifically, the chapter assessed the regime's performance thus far in the areas of security, the economy, and foreign policy. In the area of security sector reform, some progress has been made to establish civilian control over the military and security establishments. However, much work still needs to be done. The security sector is quite critical, given Ghana's history of incessant military intervention in politics. Thus, the military would need to be democratically and constitutionally contained, so that the requisite stability can be provided for the execution of the state reconstitution project.

As for the economy, while there has been very good economic growth, there are still major hurdles to overcome. For example, the standard of living for ordinary Ghanaians remains quite low. This means that the growth of the economy is not translating into improvement of the living standards of ordinary Ghanaians. Another serious problem is the increasing worthlessness of the cedi, the national currency. One of the resultant effects is that imports are very expensive. Also, there is the problem of rampant corruption in the public sector. This problem would need to be addressed, if the fruits of economic development are to be shared by ordinary Ghanaians as well.

In the foreign policy arena, the Kufour regime's cosy relationships with some of Africa's despots—the late President Eyadema of Togo and President Compaore of Burkina Faso—during its first term of office, raised serious concerns about the Kufour government's commitment to democratization and the democratic reconstitution of the state. It is very important, as President Kufour enters his second and final term of office, for the NPP-led government to draw a distinction between the "national interest" and personal and "partisan interests."

Finally, with the renewal of his mandate to govern, it would be interesting to see how President Kufour would continue to address the challenges of state reconstitution. Clearly, President Kufour has another opportunity to institutionalize the contours—economic, security, social, and political—of the democratic reconstitution of the Ghanaian state. The performance of the Kufour regime during its second term of office would be pivotal to the future of the state reconstitution enterprise in Ghana.

Notes

1. Emmanuel, Kwesi-Aning, "Spirituality and Politics in Ghana: The December 2000 Elections," unpublished paper (Accra, Ghana, 2003).
2. The new government of the National Redemption Council (NRC) was headed by the late General Ignatius Kutu Acheampong. He was one of the leaders executed by Jerry John Rawlings in 1979. Interestingly enough,

the families of these executed officers handed the Kufuor government a potentially dicey political and security problem in 2001, by appealing to the regime for help in locating the mass grave where the bodies were dumped, so that they can be given a proper burial. This generated heated debates in the country. See "We Want the Bodies," *The Guide*, March 20, 2001.

3. See E. M. Nyicor Ametor-Quarmyne"Falsehood Packed for Sale," *The Insight*, May 15–16, 2002, p. 3.

4. Joseph Osegu Boateng, "Controversy Over 22 Billion Per Deal," *The Insight*, June 7–11, 2002, pp. 1 and 4. In this deal to remake the image of Ghana, the assistant government spokesperson, Kofi Amponsah-Bediako, denied the existence of any such contract to "re-brand" Ghana. The minister for Information and Presidential Affairs, Jake Obetsebi-Lamptey, on the other hand, confirmed the existence of such a deal and justified the need for such a contract.

5. At this time, Rawlings established an Armed Forces Revolutionary Council headed by himself and a council consisting of 14 other officers and junior ranks.

6. Rawlings again made incursions into the body politic, overthrowing the government headed by Hilla Liman of the People's National Party (PNP). Rawlings eventually established a Provisional National Defense Council (PNDC) and a host of supportive organs, including the Peoples'/Workers' Defense Committees (P/WDCs). He eventually changed this name to the Committees for the Defense of the Revolution (CDRs) and other Private Voluntary Organizations (PVOs).

7. The slogan of this party, *Akatamanso*, represented by an umbrella, symbolized a party that is inclusive and that welcomes all shades of people and opinions.

8. For details of the accusations and the evidence compiled by the NPP and levelled against the PNDC, see NPP, *The Stolen Verdict* (Accra: NPP, 1992).

9. B.O. Garblah, "Lack of Internal Democracy Brought the NDC Down," *The Ghanaian Chronicle*, February 22–26, 2001, p. 8.

10. It can probably be posited that the election of 2000 was the most"spiritually" influenced in Ghana's contemporary political history. For one such example, see O. Lartey, Kufuor's. "Victory is an Act of God," *The Ghanaian Chronicle*, January 8–9, 2001, pp 4–5. For a more detailed analysis, see Emmanuel, Kwesi-Aning, "Spirituality and Politics in Ghana: The December 2000 Elections," unpublished paper (Accra, Ghana, 2003).

11. NPP, *An Agenda for Positive Change: Manifesto 2000 of the New Patriotic Party* (Accra: NPP, 2000).

12. Ibid., p. 1; First Sessional Address of President J.K. Kufuor to the 3rd Parliament of the 4th Republic, p. 2.

13. Center for Democratic Development (CDD), *Civil-Military Relations in Ghana*, CDD Report 6 (Accra: CDD, 2000).

14. See NPP, *Agenda*, p. 40.

15. A.K. Salia, "Move to overhaul CID: Don't Rush It," *Daily Graphic*, March 20, 2001, p.1.

16. *The Chronicle*, March 20, 2001; see also "Purging the Armed Forces: The Secret Behind the Changes in Military," *The Free Press*, pp. 1 and 8.

17. M. Bratton and R. Mattes, *Support for Democracy in Africa: Intrinsic or Instrumental?* AfroBarometer Working Papers, no. 1 (East Lansing: Michigan State University Press, 1999).

18. These points were explained in detail during several meetings with General E. Sam, former Chief of Defense Staff (CDS) under former President Hilla Liman's rule, "Take Control of Military for Stability," *Daily Graphic*, February 6, 2001, p. 17.

19. Statement by the minister of Defense. For a more recent discussion of the issue, see *The Daily Dispatch*, "210 Billion for 2,000 Soldiers," June 7, 2002, pp. 1 and 8. According to the report, "The NPP government . . . inherited a number of political, security and economic 'landmines.' " . . . One problem which fits the security and economic "landmines" is the issue of roughly 2,150 warrant officers (WOs) and other ranks in the Ghana Armed Forces, who were retired in 2002.

20. For a detailed analysis of the difficulties involved here, see E.K. Aning, *Democratic Governance and the Security Sector*, unpublished working Paper (Accra, 2001).

21. A number of the ideas in this section are from Luc van de Groor, *Military and Security Institutions in Developing Countries: Challenges in Civilian Control Governance and Conflict Management*, paper presented to a workshop at Clingendael Institute, January 16, 2001, especially pp. 1–3.

22. A Kofoya-Tetteh, "Take Firm Control of Military for Stability," *Daily Graphic*, February 6, 2001, p. 16; A.K. Salia, "Military Spending Can't be Exposed," *Daily Graphic*, February 28, 2001, pp. 16–17.

23. I am grateful to Nicole Ball for sharing some of these ideas with me. For example, see her *Spreading Good Practices in Security Sector Reform: Policy Options for the British Government* (London: Saferworld, 1999).

24. Ibid. Interestingly enough, this was in sharp contradiction to the approach and time frame discussed in "An Agenda for Change," in *Agenda for Positive Change*, p. 8.

25. *Daily Graphic*, February 6, 2001, p. 1. This was joint police and military led by Chief of Police Operation, Yaw Adu-Gyimah, who was subsequently transferred to the Central Region, suspended, and eventually indicted for supplying some armed robbers with some of the seized guns.

26. In an interview given by Yaw Adu-Gyimah in Accra on March 22, 2001, he indicated that the number of guns retrieved was a national security issue and could not be divulged to the public. Eventually in early 2002, a ridiculously low figure was given as the total number of retrieved weapons from people. For a critique of weapons-buy-back programs, see Emmanuel Kwesi Aning, *Security in the West African Sub-Region: An Analysis of ECOWAS' Policies in Liberia* (Copenhagen: Reprocentre, 1999), pp. 292–320.

27. Also present were Vice President Jacob Zuma of South Africa, President Abdoulaye Wade of Senegal, and a host of other dignitaries. In a statement, Vice President Zuma characterized the smooth transfer of power as "a celebration of democracy in the continent. It is further evidence that Africans can run their countries peacefully and efficiently." "Zuma Completes Visit to Ghana," *Pan-African News Agency*, February 21, 2001.

28. NPP, *Agenda*, p. 45.

29. Ibid.

30. For a crude, biased, and unsophisticated apolitical analysis of the Kufuor trip that blatantly attacks critics of the maiden foreign policy trips of the President as "an open demonstration of paranoiac impudence," see F.K. Koranteng, "The Furore over President Kufuor's Visit to Togo," *The Ghanaian Chronicle*, February 6–7, 2001, p. 6.

31. Two editorials in *The Ghanaian Chronicle* of January 15–16, 2001 and January 17–18, 2001 are more balanced in their assessment of the president's trip and raise interesting questions and issues.

32. See *Final Report of the Monitoring Mechanism on Angola Sanctions*, UNSC Document S/2000/1225, established by UN Security Council Resolution 1295 of 2000, pursuant to Resolution 864 of 1993 concerning Angola. For the specific sections dealing with the Togolese role in sanction-busting, see pp. 16–17. With respect to Burkina Faso, see pp. 17 and 19.

33. J. Kamara, "Closing in on Arms and Diamond Rackets," *West Africa*, January 15–21, 2001, p. 17; *Angola's War Economy: The Role of Diamonds and Oil*, ed. J. Cilliers and C. Dietrich (Pretoria: Institute for Security Studies, 2000); "Kufuor's Security Dilemmas," *Africa Analysis*, vol. 364, January 26, 2001, p. 3.

34. P. Fabricius, "Glimmer of Hope for Angolan Peace Talks Resuming," *The Star*, February 12, 2001.

35. Jonas Savimbi had the use and support of some of the apartheid regime's most efficient forces to fight his anti-communist campaigns. Among these were the 32 "Buffalo" Battalion; the Reconnaissance Commandos (Reccies); the Parachute Brigade (Parabats); and the paramilitary "Koevoet"(Crowbar). Their duties were to destabilize apartheid's enemies. One of these groups, the 32 "Buffalo" Battalion, deserves special mention. It was established by the South African government as a special unit to recruit Angolans into the South African army. It was mainly composed of former Frente Naçional de Libertação de Angola (FNLA) forces, Portuguese-speaking Angolans who cooperated with Jonas Savimbi's União Naçional para a Indepêndencia Total de Angola (UNITA), and became South Africa's most decorated combat unit since 1945. Comprising 70% Zimbabweans and black South Africans, most of whom were described as "soldiers of fortune," these men had fought for Ian Smith in Rhodesia, and in Angola and Namibia against the MPLA and SWAPO, respectively. For a detailed analysis of the interconnections between Savimbi and other mercenary groups, see E.K Aning, "Africa's

Security in the New Millennium: State or Mercenary Induced Stability?" *Global Society: Journal of Interdisciplinary International Relations*, vol. 15, no. 2, April 2001, pp.149–171.

36. NPP, *Agenda*, p. vi.

37. Ibid., "Justification for Re-launching Economic Growth" at section 2.2.2.4, p. 7.

38. Ibid., section 2.2.2.5. Emphasis in the original.

39. See Sessional address of the President, in Y. Osafo-Maafo, *The Budget Statement and Economic Policy of the Government of Ghana for the 2001 Fiscal year*, presented by the minister of finance, March 9, 2001.

40. For the most sophisticated analysis of earlier economic strategies, see Eboe Hutchful, *Ghana's Adjustment Experience: The Paradox of Reform* (Oxford: James Currey, 2002), especially Chapter 8 from pp. 140 ff.

41. The drive to hunt for alleged stolen wealth apparently has not been successful. See for example, *The Insight*, " 'Ex-Ministers' Foreign Accounts: Government Draws a Blank," May15–16, 2002, pp. 1 and 4. According to the paper, "The search for the foreign accounts of Ministers of the Rawlings regime appears to have drawn a blank. Well-placed sources in the security establishment say Francis Poku, National Security Coordinator, has been following leads which have taken him nowhere."

42. World Bank and Ghana Center for Democratic Governance, *The Ghana Governance and Corruption Survey: Evidence from Households, Enterprises and Public Officials* (Accra: CDD, 2000).

43. See speech delivered by Alhaji Aliu Mahama at the official launching of the above publication, February 8, 2001.

44. Two documents are helpful in understanding the economic plight of both the government and the people of Ghana. See K. Armah, *Proposed Policy Measures for the New Administration: A Recipe for Good Economic Governance*, mimeo, February 2001; K. Kote-Nikoi, Fiscal Trends and the Implications for Poverty Reduction, mimeo, October 2000.

CHAPTER 5

Reflections on the Postcolonial State in Kenya

Anne Nangulu-Ayuku

Introduction

Kenya is a richly mixed ethnic and racial society. The country's people come from a wide range of African communities incorporating two major immigrant groups of Asians and Europeans.[1] As noted by William Ochieng', the people we today call Kenyans have existed in this geographical segment of East Africa for a very long time, and in ever-changing cultural costumes and circumstances. Some, like the Okiek, appear to be indigenous; the Bantu, Cushites, and Nilotes arrived in Kenya at different times from different parts of Africa; the Arabs, Asians, and Europeans also arrived at different times from their parent continents.[2] Ochieng' further notes that, forced from 1895 into a kind of colonial "polygamous existence" by the British, the various Kenya peoples have, for over the last 100 years, struggled and coexisted, even as each ethnic group has at the same time attempted—as in a polygamous matrimony—to cater to its separate aspirations. And long after the formal departure of the British (with the attainment of Kenya's independence in 1963) the "polygamous" nation-state promises to endure.[3]

In any case, Kenya is not an easy country to govern; it has over 40 ethnic groups, volatile politicians, a sophisticated and powerful elite representing a variety of different and sometimes conflicting interests scattered over a wide and varied geographical landscape.[4] Against this background, this chapter analyzes the nature and dynamics of precolonial African societies/states and of the colonial and postcolonial state in Kenya. It also examines various strategies for reconstituting and reconstructing the postcolonial state to meet the needs of Kenyans now and in the years to come.

African Societies/States in the Precolonial Period

Kenya is, as practically all contemporary African states, an artificial creation of the colonial powers. It lumps together at least 42 separate ethnic groups, some (like the Abaluhya and Mijikenda) further subdivided by distinct geographical and cultural differences. These groups have come to develop a common name and identity only during the last few decades. In the precolonial period, all these groups had their own history, distinct social and political structures, and certain patterns of interaction with neighboring peoples.[5]

Besides, almost all Kenya's ethnic groups were characterized by what has become known as "egalitarian-segmentarian" structures in contrast with more hierarchical forms of social and political organization as, for example, the chieftainships and kingdoms in the neighboring Uganda. Minor exceptions were the small "kingdom" of Wanga among a subgroup of the Abaluhya and more hierarchical structures due to external, mainly Arab, influences, among some of the coastal communities (e.g., the Swahili). As noted by Berg-Schlosser, the main elements of these structures were, in a horizontal sense, a system of clans and lineages based on actual or perceived lines of common descent. He further notes that, vertically, the majority of these groups were divided by a system of age-sets that were set apart by distinct initiation procedures and the members of which had almost equal, but, depending on sex and age, functionally distinct rights and duties.[6]

In addition, all of them without exception, whether they were farmers (e.g., the Kikuyu and Abaluhya groups) or pastoralists (such as the Nandi and Maasai), whether they were centralized or whether they operated the age-set system, the generational system was the basic political and social institution. In localized day-to-day behavior, it determined the status and duties of all individuals. The generational system defined the hierarchy of age, wealth, prestige, and authority that permeated every aspect of life. Therefore, it can be argued that there was no one single state in what is now Kenya during the precolonial period. Furthermore, as noted by Ochieng', ethnic societies in precolonial Kenya lacked any form of centralized, traditional bureaucracy.[7] But, this does not mean that they had no government. As a matter of fact, the majority of people in precolonial Kenya had elaborate systems of lodges, sectional relations, and codes of justice, all of which contributed to the corporate polity of their respective social groups.[8]

It can further be argued that early Kenyan societies tended to be decentralized communities of small clans or lineages of more or less equal status. The political history of Kenya in precolonial times was thus essentially the history of how these separate families, lineages, and clans came together to form first small neighborhood political organizations and, then, larger and more effective societies. Again, in Kenya, without exception, each political system supported and was in turn supported by its own form of religion and rituals. These rituals were applied to the consecration of accepted customs and authority and to all those situations where decisive change in custom and authority was found desirable or necessary. That is why African religions have ideally displayed, or have been intended to display, a complete rounded explanation of life.[9]

Specifically, in the nineteenth century, scattered all over present Kenya, was a number of differing Bantu- , Nilotic- , and Cushitic-speaking peoples. Only in the interlacustrine areas of East Africa had there developed centralized political states. Between the Rift Valley lakes and the Indian Ocean, however, the typical polity was small and generally clan-oriented. Most of the Bantu speakers were agriculturalists, though wherever conditions were suitable they did keep and prize livestock. Pastoralists such as the Turkana, Galla, Maasai, and Nandi controlled substantial areas of territory between the agricultural Bantu groups. Along the coast were the Swahili city states, dominated at the beginning of the nineteenth century by a small ruling class of local trading Arabs. The population in these coastal cities was mixed, the dominant languages being Swahili, and the tempo of life considerably different from that of the interior villages.[10] As noted by John Lonsdale, indeed, the most distinctively African contribution to human history could be said to have been precisely the civilized art of living fairly peaceably together *not* in centralized states.[11]

In sum, none of today's major ethnic groupings in Kenya had a common form of political organization and decision making that simultaneously extended to all members of the community. Most were characterized by significant internal subdivisions that included the possibility of traditional forms of warfare, as for example, among subgroups of the Maasai, against one another.[12] However, it is important to note that the relations between and within Kenyan groups are today largely determined by the economic and political relations of the new state. Today, ethnic relations in the country are conducted within the context of a Kenyan state structure. Thus, superimposing the umbrella of a single political entity has created interactions among groups who had little or nothing to do with one another in the past, thereby completely transforming their former relations.[13]

The Colonial State

The formal imposition of colonial rule in Kenya came with the declaration of the East Africa Protectorate in 1895. As a result, Kenya became a British Protectorate and remained so under the administration of the British crown until 1920. In 1905, the direction of the Protectorate's administration shifted from the Foreign Office to the Colonial Office. Two years later (in 1907), the European settlers were granted a legislative council; and in the same year the headquarters of Kenya was moved from Mombasa to Nairobi. It should also be mentioned here that the period 1894–1912 was characterized by geographical surveys, fortress building, and military conquest all over Kenya. Thereafter, in 1920, Kenya was declared a British colony. Thus, the territory, Kenya, was seized by war and became a conquered state. Indeed, Kenya was transformed from a land of free, teeming nationalities into a coherent colonial state, with a legislature and international boundaries. Once again, this transformation was the work of force.[14]

The Establishment of Colonial Rule: The Administrative Structure and the Penetration of Capitalism

In the meantime, the presence of the colonial government was made known through the appointment of governors by the Colonial Office in Britain, as well as provincial and local administrators, for example, Provincial Commissioners (PCs), District Commissioners (DCs), District Officer's (DOs), police officers, chiefs, headmen, and members of the Local Native Councils (LNCs) among others. Besides, the establishment of administrative centers (e.g., Mombasa, Machakos, Nairobi, Murang'a, and Kisumu to name a few); the creation of administrative boundaries; and the levying of taxes as a major source of revenue for the colonial state were all manifestations of the establishment of colonial rule in Kenya.[15]

From the very beginning, Africans were compelled to pay taxes from the sale of livestock (slaughter cattle, goats, and sheep), livestock products (ghee, hides, and skins), farm produce, and from wage labor. The African population in the colony also paid a hut tax and a poll tax. A hut tax at the prescribed rate was payable on each hut (dwelling house) owned or occupied by the tax payer. Initially, the age of liability for payment of the poll tax was 16 years. This was later raised to 18 years by the Native Hut and Poll Tax (Amendment) Ordinance of 1936. A poll tax at the prescribed rate was payable by all able-bodied African males who were not liable to pay hut tax. Hut and Poll tax collection fell under the DOs.[16] Taxation performed two main functions in the Kenyan colony. It sustained the colonial system by providing the necessary revenue. It also created a basis of African dependency on the colonial economic system through the monetization of aspects of the local economy since taxes were paid in British-denominated currencies.

Another policy of the colonial state that continued to affect Kenya long after the formal end of colonialism was the imposition of definite boundaries between and among different African groups, based on the policy of divide and rule. Colonial administrators argued that boundaries were necessary in the allocation of resources, mainly land, for cultivation and grazing between and among different African groups. They also argued that establishment of boundaries would eliminate interethnic conflicts over grazing pastures and water, particularly among herders (e.g., between the Pokot and Turkana, Maasai and some Kalenjin speakers, and Kenya Somali and Rendille among others) whom the administration believed were warlike. Thus, in the view of the colonial administrators, boundaries were necessary for maintaining law and order.[17]

Significantly, the creation of definite boundaries also made it easier for the colonial state to alienate African land for European settlement, mainly in Kenya's high fertile areas (e.g., land occupied by the Kikuyu and Maasai at the time), and to confine Africans to mostly low yield areas, dubbed African reserves. It also made it possible for the colonial state to divide the colony into provinces, districts, divisions, and locations.

Besides the creation of various administrative units and related boundaries, the colonial administration also went ahead and established Local Native Councils (LNCs) in African occupied areas. The LNCs were a legislative branch that consisted of chiefs (nominated) and one elected member from each location. At the same time, there were varying numbers of headmen, depending on the size and population of the location who acted as assistants to the chiefs. The duties of the LNCs included adjustment of salary scales of its employees, making of by-laws, imposing cess (levies) on grains and livestock products, licensing local traders, and effecting a proper use of the land. From time to time, the LNCs were audited by Local Government Inspectors who made sure that whatever levies collected contributed to revenue needed in running the administration.[18]

Generally, the LNCs in various parts of the colony served important government functions in African occupied areas. The colonial state used chiefs and LNCs to pass on government policies to the African population. For instance, beginning in the 1920s through the 1950s, the LNCs were used in implementing livestock destocking policies, soil conservation, and better farming methods dictated by colonial administrators. Besides, one of the ways in which the colonial state could provide its minimal economic assistance to African farmers, herders, and traders was through the LNCs. Therefore, in the absence of sufficient economic incentives and the failure to involve, for example, African producers in measures designated to increase food and cash crop production, the colonial state relied heavily on chiefs and the LNCs to implement its policies and to spread the necessary propaganda. In addition, as part of the local government, the LNCs also became a source of wage labor and salary employment in African occupied areas.[19]

In addition to the LNCs, a local police force that functioned as a law enforcement body at the disposal of chiefs to help in carrying out administrative orders, particularly, tax collection, was established. The local police, or Tribal Police as it was referred to by the British administrators, was regularized by the Tribal Police ordinance of 1929. By this ordinance, provision was made for the establishment of units of local police in accordance with the principle that it was the duty of Africans to police themselves in the colony. Besides, the local police force served as a direct link between the local councils and the central administration. This meant that recruitment of the local policemen was not only based on the physical and mental capability, but also those individuals holding a certain prestige in their communities. At the same time, the colonial state carefully avoided enhancement of the local police to a stage where the LNCs could be subordinated to it.[20] Thus, the policy of the colonial state in the administration of Africans was to govern through councils, the local police, chiefs, and headmen, and in limited proportions entrusted these institutions with a measure of local responsibility and authority.[21]

In sum, it can also be argued that at the same time as the foundation of colonial rule was being laid at the local level, a central government authority was taking shape in the capital city (Nairobi) of colonial Kenya. Initially consisting of a small bureaucracy supporting a governor, the colonial state was, from the very start, characterized by a powerful executive backed by a military force. Most executive and legislative functions were vested in the governor. There was thus little in the way of separation of powers. When a judicial branch was established, it was hardly independent. In Kenya, moreover, European administrators served as arresting officers, prosecutors, and judges for most criminal cases outside the capital. An all-powerful executive and the absence of separation of powers would long characterize the authoritarian state in colonial Kenya and beyond. Nevertheless, the colonial state remained essentially small both in terms of the field administration and the central bureaucracy during the colonial period.[22]

Besides establishing control over African groups, the colonial state was concerned also to promote the penetration of commercial capitalism. Indeed, the state was the primary agent of economic change in the early period of foreign rule. It had to facilitate the penetration of capitalism and the growth of capitalist social relations and mediate the colony's external dependency.[23] This was far from a simple task as the colonial state was forced to straddle two levels of articulation "between the metropolitan and the colony as a whole as well as within the colony itself."[24] Moreover, as noted by Robert Maxon, the colonial state served as an instrument of primitive accumulation by introducing taxation, creating marketing, and financial structures, appropriating land and livestock, instituting forced labor, and building port facilities and railways.[25]

The colonial state thus took a direct hand in facilitating production for export that became a hallmark of the Kenyan economy. It fostered both estate and mixed farm production in the agricultural sector. Despite the limited financial resources at its disposal, the colonial state used a combination of economic pressure and outright coercion to promote commodity production and/or work for wages on settler farms and estates among African households. By 1914, the colonial state had mediated the capitalist penetration in Kenya. In the process, moreover, it adopted a pattern of state policies that would continue throughout the colonial period.[26]

The Postcolonial State

Kenya became independent from British colonial rule on December 12, 1963, and exactly one year later, became a republic. After Kenya's achievement of political independence, the postcolonial state was concerned with the consolidation of power and economic development. The political and economic strategy that it adopted was referred to as African socialism.[27] In more conventional terms, it may be described as a capitalist strategy, both in domestic policy and in policy toward the global system, modified by the intention (not discernibly reflected in policy) of redistributing some of the state gains to the poorer sections of the community (although this is yet to happen). Private ownership has been encouraged and the public sector has expanded rapidly as has state intervention in the economy. In this respect, Kenya's development resembles that of many other global economies, as one of a managed capitalism or mixed economy, as it is sometimes described.[28]

Furthermore, on the domestic front, the postcolonial state has favored private ownership as the mode of production in both agriculture and industry.[29] Small-scale entrepreneurs have also been encouraged by the provision of credit and technical facilities. Internationally, the government has encouraged the integration of the Kenyan economy into the world capitalist system. Foreign aid and foreign missions have been welcomed. As a matter of fact, right from independence, Kenya's leadership during the Kenyatta and later on, the arap Moi era opted for a clear strategy of economic growth, based on a determination to keep existing ties with Western countries and gain foreign aid and investment. Significantly, Kenya's economy before and after independence was and still is primarily an agricultural economy with only a very small manufacturing sector.[30]

Thus, it can be argued that nothing came out of the so-called African socialism phase of the Kenyan political economy. In the words of Eric Aseka, leaders of the independence era subscribed to the ideology of African socialism not as a practical demonstration of "Africanness" in either development planning or national reconstruction, but as an instrument of preserving capitalist relations of production and exchange.[31] In this case, despite the euphoria of independence, decolonization in Kenya then appears to have permitted a significant deepening of the new nation's participation in the production networks of the world's capitalist economy. In fact, the country's postcolonial development plans have enmeshed the economy into this capitalist web despite the idealist dream of African socialism as an ideological motif. Indeed, African socialism as a development strategy failed to establish a major turning point in Kenya's trajectory of economic development.[32]

Worse still, as noted by Peter Ndege, Kenya's essentially capitalist policy led to perverted development.[33] For this reason, the country experienced rapid economic growth only up to 1973. It has since then declined.[34] In fact, Kenya's economic performance in the first decade of independence was steady; and this was partly because, as part of a capitalist strategy for development, the country absorbed substantial foreign

aid and remained at or near the top of the aid-receiving league throughout the Kenyatta years (1963–1978). For example, in the three years
1973 to 1975, the net flow of private capital totaled K£ 36.3 m, K£ 55.7,
and K£ 20.9 m while the country's overall debt servicing stood at around
2.8 percent of the total expenditure.[35]

However, as noted earlier, steady economic performance was short-lived.
Like other African countries, Kenya was badly hit by the continuing oil
price rise of the 1970s and unfortunately, despite a long period of petroleum exploration, it has as yet no oil of its own. For instance, oil
accounted for 82 percent of Kenya's primary energy consumption at the
beginning of the 1970s with hydroelectricity providing 17 percent and
coal and coke, a mere 1 percent.[36] In March 1980, petrol prices went up
15.5 percent to Kshs. 4.82 a liter; and in June 2002, kerosene and petrol
sold at an average of Kshs. 35 and Kshs. 55 per liter respectively.
A reminder, if one was needed, that oil price rises had become a permanent
feature of economic life. In this case, Kenya is in the category of highest
oil-dependent countries.[37] Thus, since the 1970s, Kenya has been
overdependent on imported fuel and foreign aid, with devastating
impact on the country's socioeconomic life.

Despite overdependence on imported fuel and foreign aid, the state
in Kenya, as it is in Africa as a whole, has been a major actor in socioeconomic and political development. As noted by Amukowa Anangwe,
where it is not fully involved in development, planned socioeconomic
changes are at risk of not being implemented. Indeed, development
performance in Kenya may be directly related to what the state could
do or not do through either the public service or the other public
actors such as members of parliament, cabinet ministers, the councilors, and other quasi-government agencies, for example the cooperative
societies.[38]

Nevertheless, the efficacy of the state as an instrument of development has been in doubt for sometime. On one hand, in an age of structural adjustment, liberalization, and privatization, the international
community has undergone a major reversal in its appreciation of the role
of the African state (e.g., the postcolonial state in Kenya) in socioeconomic development. As noted by Martin Doornbos, formerly the
exclusive recipient, partner, and rationale of international aid needed for
socioeconomic development, the African state's "most favored" status
appears today to have been eclipsed in the eyes of donors by a veil of
assumed obsolescence.[39] Doornbos further notes that aside from the
chains of the debt burden, the autonomy of the African state is increasingly being bypassed and eroded by the international community in several

critical ways. For instance, there is, (1) advocacy of privatization, and increasing involvement of private enterprise in aid arrangements; (2) significant diversion of aid funds and the planning and disbursement of food aid via nongovernmental organizations and related channels; and (3) the rapidly growing donor specialization and involvement in selected sectors and/or regions within African countries, facilitating a gradual shift of policy preparation activities to European donor headquarters, away from national sectoral coordinating ministries or organizations.[40] This clearly illustrates that, the donor community no longer trusts the African state (e.g., the postcolonial state in Kenya) as the custodian of foreign aid and as the instrument of socioeconomic development.

Given the limited financial and staffing resources vis-à-vis collective external expertise, the role of the national government often becomes necessarily limited to accepting—or possibly refusing to accept—ready-made policy packages prepared elsewhere, or already agreed upon by the main donors. Some governments, for example, the Kenya government, for sometime managed skillfully to play off one donor against another, but increasing insistence on donor coordination is now making this more difficult and closing off this limited room for maneuver.[41]

Worse still, majority of Kenyans no longer trust the state as the custodian of foreign aid and as an instrument of socioeconomic development. This is partly due to the fact that at independence, there were expectations about the role the state would play as the prime mover in all development efforts. Whether in agriculture, industrialization, education, or other sectors, the burden of formulating and implementing the policies that would transform society was laid squarely on the government. The state was to pull the whole society along in an all-out development drive on several fronts.[42]

In particular, the state was to direct the economy and, through product marketing and other mechanisms, seek to extract a surplus that it would redirect partly for the maintenance and expansion of its own apparatus, as well as redistribution to other sectors. As was increasingly realized, however, the high expectations bestowed on the state could hardly be fulfilled under the prevailing conditions (e.g., overdependence upon foreign aid and the debt burden; as well as misuse of public funds for personal gain by bureaucrats). They proved ill-founded both vis-à-vis the state and the civil society it confronted. In case after case, high expectations were followed by profound disillusionment, and the role attributed to the African state changed from the prime mover of development to that of its main obstacle.[43]

This view is shared by Van de Walle, in his analyses of the African state. He notes that between 1960 and 1989, and rather regrettably ever since 1990, with a handful of exceptions, the postcolonial state in Africa has been largely antidevelopmental. Parasitic, self-seeking, and inept, it has been simultaneously very coercive and extremely weak, forced to prey on civil society—with devastating effect—just to survive.[44] He further notes that the bureaucracy's effectiveness has typically been undermined by a patrimonial logic in which state assets are routinely plundered for political advantage of the regime and state-society relations have been characterized by clientelism rather than citizenship; the state, powerless to elicit respect or loyalty from the populace, has typically used threats and coercion to achieve minimal—usually passive—acquiescence.[45]

In view of the foregoing character and nature of the postcolonial state and its bureaucracy, it is little wonder then that there was, for three decades after independence, little or no development. There was some growth on the economic front, though this was hardly enough to appreciably improve the quality and standards of living of millions of Africans. Thus, the verdict of the World Bank and virtually by all other "development" partners of Africa that the first three decades of independence were lost is not wholly off the mark. By implication, this laid the ground for a prolonged dialogue on structural position of the state that, in amended form, has continued until virtually to the present.[46]

However, this does not mean that the role of the state in Kenya's socioeconomic development has been curtailed. In fact, the state in Kenya has been and may have to remain the mainstay of the country's socioeconomic development for sometime to come. This is due to the fact that to date, it continues to play an interventionist role in development in spite of its well-known weaknesses and persistent prodding by the multilateral and bilateral agencies for it to adopt "privatization" as an integral part of measures to stimulate the country's socioeconomic development.[47]

State, Politics, Ethnicity and Resource Allocation

As noted above, Kenya became independent in 1963. Indeed, it can be argued that the newly independent state was very much founded on ethnic politics. The foremost parties with nationwide support, Kenya African National Union (KANU) and the Kenya African Democratic Union (KADU) were deeply entrenched in ethnic politics. KANU was formed on March 27, 1960; and KADU on June 25, 1960.[48] There were hardly what can be called ideological differences between the two in their set-up. KANU was mainly backed up by the Kikuyu and the Luo, and favored a unitary centralized political system that was fiercely opposed by KADU, a party that represented the so-called small ethnic groups. KADU was in reality a coalition of ex-ethnic inclined parties such as the Maasai United Front, the Kalenjin Alliance, the Coast African Political Union, and the Kenya African Party. KADU's agenda was the formation of a federal type of political system that would guarantee the interests of the "small" ethnic groups against the perceived Kikuyu-Luo alliance. The leadership of both these parties and the several coalitions was clearly ethnic in origin and relied on working up ethnic emotions in mobilizing support from ordinary citizens.[49]

Moreover, KANU and KADU coexisted as the two main political parties in Kenya until November 10, 1964, when KADU, responding to the political realities of the day, and to the incentives from the KANU government, dissolved itself and its members joined KANU. In November 1962, a splinter group from KANU, known as the African Peoples Party (APP) had been formed, but it too dissolved itself and its members returned to the fold in 1964. Apart from a short break, between 1966 and 1969, when disagreements in KANU's leadership ranks led to the formation of the Kenya People's Union (KPU), Kenya remained a one-party state, as a factual reality, up till 1982 and then by legal requirement, up to 1992.[50]

It should be noted that in the entire period of single-partyism, Kenya's guiding political ideology was built around the vital importance of national unity; the underplaying of racial and ethnic differentiations; and around the goal of social harmony and tranquility—the governing principles for these values being provided by the president and his government. This ideology was a major factor in shaping the national constitution, and regulating the pattern of government, as well as determining the interplay between the principal constitutional organs (the Executive, the Legislature, and the Judiciary) and the general population.[51]

From 1990, it proved rather more difficult to sustain the basic messages of unity as the foundation of a one-party system, especially in light of widespread international lobbying for pluralism and for broad-based electoral choice as a foundation for good governance, transparency, and accountability. The strident new ideology that was backed up with international and assistance packages, dictated the adoption of multipartyism in virtually all African countries.[52] Therefore, in 1991, the Kenyan

Constitution was amended (with the scrapping of Section 2A of the Constitution that had made Kenya a *de jure* one party state) to allow more parties. This saw the rise of Ford Kenya (Ford-K), Ford Asili (Ford-A), Social Democratic Party (SDP), Democratic Party (DP), National Development Party (NDP), and other smaller parties.[53] Thus, Kenya held its December 1992 and December 1997 general elections as a multiparty state. In both multiparty elections, KANU won and retained its status as Kenya's ruling party since independence.

In the meantime, following negotiations between KANU and NDP, on March 18, 2002, the two parties merged to form New KANU. However, the KANU/NDP merger was short-lived. After seven months, in October 2002, New KANU split and members of the dissolved NDP left the party for the opposition. They were immediately joined by high ranking KANU members, including Professor George Saitoti, after being dropped as the vice president. The split in New KANU was caused by intense protests following President Moi's choice of Uhuru Kenyatta (son of Kenya's first president, the late Jomo Kenyatta), as the party's presidential candidate in the December 27, 2002 general elections. As stipulated in the Kenyan Constitution, Moi who had served more than two terms in office was officially out of the race for the country's presidency, in the December 2002 general elections.[54] It is no wonder that Moi went ahead and imposed Uhuru Kenyatta as KANU's presidential candidate, hoping that he would protect his interests while in retirement. But this did not sit well with other New KANU members, causing a split in the party.

Significantly, the splinter group from New KANU went ahead and formed a political pressure group—the Rainbow, demanding free and fair elections for the country's leadership as opposed to imposing leaders on the electorate. At the same time, members of the Rainbow joined a little known registered party, the Liberal Democratic Party (LDP), to enable them officially join opposition politics and use the new party to fight it out with KANU in the December 2002 elections. However, after realizing that LDP might have little impact on Kenya's political land-scape as an opposition party, its members opted to negotiate with the National Alliance (Party) of Kenya (NAK), for opposition unity, and with one agenda, to remove KANU from power in the December 2002 general elections. It is worth noting, that NAK, an amalgamation of opposition parties, including DP and Ford-K as major parties in the Alliance, was formed to countercheck the political strength of New KANU, and mainly aimed at uprooting Moi's political hegemony.

Therefore, in less than a month after the split in New KANU, NAK merged with LDP and formed the National Rainbow Coalition (NARC).

Immediately, NARC was registered as a party, serving as a coalition for 13 political parties. Major opposition parties incorporated in NARC included DP, Ford-K, and LDP. Besides, NARC settled for Mwai Kibaki, a former vice president in Moi's government, as the party's presidential candidate in the election. Other political parties, apart from NARC and KANU that fielded presidential candidates for the elections were Ford People (that split from Ford-A, candidate—Simeon Nyachae), SDP (candidate—James Orengo), and Chama Cha Umma (CCU, candidate—Waweru Nge'the).

Generally, on the eve of the elections, Kenya had 51 registered political parties. However, a look at the list of registered parties reveals that many were hardly known to the public and some could as well be described as spurious. Some did not have physical addresses and have never participated in any election. Neither did they file returns with the Registrar of Societies. While the government in general, and the Registrar of Societies in particular, would defend themselves that they were simply obeying the Constitution by enhancing the freedom of association, a number of would-be serious political parties such as the United Democratic Movement (UDM), were denied registration for KANU's political expedience. Besides, it is no secret that certain personalities close to the establishment used parties as commercial ventures where they capitalized on their influence to register parties through proxies. Such parties where later sold to the highest bidder, mainly individuals who had fallen out of favor with the leadership of mainstream parties.[55]

Despite numerous parties in Kenya, NARC and KANU were the two main rival parties in the general elections. It is worth noting that for the first time in more than two decades, the ruling party, KANU, presented a presidential candidate other than arap Moi and that regardless of whichever party won the presidency, arap Moi had to relinquish power. What was thus certain was that come January 4, 2003, there was going to be a new tenant in Kenya's state house, and Kenyans hoped that President Moi would be their last dictator. Kenyans hoped that the next person to swear the oath of office as the country' third president would be a respected citizen and one who is a subject to the laws of the land.

After Kenya's independence on December 12, 1963, the postcolonial state was concerned with the consolidation of power and economic development. However, power and wealth were disproportionately distributed between and within an already ethnically and socially differentiated populace. Few became politically powerful and wealthy; the majority remained depoliticized, oppressed, and poor.[56] As noted by

Atieno-Odhiambo, Kenyatta's state snatched power from the British, and put it into the hands of his men (the Kikuyu).[57] Therefore, as early as 1966, the problem of ethnicity in terms of state resource allocation had become a major issue as was evidenced in the parliamentary debates, with a majority of members accusing the government leadership of overenrolling the Kikuyu people in the civil service at the expense of members from other ethnic groups. A majority of them advocated for promotion and employment to be on the basis of qualifications and experience rather than origins.[58]

As if that was not enough, in the 1970s, most of the top posts within the civil service, state corporations (popularly known as parastatals in Kenya), and government departments continued to be dominated by people from the Kikuyu ethnic group. As noted by Nyukuri Kundu, such nepotism was a major cause of high level corruption during the Kenyatta era.[59] The same charge was leveled against the Moi government. As observed by Atieno-Odhiambo, on his accession to the presidency in 1978, Daniel Toroitich arap Moi sought to shift the locus of his patrimonial state from the Kikuyu to the Kalenjin. The way to do that was to create a parallel Kalenjin elite within the military and the public service sector. Almost any among them with university education and who subscribed to the credo of total loyalty to the Moi government soon attained elevated status. Furthermore, the Moi intrusion was particularly visible at the level of state institutions. In typical elite competitive rivalry, the former Kenyatta team often cried foul, and in the aftermath of the Structural Adjustment Programs, often accused the Kalenjin elite of destroying those same institutions that Kenyattta had built. On the ground though, the reality was different, for the second and third in command at these institutions remained intact in the hands of those Kikuyu from the Kenyatta era. It became an uneasy partnership but it still worked.[60]

Indeed, the mass media and parliament reported debates about the Kikuyu and Kalenjin domination in top posts within the civil service, state corporations, and other government departments. Whether the claims were true or not, the one thing that came out clearly was the suspicion and fear that surrounded the leaders from other ethnic groups as they confronted each other over the extraction sand allocation of state resources.[61]

Furthermore, another area to illustrate disparity in resource allocation and discrimination in Kenya's postcolonial state is the educational sector. Generally, since independence, education has taken an ethnic character as well as discriminative in nature. While state policy of expanding educational opportunities and the use of Kiswahili and English as media of instruction have the potential of breaking down ethnic barriers, the majority of students attend school only with fellow ethnic-group members at the primary level. Besides, the well-to-do and politically connected tend to have access to educational opportunities both within and outside the country. The ethnic character has been publicly aired, as some ethnic groups, particularly the Kikuyu during the Kenyatta era and the Kalenjin during the Moi era, are said to have had more, and on average, better-equipped schools and training institutions than, for example, the Mijikenda at the Coast and Somali among other pastoralists of North Eastern Kenya. Besides, girls continue to lag behind boys in school attendance, despite their greater number in the population as a whole. This continues to be pronounced at the secondary stage, and even more so at the university level. Although the state has attempted to provide facilities for those districts and provinces that have lagged behind in school enrollment and university entry, the effort is yet to be realized. Thus, there is an entrenched pattern of educational discrimination against girls and young women, against pastoralists, the poor, and ethnically marginalized groups.[62] The postcolonial state in Kenya still faces the challenge of redressing educational imbalances and providing an appropriate educational system for the present and future generations. Generally, resource allocation in Kenya has been characterized by ethnicity and sectionalism. This has created dissatisfaction, with the majority of the population, particularly in rural Kenya, with the government being accused of neglect and marginalization.

Thus, the ethnographic nature of the postcolonial state in Africa means that exclusion of members of a certain ethnic group from political power implies exclusion from the material and social resources controlled by the state. Therefore, the struggle over the control of the country's social and economic resources is then waged on the political level in the form of ethnic conflicts.[63] This is a scenario that has preoccupied Kenya since independence and reached climax in the 1990s.

Ethnic Conflicts, the Struggle over Resource Control and State Security

Specifically, the worst ethnic conflicts since independence erupted mainly in the Rift Valley, Western, and to some extent, Nyanza Provinces of Kenya in the 1990s. During the first half of 1992, it was officially reported that 240 persons were killed in the three provinces. Informal estimates raised the number slained and wounded to thousands.[64]

The fighting included the Kalenjin attacking the Luo who they claimed were stealing Kalenjin cattle, and the Nandi and Pokot assaulting Luhya farmers in the long-festering land disputes and cattle theft. Kalenjin and Gusii clashes disrupted tea production in Nyanza and Rift Valley provinces. Tea is Kenya's second largest foreign exchange earner. Generally, the clashes sent shock waves of insecurity throughout the whole country.

Yet, of all the areas where ethnic clashes occurred during the early 1990s, Molo and Olenguruone Divisions of Nakuru District and Enosupukia in Narok District comprised the largest. The peak of clashes in Molo and Olenguruone covered the period mid-February to August 1992. Notably, in the two areas, clashes pitted the Kalenjin (mainly Kipsigis) on one side, and non-Kalenjin (mainly Kikuyu, Gusii, Luhya, and Luo) on the other.[65] In the case of Enosupukia, the most involved groups were the Maasai and Kikuyu. It is asserted that in October 1993, a total of 500 Maasai morans attacked non-Maasai in the area and about 30,000 people (mainly Kikuyu) were thrown out of their homes.[66] A number of Enosupukia residents forced out of their homes fled to Maela where a camp was set up near Maela town in December 1993 and housed around 12,000 people.[67] At this time, it had become clear that displaced families would not be able to return to their farms because of instability. Therefore, since 1994, some of the clash victims have managed to buy one or two acres of land in various parts of the country, in the hope of starting a new life. Others have been tracing their kinsmen in search of "accommodation." The remaining groups are still seeking refuge mainly in Central and Rift Valley Provinces, and in other parts of Kenya. At the moment, they are Kenya's internal refugees.

Worse still, in North Rift Valley, ethnic conflicts have erupted, over the years, between the Pokot and Turkana on one hand, and Pokot and Marakwet on the other. Specifically, border relations in the history of the Pokot and their neighbors have been varied and complex. Their relationships range from years of some understanding and agreements to share scare resources (grazing pastures and water), leading to temporary peace and, at times leading to escalating conflicts, contributing to both livestock and human insecurity in the area. For instance, the Pokot/Turkana conflict that flared up at the end of 1967, escalated in 1969 to a point that not only human casualties reached unprecedented peak; but the theft of livestock, most of which were never recovered, took such proportions that many of the Pokot stock owners were left destitute.[68] Besides, a prolonged drought in the first quarter of 1972 was also responsible for the deterioration of grazing, and contributed to conflicts between the Pokot/Marakwet and Pokot/Turkana. Particularly West Pokot was hit many times by the Turkana raiders in 1972, 1974, and 1976.[69] Several deaths were reported and a number of animals taken.

Furthermore, from the mid-1990s to the end of 2002, cattle raiding was still rampant in the North Rift Valley. For example, in November/December 1995, the Pokot raided the Turkana more than three times on the Pokot/Turkana border, at Nadome, Lomelo, and Napeitum and, left at least 44 people dead and about 12,000 animals stolen.[70] In retaliation, Turkana raiders attacked the Pokot near Tanguilbe, once again on the border, killing three people and taking more than 4,000 cattle.[71] What began as a mere scramble for pasture and water due to drought degenerated into full-scale interethnic warfare between two traditionally hostile communities.

In response, the government deployed security forces to contain the situation and bring the culprits to book. However, it has always been difficult to fix the whole blame on either one side or the other on border/cattle raids. Evidently, every raid particularly Turkana raids, evoked attempted retaliation from the Pokot and vice versa. Therefore, as each raid from either side exacerbates the conflict, it has remained difficult to sort out culprits and see a decisive end to it. Significantly, perpetual ethnic conflicts in North Rift Valley are a threat to state security in Kenya as a whole.

Several incidents of ethnic conflicts and related massacres have regularly taken place in other parts of the country as well. In particular, ethnic conflicts have erupted in Likipia, Samburu, Garissa, Transmara, and Tana River Districts. For example, on the Gucha-Transmara border, the war is between the agriculturalist Gusii and the pastoralist Maasai. Maasai herders have been accused of grazing their animals on fields cultivated by the Gusii and also stealing Gusii animals from time to time. In the case of Laikipia, Samburu pastoralists are accused of driving their animals into Kikuyu-owned farms, and more often than not, shoot the farmers as well. In Tana River, the contest is between the Pokomo and Wardei on one hand, and the Orma on the other. The Pokomo and Wardei want a permanent land tenure system, based on individual land ownership, to enable them cultivate and invest in their farming enterprises. On the other hand, the Orma want an open land tenure system, based on traditional communal land ownership (still practiced in the area), for easier access to pasture and water for their animals. Ethnic clashes as a manifestation of struggles over resource control, with chilling repercussions, have erupted from time to time in various parts of Kenya.

Kenya's urban areas, in particular, large cities such as Mombasa and Nairobi have not been spared from interethnic clashes that have ravaged some rural areas. For example, in August 1997, one of the most serious security breaches ever recorded in independent Kenya occurred in the densely populated Likoni area of Mombasa when a large gang assaulted the local police station, a nearby police post, and the District Officer's office. All of these were set ablaze, at least six police officers were killed in cold blood, and an armory ransacked. The raiders then controlled the area for seven days, terrorizing nearby residential and business areas. In the process, they killed more than 40 people, before the security team finally caught up with them in the south coast area, where also they had terrorized a number of villages. It was only then that details began to emerge that the terror gang was a well-organized group that had been recruited and trained by "unknown individuals" for some wholly economic and political objectives.[72]

It was reported, for instance, that raiders who went around villages in Likoni burning and killing, specifically sought out members of upcountry ethnic groups. Likoni is heavily populated with immigrant workers, especially the Luo, who have been in the area since the colonial period, providing labor at the docks and have branched out into other occupations. The immigrant community was instrumental in handing Likoni constituency to an opposition Member of Parliament running on a Ford-K ticket, in the 1992 general elections.

Whatever the case, between August and October 1997, approximately 75 people were killed in the Coast province and 4,000 were displaced following attacks on the upcountry people. The locus of responsibility for these attacks remains unclear as it may be national, local, or both. The timing of the attacks not only in Likoni but also in other parts of country in 1992 and 1997, suggests an electoral calculation, but the planning intimates official involvement, perhaps KANU hard-liners wanting to create a political climate of fear among opposition party supporters. The attacks against the upcountry people in Likoni, however, mirrored a local desire to rid the region of a more powerful population that is thought to retard local prosperity and advancement. Meanwhile, the violence, and the inability or unwillingness of the Moi administration to stop it, revived fears that top KANU politicians had employed private armies and thugs to terrorize the population, particularly those in opposition.[73] There is, of course no tangible evidence that any politician was responsible for the Likoni mayhem or ethnic conflicts that have rocked the country since the early 1990s. But it goes without saying that a daring raid executed with such a high degree of organization is certainly no ordinary crime. Of importance, it had a far-reaching impact on the country's tourist industry and posed a threat to peace and security.

In 2001, residents of Kibera, one of Kenya's largest slum areas in Nairobi, refused to pay house rent. They were encouraged to embark on a rent strike by a section of political leaders (claiming rents charged were too high). Their action sparked off a violent confrontation between them and their landlords in which a considerable number of slum dwellers were killed and many more rendered homeless.[74] In the following year (specifically in March 2002), residents of Kariobangi North, also a heavily populated residential area in Nairobi, were treated to a night of horror, as a mob rampaged through the estate, hacked 20 people to death and left a further 28 fighting for their lives after the mayhem.[75] These cases demonstrate, in particular the Kibera incident, that violence is being encouraged as an accepted means of conducting day-to-day economic activities. It also seems to have escaped the notice of those involved that there are socially acceptable and legally sanctioned methods of mediating transactions.

Worse still, it has become an accepted part of national life for one community to take up arms against another in the competition for resources. In doing so it is increasingly becoming clear that political and other leaders in Kenya have encouraged their own communities to go to violent lengths to "evict outsiders" (in reference to members of other ethnic groups) and reclaim "ancestral resources." For example, West Pokot leaders, in particular members of the parliament (MPs) from the area, have argued from time to time that "a good part of the Rift Valley is their ancestral land and it is their sworn duty to drive out outsiders."[76] This partly explains persistent conflicts and related atrocities between the Pokot and their neighbors (in particular the Abaluhya groups, Marakwet, and Turkana) in North Rift Valley.

Generally, since the early 1990s, thousands of people have either been hacked to death, shot with arrows or guns, or murdered, but not a single person has been prosecuted and punished for taking part in the orgy of blood. It is public knowledge in Kenya that although suspects have been arrested and held in police cells for various length of time, and though some have appeared in court, both the masterminds and the instruments of these massacres have benefited from an unusual and consistent impunity. This act points to the fragility of law and order in Kenya and the helplessness of the security services in the face of it. As a matter of fact, in some incidents, cattle raiders or the mob are better armed than government forces. This is a clear indication that the Kenyan state is losing control over matters pertaining to peace and security. Furthermore, this continuation of a callous pattern of lawlessness raises serious questions about the survival of Kenya as a peaceful haven in a region torn apart by conflict. Thus, it can be argued that the pattern of massacres and mayhem in Kenya has become so sustainable that it might be fair to classify the country as being in a constant state of war.[77]

The Corrupt State

While ethnic conflicts are a major threat to state security in Kenya, corruption has undermined the country's socioeconomic and political development—the very foundation of the Kenyan state. At any rate, corrupt practices in Kenya stretch back to the early years of the establishment of colonial rule. As noted by Bruce Berman, until the late 1920s, the colonial administration made no provision for salaries for the chiefs' retainers, forcing the chiefs to provide funds out of their own resources and virtually ensuring a search for additional source of income. Corruption and bribery thus became the vital "fuel of the local administrative engine."[78] Collaboration with the colonial state made it possible for the chiefs to extract a tribute from the population that helped make them by far the wealthiest men in their locations.[79]

This view is shared by Maxon, who notes that the consolidation of colonial rule at the local level, moreover, went hand in hand with appeals to personal gain and bribery. For example, inadequate pay for colonial chiefs increased the inclination of some to turn to corruption.[80] It should also be noted here that in the Kenya system of direct administration, the chiefs were almost wholly creations of the colonial state.[81] Just as chiefs were a colonial creation, colonial corruption in Kenya, in the words of Robert Tignor, "stemmed directly from the functioning of the colonial system and was not a traditional inheritance."[82]

Furthermore, the officers of the colonial administration were well aware of the corruption and abuse of power by the chiefs as well as the bitter political struggles that often swirled around them, though fully detailed information on the situation in a particular district/African occupied area was often difficult to come by. Although flagrantly corrupt and brutal chiefs were sometimes removed from office, depositions were likely to have been because such chiefs involved were regarded as ineffective and "inefficient." Indeed, where a chief was effective and useful from the standpoint of the colonial administration, there was a tendency to see the corruption and abuse of his powers as the inevitable price of control, or to dismiss such reports as politically motivated charges by a chief's opponents who would act in the same way if they had held the post.[83]

Moreover, at first, chiefs were permitted to try civil and minor criminal disputes in their own courts, but the opportunities this provided for manipulation and corruption were all too apparent. This experiment was followed by an attempt to use the councils of elders that traditionally administered African law, and a policy of developing Native Tribunals began.[84] The chiefs were excluded from the tribunals. The members were appointed by the Provincial Commissioner after some effort at informal consultation, ostensibly from the ranks of the traditional elders and other locally influential persons. It is worth mentioning that the essential ethos of the tribunals was shifted from that of the traditional indigenous objectives of reconciliation and conflict resolution to the administrative objective of enforcement and punishment of civil and minor criminal infractions.[85]

It should also be noted here that the competence of the tribunals in administering criminal law was doubtful. Indeed, there was considerable confusion about what law the tribunals actually administered. The tribunals were also troubled by the problem of corruption. The tribunal elders received only meager salaries from the government that they supplemented by the traditional method of collecting fees from the parties in case. This practice led to a suspicion among many administrators of widespread corruption in tribunals that was difficult to prove.[86] For most Africans, the Native Tribunals were thus not substantive developments of traditionally legitimate institutions and practices, but rather, along with the chiefs, an integral part of the structure of colonial domination. However, for a crucial minority in African-occupied areas, they provided an additional source of power and wealth and another element sustaining their consent to the acquiescence in the colonial presence.[87]

Thus, colonial administrators recognized corruption and related abuses in the administrative structure of colonial rule, but, more often than not, they did nothing to discourage or stamp out extortionate practices.[88] Corruption thus became part of the colonial administration almost from its inception. Given this background, it can be argued that corruption is not a new phenomenon in Kenyan history. Of importance to this study, at independence, the postcolonial state inherited the colonial administrative and economic structures, and with it inherited corrupt practices too.

In fact, since independence, Kenya's public sector has been characterized by bureaucratic political inefficiency and corruption. While inefficiency has manifested itself in government's inability to implement the country's development plans, corruption has led to the misuse of authority for personal gain, in the form of diversion of public resources, outright theft of funds, and the granting of favors to personal acquaintances by the civil servants, politicians, and heads of parastatals.[89] As a case in point, the Agricultural Finance Corporation (AFC), the Kenya Seed Company (KSC), and the National Cereals and Produce Board (NCPB), among other state-run corporations, have been infested with inefficiency and corrupt practices that in one way or another have continued to block the country's economic growth.

Specifically, the AFC was established in October 1963. Its main objective was to assist in the development of the country's agricultural sector, by making government loans available to both large and small scale farmers. The funds were aimed at supporting food and commodity production in various parts of the country. As part of government policy, AFC funds were also extended to livestock keepers, particularly those raising dairy animals on one hand, and beef cattle on the other; this was designed to increase production to meet the needs of the local and export markets.[90] Generally, since the 1960s, the AFC has operated as a specialized farm credit institution that only offers agricultural loans and does not lend to other sectors of the economy. Moreover, it does not take deposits or provide any other financial services. Administratively, it is an integral part of government bureaucracy rather than an independent financial institution. This is also due to the fact that it is mainly funded by the Kenyan government and external donors. This also means that as a government agency, it is supposed to be more accessible to *wananchi* (citizens) and provide services according to the agricultural needs of the country.[91]

However, the AFC like other state corporations (e.g., the KSC) has been riddled with corruption among high-ranking office holders. It is known for mainly serving the interests of the politically connected, barely meeting the needs of the smallholding producer who needs its services most. For instance, independent newspapers such as the *Daily Nation* and *Economic Review* among other publications in Kenya have, over the years, given extensive coverage to how a good number of Kenyan politicians have identified AFC as an agency well-placed to deliver personal patronage, either as a source of loans for themselves, or employment, and loans to their supporters and kin.[92]

It should also be mentioned here that government finance corporations like any other state corporations were run by presidential appointees, most of whom were by no means experts in banking and financial matters. More disturbing was the fact that state financial corporations (AFC included) are not subject to inspection and reporting requirements that commercial banks go through, and are not monitored by the Central Bank of Kenya. Thus, it is not surprising that they are plagued with corrupt practices, inefficiency, and financial mismanagement, at times eventual collapse, without realizing their assigned duties of enhancing the country's economic development.

The activities of the AFC illustrate more than a misappropriation of state funds; they show poor planning on the part of the government, in this case, in the allocation of credit needed to enhance countrywide crop development as a step toward striving for national food security. Therefore, it can be argued that there is need for an overhaul of government planning for allocation of credit to producers and accountability for its distribution. Besides, the government needs to streamline its lending and loan repayment mechanism and the auditing of state funds. AFC funds, among others, must be based on accountability and transparency, as opposed to corrupt means, if the government is indeed serious in striving for the country's socioeconomic development.

The KSC was formed in 1964, and ever since then it has been the main producing and selling body of hybrid/improved maize seed among other seeds (e.g., vegetable seed) needed by farmers in Kenya.[93] However, Kenyan farmers have complained from time to time about the highly priced and yet low quality seed supplied by the KSC, leading to low productivity, with far-reaching consequences on their earnings and the farming sector as a whole. However, since the KSC is a state-run corporation, nothing much has been done to look into the plight of farmers.

In the early 1980s, the Kenyan government established the NCPB as a state-run corporation to deal mainly with the marketing of cereals. Since then, it has monopolized the buying, processing, and marketing of maize and to some extent, wheat in Kenya. However, the management control that is in place at the NCPB does not provide quality service to maize and wheat farmers; it leaves them to the hazards of a poor marketing practice (e.g., delayed payment for produce delivered, and too low prices, compared to expenses incurred by farmers on inputs), while they (NCPB office holders) immerse themselves in management malpractice and corruption. This is more the reason why the formation of a power-sharing structure—that is involvement of farmers in the management of cereals (especially marketing of the produce)—may just provide the necessary relief for Kenyan farmers.

Other sections of the Kenyan society infested with corruption are the police force, the judiciary, as well as the private sector among others. As a matter of fact, a report released by the Kenyan chapter of an international watchdog on graft—Transparency International (TI) in January 2002— noted that the police force was perceived to be the most corrupt government department. According to the report, the most notorious bribe takers in the police force are traffic police, officers on patrols, at report desks, and investigators.[94]

For instance, traffic police have developed many creative ways of collecting bribes (mainly in the form of money) in order to avoid arrest. Some are known to operate from kiosks and butcheries near traffic police checkpoints, the most common areas of soliciting bribes from motorists. Specifically, commuter-taxi (popularly known in Kenya as *matatu*) drivers and touts and other motorists are known to bribe police officers at road-blocks through handshakes, dropping crumpled currency notes, placing notes in driving licenses, leaving money with third parties at kiosks, butcheries, and petrol stations. In some cases, road users (motorists, cyclists, and pedestrians) are not well-versed with various fines on traffic offenses, and consequently are easily intimidated by traffic police officers into giving bribes. Moreover, money collected as bribes by police officers at roadblocks and traffic checkpoints is shared with senior police officers. Given the rot in sections of the police force, the Kenyan public has lost confidence in the country's police force as a whole.

In 2002, the Kenyan chapter of TI released another report ranking two other government departments, apart from the police, as the most corrupt in the country: the Ministry of Public Works and the Immigration Department. The report was immediately condemned by the two departments that denied the allegations. In the report, the Mombasa Town Council was named as the place where a bribe was most likely to be demanded, followed by the Prisons Department, Ministry of Lands, and the Attorney General's Chambers.[95] It should also be noted here that the Attorney General's Chambers is the heart of the country's legal system. Given the fact that it was listed as one of the corrupt departments, it clearly indicates the level of corruption in Kenya's judi-cial system. In fact, the Kenyan public and professionals, amongst them lawyers, have made known their sentiments to the government about the kind of judges and other members of the judiciary that currently run the country's legal system. In particular, members of the judiciary are known to be corrupt and unprofessional in the dispensation of justice. For instance, many magistrates and judges are known to receive bribes (e.g., large sums of money) and consequently they are liable to throw out cases or lessen sentence for those involved in crime. In such incidents, those involved in crime may be well-to-do members of the society, among them senior government officials and their kin. Generally, the judiciary in Kenya is tainted with allegations of corruption, inefficiency, and lack of professionalism.

According to TI's 2002 ranking, Kenya was adjudged as the sixth most corrupt country in the world. Kenya's level of perception of corruption was surpassed only by Bangladesh, Nigeria, Paraguay, Madagascar, and war-ravaged Angola.[96] Kenya's corruption was reported to involve government officials, mainly demanding bribes (in the form of money) from members of the public as well as from local and foreign investors. It was further reported that they also demand free shares and directorships in private businesses. In addition, they demand fully paid trips and scholarships (for themselves and their kin) to enable them pursue their businesses and further studies inside and outside the country. As noted by TI Chairman, Peter Eigen, "Kenya's political elites and their cronies continue to take kickbacks at every opportunity."[97] He further noted that "hand in glove with corrupt business people, they are trapping the whole nation in poverty and hampering sustainable development."[98] TI concludes that corruption in Kenya is rampant, affecting all government institutions, the private sector, as well as the country's citizens.

Generally, corruption remains one of the greatest problems affecting Kenya's socioeconomic development. As a matter of fact, the decline in agricultural production, growing unemployment, and more than a half of the country's population living in absolute poverty are partly attributable to the fact that the corrupt elite in Kenya have acquired their riches at the expense of ordinary citizens.[99] As noted by Aseka, in over three decades of independence, corruption has created multimillionaires in Africa (Kenya included), while plunging into misery, nearly a half a billion human beings. Moreover, revelations of high-level corruption in the 1994 Annual Report of the Auditor General, generously advertised by the press, were deeply embarrassing to the state elite.[100] The fact that the states elites have never been fully able to muzzle such reports is a tribute both to a few courageous civil servants and journalists who risk their careers to pursue these investigations with a desire to live in a corruption- free Kenya. It also illustrates the fact that Kenyans are ready to fight and eliminate corruption, but, the political will of the ruling elite is still wanting.

Most of the funds in Kenya meant to meet the country's budgetary needs are lost to corruption and theft of public resources. As observed by Simeon Nyachae, the most amazing feature of this is that in the absence of political will on the part of the Kenyan government to fight corruption, a weak judiciary and an overpoliticized economic management environment, it is frustrating to hardworking Kenyans to read in audit reports and newspapers the colossal sums of public funds lost, year in year out, through corruption.[101] Nyachae further notes that until a system of firm and decisive governance that will not tolerate corruption is instituted, and until Kenyans have mechanisms for punishing the many overnight millionaires who run the government through their mobile phones, managing the budget will permanently remain elusive.[102]

While Kenya relies mainly on foreign aid from governments and loans from local and international banks for the country's socioeconomic development, most of these funds are lost through corrupt practices. For example, by April 2002, nonperforming and unsecured loans from local banks in the hands of the politically connected people accounted for about 39 percent of the total credit advances and this had affected and continues to affect the banking industry. What the godfathers of the bad debt forget is that, most of this money is loaned out of depositors' funds in public institutions like the National Bank of Kenya and the Kenya Commercial Bank. Some of these funds are banked in institutions out of the country where it is helping other economies grow. It is clearly immoral to siphon funds from the local economy to help other economies to grow.[103] This is not only theft as well as corruption of the highest order, but, a criminal offence.

In sum, corruption remains one of the greatest problems of the Kenyan economy. It undermines economic development by introducing distortion and inefficiency in the economy. Not only does it preclude ordinary citizens, especially the poor, from access to public services, but it also makes them poorer by making them pay for services they should not pay for. Consequently, in Kenya, corruption has enriched the politically connected at the expense of ordinary hardworking citizens, both rural and urban dwellers, most of them who have been "boxed into a corner of absolute poverty." Indeed, unless corruption is eradicated, it has and will continue to have devastating impact on Kenya's socioeconomic development.

The State and Human Rights

While Kenya has been tainted by corrupt practices, the country's record on human rights is equally sordid. As a matter of fact, Kenya's ruling elite, especially during the Moi era, had no respect for human rights. Yet, human rights are regarded as inherent in the human being and are not surrendered to the government when people form a political community. They are necessary for human beings to live in dignity, to fulfill their potential, and to satisfy their physical and spiritual needs among others. They empower citizens and residents, giving them a central role in decision making in organs of the state, and the right to associate to protect their vital interests against violation by the state. They limit the power of the state and protect against the excesses of "majoritarianism." Many rights, such as the right to vote, the freedom of expression and of the media, and access to information, apart from accountability of public authorities are necessary for the establishment and protection of democracy. They justify special treatment of minorities and other disadvantaged groups in society. Rights define the relationship of the state to the people; in this way, they provide a framework for the entire constitution. Therefore, today is it is hard to imagine a constitution that does not contain a bill of rights.[104]

As a matter of fact, the Kenyan Constitution has a Bill of Rights. Chapter 5 of the Constitution underlines protection of fundamental rights and freedoms of the individual. These include the right to life, liberty, security, and protection of the law; the right to freedom of conscience, expression, assembly and association, and the right to privacy. The constitution also protects the individual from being subjected to torture or to any cruel, inhuman, or degrading treatment. The penal code further sets out the punishment to be meted out to any person who subjects another to such treatment.

Yet, Kenya's human rights performance has been challenged both internally and internationally for its poor record. Accusations are legion about gross violation and denial of rights and liberties including the sanctity to secure protection of the law and even right to life. Numerous cases have been highlighted of violations of such fundamental rights and freedoms enshrined in the Constitution as protection against arbitrary search or entry, protection against inhuman treatment, freedom of conscience, freedom of expression, freedom of assembly and association, and freedom of movement. Such accusations have often met with vehement government denials, all without avail.

A good example to illustrate Kenya's poor human rights record is the case of Robert Ouko. Ouko, who was foreign minister in Moi's government, was murdered in mid-February 1990 under mysterious circumstances. At the request of the Kenyan government, a team of Scotland Yard investigators from Britain began an investigation into the murder on February 20, 1990. The final report on the same was delivered to the Kenyan government on September 28, 1990, and had not been released to the public by the end of 1990.[105] In fact, the report was shelved without any explanation. In a twist of events, President Moi who had promised to find and punish perpetrators, appointed a Judicial Commission of Inquiry on October 1, 1990 to continue the investigation into Ouko's death. At the end of the year, the commission was still recording testimonies.[106] In another twist of events, President Moi disbanded the commission in 1991, before it had completed its work. By the end of 2002, there had been no official conclusion on the death of Ouko.

Torture is proscribed under the constitution, but since the early 1980s, there have been credible reports of police brutality and abuse of prisoners by those in charge. For instance, Koigi wa Wamwere and his co-accused, who were charged with treason in late 1990, alleged that they were tortured and subjected to inhuman treatment. In an affidavit filed on December 17, 1990, Wamwere claimed to have been subjected to psychological abuse and physical discomfort in an effort to compel him to make false statements.[107] Generally, cases of suspects claiming that they were tortured by the police during interrogation are very common. A number of them have reported to the court that they were stripped naked during interrogation and kept incommunicado in dark rooms flooded with water for hours, even days. In such a situation, they were not allowed to speak freely with their attorneys, relatives, or other visitors.

In many cases, the number of which is difficult to gauge, Kenyans have been held in police custody for periods ranging from a few hours to several days (even months) without being charged or officially detained under specific authority. Particularly in the 1980s and early 1990s, the purpose seemed to be the intimidation of government critics. Besides, some of the government critics have been threatened with exile or were forced into exile by the government as a means of intimidation or punishment. As a case in point, one of the government's most outspoken critics, Gibson Kamau Kuria (an attorney by profession), was allowed to leave the country on July 11, 1990, after spending four days in the U.S. embassy in Nairobi. Kuria, a former political detainee, went into hiding on July 5, 1990, to evade detention, after former cabinet ministers Kenneth Matiba and Charles Rubia were detained. Kuria had been detained earlier in 1987 for ten months as he prepared to sue the government for allegedly torturing prisoners. Consequently, he received the 1988 Robert Kennedy Memorial Human Rights Award, though the government refused to give him a passport to attend the award ceremony in the United States. As a matter of fact, in 1989, his colleague, Paul Muite, went there and accepted the award on his behalf. But the Kenyan government confiscated his (Muite's) passport when he returned home. The passport was later on returned to him after a series of court cases.[108]

It should also be noted here that there are no known instances of Kenyan citizenship being revoked for political reasons. Besides, the Kenyan government does not generally prohibit emigration of its citizens.

However, in some cases, it does prevent citizens (usually its critics) from traveling abroad. Furthermore, the government does not regard the issuance of passports to its citizens as a right and reserves the authority to issue or deny passports at its discretion or to request their return.

Generally, the government reacts negatively to criticisms of its human rights record, at home and abroad, and it discourages Kenyans from providing external and internal human rights groups with information. President Moi, from time to time, publicly attacked expressions of concern from outside groups on the human rights situation in Kenya, particularly comments on the poor state of the country's prisons, as interference in Kenya's internal affairs. Yet, it is true that prison conditions are poor and sometimes dangerous to life and health. For instance, it is common knowledge in Kenya that prisoners are underfed; lack adequate clothing and bedding; have little or no access to medical care; and there are outbreaks of dysentry among other ailments due to unsanitary conditions and deaths are common phenomena. According to the Center of Human Rights and Democracy (CHRD), in most police cells, more than 70 suspects are heaped in a ten by ten feet cell, a situation that endangers the lives of inmates. Furthermore, as noted by human rights activists, suspects are tortured, harassed, and even raped by the police. In some cases, women inmates are removed from the cells by the police at night to engage in sex with crooked police officers, before being returned to custody at dawn. At the same time, relatives of suspects held at various police stations in the country are, most of the time, harassed and are allowed to see their arrested family members only after giving bribes to the police. Besides, the police are known to hold on to suspects at the police stations longer than required by the law (without charging them to court), hoping that in the process of waiting the suspects' relatives would strike a deal (through bribery) for their freedom.[109] Generally, there is rampant violation of human rights in Kenya's prisons as well as police stations.

The Kenyan government's main defense on its human rights record was based on its perception of what it referred to as the security of the state. Yet, it is common knowledge in Kenya that the state has arbitrarily interfered with privacy, family, and home of its citizens without any link to the issue of security of the state. For example, in May 1990, the City Commission demolished Muoroto shanty village in the central part of Nairobi, leaving several thousand people homeless. Once again, on November 21, 1990, the City Commission demolished Kibagare village on the western outskirts of Nairobi, leaving about 30,000 people homeless.[110] The government offered little explanation, except the claim that slums were inhabited by criminal gangs who constituted a security risk. More recently, in 2001 and 2002, kiosks operated as the only means of survival for a number of Kenyans in the country's urban centers, in particular, in Nairobi, Mombasa, and Kisumu, were demolished, and according to government officials, the demolition was part of an effort to clean up the urban environment.

Given the gross record of human rights violations in Kenya, there is need for state reconstitution to take human rights into consideration. This is also in line with the fact that Kenya is part of the international community and it is a party to a number of international human rights treaties (such as the rights of the child and the elimination of discrimination against women). Under these treaties, the country is supposed to report periodically on its own performance in meeting the standards laid down. Under its treaty obligations, the Kenyan government is required to let human rights and related organizations within the country have the opportunity to comment on the government's human rights performance. Furthermore, the constitution obligates the Kenyan government to respect the human rights of its citizens and to publish and make public a regular a report on its human rights record. The government is also required, under the constitution, to provide adequate opportunity for public discussion of its human rights report. However, Kenya's performance in meeting this reporting requirement has been dismal.[111]

Under the constitution, it is the obligation of the Kenyan government to make sure that the basic rights of society for food and shelter are met. The government also has a duty to ensure solidarity rights, that is, rights that pertain to the whole community: the right to clean, healthy, and sustainable environment, to peace, to nurturing of one's culture, and to development. Furthermore, citizens should have the right to education as well as employment without favor or discrimination. With regard to employment, the work situation should also involve certain rights: the right to choose one's occupation, the right to fair treatment within work, to equal pay for men, women, and people with disabilities, and to adequate standards of health and safety at work. These rights are a step forward in taking care of the needs of members of the society, in particular women and those with disabilities who tend to be marginalized in matters of resource allocation.

Generally, these rights are important for the community/state as well as for the individual. The Kenyan state must achieve, "at the very least, minimum levels of each of the rights" and to give priority to achieving this minimum level. Beyond that, the duty of the state is to "respect, protect, promote and fulfill" the rights. Respect means not to interfere itself with the rights; protection is against infringement by others; promotion involves education and encouragement; fulfillment involves the positive action of the state to achieve the right. In fact, this way of analyzing the duty of the state fits perfectly with its duty with respect to civil and political rights too.[112]

With regard to political rights, the rights of political participation, including the right to vote, freedom of speech, of assembly, of association, and the right of obtaining access to information held by the government—often called the freedom of information—should be upheld by the state, and more important, should be enshrined in the constitution. Furthermore, the rights of people accused of criminal offenses to fair treatment when arrested and detained, and to a fair trial should also be upheld by the state and endorsed in the constitution. Moreover, the rights of prisoners, for example, right to visitation by attorneys and family members, and conjugal rights, should also be upheld by the state. Generally, the duty of the state is to promote and fulfill fundamental human rights in society.

The State and Gender

Both the Kenyan government and the public recognize gender disparities in various sectors like education and business. Although roughly equal numbers of girls and boys enroll in the first year of primary education, fewer girls than boys proceed to secondary and higher education levels. As a matter of fact, men outnumber women almost two to three in higher education. Girls drop out mainly due to social, economic, and cultural factors. For instance, poverty is a worrisome problem facing most Kenyan families. However, much as poverty permeates the country, it is the Kenyan women who bear the brunt of poverty in the country. Whenever parents are unable to raise school fees for their children, girls are always the first ones to be forced to drop out of school.

Traditional culture and attitudes have hindered women's advancement in education. Although the Moi government passed a law providing for free and compulsory education for boys and girls at primary level, the traditional practices of elderly men marrying young, school-age girls continues with impunity. The practice, for example, among the Maasai of Kenya, sees girls as young as 10 years being married off to men as old as 60 years. In this case, the affected girls are forced to drop out of school and will never realize their full potential in life.

Worse still, the Kenyan society is a patriarchical society, and by virtue of tradition, women are not given much consideration when it comes to inheriting property, especially land from their parents. Yet, land is the main means of production, and since inheritance is passed on to male members of the society, very few women own property or businesses. Ironically, in Kenya's rural areas, women account for 75 percent of the total agricultural work force. They work on their parents' farms (before marriage) and on their husbands' farms (while in marriage), without owning the land. It should also be stressed here that legally, women can own property and businesses (only if they can purchase them), and are increasingly active in the modern economy. However, the number of women who own property in Kenya, and serving in professional roles is still limited. As a matter of fact, female unemployment in Kenya is double that of men. But women sometimes receive lower rates of pay than men who perform the same jobs. Disparities in fringe benefits also occur; for example, some businesses give housing allowances to men but not to married women.[113] Thus, low levels of education by women, coupled with retrogressive sociocultural practices have resulted in women's low participation and representation in decision-making positions. Consequently, they lack full access to economic opportunities and resources.

According to the United Nations Population Fund (UNFPA), no fewer than 1.3 billion people worldwide are trapped in the cycle of poverty.[114] Men and women stuck in grinding poverty lack real choices, opportunities, and basic services to improve their situations. Due to inequality and discrimination, women suffer the most. Besides, the World Bank's development indicators for 2001 show quite starkly that the poorest mothers face the highest risk of death. For instance, globally, every minute, a woman dies during pregnancy and childbirth due to lack of adequate care and proper treatment, all pegged to poverty.[115]

A 1999 service provision assessment survey carried out by Kenya's Ministry of Health and the National Council for Population Development indicated that many maternal facilities lacked the equipment, supplies, and medicines to handle obstetric complications.[116] Generally, though women make up about 52 percent of Kenya's population of about 30 million people, more than three quarters of the women do not have access to choice of safe obstetric care. A considerable number of Kenyan women die each year from mostly preventable causes related to pregnancy and childbirth.

Perhaps, nowhere is the need for productive health services more urgent than in the fight against HIV/AIDS. Based on the findings of United Nations Population Fund (UNFPA) globally, everyday at least 14,000 people are newly infected by HIV/AIDS, and half are young people under the age of 25 years.[117] Many know little about the disease and how the virus is transmitted. Of all groups, women and the youth are the most vulnerable. In some African countries (Kenya included), teenage girls are five times more likely to be infected with HIV/AIDS than boys of the same age.[118]

Related to productive health, it should also be mentioned here that Kenya's population growth rate substantially declined from 4.1 percent per annum in 1979 to 2.3 percent per annum in 2002.[119] In fact, Kenya is lauded across the population development circles for being the first sub-Saharan African country to adopt an official family-planning policy. The main objective of the policy was to reduce the population growth rate that was considered to be too high for the achievement of the country's development objectives. As a result, since the early1980s, Kenya has witnessed a reduction in the rate of population growth, but the government and citizens alike are still clamoring for more reduction that would practically translate to two children per family. This can be achieved by integrating population needs in development process. Both men and women should be involved in population development processes in order to protect the integrity of the family.

Safe motherhood should be encouraged by concerned state officials (especially those in the health sector and clinicians), given the fact that, in Kenya, an estimated 590 out of every 100,000 women die during childbirth.[120] Therefore, complications during pregnancy should be tackled to ward off problems during childbirth. Nongovernmental organizations should focus on carrying out research and set aside resources to combat sexually transmitted diseases, for example, HIV/AIDS that put reproductive health in jeopardy. They should undertake this task with the realization that smaller and healthier families, fewer sexually transmitted infections, and safer childbirth are major benefits to society and form part of the agenda for reconstituting the health sector. Reproductive health services provided by the state and nongovernmental organizations can empower women and young people by providing them with HIV/AIDS life-saving messages and skills that can help stop HIV/AIDS from spreading and reduce suffering and socioeconomic disruption. The greatest deficits in access to health services can be found in the poorest segments of the population. By channeling state resources to healthcare, several important objectives can be realized: lives can be saved, population growth stabilized, the spread of HIV/AIDS slowed, and gender equality fostered (since both male and female will have access to same health facilities).

Thus, as part of state reconstitution, there is need for various interventions in the domain of women's reproductive health and Kenya's health sector in general. Therefore, it is the duty of the Kenyan state and nongovernmental development organizations to fund reproductive health in the country; increase access to family planning (particularly among the country's rural and urban poor); combine family planning and poverty alleviation programs to save lives; and reach young people with information and services.

Gender equity is part of the key to sustainability. Sadly, despite being the key to development, women are less likely than men to own land, or have access to credit, adequate employment, or economic security in old age. Besides, girls from poor households receive less schooling, less food, less healthcare, and less pay for their work. In this case, better education and income for both men and women will translate to better standards of living.

Women invest more of their income and time in their families than most men. When women engage in development, families, societies, and nations gain substantially—economically, politically, socially, and culturally. Thus, it can be argued that when women are empowered—through laws that ensure their rights, healthcare that ensures their well-being, and education that ensures their active participation in the country's development agenda—the benefits go far beyond the individual; they help the family, the community, and the nation. Therefore, while the Kenyan state, nongovernmental organizations, and their partners work to close the poverty gap, they must also work to close the gender gap.

In sum, the Kenyan state and its partners should work to promote healthcare and universal education; increase access to credit facilities (particularly targeting the poor, regardless of gender); create income-generating opportunities, partly by adopting cost-effective and efficient technologies to promote industrial and agricultural enterprises that will benefit members of the society (especially the rural and urban poor regardless of gender); pass laws allowing women to own land; and take culturally sensitive action to remove barriers to women's economic and political empowerment. It is crucial to bear in mind that for Kenya to develop, the state has the responsibility of promoting gender issues by reducing inequality and enhancing both male and female's participation in development.

The Rape of the Environment

Besides issues pertaining to human rights and gender disparities in development, a great deal of concern in Kenya today is expressed over environmental degradation that has occurred in various ways. For instance, pollution of land, air and water, waste disposal problems, unplanned building development (especially in Kenya's urban areas), and deforestation (mainly for timber and charcoal used as a source of energy for cooking in homes) are main causes of compliant.

According to a 2002 audit report carried out by the Economic Commission for Africa (ECA), Kenya's environmental management is among Africa's worst. Of the 38 African countries audited for environmental sustainability from 1975 to 2002, Kenya is third from the bottom, ahead only of Tunisia and Morocco (on top of the chart is Gabon, Burkina Faso, and Guinea, in that order). It should also be noted here that the Addis Ababa-based ECA is the regional United Nations arm mandated to support the continent's 53 member states' economic and social development, foster regional integration, and promote international cooperation.[121]

In the ECA report, four indicators—forest cover, arable land, carbon dioxide emissions, and population density—were used to capture a country's natural capital and how it is managed. Countries like Kenya, at the bottom rank of the ratings, are reported to have little forest cover, high carbon dioxide emissions, and a high population density. Gabon which tops the list is described as having reduced its carbon emissions and having the greatest forest cover, and low population growth and density. Kenya finds itself in this position, as noted by the ECA's report, because it pursued poor environmental management policies. As a case in point, between 1986 and 1994, an estimated 46,945 hectares of forest land in various parts of the country were lost through the felling of trees to meet industrial and domestic needs. By the year 2000, the Mount Kenya region had lost 80,000 acres of tree cover to the timber industry as well as to charcoal burners/traders. Furthermore, in 2000 alone, 1,393 acres of Nairobi's Karura forest were also lost through tree felling: Maragoli forest in Vihiga district had been completely destroyed.[122] Worse still, in 2001, the Kenyan government, through its Ministry of Environment and Natural Resources, de-gazetted 167,000 acres of forested areas, 10 percent of the entire national forested land, and opened them up for human settlement as well as farming enterprises.[123] Undoubtedly, this new government policy raised eyebrows among Kenyans on the role of the Kenyan state in environmental sustainability. This was due to the fact that after the new policy was put in place, it was estimated that Kenya's forest cover dwindled to 1.7 percent, against the internationally approved 2 percent limit.[124]

Generally, as noted by the ECA report, deforestation is one of the most pressing environmental problems in many African countries. Studies indicate that between 1990 and 2000, Africa's annual deforestation averaged 0.8 percent, the highest rate throughout the world. While most forests are lost through the massive illegal logging, a huge number is said to be lost through a demand for firewood and charcoal.[125]

Countries in various parts of the world are experiencing rapid loss of forest cover, and already are or are going to be highly susceptible to climate change, drought, cyclones, landslides, floods, and bushfires. In the case of Kenya, there are already fears that, the country's rate of forest depletion might make it more vulnerable to climate change and floods. As a matter of fact, in Murang'a (in Central Province of Kenya), huge landslides and flooding linked to deforestation in 2002 alone left deaths in their trails. Thus, any climate change and shifts in rainfall pattern (now and in the future) would have devastating environmental impact on Kenya, as well as various parts of Africa and the world as a whole.

More frightening, as far as environmental degradation in Kenya is concerned, is the growing trend of allocating public places, parks, and forests to individuals—mainly powerful politicians, their relatives, and civil servants for conversion into commercial infrastructures. In virtually all such cases, there seems to be the least concern, even in the rapidly expanding urban centers such as Nairobi, Kisumu, and Mombasa, for the long-term preservation of spaces for essential public facilities such as schools, health and recreational institutions, cemeteries, shopping centers, parks, and gardens among others, let alone for environmental protection, an issue of the immediate future.[126]

As a matter of fact, large portions of the historic City Park and Karura Forest, both on the outskirts of Nairobi, have been dished out to politicians and bureaucrats, who in turn have sold them for untold fortunes to private as well as commercial developers. Besides, the indigenous forest bordering the Jamhuri Park in Nairobi is virtually gone, wiping out a rich diversity of plants and animals that were invaluably beneficial to the city's human future. In its replacement are residential homes (mainly for rental) among other commercial entities. To the east and southeast of Nairobi city, unplanned godowns and factories, as well as residential build-up, are swallowing the Embakasi plains and encroaching on the Nairobi Game Park. Large proportions of Wilson Airport on the outskirts of Nairobi have also gone to private developers. If unchecked, the trend is likely to trigger large-scale extinction of species. Ironically, ecotourism associated with Kenya's animal and vegetation species contributes almost a third of the total tourism industry, currently one of the largest sectors (in terms of income generation) of Kenya's economy.[127]

With the seemingly uncontrollable scramble for open spaces, parks, and forests, urban Kenya is rapidly and irreversibly becoming home for planned as well as unplanned commercial infrastructures, without any consideration for environmental conservation. At a time when a considerable number of countries in the world are spending billions in designing their cities and towns to pave way for green parks in the midst of concrete infrastructures, Kenyans (particularly the bureaucrats) are busy desecrating the last remains of once-lush spaces in the country's urban centers. Kenyan authorities, it would appear, are yet to realize that it is easier to prevent environmental ruin than cure it.

Kenya's problem is lack of proper environmental management policies, and it is no wonder that the country was heavily criticized for it during the 2002 Johannesburg World Summit on Sustainable Development. Environmentalists and conservationists believe that with proper policies, forests in Kenya as well as other parts of the world, can be used renewably and sustainably. Therefore, the Kenyan government and citizens alike have an obligation to protect forests and engage in vigorous and continuous afforestation programs. As part of environmental conservation, the Kenyan government needs to practice, and where applicable, put in place policies that require waste minimization and recycling; address issues of water conservation and purification; and promote the use and development of energy-efficient technology, and the use of renewable resources (e.g., invest in solar energy). The government must set up and ensure the effective functioning of a system of environmental impact assessment and environmental audit and monitoring; and ensure that environmental standards enforced in Kenya keep up with those in other developing countries internationally.[128] Thus, both the Kenyan state and Kenyan citizens have to prioritize environmental conservation and sustainability as part of the country's development agenda to enhance human development now and in [the] future.

The Kibaki Era: Toward the Reconstitution of The State?

The Kenyan political landscape experienced a seismic change during the 2002 elections: The Rainbow Coalition, an alliance of political parties, defeated the ruling Kenyan African National Union (KANU) that had ruled Kenya since independence. Mwai Kibaki, a former KANU chieftain and one-time vice president of Kenya, during the Moi era, was elected president. The defeat of the ruling KANU was greeted with great joy across Kenya. The majority of Kenyans were excited because the defeat of KANU portended well for the future, especially after more than four decades of political repression and economic and social malaise. So, despite the new president's previous association with the KANU cabal,

Kenyans accepted his claim of being a "born again democrat." In his inaugural address, President Kibaki fueled the hopes for renewal, when he outlined the basic caveats of his government's campaign to reconstitute the Kenyan state; they included the establishment of a new political order based on multiparty democracy, pluralism, and the respect for fundamental human rights; the institution of economic reforms, including a concerted effort to end the scourge of rampant corruption; and addressing the myriad social problems confronting Kenya. As part of the state reconstitution efforts, the Kibaki administration established new state institutions such as the Anti-Corruption Commission and set into motion the redesigning of some of the existing state institutions.

Although a detailed assessment of the state of the reconstitution project under the Kibaki regime needs to be conducted, the preliminary results indicate that the new Kenyan government is facing major challenges. For example, the anticorruption campaign is failing to contain the spread of this "menacing disease" in the public sector. In fact, critics argue that the hurdles being experienced by the anticorruption campaign and the broader state reconstitution process are the resultant of the lack of commitment by the Kibaki administration to serious reform.

Consequently, the Kibaki government is beginning to lose public support. Clearly, if the state reconstitution project is to get on track, then the Kibaki regime must demonstrate through deeds that it is determined to reconstruct the negligent and corrupt Kenyan state for the betterment of the majority of the people of Kenya.

The Kenya We Want: Reconstituting and Reconstructing the Kenyan State

Based on the above analyses of various problems that have crippled the Kenyan state, there is an imperative to reconstitute and reconstruct it so that it can meet the needs of its citizens. However, it should be pointed out that the journey on the road to reconstituting and reconstructing the Kenyan state will be long and arduous. This is partly due to the fact that the Kenyan government under the leadership of both Presidents Kenyatta and Moi lasted for too long and they both treated the Kenyan state as their personal property. Even within corporate boardrooms of companies, long tenure breeds vested interests and stagnation of ideas. An analysis of the public sector in Kenya since independence points to the fact that both Kenyatta and Moi treated the civil service as their personal property. Over the years, together with their cohorts, the two presidents filled the expanding ranks of the civil service with political appointees and selected top administrators on the basis of personal loyalties. In turn, top civil servants treated their administrative duties as personal service to the president and behaved as if obedience and respect to the head of state was most important. The virtues and principles of running bureaucracies such as hierarchical authority, expertise, neutrality, and efficiency were totally ignored. The consequence was that a considerable number of civil servants was forced to become corrupt and to reluctantly become, in this case, accomplices of corrupt politicians. Distribution of state jobs by political patrons to their followers eroded meritocracy and efficiency in the civil service and demoralized honest public servants.

Therefore, as part of state reconstitution, Kenya's public sector needs to be reformed. In retrospect, Kenya as well as others African states made the wrong assumption when they uncritically agreed with the World Bank prescription that the starting point of reforming the civil service was by way of "down-sizing" the state.[129] It is now clear that as part of state reconstitution (specifically in the post–Moi era), the Kenyan government needs to come up with ways of depoliticizing the civil service. This will involve comprehensive and far-reaching reforms that will include recruitment of managers and top civil servants based on merit and not on political patronage. Besides, the Kenyan state will have to reinstitute meritocratic procedures (eroded mainly during the Moi era) for hiring and promoting civil servants.

Kenya's political system needs to be reconstituted, especially in its role as a wealth-generating institution. Kenyans would like to see civil servants as well as other members of the society make their living and generate income from a reformed public sector; and from the productive agricultural and industrial/business sector than from political patronage. In this case, there is need for economic reform, given the fact that the long-serving Kenyan presidents, Moi in particular, were opposed to economic reforms, especially, when such reforms threatened to eliminate the privileges and rents that their cronies reaped from the state.

Therefore, in the post–Moi era, economic reforms, if implemented properly, may diminish or completely eliminate some of the patronage resources altogether. Take, for example, the case of unsecured loans acquired by the politically well connected from state-owned banks, such as the National Bank of Kenya and Kenya Commercial Bank. As noted earlier, the National Bank of Kenya has been crippled by political loans. If the post–Moi government decides to fully embrace the policy of privatization of state-owned banks, then it will insulate these banks from powerful rent seekers. The state-owned banks will be relieved of the problem of political loans and the mess they create in the banking sector and the country's economy as a whole.

It should also be emphasized here that economic reforms for the common good can only work if there is the will on the part of the country's leaders and citizens alike to implement them. Besides, one of the cardinal principles of the Kenyan Constitution is that every five years, Kenyans must have an opportunity to change their representatives in the country's political system. These same representatives/leaders are empowered by citizens to manage the country's political, economic, and social set-up, for the common good. That principle is what defines Kenya as a representative democracy. Therefore, depending on how the post–Moi transition is managed, and if the politicians elected in the December 2002 elections are people who are not anchored in the present networks of rent seekers, then the new team in office will be able to change the economic environment in Kenya in a very profound way.[130]

As part of state reconstruction, programs should be set in place to address infrastructural problems that discourage private investment, including transportation, water supply, and power generation, which were partly crippled due to corrupt practices in the Moi era. Besides corrupt practices, in the past, budgetary allocations were not guided by specific prioritization of Kenya's development needs. The Kenyan government and citizens need to focus on development programs that will help resolve the country's most intractable problems like poverty, unemployment, the challenges of malaria, spread of HIV/AIDS, and the expansion of the educational sector among others. Kenyans should target sectors that will not only aid quick economic growth and help address employment and poverty, but also sustain the inevitable expansion in the educational sector.

In the key sectors of the economy, women form the critical bedrock that sustains such sectors as small-scale farming and, to a large extent, the informal sector. In this case, long-term-oriented projects should be set in place, by both the private and the public sectors, which can give credit to the small-scale farmers and those in the informal sector (popularly known as *Jua Kali* in Kenya) to boost their income-generating activities as one way of fighting poverty. Besides, this is one way of directly targeting the improvement of Kenyan women's and family income and that of the urban and rural poor in general, and thus contributing to poverty alleviation among various groups in Kenya.

Apart from social and economic reforms, another section of the Kenyan state that needs urgent reform is the judiciary. As noted earlier, a considerable number of Kenyan judges as well as other members of the judiciary are corrupt and unprofessional in the dispensation of justice. The appointment of judges in Kenya is not through a process initiated by the Judicial Service Commission (JSC) as stipulated by the constitution. Instead, the appointments are effected through lobbying of the president by various interest groups. The president, then directs the JSC to ratify the appointments. There are no criteria used to determine the work ethics and professional standards that one should demonstrate before appointment.[131] The ideal situation should be that the JSC identifies prospective candidates and submits the names to the president for approval. It is therefore imperative that an effective, efficient, and transparent procedure of appointing judges and other judicial officers be put in place. In short, the JSC should be restructured in order to ensure that it is independent and effective and not subject to the direction and control of any other person or authority in the exercise of its functions. Membership of the JSC should be broad-based, consisting of members trained in legal matters and drawn from various sections of the society regardless of gender and stakeholders.

I support the view of Kenyan professionals, in particular, lawyers, that in its restructured form, members of the JSC should comprise persons of high moral character and proven integrity. The JSC should also carry out the following functions: (1) To recommend to the president, persons of highest integrity after rigorous vetting for appointment as judges, including the chief justice;(2) to review and make recommendations on terms and conditions of service of judges, magistrates, and other judicial officers; (3) to receive and investigate complaints against judges, magistrates, and other judicial officers, and discipline them in accordance with the law of the land. For instance, where necessary, appropriate action be taken for removal of any judges or judicial officers found guilty of misconduct; (4) to advise the government on improving efficiency in the administration of justice and access to justice, including legal aid. For instance, the present failure to ensure full legal presentation of all proceedings involving persons accused of capital offenses should be addressed;(5) there is also need to encourage gender equity in the administration of justice; and (6) last but not least, the JSC should address any other judicial function as may be prescribed by the Constitution or any other legislation enacted by parliament.[132]

In addition to the above recommendations, it can also be argued that Kenyan courts will fail to serve the public interest if their doors are effectively closed to the poor and disadvantaged. In this case, the restructured JSC should be mandated to advise the government on improving access to justice, particularly to marginalized members of the society, for example, women, those with disabilities, and the poor in general. Similarly, consideration should be given to the development of alternative methods of dispute resolution, in particular, ethnic conflicts, possibly by building on traditional local tribunals or customs as a means of enhancing access to justice.[133] Generally, the judiciary should be independent from other arms of the government for it to work efficiently. Specifically, all judicial staff should enjoy freedom from the executive, or the political patronage structure. Besides boosting efficiency in the dispensation of justice, to some extent, judicial independence could also shield the judiciary from the threat of corruption.

As noted earlier on in this chapter, the evil of corruption confronts the Kenyan state on many fronts. Corruption has continued to threaten all aspects of economic development and social order in Kenya. Even the post–Moi government has not been able to deal effectively with the menace of corruption. This may indicate that corruption has its roots in the sociopolitical structure of the country. Therefore, as part of state reconstitution, effective constitutional institutions, such as the establishment of special corruption courts are needed to fight corruption. As a matter of fact, special corruption courts were launched in Kenya on April 25, 2002, at the Nairobi law courts, by the Chief Justice, Bernard Chunga. The launching of the courts followed proposals by a team of British experts hired by the Kenyan government to assist (in terms of suggestion and recommendations) in the war against graft. The experts, led by Graham Stockwell, suggested that permanent reputable judges be appointed to run the courts. They also proposed that a team of special prosecutors be put in place to deal with corruption in both the public and private sectors. Besides the launching of corruption courts in Nairobi, similar courts will be established in various parts of the country to deal with graft-related cases.[134]

With effective institutions such as anticorruption courts in place, those found guilty of corrupt practices, for example, government officials and their cronies who have misappropriated funds meant for public projects, should be jailed and their wealth confiscated by the state for the common good. Furthermore, as a way to stamp out corruption in the country's political and economic system, those running for office, including aspiring presidential candidates, ministers, and parliamentarians, must declare their assets and account for the same, as a prerequisite to serving in a public office. High-ranking officers in the public service and state corporations, as well as private institutions, must also declare and account for their wealth. In addition, heads of state corporations and holders of key government offices should be subjected to job interviews by, for example, the Special Parliamentary Select Committees, to ensure that qualified candidates, who are free from corrupt practices, occupy office. At the same time, the war on corruption should be broad-based, involving the input of the government, the private sector, nongovernmental agencies, and Kenyan citizens. Generally, there should be a change of attitude among Kenyans toward corrupt practices. Kenyans should be ready to fight graft in their midst, specifically by refusing to receive or give bribes. All in all, collective effort is needed to uproot corruption in Kenya.

The Kenya government has taken the security of its citizens for granted. Both the ethnic violence that continues to rock the country and the high rates of crime in urban and rural areas, call for urgent attention. The country's police officers entrusted with providing security have been linked to violent crimes, for example, armed robberies, burglaries, and auto theft, as well as graft, mainly in Kenya's capital, Nairobi, and other parts of the country. However, most police officers argue that the police force lost its glory due to neglect, frustration, and isolation. They further argue that the Kenya government has neglected the country's security docket and police officers operate under very difficult conditions. For instance, they cite the case of Nairobi, and note that Nairobi's Central Police Station was built by the colonial state to serve the central business district. Over the years, Nairobi's business district has expanded and it has also experienced a huge population increase, but the Central Police Station has not been expanded or new ones established to cater to security measures in the city. At the same time, many estates and slums have sprung up in Nairobi, but very few police stations have been set up in these areas to provide security. In this case, the sluggishness on the part of the government in providing the police force with adequate facilities and equipment (e.g., arms, vehicles, and telephones among other communication gadgets) have worsened the situation, since criminals have become more violent and in some cases better-equipped than a considerable number of police officers. Ironically, most senior government officials have an average of three government vehicles at their disposal, yet some police stations do not have a single automobile. Low-ranking police personnel, for example, constables, are poorly paid and poorly housed. A police constable earns only Kshs. 4,800 (about $65) a month and a good number of them (together with their families) share houses in the police quarters. For instance, it is not rare to find two or three police families living in a house meant for only one family.[135]

Therefore, as part of state reconstitution, the Kenyan government needs to invest in the security sector. Provision of arms, vehicles, and other equipment to the police force is the government's responsibility and should be provided at all times to boost state security. Police officers need to be paid appropriately and provided with adequate housing or housing allowance to cater to their accommodation needs. The Kenyan government has no option but to invest in the country's security, given the fact that the ongoing political instability in East Africa and the Great Lakes region (Rwanda, Burundi, Uganda, Sudan, Ethiopia, and Somalia) poses a major threat to Kenya.

In addition to reconstituting the police force, the way out of incessant crime and insecurity is to improve the economy and ensure that the youth and all eligible people are engaged in gainful employment. In sum, the police force needs to be restructured to be able to protect citizens. Kenya has only about 30,000 police officers serving a population of over 30 million people. This translates to 1 police officer for every 1,000 people. The ratio recommended by the United Nations is 1 police officer to every 400 people.[136] Furthermore, police officers should be trained in matters related to human rights, conflict resolution and, public and media relations. At the same time, police officers who engage in corrupt practices and violence should be dismissed from the force. Generally, they should be dealt with in accordance with the law of the land. Arguably, there is need to develop the police force into a dynamic institution that is in touch with emerging global realities in mattes related to security and provide adequate security in the Kenyan state. Thus, there is need to reorient police officers in matters of state security and rights of the citizens right from the constable to the police commissioner. Indeed, there is need to reconstitute and reconstruct the Kenyan state to meet the needs of its citizens now and in the years to come.

Conclusion

As noted in this chapter, many different forms of social and political organizations existed in precolonial Kenya, ranging from one centralized kingdom (the Wanga Kingdom) to acephalous societies. Generally, African groups in Kenya lived in acephalous states, organized around the family, kinship group and the clan, though this did not necessarily mean that they had no government. However, with the establishment of British colonial rule in Kenya in the late nineteenth and early twentieth century, the colonial state carried with it the political thrust that eroded the autonomy of the leading village heads and clan leaders, as well as leaders of various ethnic groups. In particular, the colonial period witnessed the strengthening of state apparatus. Amongst them were the military, police force, the legal system, various government ministries, and the local government, with far reaching consequences on the traditional structure.

Nonetheless, at Kenya's independence in 1963, the same institutions set up during the colonial era were inherited by the postcolonial state. Indeed, the colonial state established social, political, and economic basis for Kenya's postcolonial administrations. However, as shown in this study, since independence, the state in Kenya has failed to deliver services to its citizens. As in other African countries, political leaders in Kenya, specifically President Kenyatta and later on President Moi and their inner cabinet members, arrogated too much power unto themselves. Moreover, corrupt practices and other forms of public malfeasance through which public funds were siphoned into private bank accounts became rife. As a result, the state ended up delivering too little to the people.

Yet at independence, Kenyans looked forward to better lives after colonialism. The leadership, in a nationalistic fervor, promised to eradicate ignorance, poverty, and disease. As a matter of fact, both the Kenyatta and Moi administrations vowed to distribute national wealth equitably, offer free education, employment, and even food for the needy. Everything was to be done in the name of the common good, general welfare, and general interest. In reality, the leaders failed to deliver on their promises. As noted by Wagona Makoba, evidence accumulated over the past three decades shows "the inability of the African state to deliver on its development promise."[137] In fact, the African state, in this case, the Kenyan state, is now perceived as the "inhibitor of social, economic and political development."[138] As a result, donor agencies have, in recent years, increasingly channeled development assistance through nongovernmental organizations and other non-state institutions because African states (Kenya included) are considered to be both inefficient and corrupt.

Therefore, as argued in this chapter, there is need to reconstitute and reconstruct the African state, in particular, the Kenyan state, to meet the needs of its people in the twenty-first century and beyond. The Kenyan government and nongovernmental organizations should promote full participation of both men and women as equal partners in the country's sustainable development. Furthermore, as part of state reconstitution, the enforcement of human rights, on the one hand, and resource allocation, on the other, for example, access to education and health facilities to all citizens is a basic duty of the state. Besides, in matters of resource allocation, the state needs to take into consideration the needs of the disadvantaged members of the Kenyan society, especially the rural and urban poor, women, children, and the elderly among others.

State organs and citizens alike should promote national unity, peace, and stability. As shown in this chapter, ethnic conflicts disrupt social, political, and economic life of society. Therefore, it is the responsibility of the state to provide adequate security and to uphold the right of the citizen to live, conduct business, own property, or work, and live in any part of the country. All in all, there should be collective effort on the part of the government, nongovernmental organizations and citizens alike to reconstitute and reconstruct the Kenyan state, by, for example, fighting corruption; working toward poverty alleviation programs; promoting equality for all citizens in the dispensation of justice; facilitating access to employment opportunities, as well as to education and health facilities, regardless of gender, and promote environmental conservation for the common good. Indeed, there is need for state reconstitution and reconstruction in Kenya, if the state has to meet the needs of its citizens today and in the years to come.

Notes

1. Guy Arnold, *Modern Kenya* (London: Longman Group Limited, 1981), p. 1; and Anne Nangulu-Ayuku, "Politics, Urban Planning and Population Settlement: Nairobi, 1912–1916," *Journal of Third World Studies,* vol. XVII, no. 2, 2000, pp. 171–204.
2. William R. Ochieng' "Afterword," in *Kenya: The Making of a Nation 1895–1995,* ed. Bethewell A. Ogot and W. R. Ochieng' (Maseno: Institute of Research and Postgraduate Studies, Maseno University, 2000), pp. 224–228.
3. Ibid., p. 224.
4. Arnold, *Modern Kenya,* p. 19.
5. Dirk Berg-Schlosser, "Ethnicity, Social Classes and the Political Process in Kenya," in *Politics and Administration in East Africa,* ed. Walter O. Oyugi (Nairobi: East African Educational Publishers, 1994), pp. 247–293.
6. Ibid., p. 249.
7. William R. Ochieng', *A History of Kenya* (London and Nairobi: Macmillan Publishers Ltd., 1985), p. 44.
8. Ibid.
9. Ibid.
10. Ibid., p. 67.
11. John Lonsdale, "States and Social Processes in Africa: A Historiographical Survey," *African Studies Review* vol. XXIV, nos. 2 and 3, 1981, pp. 139–225.
12. Berg-Schlosser, "Ethnicity," p. 250.
13. Ibid., p. 249.

14. Great Britain, *Colony and Protectorate of Kenya Annual Report, 1922* (London: His Majesty's Stationary Office, 1923), pp. 3–4; E S. Atieno-Odhiambo, "Mugo's Prophesy," in Ogot and Ochieng', eds., *Kenya: The Making of a Nation*, pp. 5–15; and Ochieng', "Afterword," p. 224.

15. The colonial administration was based on centralization of power. For instance, a number of policies and related orders from the Colonial Office in Britain were relayed to the Governor, who then passed them through the established hierarchy of government all the way to the village level where they were executed by chiefs and headmen on behalf of the colonial state. Almost all these aspects of the colonial administrative machinery (minus the Colonial Office) were inherited by Kenya on its independence and perpetuated by the postcolonial state.

16. Great Britain, *Colony and Protectorate of Kenya Annual Reports, 1931 and 1937* (London: His Majesty's Stationary Office, 1933 and 1938), pp. 55 and 57.

17. Anne Kisaka Nangulu, "Food Security and Coping Mechanisms in Kenya's Marginal Areas: The Case of West Pokot," PhD Dissertation, West Virginia University, 2001, p. 35.

18. Ibid., pp. 41 and 46.

19. Peter Odhiambo Ndege, "Struggles for the Market: The Political Economy of Commodity Production and Trade in Western Kenya 1929–1939," PhD Dissertation, West Virginia University, 1993, pp. 199–200; and Robert Maxon, "The Years of Revolutionary Advance, 1920–1929," in *A Modern History of Kenya*, ed. W.R. Ochieng' (Nairobi: Evans Brothers Ltd, 1989), pp. 71–111.

20. Kenya Colony and Protectorate, *Native Affairs Department Annual Report, 1931* (Nairobi: Government Printer, 1932), p. 73; Great Britain, *Colony and Protectorate of Kenya Annual Report, 1938* (London: His Majesty's Stationary Office, 1939), p. 50; and Nangulu, "Food Security," pp. 46–47. It should also be noted that the local police was not the same as the regular police in almost all their functions. Besides, in 1953, the LNCs were replaced by the African District Councils to consist of one nominated and one elected member from each location.

21. As mentioned earlier, these institutions in the Kenya colony were answerable to the DOs, DCs, PCs, the Governor and then to the Colonial Office.

22. Robert M. Maxon, "The Colonial Roots," in *Politics and Administration in East Africa*, ed. Oyugi, pp. 33–65.

23. Ibid., p. 36; and Tiyambe Zeleza, "The Establishment of Colonial Rule, 1905–1920," in *A Modern History of Kenya*, ed. Ochieng', p. 39.

24. J.M. Lonsdale and B.J. Berman, "Coping with the Contradictions: The Development of the Colonial State in Kenya," *Journal of African Studies*, vol. 20, 1979, p. 90.

25. Maxon, "The Colonial Roots," p. 36.

26. Ibid.

27. For details see *African Socialism and its Application to Planning in Kenya, Sessional Paper No. 10* (Nairobi: Government Printer, 1965).

28. Frances Stewart, "Kenya: Strategies for Development," in *Papers on the Kenyan Economy: Performance, Problems and Policies*, ed. Tony Killick (Nairobi: Heinemann, 1981), pp. 75–89; and Nangulu, "Food Security," pp. 121–122.

29. Many Kenyan industrial establishments are primarily concerned with the processing of food and other agricultural products.

30. Stewart, "Kenya," pp. 76–77; William R. Ochieng', "The Post-Colonial State and Kenya's Economic Inheritance," in *An Economic History of Kenya*, ed. W.R. Ochieng', and R.M. Maxon, (Nairobi: East African Educational Publishers, 1992), pp. 259–272; and William R. Ochieng', "Independent Kenya, 1963–1986," in Ochieng', *A Modern History of Kenya*, pp. 202–218. Jomo Kenyatta became Kenya's first president, and following his death in August 1978, Daniel Toroitich arap Moi succeeded to the presidency.

31. Eric Aseka, "The Post-Colonial State and the Colonial Legacy," in Ogot and Ochieng', eds., *Kenya: The Making of a Nation*, pp. 92–105.

32. Ibid., pp. 99 and 101–102.

33. Peter Ndege, "Modernization of the Economy, 1964–1970," in *Kenya: The Making of a Nation*, ed. Ogot and Ochieng', pp. 106–117.

34. Ibid., p. 116.

35. Arnold, *Modern Kenya*, p. 25.

36. Ibid., p. 35.

37. Ibid., pp. 35 and 37; and *Saturday Nation*, June 15, 2002. *Saturday Nation* is published weekly by the Nation Group, Nairobi.

38. Amukowa Anangwe, "Public Service and Development in East Africa," in *Politics and Public Administration in East Africa*, ed. Oyugi, pp. 71–105.

39. Martin Doornbos, "The African State in Academic Debate: Retrospect and Prospect," *The Journal of Modern African Studies*, vol. 28, no. 2, 1990, pp. 179–198.

40. Ibid., pp. 187–189.

41. Ibid.

42. Ibid., p. 182.

43. Ibid., p. 183.

44. Nicholas Van de Walle, "Crisis and Opportunity in Africa," *Journal of Democracy*, vol. 6, no. 2, 1995, pp. 128–141.

45. Ibid., p. 132.

46. Omoniyi Adewoye, "Leadership and Dynamics of Reform in Africa," in *Reflections on Leadership in Africa: Forty Years After Independence*, ed. Haroub Othman (Brussels: VUB University Press, 2000), pp. 39–48; and Doornbos, "The African State," p. 183. This book cited here on, *Reflections on Leadership in Africa*, is based on essays in honor of the late Mwalimu Julius K. Nyerere, on the occasion of his 75th birthday.

47. Anangwe, "Public Service," p. 73.

48. J.B. Ojwang', "Government and Constitutional Development in Kenya, 1895–1995," in *Kenya: The Making of a Nation*, ed. Ogot and Ochieng', pp. 148–158.
49. Frank Khachina Matanga, "Leadership and Politics in Kenya," in *Kenya: The Making of a Nation*, ed. Ogot and Ochieng', pp. 159–170.
50. Ojwang', "Government," pp. 156–157.
51. Ibid.
52. Ibid.
53. It should be mentioned here that Ford Kenya and Ford Asili are products of the formation of the Forum for Restoration of Democracy (FORD) in 1991 and its eventual split into Ford Kenya and Ford Asili.
54. Kenya's current Constitution stipulates that the country's president can serve for a maximum of two consecutive five-year terms. Thus, general elections are held every five years.
55. Fred Oluoch, "Why Fringe Parties are Here to Stay," in *Daily Nation*, November 18, 2002. *Daily Nation* is published by the Nation Group, Nairobi.
56. Ndege, "Modernization of the Economy," p. 106.
57. E.S. Atieno-Odhiambo, "The Kenya Elite: Historical Anthropology and Political Sociology of an African Formation," in *Kenya: The Making of a Nation*, ed. Ogot and Ochieng', pp. 139–147.
58. Matanga, "Leadership and Politics," p. 161.
59. Nyukuri Barasa Kundu, "Ethnicity and the Challenge of Nationhood in Kenya," in *Kenya: The Making of a Nation*, ed. Ogot and Ochieng', pp. 171–186.
60. Atieno-Odhiambo, "The Kenya Elite," p. 145.
61. Kundu, "Ethnicity," p. 177.
62. Robert M. Maxon, "Social and Cultural Changes," in *Decolonization and Independence in Kenya, 1940–93*, ed. B.A. Ogot and W.R. Ochieng' (Nairobi: East African Educational Publishers, 1996), pp. 122 and 129; and Norman Miller and Rodger Yeager, *Kenya: The Quest for Prosperity* (Boulder, CO: Westview Press, 1994), pp. 87–88. Women make up about 52% of Kenya's population. However, because of customs (particularly among pastoralists) and poverty, girls are forced into marriage at school-age, and thus, there is a tendency to send boys, instead of girls, to school
63. Oanda Ogachi, "Economic Reform, Political Liberalization and Economic Ethnic Conflicts in Kenya," *Africa Development*, vol. XXIV, nos. 1 and 2, 1999, pp. 83–107.
64. Republic of Kenya, *Kiliku Report: Report of the Parliamentary Select Committee to Investigate Ethnic Clashes in Western and Other Parts of Kenya* (Nairobi: The National Assembly, 1992), p. 13.
65. Ibid., pp. 11–13.
66. Amnesty International, "Women in Kenya, Repression and Resistance," (London: International Secretariat, 1995), p. 15.

67. Ibid., p. 16.

68. Republic of Kenya, *West Pokot District Annual Reports, 1967 and 1969* (Kapenguria: District Commissioner's Office, 1967 and 1969), pp.3–4.

69. Republic of Kenya, *West Pokot District Annual Reports, 1972 and 1976* (Kapenguria, District Commissioner's Office, 1972 and 1976), pp. 17, 29 and 52.

70. *Daily Nation*, February 14, 1996.

71. Ibid.

72. *Economic Review*, August 18–24, 1997. *Economic Review*, now out of print, was a weekly news magazine, published in Nairobi by the Economic Review Limited.

73. Frank Holmquist and Michael Ford, "Kenya Politics: Toward a Second Transition?" *Africa Today*, vol. 45, no. 2, 1998, pp. 227–258.

74. For more information on clashes in Kibera see "Ten Feared Dead in New Kibera Clashes Over Rent," in *Daily Nation*, 5, December, 2001.

75. For details on mayhem in Kariobangi see *Daily Nation*, March 5, 2002 and March 8, 2002.

76. Ibid.

77. Mutuma Mathiu, "A Trial of Blood and Tears, Losing Control Over Peace and Safety," in *Daily Nation*, March 8, 2002.

78. Bruce Berman, *Control and Crisis in Colonial Kenya: The Dialectic of Domination* (Nairobi: East African Educational Publishers, 1990), p. 212.

79. Ibid.

80. Maxon, "The Colonial Roots," pp. 35–36.

81. Berman, *Control and Crisis*, p. 209.

82. Robert Tignor, *The Colonial Transformation of Kenya: The Kamba, Kikuyu and Maasai from 1900–1939* (Princeton: Princeton University Press, 1976), p. 55.

83. Berman, *Control and Crisis*, p. 213.

84. Ibid., pp. 214–215. The Native Tribunal Ordinance was passed in 1930. It gave the colonial administration wide discretion in establishing the form and functions of African Courts.

85. Berman, *Control and Crisis*, pp. 214–215.

86. Ibid.

87. Ibid., p. 216.

88. Robert M. Maxon, *Conflict and Accommodation in Western Kenya: The Gusii and the British, 1907–1963* (London: Associated Universities Press, 1989), pp. 49–50.

89. Peter O. Ndege, "The Decline of the Economy 1973–95," in *Kenya: The Making of a Nation*, ed. Ogot and Ochieng', pp. 204–223.

90. Zachary Theodore Onyonka, Agricultural Development Banking: A Case Study of Kenya, PhD Dissertation, Syracuse University,1968, pp. 59–60; and Jo Anne Paulson, The Structure and Development of Financial Markets in Kenya: An Example of Agricultural Finance, PhD Dissertation, Stanford University, 1984, pp. 15 and 108.

91. Paulson, "The Structure and Development of Financial Markets," pp. 15 and 25–26.

92. Ibid., pp.108–109.

93. Nangulu, "Food Security," p. 128.

94. Stephen Muirui, "Police Graft Shock Revealed in Report," in *Daily Nation*, September 4, 2002.

95. Peter Eigen, Chairman, Transparency International, quoted by Eric Shimoli, "Kenya Slips Further Down the Graft List," in *Daily Nation*, August 9, 2002.

96. Ibid.

97. Ibid.

98. Ibid.

99. Alexander G. Higgins, "Poverty Getting Worse in Poorest Continent," in *Daily Nation*, June 20, 2002. As reported by Higgins, a United Nation's Report on the "Least Developed Countries," indicates that in Africa's poorest countries, nearly 65% of the people are now living on less than a dollar a day.

100. Michael Bratton and Nicolas Van de Walle, *Democratic Experiments in Africa: Regime Transitions in Comparative Perspective* (Cambridge: Cambridge University Press, 1997), p. 250; and Aseka, "The Post-Colonial State," p. 104.

101. Simeon Nyachae, "Why Balancing Kenya's Budget is a Real Nightmare," *Sunday Nation*, April 28, 2002. Simeon Nyachae is a legislator and a former Minister of Finance in Moi's government. *Sunday Nation* is published by the Nation Group, Nairobi.

102. Ibid.

103. Ibid.

104. This information is cited from "The People's Choice: Draft Report of the Constitution of Kenya Review Commission," serialized as Special Report by the *Daily Nation*, September 19, 2002.

105. This information is based on a Special Report on "Human Rights in Kenya," in *Finance*, August 16–31, 1991. *Finance* was a news magazine, now out of print, published twice monthly by Finance Institute Limited, Nairobi.

106. Ibid.

107. Ibid.

108. Ibid. Gibson Kuria managed to return to Kenya when Moi subsequently invited Kenyans in exile to return home without fear of arrest.

109. This information is cited from *Weekly Citizen*, vol. 5, no. 40, October 7–13, 2002. *Weekly Citizen* is a weekly newspaper published by Headline Publishers, Nairobi.

110. Ibid.

111. Cited from "The People's Choice," *Daily Nation*, September 19, 2002.

112. Ibid.

113. Cited from *Finance*, August 16–31, 1991, based on a Special Report on Human Rights.

114. Dan Teng'o, "Spotlight on Women and Youth as the World Marks Population Day," in *Daily Nation*, July 11, 2002.

115. Ibid.

116. Ibid.

117. Thoraya Ahmed Obaid, "More Resources for Women and Productive Health," *Daily Nation*, July 11, 2002. Obaid is Executive Director, UNFPA.

118. Ibid.

119. Dan Teng'o, "Major Challenges Facing Kenya's Population, Aids and Poverty," in *Daily Nation*, July 11, 2002.

120. Ibid.

121. Cited from Arthur Okwemba, "Kenya Scores Poorly in Conservation," in *Daily Nation*, October 3, 2002.

122. Ibid.

123. Ibid.

124. Ibid.

125. Ibid.

126. This information is based on "The Rape of Urban Kenya," *Finance*, August 16–31, 1991.

127. Ibid.

128. Cited from "The People's Choice," *Daily Nation*, September 19, 2002.

129. For details on World Bank prescription on "down-sizing" in Kenya and its effects, see Anne Nangulu-Ayuku, "Structural Adjustment, Retrenchment," and "The Golden Handshake": The Kenyan Experience," in *The Third World on the Brink of the Twenty-First Century*, ed. Nancy Schumaker and Marcia Jones(Georgia Southern University, Statesboro: Office of Publications and Faculty Research Services, 1997), pp. 100–110.

130. Jaindi Kisero, "Kenyan After Moi: The Challenges that Lie Ahead," in *Daily Nation*, August 7, 2002.

131. Lilian Nduta, "Why Lawyers Want a Total Overhaul of the Judiciary," in *Daily Nation*, April 24, 2002.

132. This information is cited from a Special Report on "Reforming the Judiciary in Kenya," *Daily Nation*, May 21, 2002.

133. Ibid.

134. Cited from "Chunga to Launch Special Graft Courts," *Daily Nation*, April 24, 2002.

135. This information is based on "Funding and Public Support the Key to a Finer Force," *Daily Nation*, August 14, 2002.

136. Ibid.

137. J. Wagona Makoba, "Nongovernmental Organizations (NGOS) and Third World Development: An Alternative Approach to Development," *Journal of Third World Studies*, vol. XIX, no. 1, 2002, pp. 53–63.

138. Ibid.

CHAPTER 6

Reconfiguring and Reinventing State-Society Relations in Mauritius

Sheila Bunwaree

Introduction

The World Development Report devoted its 1997 issue to the question of the state. The actual title of that issue was "The State in a Changing World." The report argues that the new worries and questions about the state are many and various, and that different parts of the world have gone through different experiences. It also speaks about the "collapse" of states in several parts of the world. Although it does not specifically refer to Africa, one is fully aware that Africa and some other parts of the developing world are often implied when notions such as "collapsed," "aborted," "weak," "criminalized," etc, are used as adjectives to qualify the state. Whatever the term and its appropriateness, the reality is that all states have a role to play and need to be "legitimate" if they are to continue existing. States can only be legitimate if state-society relations are premised on equality and creation of opportunities for everyone. Many countries in Africa have experienced a rolling back of the state as they implemented the IMF/World Bank-dictated Structural Adjustment Programs (SAPs). SAPs have, more often than not, led to worsening social conditions and increasing poverty. The intensification of poverty and different forms of persistent maldevelopment in different parts of the continent call for a reexamination of the role of the state.

SAPs have, in many cases, affected the legitimacy of governments in Africa. The erosion of the legitimacy of the postcolonial African state has had implications for its political capacity to implement effective public policies. The efforts to retrench the state not only helped to curb its social reach, but also further undermined the postcolonial contract, on the basis of which the state sought to construct ideological legitimation, build political alliances, relate with the opposition, and secure the cooperation or support of autonomous centers of power.

Mauritius is often cited as an exception, as a "success story" and a model to emulate, but this chapter argues that the country has a long way to go before it can be a real model. Democracy can only make sense if the rights of all citizens are respected and everyone, irrespective of gender, creed, ethnicity, race, and class is given an equal chance. Mauritius has done very well in the postcolonial period. Energies have been channeled into developing the economy of the island and consolidating its democracy. The chapter however argues that the Mauritian developmental state has to be reconfigured so that the democratic state of Mauritius becomes more inclusive. Mauritians of African descent, commonly known as the "Creoles," and women are the most disadvantaged citizens. As Mauritius attempts to plunge further into the global system, these two groups run the risk of being further marginalized. The chapter also questions the notion of the developmental state itself and argues that a state cannot be developmental if large segments of the population are increasingly pushed to the margins of society. The chapter contends that it is imperative to reengineer the Mauritian developmental state so that all citizens are treated on equal terms. If that is done, state-society relations can be greatly improved.

One of the most important tasks facing the African continent in this new millennium is the construction of democratic developmental states. The structural adjustment programs of the last two decades have simply not worked to the advantage of the average citizen. Emasculating the state reduces the ability of the state to provide for its citizens. This does not mean that neoliberalism should be substituted by a strong dirigiste project. T. Mkandawire and C. Soludo contend that two important lessons can be drawn from Africa's development experience. The first lesson is that the failure to mobilize the resource allocative functions of the market can only contribute to the inflexibility of the economy. A second lesson is that the failure to recognize the weakness of market forces in a number of fundamental areas can lead to failed adjustment policies.[1] Development policies will therefore have to be keenly responsive to the capacities and weaknesses of both states and markets in Africa and seek to mobilize the former while correcting the latter. Dogmatic faith in either planning or markets will simply not do.

Mauritius, from its early days, pursued state capitalist policies and both its growth and developmental record were impressive for a while, but the growing poverty of recent times highlights how certain groups have been subjected to a narrative of exclusion. This has led to the questioning of the quality of state-society relations as well as the nature of Mauritian democracy. Like other African countries, Mauritius adopted an economic structural adjustment program but it resisted IMF/World Bank conditionalities such as abolition of free education and free healthcare. This has caused some to refer to SAPs as being human-faced in Mauritius but whether its human-faced aspect has extended itself to all layers of Mauritian society is the question that needs to be asked.

The first part of this chapter provides a brief history of Mauritius and it examines the development of the Mauritian state. It looks at the evolution of the constitution and questions the "best loser" system adopted by Mauritius. It also argues that the state fails to give due recognition to women. Whilst ensuring the representation of the various ethnoreligious groups within its political space, gender as a category has remained unimportant. The first part of the chapter also examines the factors that have contributed to making Mauritius a seeming "success" story.

The second part of the chapter concentrates on Mauritius as a developmental state. The literature on developmental states is quite substantial and refers mostly to the East Asian countries. I do not pretend to offer here an exhaustive review of the expanding literature on developmental states. For the purpose of this chapter, it will suffice to map its broad contours and examine the degree to which it is relevant to Mauritius. The chapter however argues that Mauritius has a long way to go before it can truly qualify as a developmental state.

The third part of the chapter addresses the challenges currently facing Mauritius. The loss of the country's only comparative advantage, that is, cheap labor, the dismantling of the multifiber agreement and the loss of protected markets, rising unemployment, and a rapidly ageing population are some of the difficulties that Mauritius faces at the beginning of this millennium. The chapter argues that the already ethnicized and gendered labor market that is rapidly thinning down poses a real challenge to the state. The riots of February 1999 reflect the frustration and alienation that some sections of Mauritian society experience.

The chapter's concluding section argues that the asymmetry in the distribution of entitlements is likely to grow in this increasingly liberalized and globalized era. Thus, there is an urgent imperative to further democratize Mauritian development. In other words, a new social contract should be developed where each one can sustain his/her livelihood in dignity. The present discontent with Mauritian democracy needs to be urgently examined and addressed so that the developmental state of Mauritius is reengineered to make the small multiethnic island a more just society.

A Deterritorialization of People from Across the Globe

Mauritius, located in the South Western Indian Ocean, forms part of the Mascarene group, the other two islands being Reunion and Rodrigues. Mauritius had no indigenous population. Portuguese explorers were the first people to arrive on the island during the first decade of the sixteenth century but there is no evidence of their permanent settlement on Mauritius. The Dutch were the next to arrive but they too failed to settle in the island permanently. Sugarcane was introduced by the Dutch who also established a sugar industry that is even today an important contributor to the Mauritian economy. In 1715, the French took possession of the island in the name of the French East India Company. The island became known as Isle de France. In 1810, the British conquered the island and it was thenceforth called by its former Dutch name, Mauritius.

At the end of French rule, social relations had become much more complex. A sharply differentiated society with extremes of wealth and poverty and an elite deeply committed to, and dependent, on slavery were the major social legacies of the period. The socioeconomic institution of slavery destroyed the slaves' mother tongues and traditions. A new language, Mauritian Creole that is largely based on French developed. Today, Creole is the common language of the different elements of Mauritian society but it is not officially recognized.

The colony's inclusion into the British imperial system set the stage for a series of major social and economic transformations. Three main developments dominated life in Mauritius during the nineteenth century: the abolition of slavery, the bringing of indentured laborers from India, and the transformation of the Mauritian economy from one based on maritime economic activities to that based on the production of sugar for export. Indentured labor that was "tantamount to slavery" contributed to the prosperity of the sugar industry, but the arrival of the indentured laborers had another significant impact. It changed the demographic character of the island. Within three decades (1835–1865), the Indians became, and still remain, the island's largest population group. The ethnicity of the island became more diverse too. By the 1930s and 1940s, the Indian population changed the face of Mauritian politics. With Chinese immigrants beginning to settle on the island in the 1830s, Mauritius developed into a pluriethnic and polylingual society.

The people of Mauritius represent a deterritorialization of peoples from across the globe and this is perhaps why many Mauritians' "imagined communities" lie elsewhere. Speaking about the obstacles to the development of a Mauritian nationalism, Larry Bowman writes, "The idea of escape or return to a homeland is deeply rooted in historical experience and has hindered the development of a Mauritian nationalism."[2] Although Bowman's reference to the return to a homeland is not translated in practical terms, it is very telling in the sense that many Mauritians' "imagined community" tends to lie elsewhere.

Subdivisions that are important in Mauritius exist within the broader categories. Apart from the Hindu-Muslim split, the Indo-Maurtian group is also divided by ancestral language and caste. The Hindus form approximately 52 percent of the population, Creoles of African ancestry form 27 percent, Muslims 16 percent, Chinese Mauritians, some 3 percent and Mauritans of French ancestry constitute approximately 2 percent of the population.

The Formation of a State: The Shift from Class to Ethnic Factor

During the 1930s and 1940s, many Mauritians experienced severe economic hardship. This led to riots, violence, and industrial unrest. Fierce political struggles between the dominant minority, the Franco-Mauritians who represented the French sugar oligarchy, and the oppressed majority took place. The beginning of organized class struggle and the gradual decline of the sugar oligarchy was first signaled by a strike in 1937 followed by another one in 1943. In 1938, a labor ordinance was passed allowing workers to form trade unions and workers' associations. Several organizations mushroomed. They tried to organize Creoles and Indians to press for political and economic demands more effectively.

A final blow to the political monopoly of the French elite came after a constitutional reform was implemented in 1948 and an election was held in the same year. An extended franchise based on a simple literacy test allowed 71,569 people to participate in the 1948 elections and Mauritius, for the first time, had a representative government. The Hindu representatives of the Indo-Mauritian group swept the polls and secured 11 of the

19 elected seats. The Creoles won 7 seats and the Franco-Mauritians won only 1 seat.[3] Political power now transferred to the hands of the Indians and Creoles did not, however, bring with it economic power.

Mauritian political life changed significantly after 1948. The emphasis was much more on communal groups than on class. The two decades preceding independence in 1968 were marked by different ethnoreligious groups expressing deep concerns about communal power, security, and privilege. In the decade preceding independence, however, the emphasis shifted from class to communal/ethnic divide. According to B. Benedict, ethnic and religious affiliations became political symbols as well as the means of mobilizing each section of the population against others.[4] Between 1948 and 1960, elections were held three times (1948, 1953, and 1959). The results of the 1948 elections provided a clear indication of the future of Mauritian politics. In political terms, the educated Hindus were the real victors, but by nominating 12 conservatives to the legislative council, Governor Mackenzie-Kennedy made it hard for the elected Hindus to influence government policies. With the three officials and two elected conservatives certain to join the 12 nominees on crucial votes, dramatic political initiatives put forward by the Hindus and rejected by the British or the Franco-Mauritians had no chance of being implemented.

Mauritius became independent in 1968. Unlike many former colonies that achieved their statehood initially by fighting wars of national liberation against the metropolitan powers, Mauritius, like some other parts of the British Empire, achieved its independence through political concessions from Britain. Although many countries can speak of their independence as fueled by nationalist sentiment, Mauritius experienced a different situation altogether. No nationalist sentiment existed in Mauritius. Anticolonial feelings were expressed by the Hindu majority, but the other ethno-religious groups preferred to retain ties with the colonial ruler. Fear of a "Hindu" hegemony was prevalent. Violence flared in May 1965 with riots between Creoles and Hindus. Several people were killed and the British sent in troops who remained in the country until the end of the year. In order to reduce tensions and dampen fears of the different communal parties, the British proposed a plan to establish a new electoral commission to deal with issues of representation. The electoral commission submitted its report in May 1966.

Ethnoreligious Communities in the Political Space

The proposals that emerged from the commission have continued to shape Mauritian elections till today. Single member constituencies were scrapped on the ground that they tended to overrepresent the Hindu community. They were replaced by 20 constituencies with three members each. In addition, eight seats were to be allocated after the elections to the "best losers" representing communities underrepresented in the main election. Commenting on the electoral system, The 1997 *World Development Report* notes as follows:

> The designers of the electoral system, anxious to avoid creating institutions that might exacerbate the country's divisions, structured the system to force the main parties to seek support from all communities. Moreover, Mauritius governments have generally chosen broad based growth and distributive policies over ethnic preferences. Formal preference in employment and education has never been used. And all governments since independence have had to form multiethnic coalitions in order to assume and maintain power.[5]

Mukonoweshuro also contends that Mauritian politicians "have woven a political spoils system which has ensured that each ethnic group has an established stake in the system, thus ensuring its legitimacy by all the ethno religious communities on the island."[6]

Whether representation of ethno-religious communities in the political space is enough to ensure legitimacy is a question that should be asked. The legitimacy of the Mauritian state has no doubt been consolidated by other factors but as Mauritius's vulnerability increases and different kinds of tensions/conflicts emerge between the state and citizens, there is a need to revisit the role of the state and perhaps to reengineer it. Implications of the "Best Loser System" have also been highlighted by the *International Herald Tribune* that regards it as a major perpetrator of communalism and as having the potential to divide.[7] Although some people argue that the "Best Loser System" breeds communalism, splits Mauritian society, and hampers the development of a Mauritian nation, others think it helps to tame communalism and is a contributory factor to the political stability *a la mauricienne* and a democratic system, a rather rare quality in the rest of the African continent and other parts of the third world. The "Best Loser System" may well be contributing to a better representation of the various ethno-religious groups in the political space but its gender insensitivity makes us question the quality of Mauritian democracy. No efforts were made to ensure the representation of women as if they did not form part of the Mauritian citizenry.

State legitimacy was not, however, only a consequence of each ethnic group feeling represented, it was also strengthened by the consolidation of democracy and the welfarist approach of successive governments. Mauritius has regular elections by the ballot, a lively civic culture, a vibrant free press, and a relatively impressive economic growth. In addition to making the male component of its diverse ethnic groups feel politically represented and secure, the state also focused on consolidating the economy and improving the quality of life of its people.

In the late 1960s and early 1970s, Mauritius had to grapple with massive unemployment, huge balance of payments problems, rapidly expanding population, soaring prices, and a stagnating monocrop economy. Yet, in less than a decade, Mauritius managed to diversify its economic structures and gained the status of a small "tiger" economy. It created an export-processing zone, developed a strong tourist industry and more recently, a financial and offshore center. Parallel to these developments, Mauritius provides free health, free education, and old age pensions to all its citizens. The Government's Vision 2020 report explains that it is these free services that have contributed to the "exceptional social cohesion which have underpinned our past economic development."

Mauritius has very quickly learned that a strong social scaffolding is important for economic stability. Social policy thus proved to be one of the most important prongs of the country's development model and this contributed to consolidate the legitimacy of the government.

The Restoration of Democracy

What also contributed to state legitimacy in Mauritius is the leaders' ability to recognize the importance of democracy and the need to sustain it. Democracy was interrupted briefly but restored again. Alarmed by the growing popularity of the radical MMM (Mouvement Militant Mauricien) Party, the government moved to postpone elections scheduled for 1972. The MMM responded by organizing a series of general strikes, prompting the government to enact the Public Order Act of 1971 that allowed it to pass the state of emergency proclamation. In the face of growing popularity of the MMM, a rather left wing radical party, led by a Franco-Mauritian, Berenger, the government declared a state of emergency, suspended 12 trade unions, arrested numerous union leaders, banned political meetings, and shut down the MMM newspaper.[8] Justifying the government's action, Prime Minister Ramgoolam argued as follows:

> There is a need for Emergency Powers to achieve stability. We cannot
> risk another attempt to starve the Government and the country into

submission by wildcat and illegal strikes. We cannot permit attempts to destroy democracy in this country and replace it by dictatorship. We cannot permit violence, sabotage, and subversion because these things will destroy the climate of confidence upon which our social development is founded.[9]

Whether Ramgoolam was genuinely convinced about the above or whether this was mere rhetoric to try and retain political power are questions that may be asked. It may well be that there was a combination of both. However, Ramgoolam was voted out of power in 1982 when the MMM had a landslide victory.

What differentiated Mauritius from other postcolonial African states, however, is that Mauritius opted to espouse its democratic route again, in a very similar vein to India that, after the period of emergency under Prime Minister Indira Gandhi, decided to continue with regular, normal elections. Mauritius did not adopt the one-party state nor did it seek to move toward a permanently authoritarian regime. The MMM leaders were freed, press censorship was lifted, and the 1976 elections were held as scheduled. In these elections, the MMM won more seats (34 out of 70) than any other single party, but the MLP (Mauritian Labor Party) with 28 seats, formed a coalition government, with the conservative PMSD (*parti mauricien social democrate*) that had won 8 seats. This coalition governed the country until 1982—midway through the economic crisis of 1978–1984.

Mauritius's "success" story may also be attributed to the type of structural adjustment program and the manner of its implementation. While the overall stance of SAPs is to restructure the economy through the reduction in the share of the public sector, the stimulation of entre-preneurship and export orientation, the pursuit of price liberalization, and the implementation of a "user pays" policy with regard to public utility, the Mauritian state has tried to implement a policy of adjustment with a human face. It combined growth with equity through employ-ment creation, cushioning the impact of adjustment measures on partic-ular groups and giving incentives to small businesses. R. Bheenick argued that the government was committed to reform but maintained "an intensive policy dialogue" with the World Bank and the IMF; this meant that the structural adjustment loan was supported rather than dictated by the World Bank.[10] The Mauritian government took great pride in the fact that it resisted the IMF request to abolish both free edu-cation and subsidies on food. This decision certainly enabled many people to benefit from education. The policies of economic diversification adopted in the postindependence period and the SAP with a human face have contributed to making Mauritius a middle income country. But the whole process was not without pain. As R. Gulhati and R. Nalhari have noted:

> The macro economic stabilization, mainly through curtailment of aggregate demand, involved quite a painful adjustment, consisting of rising unemployment, declining real wages and disciplined austerity. The government persevered with reforms even though it meant a considerable loss in economic growth and a perceptible setback in the welfare of low income groups. Very little was done to "sweeten the pill" for the underprivileged social groups.[11]

Although mention is often made of the underprivileged groups, no one knows exactly how many they are and whether their children have, over the past two decades of "successful" development, been able to climb the social ladder. Statistics are not collected along ethnic and gender lines in Mauritius, but there seems to be a clear indication that the "ti kreol" are disproportionately represented amongst the poorest stratum of Mauritian society. Creoles, that is, people of African descent, are not a homogeneous group in Mauritius, but there is increasing recognition that some sections of this group are the most marginalized. When members of disadvantaged communities take stock of their plight and begin to realize that the fruits of development are too inequitably shared, tensions/conflicts begin to rise. Such tensions pose a threat to peace and stability. They also give rise to important questions regarding state-society relations. Accumulated frustration of two generations or more may start taking its toll when resources become increasingly scarcer and social mobility for the poorest strata, particularly women, becomes more difficult. Windows of opportunity that existed in the first phase of industrialization do not exist any more. Now that the economy is attempting to shift to an information-based economy, the emphasis is much more on mental rather than manual labor. Also, there is greater emphasis on scientific and technical fields where girls and women remain largely invisible.

The Developmental State

The literature on developmental states is quite substantial and refers mostly to the East Asian countries. I do not pretend to offer an exhaustive review of the expanding literature on developmental states here. For the purpose of this chapter, it will suffice to map out its broad contours and examine the degree to which it is applicable to Mauritius.

The success of the East Asian countries in the second half of the twentieth century has attracted the attention of many people. Countries such as Japan, Korea, and Taiwan have, during the post–World War II period, enjoyed impressive rates of growth and rapid industrialization. Growth models that rely on individual entrepreneurs reacting to market signals could not predict or explain the kind of transformation that occurred in East Asia. Ha Joon Chang argues that the state played a critical role in this unprecedented process of economic and social transformation and this explains the reason why such states were described as developmental.[12] More precisely, Chang defines the developmental state as one that considers the objectives of long-term growth and structural change seriously and that at the same time has the potential of creating and regulating the political and economic relationships, necessary for sustained industrialization.[13] According to Chang, conflicts are bound to happen during the process of change but political management of the economy helps to mitigate these and that an engagement with institutional adaptation and innovation are also required to achieve the overall objectives of growth and structural change.[14]

Writing about developmental states, A. Leftwich argues that "developmental states may be defined as states whose politics have concentrated sufficient power, autonomy and capacity at the center to shape, pursue and encourage the achievement of explicit developmental objectives, whether by establishing and promoting the conditions and direction of economic growth, or by organizing it directly, or a varying combination of both."[15] Woo-Cummings explains that the developmental state is "a short-hand for the seamless web of political, bureaucratic, and moneyed influences that structure economic life in capitalist North East Asia."[16] According to Theda Skocpol, a state's means of raising and deploying financial resources tells us more than could any other single factor about its existing and immediately potential capacities to create or strengthen state organizations, to employ personnel, to co-opt political support, to subsidize economic enterprises, and to fund social programs.[17]

What one derives from the Asian experience is that state capacity must not be explained only in terms of the skills and aptitudes of the technocrats within the state, but also in terms of effective institutional building and development. More importantly, a developmental state must be socially anchored. According to P. Evans, developmental states combine "Weberian bureaucratic insulation with intense immersion in the surrounding social structure. How this contradictory combination is achieved depends of course, on both the historically determined character of the state apparatus and the nature of social structure in which it is embedded."[18]

These various definitions seem to indicate that there are three core elements attached to the understanding of developmental sates. The first centers on the idea of autonomy of the government. In other words, the government can operate freely and independently from the pressures of particular interest groups. The second element is the capacity of the state to steer the country's development. Capacity here refers to the cooperation and agreement between bureaucratic and political elite to move in the same direction with developmental objectives in mind. And the third element is the development of an industrialization strategy that is home-grown and to a large extent, a nationalistic one. Here, cooperation between the state and the local private sector is emphasized.

If we go by these definitions, Mauritius can be regarded as a developmental state. Very early in the postindependence period, Mauritian politicians and the local bureaucracy promoted and directed the conditions for economic growth. The bureaucracy is the prime mover in Mauritian society. In addition to working out the means to diversify the economy, the government spared no efforts to find ways and means of raising revenue to provide more social services to its people. The state also used its intellectual elite to develop a host of institutions to help consolidate the economy. Mauritius's intellectual elite have emerged from that segment of the population that was given the opportunity to climb up the social ladder. Expansion of educational opportunities and the *grand morcellement* have contributed immensely to the social mobility of the working class, particularly people of Indian descent. This mobility has also contributed to a political class and a bureaucracy that, with time, gained increasing political power whilst economic power remained in the hands of the white sugar plantocracy.

The intellectual elite together with the other stakeholders such as the government, the private sector, and the NGO community contribute to the policymaking process in Mauritius and often manage to obtain some form of "consensus." Mauritius has managed to juggle with policies and minimize tradeoffs that often exist between economic dynamism and social justice. In short, small, isolated and dependent Mauritius has achieved some sort of "democratic corporatism." In his study of small European countries, P. Katzenstein describes democratic corporatism as an ideology of social partnership expressed at the national level; a relatively centralized and concentrated system of interest groups, and voluntary and informal coordination of conflicting objectives through continual political bargaining between interest groups, state bureaucracies, and political parties.[19]

What is often referred to as "social dialogue" in Mauritius perhaps comes close to the ideology of social partnership to which Katzenstein refers. The "social dialogue" is in fact an ideology based on the twinning of economic and social policy that is considered to be vital for the maintenance of social harmony in an ethnically diverse society such as that of Mauritius. This "social dialogue" however excludes women's voices. Female labor continues to be on the margins of the Mauritian labor market. Female unemployment is once more on the rise amounting to something like 12 percent while that of men is only 4 percent. Unlike class and ethnic tensions that often erupt into open conflict and violence, gender contradictions and cleavages do not command the same urgency and intensity of political response.

Social Engineering Through the Sugar Export Tax

Although early Mauritian development plans included the establishment of "Export-Processing Zones," (EPZs) the island's first try at industrialization primarily relied on an import-substitution strategy. It was soon discovered that Mauritius did not possess the labor supply, capital, and markets necessary for an internally oriented process of industrialization. Still, some economic diversification was accomplished in the 1970s when good weather and bumper harvests produced the economic growth (10 percent from 1971–1975) necessary to provide funds for welfare and diversification efforts by the state. In the early 1970s, manufacturing employment grew from 5 percent to 20 percent of the labor force. At the very least, these years built up the country's infrastructure, a necessity for any further industrialization. Still, the island remained a society of great social inequality where the top 10 percent of income earners received 46.7 percent of the total income while the bottom 40 percent got less than 20 percent.

The logic of Mauritian development planning seems to have been to boost sugar production in order to accumulate both private capital and public revenues as a basic resource for a more diversified and industrialized economic development. Following the recommendations of the Meade Report, the state decided to tax sugar exports and to use public revenues to provide jobs through a public works program and state-supported economic diversification.

The imposition of an export tax on sugar had been for quite a while within the plans of the MLP. It was mentioned as early as 1949. The advocates of the tax believed that various state- negotiated sugar marketing agreements guaranteed planners a healthy profit and a margin of rent that could justly be taxed to produce revenue for social and economic development. Contrary to the advice in the Meade Report, the sugar tax applied most harshly to the large estates, while small cane growers were assisted and subsidized by the state. This reversal of the agricultural priorities of the colonial state was in part due to the new Mauritian government's need to be responsive to its own constituencies and electoral supporters.

This policy decision was a crucial factor in the development of Mauritius. It was perhaps the beginning of an articulation between the social and the economics of the matter. The decision to tax sugar exports was made—and perhaps could have only been made—by a relatively autonomous state bureaucracy, a developmental state. The fact that the Mauritian bureaucracy was free enough from the influence of the sugar oligarchy meant that it could ensure the government's decision of imposing a significant tax on the large sugar estates. Writing about the sugar export in Weekend, a weekly newspaper, E. Dommen argued that the "tax allowed government to fund its social program, health, education, and food subsidies and . . . rural electrification. . . . The expenditure was . . . a way of meeting important consumption needs so that social peace could be maintained while wages were low."[20]

The issue of the sugar export levy was so controversial that the PMSD that represented the oligarchy, left its coalition with the MLP when the tax was decided. Sugar export levy remained contentious and was redebated every time the levy was raised, as had been done several times. The large planters consistently opposed the sugar tax and any increase in its terms. The state evidenced its autonomy by implementing it, continuing it, and increasing it.

From a "Tiger Economy to a Miracle in Trouble"

Travails of Success

It is somewhat surprising that the small, isolated, resource-poor multiethnic island of Mauritius that some people described as being on "the verge of disaster" in the immediate postindependence period, was within less than a decade, able to climb to the ranks of a middle income country. Mauritius has a per capita income of about $3800 and has often been cited as an economic miracle, the "tiger" of the Indian Ocean. But the "tiger" economy is now in trouble.

In fact, the riots of 1999, the fall in its position on the Human Development Index ranking the rise in the level of unemployment, a reversal in infant mortality rates, rising income inequality, and increasing levels of deprivation experienced by some segments of Mauritian society are only a few examples of the symptoms of strain. The *Vision 2020 Report* mentions an array of societal breakdowns, for example, drug addiction and drug trafficking, alcoholism, higher levels of crimes, muggings and attacks on the aged, burglaries, prostitution, juvenile delinquency, domestic violence, divorce, suicides, child battering, and sexual abuse. The Social Fabric Phase Two Study (1999) in fact confirms *Vision 2020's* argument that many of these problems are associated with poverty and deprivation. A weekly paper, *Weekend*, drew attention to *la prostitution alimentaire.* It highlighted the fact that some women, especially in Rodrigues, prostituted themselves in exchange for food. If development means the expansion of choices and increased "capabilities," the prostitution /poverty linkage referred to highlights the level of maldevelopment existing in the country.

In Mauritius wealth is highly concentrated in the hands of a few. Labor is the only asset that the poor possess, and as globalization unleashes its forces unabated and windows of opportunity shrink for many, the gap between the rich and the poor increases. The export-processing zone contributed to the mid-1980s boom that in turn led to a growing middle class. But now the country faces new challenges, including the fact that many families' livelihoods are threatened in this jobless era.

The labor market, a major provider of livelihoods, is often regarded as segmented in Mauritius. There is some sort of a cultural division of labor correlated with ethnic identity. The public sector is mostly filled by Whites, Mulattoes, and very few Creoles. The Franco-Mauritians, commonly known as the sugar barons (*Grand Blancs*), remain the country's wealthiest group and have invested in the manufacturing sector and tourism. They are followed by the Chinese who dominate this sector, though there are wealthy Muslim textile and grain traders as well. At the bottom of the socioeconomic scale are the Hindu plantation workers, Muslims working in petty jobs within the informal sector and Black Creole factory workers, dockers, and fishermen.

In addition to its being ethnically segmented, the Mauritan labor market remains terribly gendered. A glance at female labor market participation rates and the sectors in which women are most represented is an indication of the extent to which the labor market is gendered. Women continue to be overrepresented in low skilled, low status, and low paid jobs. Some 38.7 percent of women are considered to be economically active while male participation rate is approximately 78.7 percent. The vast majority of women are employed in the EPZ.

The latter is one of the few sectors of the economy that attracts more women than men. The sex-based occupational segregation is striking in Mauritius. Except for the EPZ, women have a marginal presence in most occupations.

The employment effect of the EPZ was substantial during the 1980s, but now the EPZ is experiencing a slowdown in employment creation. When jobs are created however, they are either for migrant workers or newcomers to the labor market. Workers made redundant as a consequence of closures find it extremely difficult to find new jobs and their livelihoods are threatened. Emerging jobs in the labor market often demand skills that the redundant workers do not possess. Moreover, there is increasing reliance on foreign workers based on the argument that they are more productive and are willing to do overtime labor. The reality is that the migrant workers work in very exploitative conditions.

Amartya Sen is right in saying that the only asset that the poor possess is his or her labor, but when the poor are stripped of the opportunity to work, the fundamentals of the macroeconomic policies and the functioning of the state need to be scrutinized.[21] States across the globe are becoming increasingly "powerless" but we need to ask whether they are truly powerless or allowing themselves to be increasingly dominated by the logic of the market and the movements of international capital that are benefiting the "privileged few."

Mauritius experienced full employment in the 1980s, and but now the country is moving into a jobless era. The Creoles who are the most disadvantaged in terms of housing, education, and employment find it very hard to access an already ethnically segmented labor market that, in the new millennium, is demanding skills and aptitudes they do not possess.

The violence of February 1999 can perhaps be attributed to the growing poverty and inequalization, to borrow a term from Dahrendoff.[22] The gap between the haves and the have-nots is increasing in Mauritius. The *malaise creole*, a term that has been coined in recent years to explain the deplorable plight of some sections of the Mauritian community, is regarded by some as a major cause of the social explosion. The demonstrations of February 1999 rapidly escalated out of control and the country was brought to a standstill for almost a week. Protesters vandalized public and private property in various parts of the island. Various symbols of capitalism and wealth as well as symbols representing the state such as police stations, traffic lights, government-owned buses and other vehicles such as ambulances were targeted. Looting of shops and stores took place and a few people's houses were burnt. Although the unrest degenerated into some form of communal attacks between the Creole community on the one side and the Muslims and the Hindus on the other, some people's interpretations and readings of the riots are that they were much more an indication of the frustration of the working class rather than simply the representation of the *malaise Creole*.

Encountering New Challenges in the Context of Globalization

The loss of protected markets, the emergence of cheaper sites of production, product overdependence within a narrow industrial base, slowdown of foreign direct investment, lack of skilled and qualified human power, and a worsening pensioner-worker ratio are some of the difficulties that Mauritius is currently experiencing.

The Loss of Protected Markets

The globalization and liberalization of trade under the aegis of the World Trade Organization will adversely affect many of the semi-protectionist advantages enjoyed by Mauritius under the old GATT regime. There are doubts as to whether the current LOME Convention will be renewed and if it does, there are fears that the terms of the renewal will not be as favorable to the developing countries as they used to be. Another major challenge is the dismantling of the Multifibre Agreement (MFA). The MFA that has enabled Mauritian firms to receive higher prices for their clothing exports to the European Union and United States ran out in 2005. The protected markets that the LOME Convention had provided have consequently disappeared. Mauritian textiles and clothing are now subject to the same rules of the ruthless market. The emergence of regional trading blocs such as NAFTA, ASEAN, and the European Union also has serious implications for Mauritius. Mauritius may find it very difficult to gain access to these trading blocs.

Cheaper Asian garments and the emergence of cheap labor countries such as Madagascar, Sri Lanka, and Vietnam to name just a few, are certainly important difficulties for Mauritius. *The Economist* of February 28, 1998 argues as follows:

> Surprises don't go well with the Mauritian private sector and the crisis in South East Asia came as a particularly nasty one. In the past decade Asian style policies in Mauritius produced an export led boom which transformed this previously sugar dependent economy into a mini miracle, an African tiger cub. Now Mauritian textile prices are being undercut by cheaper Asian garments.[23]

Whether Mauritius will be able to get out of its trouble and ensure "quality livelihoods" for its citizens is a question that is difficult to answer at a time when growing poverty starts making itself felt in an increasingly polarized and fractured Mauritius.

Product Overdependence and the Africa Growth and Opportunity Act

Mauritius's overdependence on one or two products within its policy of industrialization has not enabled it to widen its productive base. The latter remained very narrow and therefore fragile. Mauritius' attempts to diversify its highly concentrated export sector with 80 percent of its exports being in apparel have not been very successful. However, it has been able to diversify its markets and it now exports a great deal more to the United States though it is still operating on a quota basis. The Africa Growth and Opportunity Act (AGOA) is projected as a panacea to many problems, particularly as an opportunity to expand African exports to the United States. Some opinion leaders and policymakers argue that in order to benefit from such opportunities, Mauritian workers have to be more flexible, productive, and competitive. But Mauritian leaders fail to emphasize the various conditionalities imposed by the Africa Growth and Opportunity Act.

Labor unions in Mauritius have divergent views about AGOA. While some of them supported the government and the Mauritius Export Processing Zones Association's (MEPZA) initiative of lobbying for the passage of the law, others led by AWC (All Workers' Conference), argue that AGOA comes with too many conditionalities that can have adverse effects on people. The AWC opposes the strong private sector orientation of AGOA and has joined the coalition of anti–free trade NGOs, American Unions and U.S. garment manufacturers who oppose it.[24] WILDAF (Women in Law and Development in Africa) at their second general assembly held at Accra, Ghana, in July 1999, drew attention to the various implications that the AGOA may have on people's livelihoods and argued that with it, many African countries will have to abide by the conditionalities of the World Bank and the International Monetary Fund. WILDAF also argued that there should be a strong campaign for the removal of the conditionalities imposed by AGOA.[25]

The Difficulties of Attracting Foreign Direct Investment

The initial spurt of FDI inflows that fueled the economic boom of the 1980s is tapering off and investors are relocating to cheaper areas.

The World Investment Report (1997) draws attention to the dramatic slowdown in the growth rate of FDI in Mauritius. While annual growth rate of FDI inflows were 49.5 percent over the period 1985–1990, the figure for 1991–1997 was only 13.9 percent. In fact, the Africa Competitiveness Report speaks of Mauritius as having a very low optimism index while still remaining highly competitive. This seems rather contradictory but it may be easily reconciled if it is taken as an indication of the fear that competitiveness will also go down if the FDI inflows persist in moving away from Mauritius to other sites.

The Lack of Skilled and Qualified Manpower

Mauritius lacks skilled and qualified human power. It needs to upgrade its human resource base as well as minimize waste of its human capital. *The International Herald Tribune* in a special report on Mauritius says that the economy needs to "retool to ward off stagnation."[26] In that same article, the newspaper quoting the World Bank says:

> Mauritius will need to foster increased labor productivity by improving technology and reallocating labor to higher productivity sectors. This will require an upgrading of skills and thus a greater emphasis on education and manpower training.[27]

Mauritius has still not been able to address the inefficiencies of its education/training system. Many documents and policy papers have been produced. There was a Master Plan of Education in 1991 and an Action Plan in 1996, but neither of them has been implemented. One of the major concerns of both plans is to reduce the inefficiencies and to provide a compulsory nine-year schooling system, but this is at the level of rhetoric.

Worsening Pensioner-Worker Ratio

The Battersby Report of 1998 states that there are approximately 7.5 people of working age, for each person over pension age but this ratio is expected to fall to under 5 by 2015, and to under 3 by 2035. The steep decline in the pensioner support ratio implies that a greater part of the wealth produced by those working will need to be transferred to the pensioner population.

Mauritius has a system of contributory and noncontributory pensions. The latter covers all citizens over 60 years but the question that arises is whether the welfare state will be able to sustain itself in these difficult conditions and what will be the fate of women especially at a time where women unemployment is on the rise and when the potential for contribution toward their pensions declines. Moreover, Mauritius still does not have a "dole" system. It is only now that there is some talk about an "unemployment bill."

Overcoming the Challenges of State Reconstitution: Some Proposals

Fabianism or social democratic ideology, at a time when the ripple effects of joblessness have already started making themselves felt in the economy of as Mauritius, will perhaps need to be given a new boost if conflicts are to be avoided and sustainability ensured. As globalization hits the country, the Mauritian welfare state, a major contributor to the social scaffolding, is under threat. The political theorist, J. Gray, regards the demise of the welfare state as a direct effect of globalization. As he argues,

> To imagine that the social market economies of the past can renew themselves intact under the forces of downwards harmonization is the most dangerous of the many illusions associated with the global market. Instead social market systems are being compelled progressively to dismantle themselves, so that they can compete on more equal terms with economies in which environmental, social and labor costs are lowest.[28]

The Mauritian developmental state should revisit its welfare policies and should eradicate all gender biases. Mauritius is increasingly speaking about the passing of an Equal Opportunity Act; but whether the mere passage of an act will bring redress is a moot point. This echoes M. Esman's contention that:

> Even when laws, polices and programs appear in a formal sense to be objective and impartial, they may be skewed in implementation by public administration to favor one set of ethnic claimants over others. This ethnic skewing can be applied to matters of substantial value, including government contracts, access to land, credit, capital, business licenses and foreign exchange, and to a variety of public services such as higher education, municipal amenities, housing, water supply and recreational facilities.[29]

The *malaise Creole* that has so often been talked about in Mauritius in recent years refers to the nonpossession of many of these resources by the

Creole community and the ensuing inequality. While the enactment of laws such as the ones mentioned above reinforce the idea that everybody is given an equal chance, in reality the playing field runs the risk of remaining very uneven.

The major source of conflicts in the present era is poverty. In addition to its deteriorating human development index, worsening Gini coefficient, Mauritius is currently experiencing a reversal in infant mortality rates and its educational system continues to exclude some 40 percent of the student population at the age of ten and above, as a consequence of a fierce competitive examination called the certificate of primary education. Children who live in mostly deprived areas are pushed to the fringes of society. They lack the "cultural capital" that the schooling system requires. Modern and "successful" Mauritius does not provide a future for these kids. Steps need to be taken to address these problems.

The recent riots have again brought the issue of inequality and poverty home to Mauritians. The riots ignited some form of debate about the country's development strategies. They also laid bare the fact that the fruits of growth have not actually trickled down to the bottom layers of society. Women and the Creoles remain marginalized within the society and the steadily worsening economic conditions in the country are bound to aggravate their plight. Clearly, there is a need to formulate and implement redistributive policies that treat all ethnocultural groups equally.

Conclusion

Most of Africa is undergoing various waves of democratization and at the same time, we keep hearing of what I call a series of "Rs" and "Ds." The Rs refer to terms such as renaissance, renewal, reconfiguration, reinvention, and reconstitution, while the Ds refer to decomposition, decay, destruction, dismantling, and so on. It is perhaps important to start hearing less of the Ds and more of the Rs. The R that one chooses, should work toward the democratization of the state's development. There is widespread recognition that development is not limited to economic efficiency and growth, but includes such things as well-being, equality, dignity, the right to realize one's human potential, and above all, freedom from poverty. To be developmentally beneficial, growth must be socially equitable, pro-poor and environmentally sustainable.

Trapped in dependent development and having to confront the exigencies of the global economy, the Mauritian state has to juggle with various policies to try and maintain its competitive edge as well as its social cohesion. The visible hands of the state have, to a large extent, influenced the invisible hands of the market in Mauritius. But now that privatization, deregulation, and liberalization are the order of the day, Mauritius, the dead volcano, runs the risk of erupting again. It is therefore important for the Mauritian state to reengineer itself in such a manner so as to ensure that the macroeconomic and other development policies that it is putting in place translate into the creation of jobs for every employable person. In other words, the Mauritian developmental state should become more inclusive. Redistribution patterns and the welfare state should also be revisited so that each Mauritian citizen irrespective of gender, ethnicity, or creed is treated on equal terms.

Notes

1. T. Mkandawire and C. Solubo, *Our Continent, Our Future* (Dakar, Senegal: CODESRIA, 1999).
2. Larry Bowman, *Mauritian Education in a Global Economy* (Rose Hill, Mauritius: Edition de l'Ocean Indien, 1991), p. 64.
3. R.D. Ramdoyal, *Development Education in Mauritius* (Reduit: Mauritius Institute of Education, 1977), p. 116.
4. B. Benedict, *Indians in A Plural Society: A Report on Mauritius* (Her Majesty's Stationery: London, 1965), p. 63.
5. World Bank, *World Development Report* (New York: Oxford University Press, 1997), p. 113.
6. Eliphas Mukonoweshuro, "Containing Political Instability in a Poly-Ethnic Society: The Case of Mauritius," *Ethnic and Racial Studies*, vol. 14, no. 2, 1991, pp. 199–224.
7. See *International Herald Tribune*, June 17, 1999.
8. Bowman, *Mauritian Education*, p. 73.
9. Seewosagur Ramgoolan, Mauritius' Legislative Council Debate, June 25, 1973.
10. R. Bheenick, "Beyond Structural Adjustment," paper presented at the Seminar on Deficit Financing and Economic Management, Reduit, University of Mauritius, 1991.
11. R. Gulhati and R. Nalhari, *Successful Stabilization and Recovery in Mauritius*, EDI Policy Cast Series (Washington D.C: World Bank, 1990), p. 58.
12. Ha Joon Chang, "The Economic Theory of the Developmental State," in *The Developmental State*, ed. M. Woo-Cummings (Ithaca, NY: Cornell University Press, 1999).
13. Ibid.
14. Ibid.
15. A. Leftwich, "Bringing Politics Back In: Towards A Model of the Developmental State," *Journal of Development Studies*, vol. 31, no. 3, 1995, pp. 400–427.

16. Woo-Cummings, "Introduction," in his edited volume, *The Developmental State*, p. 1.
17. Theda Skocpol, *Social Revolution in the Modern World* (Cambridge: Cambridge University Press, 1994).
18. P. Evans, "The State as A Problem and Solution: Embedded Autonomy and Structural Change," in *The Politics of Structural Adjustment*, ed. S. Haggard and R. Kaufman (Princeton: Princeton University Press, 1992), p. 154.
19. P. Katzenstein, *Small States in World Markets* (Ithaca, NY: Cornell University Press, 1985).
20. E. Dommen, "Meade's Sugar export Tax Saved Mauritius," *Weekend*, March 10, 1996.
21. Amartya Sen, *Inequality Re-Examined* (Cambridge, MA: Harvard University Press, 1992).
22. Ralph Dahrendorf, "A Precarious Balance: Economic Opportunity, Civil Society and Political Liberty," *Rights and Responsibilities*, vol. 5, no. 3, 1995, p. 13.
23. *The Economist*, February 28, 1998.
24. *Le Mauricien*, August 14, 1999.
25. Ibid.
26. *International Herald Tribune*, September 26, 1993.
27. Ibid.
28. J. Gray, *False Dawn: The Delusions of Global Capitalism* (London: Granta Books, 1998), p. 92.
29. M. Esman, "Public Administration, Ethnic Conflict and Economic Development," *Public Administration Review*, vol. 57, no. 6, 1997, p. 528.

CHAPTER 7

The Imperative of Reconstructing the State in Nigeria: The Politics of Power, Welfare, and Imperialism in the New Millennium

Sylvester Alubo

Introduction

For almost a quarter century, Nigeria has been enmeshed in economic and political crises of varying forms, intensity, and pervasiveness. Since the restoration of civilian rule on May 29, 1999, the sharp edges of the political dimension of the crisis have become somewhat blunted. Nonetheless, the economic facets of the crises are still in place. Central to the nature of the crises and their resolution is the nature of the state. Yet, the state, its nature, structure, and other characteristics, as well as its roles in the lives of citizens, are often the least-known factors in the discussion of the crises of the Nigerian political economy. Most of the attention has focused instead, on issues such as debt burden, servicing and repayments and associated policies that reflect, as well as are constrained by the debt overhang, as if these are outside the domain of the state. In reality, the state is perhaps the most central actor in the debt management process as indeed in the entire development project. This is because in Nigeria, as in most third world countries, the state is crucial to the accumulation process and the economy in general. It, for instance, provides and maintains infrastructure without which economic development is hamstrung. The state is also a major promoter of economic activities because capital is often too dispersed and too invisible for the needs of foreign and domestic investors. The state therefore plays the important business broker and co-investor roles, crucial for the accumulation process.

In the performance of this role of entrepreneur, the state sometimes comes into conflict in the delicate balancing act between its other functions such as providing welfare to its citizens and protecting the interests of domestic and foreign entrepreneurs. I illustrate below how the state's balancing act, such as the indigenization process of the oil boom period, actually went against the material interests of foreign partners even if only temporarily. In the ensuing struggles, the foreign partners also devised ways of reestablishing their stronghold on, and exercising more direct control over the economy and politics. It is therefore important to reexamine the roles of the state in Nigeria in relation to the development project and the crises that have tended to dog this process.

In what follows, I first engage in a conceptual discourse on the nature of the state in Nigeria by situating the modern state in its political-economic past and explaining how this history has structured its present form, character, and roles. I periodize the state in Nigeria into the following epochs: (1) Colonial; (2) early postcolonial period; (3) the oil boom period; (4) the oil bust and economic adjustments; and (5) debts and globalization. I conclude by pointing out that the character, structure, and roles of the state in Nigeria's national life has, *mutatis mutandis*, retained its colonial form, and thereby proving the popular cliché *plus ca change, plus c'est la meme chose* (the more things change, the more they remain the same). Hence, the Nigerian state needs to be reconstituted.

Understanding the Nature of the State in Nigeria and its Unchanging Legacy

The formal colonization process, distinct from decades of trade links, ended the various indigenous states within the vast land mass now called Nigeria. To be sure, the colonization process was gradual, beginning from coastal areas in 1841 (the location for most of the early trading, including slave trade activities) to the eventual conquest of the Sokoto Caliphate in 1910. In line with the broader British expansionism of the era, the following hallmarks of the colonial state can be deciphered:

1. The presence of an imperial force whose preoccupation was the comprehensive domination of the indigenous people—politically economically and culturally

2. Preponderant resort to the use of force, often in unprovoked circumstancess
3. Preoccupation with the accumulation process and setting up of the necessary structures to support and facilitate this
4. Active involvement of the state as a rallying point for, as well as partner in the accumulation process
5. The neglect of the welfare of the indigenous peoples except when this threatened the colonial rule or accumulation process.[1]

These roles defined the state as part and parcel of British expansionism and the wider imperialist agenda.

To place this discussion in the context of debates on the state in underdeveloped countries, I argue that the state in Nigeria has always been a major controller of, as well as a determinant of economic activities in the process of which it is subject to various contending international and domestic influences and interests. In this sense, while the notion of the state as the executive committee of the bourgeoisie or a mere class apparatus ascribed to Karl Marx would be an overstatement; the converse that it is neutral would equally be an understatement. I argue that the state has the prime characters earlier highlighted, and that its other roles are only as these facilitate the accumulation process and the domination of the citizens in the process. As in the colonial period, popular welfare has remained on the back-burner of the postcolonial state.

Both as a result of the oil and its roles within it, the Nigerian state is said to have three distinguishing characteristics: rent seeking, prebendalism, and patrimony. The first relates to its role vis-à-vis the oil companies from which it receives huge rents. These rents are central to the oil wealth for the execution of programs and projects, and are lodged in the federation account, resulting in a situation of rich and domineering federal government from oil rents, in stark contrast to the previous era when the regional governments kept most of the revenue in accordance with the doctrine of derivation. The former mechanism of derivation as the basis of revenue sharing resulted in a situation in which the regions were much richer than the central government. These huge revenues from oil are then used as prebends that the federal government can dispense at will. As one analyst Matthew Kukah called it, it is a situation of *donatus state* (from the Latin dono-are- avi-atum to give), a benefactor that gives as it wills.[2] Such prebends strengthen the power of the central government as well as lead to its patrimonious relationship with the regional governments and the citizens. In this way, the federal government cuts the image of a generous father figure. This bolsters its internal legitimacy even when it is weak in relation to its foreign creditors.

The Nigerian state has also used its oil revenue (in addition to its large population) to become a regional hegemon. It plays key roles, especially in the West African subregion, whether in relation to the regional economic bloc, the Economic Community of West African States (ECOWAS), or even in the Organization of African Unity (renamed the African Union in 2002, apparently to copy the European Union). Nigeria single-handedly prosecuted the war to restore President Samuel Doe's power in Liberia until ECOWAS turned it into a regional force, ECOMOG. Even under ECO-MOG, Nigeria provided most of the troops and the resources, expending up to $6 billion in the process. It played a similar role in Sierra Leone when ECOMOG's mandate was extended there to address the rebel activities against the government of President Ahmed Tejan Kaba. In earlier periods, the government extended a helping hand to neighbors for road construction (Benin Republic) and for provision of electricity (Niger).

Nigeria's desire to be a key player in the West African subregion introduces further complications in the delicate balancing act. While the state facilitates the accumulation, it also plays the big father role, processes that may have little to do with the former objective. Furthermore, the state is also dialectically enfeebled as its earlier claims to independence are now glaringly impugned upon and subverted by the imposition of Structural Adjustment Programs (SAPs) and overall challenges of debt servicing and repayment. Thus, annual budget and other expressions of priority are only as permitted by the World Bank that, since the mid 1980s, has formalized its supervisory role over the economy by establishing a resident office in Nigeria.

The entrepreneurial role of the state is illustrated by the process of Nigeria's incorporation into the global capitalist system through the imposition of poll tax during the colonial period. The emerging order changed traditional subsistence agriculture to peasant production as Nigerians were compelled to pay tax using the newly introduced currency. Taxation was an imperative for the entrenchment of the new imperial order as well as for broadening the revenue base of the colonial state. In both roles, the indigenous peoples were compelled to shift emphasis to cash crop production to earn the new currency. These cash crops, effectively raw materials for European industries, led to new forms of social organization. As Gavin Williams puts it,

> Colonialism created a peasantry in Nigeria. It subordinated rural producers
> to the requirements of the metropolitan market and the colonial state. They

depended for the realization of the value of their labor on the exchange of commodity markets whose terms they could not control . . . [this structure] enabled mercantile companies and subsequently the state and indigenous capitalists to appropriate surplus value for their labor.[3]

The state moved quickly to consolidate these structures through the establishment of Produce Marketing Boards as well as manufacturing and distributive trade. The boards provided the sole outlets for peasant producers' cash crops, reproducing the same unequal relationship between center and periphery. The prices of the crops were invariably dictated by the state produce marketing boards leading to the "development of underdevelopment." Providing capital finance and other activities of multinational corporations later strengthened these structures of foreign control over the economy.

The state has had to contend with ethnic pluralism and religious politics of the Nigerian polity. With a count of over 373 ethnic groups, forging national integration has remained a constant challenge, in appreciation of which the late premier of Western region, Obafemi Awolowo, referred to Nigeria as "a mere geographical expression." There are regular contestations among ethnic groups, each struggling for vantage positions to enhance its economic and political advantages. These ethnic contestations are further compounded by religious agitations which pit Christians and Muslims against each other. Since 2000, when the Islamic legal code, the Sharia, was introduced in some states in northern Nigeria, the politics of religion has assumed predatory dimensions and has led to frequent violent conflicts. Besides the regular challenges to national integration, the ethnoreligious contestations also weaken resistance to pan-ethnic agenda such as resistance to the economic austerity programs or the military government's annulment of the June 12, 1993 presidential election. The latter instance was when an election adjudged to be the freest and fairest in Nigerian history was annulled and the acknowledged winner, Moshood Abiola, was jailed. Abiola eventually proclaimed himself president and was promptly arrested by the military. He later died in a prison without ever assuming the presidency that he had obviously won. As Sam Egwu has illustrated, this flagrant action by the military regime of General Ibrahim Babangida was "ethnicized" by the Yoruba, Abiola's ethnic group, and presented as part of the grand design to bar its members from becoming president.[4]

For most of the third quarter of 2002, President Olusegun Obasanjo faced threats of impeachment. Beginning from the House of Representatives, the threat spread to the Senate. Obasanjo was accused of several constitutional breaches. Rather than addressing the issues, the allegation took on an ethnic character. The Southwest, the president's home region, accused the North, from where most of the past military leaders came, of masterminding the plot to unseat their son. A commentator expressed this position thus: "The Northern power elite are regretting the mistake of 1999 and so, they want their power back."[5] Obasanjo himself said, along the lines of his ethnic chieftains, that the impeachment threat could lead to a civil war. Others argued that impeachment would jeopardize the nascent democracy, but without also mentioning that it is a quintessential part of the democratic process.

Here again, ethnicity was being used to scupper an important issue of whether or not the president had violated the constitution. This obvious whipping of ethnic sentiment was occurring at a time of frequent ethnic conflagration that, more than fears of impeachment, threatened Nigeria's corporate existence. As I have shown elsewhere, the return to civil rule has been dogged by regular violent ethnic conflicts in which up to 10,000 people have lost their lives.[6]

This chapter is anchored on the perspective that the state in Nigeria has continued to play the same roles: the protection of capital, capitalism, and capitalists, even if it periodically provides some welfare. Other roles are only incidental to, or only as they support the prime function. These roles are performed in the context of ethnic and religious cleavages that vitiate the opportunity to challenge the government of the day or its policies. As we now document, changing periods have made little difference as the state has played essentially the same roles in all epochs.

The State in the Early Postcolonial Period, 1960–1971

Nigeria was among the wave of countries that gained independence in a process, the then British Prime Minister, Harold Macmillan, described as the wind of change blowing across the African continent. This change was, however, limited to the personages who ran the system as the system itself remained intact. It was an externally directed economy that was inherited at independence in 1960 and with it, a situation whereby the economic basis for independence lay outside Nigeria's control. These features are the acknowledged characteristics of states in postcolonial societies, as a recent comment expressed in bold relief:

> Scholars have characterized the state in the third world formations as neo-colonial. The major feature of the neo-colonial state is its external orientations in policy thrusts, which in all cases results in the disarticulation of

the economy, as the major economic activities are geared towards extraction of minerals for export rather than production of goods for domestic consumption.[7]

This primary contradiction is central to a correct interpretation of the unchanging political economy of Nigeria. In practical terms therefore, the overwhelming influence over the state apparatus is from outside, a fact General Obasanjo appeared to understand. He once referred to Nigeria as a *trading post* of foreign investors.[8]

This disarticulation is manifest in the exportation of raw materials such as groundnuts, cocoa, cotton, palm produces, and soya beans in exchange for manufactured goods. The demand and its corollary the prices of these primary products were determined from the metropolitan countries. In terms of relationship, the situation led to what Teresa Turner and P. Badru once called a *commercial triangle*: an intimate allegiance among middle men and women from the private sector, representatives of international capital who owned and controlled the key economic activities and government officials who control the Nigerian state.[9]

This situation was radically altered from about 1973 when petroleum replaced cash crops as the major foreign exchange earner. Crude oil did rake in huge revenues which, according to one estimate, averaged over $25 billion annually between 1973 and1980.[10] But as we now examine, these huge oil revenues did not change the character of the state or the structure of its domestic or international relationships.

The State in the Oil Boom Period, 1972–1982

The exploitation of petroleum in commercial quantities, or the *oil boom* as the initial revenue surge associated with it came to be known, marked a major watershed in the annals of Nigeria's political economy. Internally, the country witnessed rapid expansion in all spheres of life including infrastructural development and popular welfare issues. As I have documented elsewhere, in addition to free and universal primary education, generous support for secondary and tuition-free tertiary education,[11] the state provided free medical care to all citizens and free meals for hospitalized patients, all of which gave some impression of the advent of the welfare state. In consonance with the *noveau riche* image, the rallying cry of the period, popularized by the then Central Bank Governor, Clement Isong and Head of State, General Yakubu Gowon was: "Money was not the problem but how to spend it."[12]

Bolstered by the huge revenues, the state sought to assert some independence over the economy variously by propping up the indigenous bourgeoisie. It provided vast opportunities for accumulation. As S. Othman has rightly observed,

> Nigerian elites have generally sought political power as a means of advancing their economic interests. They have used state power to gain accesses to a share of profitable opportunities and the finance necessary to establish themselves as the bourgeoisie. Success in business became dependent on favors granted by the state since it is the major source not only of money but also of vast opportunities, loans, subsidies and import license.[13]

Or more eloquently, as Pita Agbese argues, "access to the state constituted the principal instrument for appropriation of capital [hence] different factions of the bourgeoisie engage in intense struggles to control the state and utilize its allocative and distributive powers for their own ends."[14] The scramble for access to and control over state powers accounts in part for the regular frauds that invariably furthered accumulation and enrichment. In addition to legitimate businesses such as construction contracts and supplies, public servants in collusion with indigenous bourgeoisie devised disingenuous ways of fleecing the state as

> These [development] projects also served as avenues for fraudulent accumulation . . . several frauds were unearthed. Prominent among these were the purchase of reconditioned Leyland buses at price of new ones and the *cement armada* . . . the importation of several times more cement than was needed even in a boom economy.[15]

As Festus Iyayi has shown, the amounts lost in the process between 1978 and 1982 was up to N6 billion, which at the time was over US$10 billion![16] A more recent example is the huge fortunes of the late General Sani Abacha's family, up to $1 billion most of which was repatriated from the vaults of Swiss banks. Curiously, the "anticorruption government" of President Obasanjo struck a deal with the Abacha family allowing it to keep over $100 million of the illegally stolen public money. President Obasanjo has added in self-congratulatory manner, "I'm proud of what we have been able to achieve."[17]

The oil wealth also gave the state the economic leverage to intervene on the side of the domestic bourgeoisie, who had been agitating for state support to do "something about the domination of foreign capital in the economy."[18] Instances of such intervention include the indigenization decree through which the state compelled foreign investors to sell off up to 60 percent of shares in some businesses, or completely restricted their participation in others. It went further to establish credit and management institutions such as Mortgage Banks, Agricultural Development Bank, and Bank of Commerce and Industry to further prop up the nationalist bourgeoisie. These and similar actions require a politically and economically strong state to call the bluff of, and directly challenge the international bourgeoisie.

Politically, Nigeria pursued an aggressive foreign policy in support of the liberation efforts in the Southern African region and in the process, went against major Western countries. As part of the cold war, most of the liberation struggles in the continent were pro-people and were perceived as "communist" by most Western countries who (such as Britain in Rhodesia, now Zimbabwe, and South West Africa, now Namibia, and Portugal in Angola) were either the colonial powers from whom independence was fought, or supported noncommunist reactionary forces such as the U.S. support for UNITA.

Here again, these efforts were circumscribed by structural relationships with the imperialist center, whose support the domestic bourgeoisie needed to survive as a class. Without such support, it would be handicapped in sustaining production because of dependency for machinery, spare parts, and at the time, most of the raw materials. This organic linkage was particularly glaring in industrial production that, for the most part, relied almost exclusively on imported machinery and raw materials such as automobile assembly plants in Kaduna, Enugu, and Lagos that the state was proud to enumerate as its achievements in industrialization.

These investments also reproduced and reinforced the structures of dependency on one hand and made huge profits for foreign partners on the other. With particular reference to the Peugeot Assembly plant in Kaduna, every aspect of the business was in favor of Peugeot France and French businesses in general. The local "manufacture" amounted to over 80 percent foreign content ranging from Completely Knocked Down parts (CKDs) to accessories, all of which were airfreighted to Kano by the now defunct French Airline, UTA. A large share of even the land haulage from Kano to Kaduna went to CFAO, another French business. The same is true of other industrialization projects such as the Volkswagen (VW) Plant in Lagos in which German companies had virtual monopoly, or the Agricultural Development Project in Bakalori in which Italian businesses were the key actors.[19] In effect, the supposed industrialization during the boom period had little backward linkage to other aspects of the Nigerian economy, and hence, the perpetuation of the structures of underdevelopment.

The state ensured the patronage of the locally assembled cars by suddenly banning the importation of all private vehicles over 2000cc. Through the ban, VW and Peugeot had virtual monopolies of the Nigerian private car market. In addition, the federal government, in pursuit of "low profile,"[20] barred all cars in the newly defined offending category from its fleet and replaced them with Peugeot brands.

State entrepreneurship was cut short by other factors: the boom that hitherto masked the unchanging structural relationship between Nigeria as a peripheral country and the capitalist metropolis and also gave the state added economic and political muscles to assert its powers was short-lived; the boom had turned to a bust. This bust was manifested in the depletion of foreign reserves resulting in the inability to pay for imports. The government of the day had squandered available resources on foreign trips by legislators (all senators and members of the House of Representatives visited the United States to "see how democracy works") and massive importation of goods, especially rice.

The State, Oil Bust, and Adjustment, 1983–1996

What is today a seemingly interminable oil bust began in 1978, with a slight dip in oil revenue. This decline provided foreign investors, bolstered by indigenization attempts, the needed opportunity to reposition themselves in the Nigerian economy. A $2 billion loan was packaged for the government, supposedly as proof of the confidence of West in the economy. As experiences in later decades would prove, this was the period of austerity, a concept that was first introduced into the political lexicon later to become a household word. In effect, the loan apparently came with conditionalities that were to be enforced by the state. Suddenly, the state that had hitherto been marked by a massive expansion demanded austerity and belt tightening in all spheres of economic and social life.

If the boom was a landmark in the relationship between the state, its subjects, and international business, so too was the oil bust that, in several ways, was the antithesis. What was imagined to be a temporary measure at the time later came to dominate the development agenda. All Nigerian governments since 1978 have confronted this problem and sought to implement with incremental harshness, monetarist policies to facilitate debt servicing and eventual repayment and, ultimately, "economic recovery."

The crisis led to depletion of foreign reserves and thereby threatened the very foundation of the accumulation processes of a dependent economy. Domestically, there were widespread cutbacks in welfare programs leading to the reimposition of user fees in medical care, reintroduction of fees in primary education and massive retrenchment of public sector workers, apparently to cut down on wage bills. As of 2001, Nigeria's foreign debt portfolio stood at $30 billion. The oil bust has been characterized by the following policy shifts:

1. Commercialization of the social sector such as education and health
2. Trade liberalization
3. Acknowledged supremacy of market forces
4. Currency devaluation
5. Downsizing of civil service, the largest employer of labor in Nigeria
6. Rollback of the state through privatization and commercialization.

These policy shifts have been implemented with varying intensity such as economic stabilization during the Second Republic (from 1982), countertrade of the Buhari era (1984–1985) until the eventual formalization of IMF structural adjustment program in 1986. Before then, the crises associated with the oil bust provided the needed excuse for military coups with each succeeding regime reciting a litany of "difficulties" and "intolerable suffering" from which their patriotic zeal compelled a deliverance of the country.[21] Among these was the Babangida coup in 1985, when Nigeria had negotiated IMF support to a stalemate. Because of the unacceptable conditionality, the preceding Buhari government resorted to countertrade (modern day trade by barter) as an alternative to the chagrin of many Western countries. The Babangida coup was then hailed in the West as " 'the first IMF coup in Africa' that was expected to push the economy to the full rigors of the market mechanism."[22]

Rather than the anticipated decisive move, the new regime subjected the IMF loan to popular debate in which the Nigerian people roundly rejected the loan because of its unacceptable conditionalities. The government settled for a "Nigerian alternative" or "home-grown alternative" to the IMF conditionality.

In some respects, this initial rejection of the loan broached the way for eventual and full implementation of the unacceptable conditionality, because it is more acceptable to make sacrifices ostensibly on one's own terms than being compelled to implement externally dictated conditions. Strengthened by this reasoning, Babangida prepared the ground for the implementation of the same rejected conditions. Babangida stated this quite vividly, when he asserted,

> It is not at all clear from the evidence that additional sacrifice involved by obtaining the loan is less than the additional sacrifice entailed in not taking the loan. But what is clear is whatever action we take will involve a lot of sacrifice by our people. We must by ourselves and on our own terms do all things which will help restore our economy, no matter what pains are involved.[23]

The so-called Nigerian alternative culminated in the formal acceptance of the loan and the commencement of Structural Adjustment Program; and a policy that "pushed the adjustment program to its logical conclusion. For the first time in the history of the crisis, a regime now existed which was ready to reason along the lines of the IMF in its details by insisting on the correlation between stringent fiscal measures and a comprehensive structural adjustment that would elevate the full forces of the 'free market' to a hegemonic position in the economy."[24] These stringent conditions needed a strong state power to implement and hence, initial lip service soon gave way to gross human rights abuses. As the conditionalities took hold, they triggered protests by labor and other mass organizations. The people's resolve to fight the harsh conditions was matched by government's resolve to impose the same, and thus pitting the state against its citizens. In 1988 for example, the government responded to protest against fuel price increase by giving the security forces blanket order to "shoot- at- sight." The full logic of adjustment began to unfold as, "The monetarist strategy of crisis management pushes the state towards more authoritarian policies . . . [for] specific adjustment policies throw up specific types of politics and institutional structures."[25]

SAP was indeed characterized by the tendency to:

> Increase internal repression; respond to the demands of external interests while imposing further austerity on their citizenry though not on themselves); and to increase internal disorder and turmoil . . . they have inevitably imposed an authoritarian rule and culture on societies and have invariably defended property against people . . . they have made life arbitrary, dangerous and violent for their citizens.[26]

The experiences with SAP also called into question the nature of the "social contract" between the state and its citizens. The state seemed to have jettisoned all pretensions to welfare and concerns for the lives of the people and showed a determination to sacrifice these on the altar of accumulation and debts. Indeed, as L. Laakso and A. Olukoshi posit,

> deep-seated domestic problems in the context of a recessionary international economic environment meant that the post-colonial "social contract" and the various alliances and networks built around it to create relative political stability became increasingly unsustainable. As the economic crisis worsened in several African countries, so too did the capacity of the state to provide welfare services to the populace and patronage to the political and economic elite diminish. Battered by the economic crisis, the legitimacy of the state, and the nation-building which it pursued, was called into question as the various groups began to devise strategies and mechanisms for coping with the deteriorating domestic economic environment and the social costs which both the crisis and governmental austerity measures were exacting.[27]

It is in this sense that Giovanni Berlinguer's statement that SAP amounted to a *de facto* human experimentation with the people of the third world but without informed consent becomes apt.[28]

To conclude, SAP marked not just an exacerbation of unequal relations between the state and internal capital, it also tellingly further impinged on the state's already fragile independence ceding many controls to the World Bank, the IMF, and clubs of private finance. SAP also rendered survival precarious for the lower classes, while virtually eliminating the middle class pushing its members down the social ladder. In effect, these dynamics, along with the premium now placed on payment as the basis of access to social services, "further weakened the basis of the post-colonial social bargain that imbued the post-colonial state legitimacy and underpinned the quest for post-independence nation building."[29] SAP that paved the way for globalization has become an albatross around the necks of the Nigerian state and its citizens.

The Nigerian State and Globalization, 1997–2005

Globalization, now a buzzword in international economic discourse, is an outgrowth of SAP as well as the end of the cold war. This latter development transformed the world in accordance with the supremacy of market forces and its ideologues. As the late Claude Ake has argued, the imposition of structural adjustment and the overall Western hegemony was a part of an emergent new unipolar (unidollar) existence:[30] According to Ake, "After the Cold War, there is only one power bloc whose leaders act as though might were right. There is only one ideology, liberal democracy, only one religion, market forces."[31]

The emergent "New World Order" is what Walden Bello has appropriately described as constituting a "*dark victory*."[32] Globalization, as the new restructuring of capitalism is called, is a "sweeping strategy of the global economic roll back unleashed by Northern political and corporate elite to consolidate corporate hegemony in the home country and shore up the North's domination in the international economy."[33]

This market ideology is reinforced by the leading Western countries and presented to the rest of the world as "freedom," and the only viable path to development. The globalization process has been considerably enhanced by advances in information and communications technology, which now makes it possible to trade in stocks, goods, and services from far-flung territories at the mere click of the mouse. But like other aspects of development, access to ICT, especially the Internet, is unequal with Africa and other third world countries having less access than countries in the North; and hence, the recognition that rather than a unilinear progression, globalization "proceeds unevenly."[34] In effect, irrespective of attempts to present globalization as a natural and inexorable course of human history that is turning the world into a "global village," its class character and links with those who control the world economy cannot be denied. Hence, the issues of whose globalization and who benefits from it are crucial because "What passes for globalization is a specific type of internationalization of capital, labor and knowledge, characterized by an unrestrained and regulated search for profits and greatly enhanced by the public policies initiated by the governments of President Reagan and Prime Minister Thatcher."[35]

As part of this process, the policies of the "free world" have spun millions of threats to keep poor countries in perpetual bondage. Two complementary forces, the megamerger of major multinationals and the receding role of the state further ensured this. The past decade and half, especially the run-up to the new millennium, witnessed mega-mergers leading to massive concentrations of wealth and power in fewer hands. Virtually all industries—from media and ICT to drugs and automobile— are now controlled by 2–5 major players. This process was also accompanied by the receding roles of the state in the third world. Weakened already by SAP therapies and falling produce prices, it has been compelled to surrender to the World Bank and the IMF.

The towering role of the Bank is evident in all spheres of development, including education where the Bank now requires universities to carry out strategic planning and restructure course offering in favor of courses that are self-financing and more sellable in the job market. This policy thrust, as the eminent historian, Ade Ajayi, has warned is fraught with dangers for development and the ability of Nigerians to think for themselves:

> Although we usually deny it, our policies are, to a large extent, teleguided by the World Bank/IMF. Since 1970s, the World bank has been pushing the heretical idea that the return to the State as compared to the return to the individual beneficiary is highest in elementary education and lowest in higher education, therefore, the state must, in the name of structural adjustment, increase the allocation of resources to the elementary education at the expense of higher education. We have said it again and again that the value of education should be measured not just by how much it increases the earning capacity of the beneficiary, but by how much it contributes to overall national development.[36]

The state in Nigeria was forced to accelerate the adjustments begun with SAP and has now divested itself of share capital in businesses, including those that are profitable. Removal of trade barriers to facilitate free market and the movement of goods, wage restraint measures, and the removal of subsidies, currency devaluation supposed to make exports attractive and ensure commitment to debt serving and repayment—all these policies constitute the central plank of the Obasanjo-led Fourth Republic. Since assuming office, the Naira has been constantly devalued losing over half of its value (from $1 = 80 Naira in May 1999 to $1 = 135 Naira in October 2001) within the first two years of the first term of the Obasanjo presidency. The government has also opened up the market leading to massive importation of every conceivable commodity.[37] The importation of juices, even from countries that do not produce these, gulped up $100 million in 2001 alone. Main public corporations are also been auctioned off, the major one being the sale of the telephone company (NITEL) to a hitherto unknown consortium, International Investors, London Limited, ILL;[38] others like the Security Printing and Minting Company and the electric power company (NEPA) were also slated for the auctioneer's hammer.

The liberalization policy has also facilitated ICT investments. In addition to more cable television networks, GSM is fast replacing the conventional phones; in the congested Lagos traffic, sales of recharge cards are familiar merchandise. The government has also doggedly pursued a policy of removal of subsidy leading to a fourfold increase in domestic fuel prices; these hikes were implemented five times in as many years. It has also cracked down on the opposition arresting and detaining labor leaders in a cruel reminder of the military era. The government has stoutly defended its position as necessary steps to ensure peace and development and brushed aside all proposals for wage increase. What is more, the Obasanjo government is in the forefront of policy of continent-wide acceleration of the globalization process through the so-called New Partnership for African Development (NEPAD).

The effects of these policies have been devastating and pervasive. Aside from the impact on local manufacture and concomitant loss of jobs, there is high inflation. The more telling effects are on daily lives as divestment from social services that began during SAP has continued and led to a practice of pay or be excluded. Worse still, the virtual collapse of most social sectors has forced individuals to make their own arrangements, thus dashing all hopes of independence. As I have stated elsewhere,

> Nigerians who were offered so much hope—and expectations—are now compelled to look after themselves, the best they can. Government's presence or impact on their lives is either largely absent or even counter productive (excessive taxation for example). Thus, in both urban and rural communities, Nigerians tax themselves to provide their own parallel structures for water and power supply. The Nigerian people also maintain streets and highways just as many communities provide their own security outfits. The list is endless as even institutions like public primary and secondary schools, rickety as most have become, would have collapsed completely but for the efforts of communities via the Parents Teachers Associations. So by some cruel turn of events and long neglect, what a colleague calls a new form of "self-governance" has emerged, the very opposite of what millions toasted on October 1, 1960.[39]

Even the maintenance of major highways is left largely to gangs of youths who fill potholes with sand and stones without which many roads would be impassable. As a reward, these "maintenance crews" rely on the benevolence of motorists to toss them a few Naira.

While the emerging self-government frees the state from many of its obligations to the citizens, it also weakens the state. For example, the takeover of security functions leading to the emergence of well-organized outfits such as the Odua People's Congress, the Bakassi Boys, and *yan banga* also represent an effective takeover of state powers. Worse still, the citizens on whom the state has forced removal of subsidies now subsidize the state even in crucial areas of law enforcement. Thus, it has become the norm in Nigeria for a complainant in a police station to provide stationery, vehicle, and other logistics—and inducements—in order for the police to take up a case.[40]

The state in globalized Nigeria is weak and it faces several challenges. Its pursuit of commercialization and the removal of subsidies has led to a further decreased impact on people's lives, which leads to legitimacy crisis as well as undermines some of its powers. On the international level, its powers are further weakened both by terms of trade and its capacity to formulate truly "Nigerian" policies. Its status as an independent state is thus compromised in a process Dan Nabudere has appropriately refereed to as the *third colonial occupation*,[41] that,

> Delegitmizes nationalism and the nation building . . . and the role of the Bank, on behalf of the "donor community" also sought to delegitimize institutions of popular resistance against imperialism and neo-colonialism as well as destroying the political achievements of the African people in their earlier resistances against colonialism. It was a form of revisionist history that tried to restore the glory of colonial dependency under new conditions by highlighting the glory of the "free market" as a cure for all the ills of neo-colonialism.[42]

The "donor community" also insists on some form of democratization to coat the new forms of surplus transfer with some veneer of legitimacy. Thus, the same countries that once supported autocracy, military rule, and other forms of government without popular representation, became avid campaigners for democracy. But the brand of democracy advocated gives short shrift to popular participation in decision making, focusing instead on managerial roles and effectively "redefining democracy and bandying about the concept of good governance. In practice, the label became more important than the process such as democracies where there are no parties (such as Uganda) and in situations like Nigeria where the entire process was rife with intimidation and massive rigging."[43]

The state's patent weakness is only in relation to the outside. Internally, Nigeria is a strong state that jealously guards its strength and suppresses threats to its powers. I argue that democracy, including the wave that has attended globalization, has made little difference, as the state has merely changed in personages and not in structure and form. Thus, where it perceives threats to its powers or to the accumulation processes, it has come down hard on the citizens irrespective of professed commitments to freedom of expression and others niceties. The Bakalori Massacre in 1980, the suppression of anti- SAP protests in 1988, and the more recent suppression in Odi and Zaki Biam are ample illustrations.

The Bakolori Massacre, 1980

The Bakolori Project was part of the World Bank-initiated assault on world poverty and its Agricultural Development Programs (ADP) that would, ostensibly, simultaneously boost food production through the application of fertilizer and other inputs as well as improve the quality of life through trickle down mechanisms. The project was undertaken by an Italian company on behalf of the Sokoto State government and entailed building a dam. The dam construction dislocated over 250,000 people who were forced to move from the *fadamas* (fertile valleys) they occupied to a barren stretch of land along the highway. The peasants' frustration was compounded by the nonreceipt of any compensation. The peasants engaged in civil protests by mounting a roadblock; the state responded swiftly to what it perceived as a threat to law and order and drafted policemen who had orders to shoot on sight. Over 600 people were killed in what B. Beckman described as an "unrestrained punitive expedition."[44] The Sokoto State Government justified the action as "inevitable because the farmers' action was not only causing great losses to the State but was undermining law and order."[45]

The Suppression of the SAP Rebellion, April 1988

As part of its SAP package, the government commenced a gradual removal of fuel subsidy in 1988. The effective date was preceded by media blitz explaining how resources "freed" from removal of subsidy could be applied in other areas such as road maintenance, medical care, and water supply. The Nigerian Labor Congress countered the propaganda by pointing out that fuel was already sold at a profit at current prices. The government arrested and clamped labor leaders into detention and charged them with subversion and eventually sacked the elected leader of the NLC and appointed a sole administrator. A former personnel manager in a multinational company was awarded this job.

Government advertisement about the benefits of the higher fuel prices continued and two months after the decapitation of labor, the higher prices were implemented on April 10. Students in the University of Jos began protests that eventually spread to most other tertiary institutions and most large cities in Nigeria. The government responded with sweeping arrests and detention, and gave expressed orders to the police to shoot protestors on sight. Over 40 people were killed. The protestors were denounced "as vagabonds, mischief makers and subversives who would face the full rigors of Decree No 2 (which empowers the state to arrest and detain without trial any one considered a security risk)."[46] It closed down all tertiary institutions and used traditional rulers to appeal for peace. The increase stuck and the government scored a victory against its people.

The Odi Massacre, 2000

This incident in the oil-producing Niger Delta region relates to some complex issues that touch on youth unemployment that makes them easily enlistable for thuggery by politicians and the unresolved issues of control of oil revenue. A gang of youths who had been part of the Baylesa State Governor Diepreye Alamieyesigh's campaign apparently had problems settling to normal life after the excitement of electioneering. Some of them began to engage in extortion and black marketeering of fuel and were spoiling for action. The explosion of ethnic violence between Ijaw youths and Yoruba in Lagos gave these restive youths the opportunity they had been craving. They mounted roadblocks as a protest against the situation in Lagos and a group of seven police men sent there was abducted and killed.

The President of Nigeria responded by threatening a state of emergency if the state government did not act firmly. When a large column of soldiers sent there was ambushed by the youths, the government responded with a heavy hand and large-scale destruction:

> The troops apparently enraged by the ambush, embarked on a scorched-earth campaign. Over the next two weeks, they razed Odi with motors and heavy caliber machine guns. The soldiers killed dozens of civilians and destroyed every building in the town except a bank, a health center and an Anglican Church.[47]

Odi bears the same hallmarks of a repressive state in the relationship to its citizens.

Zaki Biam Massacre, 2001

A long-festering land feud between the Junkun and the Tiv ethnic groups erupted again in September 2001. The state sent in some peace-keeping troops to the troubled area. However, there was a long-standing accusation that some of these troops were enlisted by the Junkun faction against the Tiv, and so when 19 federal troops were apprehended by the Tiv, the captured troops were thought to be Junkun mercenary and were killed by Tiv militia.

The government responded by vowing that the killers would be punished. The soldiers were buried with full military honors and just before the burial got under way, the federal government dispatched soldiers to avenge the killing. Over half a dozen Tiv villages were burnt down and about 200 to 300 people, some of them invited for peace talks, were killed in cold blood. As the Human Rights Watch put it,

> [A] large number of soldiers arrived in several towns and villages in Benue, between October 19 and 24, in a carefully coordinated operation designed to take local residents by surprise. Several survivors and witnesses told Human Rights Watch that they felt tricked and deceived: they initially believed the soldiers were coming to protect them, especially as they pretended that they had come to discuss peace. Instead, the soldiers turned against them . . . [In Gbeji] they asked the residents on which day the market was usually held, then they went away. They returned on the October 22 [on the market day]. They told them they had come on a peace mission and wanted to discuss ways of restoring peace in the area. The residents gathered, believing it was a genuine initiative. Once a sufficient number of people had come together, the soldiers separated the men from the women and the children. They opened fire on the unarmed men. After shooting them, they poured petrol over them and set them alight.[48]

When President Obasanjo was asked about the massacre, he responded by saying he must maintain law and order and that anyone who harms a soldier should expect reprisals. The massacre in Zaki Biam bears the same trademarks as the others, an exacerbation of the legitimation crisis and a state that represses its own people.

This section has shown that in spite of a weakened state vis-à-vis external affairs, the Nigerian state remains a powerful domestic force in relationship with its citizens. Furthermore, it has become progressively "irrelevant" in the daily lives of the citizens with whom it seems to have successfully played the "Pontius Pilate" with their welfare. Citizens are compelled to fend for themselves and in the process subsidize state functions even in areas such as like law enforcement and crime control. But the same state that is enfeebled by the forces of globalization and has to be subsidized even in basic functions asserts itself when it perceives any threats to its power or to the accumulation process. In this way, globalization has made little difference as the state continues to place more priority on its entrepreneurial role than on its citizens' welfare. This seeming consistency in its role, as we turn in the concluding section, further spells out its character, the nature of development it supports, and the nature of the social contract with its citizens.

Shendam, July 2002: Disaster Averted

In the last half of July 2002, festering religious/ethnic clashes in Jos, the capital city of Plateau State in central Nigeria, spread to the southern half.

For two weeks, there was a domino effect, with ethnic strife starting from one rural community and falling on to the others. A policeman and a soldier on peacekeeping duties were abducted and killed and their weapons stolen by local militia. The commander of the joint military task force issued an ultimatum to the entire community to produce the weapons or have itself to blame. According to Brigadier General Ben Akpunonu,

> I have received orders from the Army Headquarters through the Chief of Army Staff that *we have been given seven days* from today till next Wednesday [July 23] for those weapons to be handed over to the military and police. . . . *Otherwise we shall go into those areas and deal with the situation decisively. . . . Remember what happened in other areas.*[49]

Fearing a repeat of what happened in "other areas"—an apparent reference to Odi and Zaki Biam—the people cried out through their representative in the House of Representatives. Unsure whether this would save the situation but desirous to avoid any deaths, the villagers began to migrate in droves to other areas of the state.[50] In the end, the army that had massed troops all around Shendam town and environs was prevailed upon not to invade the community.

This incident again conveys the same message as given by Odi and Zaki Biam: the state gives short shrift to due process when it perceives threats to its power. That such an ultimatum would be issued to an entire community, hard on the heels of Zaki Biam, is most revealing of the nature of relationship between the state and the civil population.

Before this, President Obasanjo visited Ikeja Cantonment, where there were bomb explosions. The residents, who pleaded with him to visit the scene of the explosion to see things first-hand, were rebuffed, and he actually told one of them to "shut up" and reminded the bewildered residents that he did not need to be there. This incident in Ikeja seems consistent with the acts of a president who ordered—at least condoned—two invasions of the army in the community in as many years. All levels of government exhibit this contempt for the people and take them for granted. In addition to separation from the people through impenetrable security cordon, sirens, outriders and tinted glasses, the people are frequently ordered around. In the September 2002 voter registration exercise, for example, many state governors orally decreed that proof of voter registration would serve as a prerequisite for payment of salaries to civil servants and for the enrolment of children into public schools.

Proposals for the State Reconstitution Assignment

As may be seen from the foregoing, the state in Nigeria shows little respect for its citizen whom it relates to as subjects. Military regimes or civilian administrations have made little difference to people's welfare suggesting that the challenge is how to reconstruct (reinvent, restructure) the state. In this section, I provide broad outlines of how this task could be accomplished, or at least begun.

Addressing the Citizenship Question

The burning citizenship question has to be seriously addressed. There are many instances where fellow citizens are told to "go home," and are expelled from particular geographical space even as the constitution guarantees the right to make any part of the country a home. The return of civilian rule has been overshadowed by outbreaks of ethnic and religious violence all of which point to the urgency of the problem. This would have to mean that concepts like "indigene" and "settler" must be abolished and replaced with residents and nonresidents. At the moment, the state supports and perpetuates the divisions through elaborate procedures of indigeneship certificates that give more opportunities to indigenes over settlers. Existing ethnic and religious divisions are similarly exploited to weaken resistance as in the June 12 presidential election saga and in the 2002 attempt to impeach President Obasanjo.

Forum to Discuss the Nature of the Nigerian State

Even after 40 years as an independent country, Nigeria is yet to come to terms with its pluralism. After ignoring years of strident calls for a national conference or some forum where the nature of one Nigeria could be discussed, the Nigerian Government finally organized a "Forum for Political Reform" in early 2005. Unfortunately, there were two major problems with the forum. The delegates to the forum were handpicked through a manipulative process orchestrated by the Obasanjo administration. The other problem was that several major stakeholders were not invited to the forum. Given the myriad problems confronting Nigeria, including ethnic and religious conflicts, it is imperative that a genuine national conference be held, consisting of the representatives of all of Nigeria's major stakeholders.

Return to True Federalism

At the moment, there is an enormous concentration of power in the central government, over virtually all matters, especially revenue. This concentration has led to fears of domination of majority ethnic groups over the minorities. At the time of writing, a contentious issue is the control of oil revenues that though produced from the ethnic minority regions—the Niger Delta—is controlled by the federal government. A return to true federalism would allay fears of domination and give the federating units more sense of belonging. It will also reduce the largely negative overbearing impact of the federal government on people's lives.

Revisiting the 1999 Constitution

The constitution on which the Fourth Republic is based was drawn up by the military regime. It was a secret document whose contents were not made public until the eve of the military's departure from office in May 1999. There was little popular participation in the process that led to the drawing up of the constitution. Its preamble alluding to "We, the people of Nigeria . . ." is rather fraudulent. It is imperative to elect broad representatives of the people to rewrite the constitution and have the opportunity to address many of the issues such as revenue sharing or the de facto division of Nigeria into six geopolitical zones.

The Role of Civil Society

Civil society needs to become more assertive in the political process. I envisage a situation where civil society through its intricate networks in the communities will begin to set the agenda for change. Many of the challenges Nigeria faces such as desertification, food security, right to healthcare, education, and gender equality could then be placed on the political agenda. At the moment, politics and electioneering revolve on the mundane and trite concepts of peace, stability, and "moving Nigeria forward." This means that various civil society groups such as women's organizations, youth groups, peasant cooperatives, and labor unions would have to break the mould and make demands. Besides forcing politicians to address issues placed on the agenda, a more vibrant civil society would prevent the state from taking the people for granted. By resorting to the use of force, many politicians show little regard for the electorate: fancy how the Deputy President of the Senate, Ibrahim Mantu, during the 2003 general elections, ran on a mission to "speak for the people, think for them and deliver them from their suffering[s] [*sic*]." No doubt, there are no easy answers but the proposals above will at least assist in the reconstruction process.

Conclusion

I sought in this chapter to provide evidence about the changing and unchanging nature of the state in Nigeria. This chapter has shown that the state has played crucial roles in economic development, first by leading the process and becoming an entrepreneur. At a later stage, state-led development became unpopular and was discounted by the "international community" that now insists on market-led reforms. Underlying the reforms is the neoliberal assumption that the forces of the market would effect a more rational allocation of resources, liberate civil society and encourage democratization and, most of all, downsize the state itself. These later changes have weakened the state, in several ways, undermined its roles, vis-à-vis the foreign partners, as many of its key functions have been surrendered to the IMF, World Bank, and private finance capital. The Nigerian state has been reduced to a debt collector and disciplinarian imposing punishment on its own citizens while providing little welfare. Citizenship in Nigeria has been virtually emptied of all material benefits.

These changes also mark and redefine the nature of the social contract between the state and its citizens. Unlike the past where welfare was central to development and nation building, it has now been placed on the back-burner and sacrificed on the altar of debt, privatization, and commercialization. In effect, the changes make a new paradigm of people-centered development difficult. As we have seen, earlier concerns about investing in people have given way to supremacy of market forces and privatization. Perhaps, because of the growing state irrelevance and the accompanying alienation from its own citizens, the state constantly bares its fangs and exhibits its strength internally whenever it perceives threats to its powers or to the accumulation process.

The state in Nigeria has effectively undergone transformation in its relationship with international capital and its citizens, but little else has changed since the colonial times. At issue therefore is the nature—or its lack—of popular participation in, and control over the state apparatus. Without this reconstruction (effected through a truly popular constitution, more participation in decision making, etc.) the structures from which these roles derive remain the same. I envisage a reconstructed (reinvented, restructured) state as a more humane one whose power would not only derive from the people, but would also show more respect for the people. Many of the acts of repression that the Nigerian state frequently visits on its citizens can only be carried out by a state that regards and treats its citizens as subjects. The Nigerian experience reveals that while constitutionalism might have opened up the political space, a lot more action of civil society is required to purge the state of what Isawa Elaigwu aptly referred to as *residual militarism and messianic arrogance.*[51] A reconstructed state would cultivate a different social contract with the people in which the latter would be central to all actions and processes. No amount of SAP, or current buzzwords like good governance, transparency, accountability, and democracy would have much meaning to the development process until the powers of the state derive more "transparently" from the people.

Notes

1. General Gowon became Head of State after the July 1967 countercoup and prosecuted the civil war (1967–1971). As the Head of State, he was in a position to know the true picture of the country's finances. Gowon was overthrown in 1976 paving the way for Murtala Mohammed.
2. Matthew Kukah, *Democracy and Civil Society in Nigeria* (East Lansing: Michigan State University Press, 1999).
3. Gavin Williams, *State and Society in Nigeria* (Indanre: Afrographica, 1980), p. 30.
4. Sam Egwu, *Democracy at Bay: Ethnicity and Nigeria's Democratic Eclipse, 1986–1995* (Jos: The African Center for Democratic Governance, 1998).
5. *Guardian*, September 10, 2002, p. 11.
6. Sylvester Alubo, "Massacre in Tivland," *Newswatch*, November 3, 2001, p. 8.
7. International IDEA, *Democracy in Nigeria: Continuing Dialogue for Nation-Building* (Stockholm: IDEA, 2000), pp. 136–137.
8. Olusegun Obasanjo became the military Head of State following the February 1976 assassination of Murtala Mohammed, to whom he was a deputy. He was in charge during the oil boom period. He relinquished power to an elected government in 1979. After serving as the President of the African Leadership Forum, an NGO, for over two decades and in the process fraternizing with civil society organizations (for example, he was a member of the Board of Directors of Transparency International), he ran into trouble with the Abacha regime and was jailed. He returned from jail to win the May 1999 Nigerian Presidential Election, and thus reenacting the Nelson Mandela feat of prisoner to President. His first term as president ended in 2003. He was reelected for a second term in 2003, amid charges of electoral fraud and vote rigging. President Obasanjo seems to have returned to concretize "trading post policies."
9. T. Turner and P. Badru, "Class, Contradictions and the 1983 Coup in Nigeria," *Journal of African Marxists*, vol. 7, 1984, pp. 4–21.

10. T. Parfit and S. Reily, *The African Debt Crisis* (London: Routledge, 1989), p. 3.

11. Sylvester Alubo, "Power and Privileges in Medical Care: An Analysis of Medical Care in Post-Colonial Nigeria," *Social Science and Medicine*, vol. 24, no. 5, 1987, pp. 453–462.

12. Sylvester Alubo, *Medical Professionalism and State Power in Nigeria* (Jos: The Center for Development Studies, University of Jos, 1994).

13. S. Othman, "Classes, Crises and the Coup: The Demise of the Shagari Regime," *African Affairs*, vol. 83, 1989, p. 442.

14. Pita Ogaba Agbese, "The Impending Demise of Nigeria's Forthcoming Third Republic," *Africa Today*, vol. 37, no. 3, 1990, p. 237.

15. Sylvester Alubo, "Mass Mobilization and Legitimation Crisis in Nigeria," *Political Communication and Persuasion*, vol. 8, 1991, p. 48.

16. Festus Iyayi, "The Primitive Accumulation of Capital in a Neo-Colony: The Nigerian Case," *The Review of African Political Economy*, vol. 13, no. 35, 1986, pp. 27–39.

17. See *Tell* Magazine, "Interview with President Olusegun Obasanjo," May 27, 2002, pp. 16–21.

18. J. Zwinginia, *Capitalist Development in an African Economy: The Case of Nigeria* (Ibadan: University of Ibadan Press, 1992), p. 75.

19. By various accounts, virtually every aspect of the Bakolori Project went to Italian companies: all vehicles (Fiat), the construction of the dam and down to wines for the expatriate workers.

20. This was a loosely defined policy of the General Obasanjo Government that included avoiding ostentation and return to traditional modesty as contained in the Jaji Declaration.

21. For a compendium of military coup speeches, see Dan Agbese, *Fellow Nigerians: Turning Points in the Political History of Nigeria* (Ibadan: Umbrella Books, 2000).

22. Y. Bangura, "Structural Adjustment and the Political Question," *Review of African Political Economy*, vol. 23, 1987, pp. 231–232.

23. Ibrahim Babangida, *Collected Speeches* (Lagos: Ministry of Information, The Federal Republic of Nigeria, 1987), p. 1.

24. Bangura, *Collected Speeches*, 1987, p. 26.

25. Ibid.

26. Morris Szeftel, "Questions About Democracy in Africa," *Review of African Political Economy*, vol. 16, nos. 45 and 46, 1989, p. 4.

27. L. Laakso and A. Olukoshi, "The Crisis of the Post-Colonial Nation-State Project in Africa," in their edited volume, *Challenges To The Nation-State in Africa* (Uppsala: Nordiska Africainstituet, 2000), pp. 16–17.

28. Giovanni Berlinguer, "Globalization and Global Health," *International Journal of Health Services*, vol. 29, no. 3, 1999, p. 580.

29. Laakso and Olukoshi, "The Crisis," pp. 16–17.

30. Claude Ake, *Democracy and Development in Africa* (Washington DC: The Brookings Institution, 1996), p. 5.

31. Ibid.

32. See Walden Bello, *Dark Victory: The United States, Structural Adjustment and Global Poverty* (Pennang: Third World Network, 1994).

33. Bello, *Dark Victory*, pp. 2–3.

34. Dan Nabudere, "Globalization, The African Post-Colonial State, Post-Traditionalism and The New World Order," in his edited volume, *Globalization and The Post-Colonial African State* (Harare: The African Association of Political Science, 2000), p. 11.

35. V. Navarroo, "Neo-liberalism, Globalization, Unemployment, Inequalities and the Welfare State," *International Journal of Health Services*, vol. 28, 1998, p. 643.

36. Ade Ajayi, "Paths To The Sustainability of Higher Education in Nigeria," *Proceedings of the General Assembly of the Social Science Academy of Nigeria*, Abuja, Nigeria, July 3–7, 2001, p. 4.

37. In one of his regular television appearances in 2002, President Obasanjo said there were over 72 brands of toothpaste on the Nigerian market, but only 5 of these were manufactured locally.

38. After the initial down payment, ILL was unable to make further payments to conclude the NITEL deal touted as the flagship sale.

39. Sylvester Alubo, "The Self-Governance," unpublished occasional paper (Jos, 2001).

40. In a recent case I am familiar with, a victim who reported a case of theft was required to provide transportation money to enable the police to arrest the suspect, feed the detained suspect and to transport the police, the accused, and his accomplice to court. He also paid N500 for two sheets of foolscap paper; an amount that could buy two reams of 1000 sheets.

41. Nabudere, "Globalization," p. 36.

42. Ibid.

43. Karl Maier, *This House Has Fallen: Midnight in Nigeria* (Boulder, CO: Westview Press, 2002), p. 140.

44. B. Beckman, "Bakolori: Peasants V.S. State and Capital," *Nigerian Journal of Political Science*, vol. 4, 1985, p. 6.

45. Ibid.

46. Sylvester Alubo, "Crisis, Repression and The Prospects for Democracy in Nigeria," *Scandinavian Journal of Development Alternatives*, vol. 2, no. 4, 1989, p. 114.

47. Maier, *This House Has Fallen*, p. 142.

48. Human Rights Watch, *Military Revenge in Benue: A Population Under Attack* (New York: Human Rights Watch, 2002), pp. 6–7.

49. I. Salami, "Army Threatens to Invade Plateau Town," *The Guardian*, July 20, 2002, p. 2.

50. Yusuf Ozi-Usman, Tiv-Jukun Conflicts, *Weekly Trust*, July 19, 2002, p. 1.

51. Isawa Elaigwu, "Ethnicity and the Federal Option in Africa," *Nigerian Journal of Federalism*, vol. 1, no.1, 1994, p. 69.

CHAPTER 8

The Postapartheid State in South Africa

Victoria Maloka

Introduction

In 1994, South Africa entered a new constitutional dispensation that has had a profound effect on the lives of all South Africans, young and old. A new culture of governance based on the supremacy of the constitution and respect for the rule of law replaced authoritarian one of the racist white minority regime that had ruled the country since 1948. The rebirth of the South African society into a constitutional democracy is the result of the national liberation struggle against apartheid, among other things. For hundred of years, black South Africans experienced severe hardships, loss of human dignity, oppression, and suffering due to apartheid and colonialism. Notwithstanding the constitutional dispensation, South Africa's new democracy is still a fragile entity, for though the battles of political plurality and universal suffrage have been won, the war against the legacies of apartheid, namely inequality, poverty, illiteracy, and unemployment, has only just begun.

This chapter examines the aftermath of the collapse of the apartheid state and the setting into motion of the state reconstruction project in South Africa in 1994. How has the new constitutional and democratic system taken shape? Has public participation and accessibility to democratic institutions and processes been successful? Are South Africans economically benefiting from their new democracy? Has South Africa managed to consolidate democratic practices over the past 12 years in terms of defining and dealing with the national question, issues of human rights, the economy, and tackling crime and corruption?

The transformation of South African society remains the government's greatest challenge since the inception of democracy in 1994. The greatest challenge, as James A. Joseph puts it, was the more daunting task of transforming the entire nature of governance.[1] This means establishing a legitimate, effective, and credible government. As in the rest of the African continent, the task of creating and maintaining a viable and legitimate state that is accessible, efficient, accountable, transparent, and equitable has been one of the critical and complicated challenges of the transformation process.[2] This is because the efforts of the political institutions and mode of governance in promoting the general well-being and prosperity of the population have as their fundamental objective, the maintenance of the privileges of a few elected people, the governing elite.[3] The postcolonial African state therefore is not perceived as an instrument of delivery of social welfare and security to its citizens, but as the accumulation of private wealth by those who preside over the state. Coupled with this lack of proper leadership ethos are an absence of political and administrative capacity, uneven distribution of resources, poverty and underdevelopment, and lack of respect for human rights, to mention but a few.[4]

In South Africa, for example, the new government inherited a political apparatus that was designed to implement colonialism and later, an institutionalized government of racial discrimination and oppression. The system was fragmented and was unable to meet the demands of the new constitutional order, as the postapartheid government had inherited a system of internal colonialism with some of the largest systematic inequalities in the world.[5] To what extent has the government managed to deal with the legacies of apartheid at the social, political, and economical level? The constitutional values and principles enshrined in the 1996 constitution provide the government with the machinery it requires to transform the country. But to what extent has transformation really taken place? I acknowledge that issues of transformation could be a study in their own right. Therefore, for the purposes of this study, transformation shall imply political achievements that were followed by fundamental economic and developmental changes that benefited every citizen, especially the previously disadvantaged black people.

In order to understand the challenges that confront postapartheid South Africa, we need to place them in their proper historical and political context. Therefore, a historical and political framework encompassing the apartheid era, right up to the period leading to the lifting of the ban on liberation movements, will be sketched out. The next section of the chapter examines the era of political negotiations and the events leading to the first democratic elections in South Africa. The chapter then undertakes a critical examination of the 1996 constitution as a prelude to a critical analysis of the present state of affairs. It examines, among other things, the national question, state of human rights, anticorruption, political parties, the economy, and the environment.

South Africa is one of the most developed and richest countries in Africa. In the aftermath of apartheid, the country has been playing a prominent role in regional issues, including developmental, political and, peace processes. Therefore, it is important to contextualize the developments in the country by looking at the southern African region at large. The chapter will look at regional integration through a discussion of the African renaissance, the New Partnership for African Development (NEPAD), and the African Union (AU).

The Political History of South Africa

The Apartheid Era

South Africa's history has been aptly described as one of a deeply divided society characterized by strife, conflict, untold suffering, and injustice that was guilty of gross violations of human rights, the transgressions of humanitarian principles in violent conflicts, and legacy of hatred, guilt, and revenge.[6] The revolutionary history of South Africa is brilliantly captured by Justice Mahomed in the constitutional court case of Azapo *v* President of South Africa:[7]

For decades, South Africa was been dominated by a deep conflict between a minority white population that reserved for itself all control over the political instruments of the state and a black majority that sought to resist that domination. Fundamental human rights became a major casualty of this conflict as the resistance of those punished by their denial was met by laws designed to counter the effectiveness of such resistance. The conflict deepened with the increased sophistication of the economy, the rapid acceleration of knowledge and education and the ever-increasing hostility of an international community steadily outraged by the inconsistency between its own articulated ideals following the Second World War and the official practices that had become institutionalized in South Africa through laws enacted to give them sanction and teeth by the parliament elected only by a privileged minority. The result was a debilitating war of internal political dissension and confrontation, massive expression of labor militancy, perennial student unrest, punishing international economic isolation, widespread dislocation in crucial areas of national endeavor, accelerated levels of armed conflict, and a dangerous combination of anxiety, frustration, and anger among expanding proportions of the populace. The legitimacy of law itself was deeply wounded as the country hemorrhaged dangerously in the face of this tragic conflict that had begun to traumatize the entire nation.

Apartheid represented a brutal, massive but almost heroic attempt on the part of the National Party to secure a correspondence between nation and territory for white people by imposing an order much more incisive than mere racial segregation. The government used legislative, economic, and administrative strategies to keep the black populace out of government. Apartheid as a system of governance was formally entrenched into the South African legal system after the 1948 electoral victory of the National Party that used the concept and program as the focus of its election campaign.[8] However, segregation policies and attempts to classify the South African population have been noticeable for centuries, though more effectively since colonialism took root in South Africa.[9] In most respects, apartheid was just a continuation, in a more systematic and brutal form, of the segregationist policies of the previous governments.

One of the first pieces of legislation to be enacted by the National Party government in 1948, the Group Areas Act, provided for the exclusive occupation by each racial group, that is white, colored, Asiatic (Indian), and Native (later termed Bantu or African). This racial segregation policy required the relocation of many South Africans. The creation of Black Homelands served the very purpose of restricting black South Africans to those areas. In addition to limiting the participation of the majority in matters of governance, this policy was a denial of sociopolitical and economic rights to the majority in the bulk of the country that was identified as white South Africa. Race was an all-important requirement for participation in political, social, and economic matters of the country. All over the country, Afrikaner nationalism was in the ascendancy. By the 1950s, whereas the rest of the African continent was experiencing a wave of decolonization, and a global backlash against racism was gathering momentum, South Africa was dramatically opposed to world opinion on issues of human rights. While Afrikaner nationalism was in the ascendancy, other forces that demanded another form of nationalism were gathering. The African National Congress (ANC), the primary organization of the liberation movement formed in 1912 as the South African Native National Congress, advocated universal adult franchise and the creation of a united democratic South Africa. At the time these thoughts were regarded as revolutionary and subversive by the then Afrikaner government. The ANC adopted the Freedom Charter as a way of articulating and consolidating black resistance. The Charter called for equal access to health, education, and legal rights and demanded that all apartheid laws and practices be set aside.[10] Furthermore, the Charter enunciated the principles of the struggle, binding the movement to a culture of human rights and nonracialism.

This period also witnessed the formation of national organizations reflecting the aspirations of other oppressed non-white groups (the coloreds and the Indians) and the creation of economic and political organizations like the South African Communist Party and trade unions that reflected the special aims and aspirations of the newly developed and doubly exploited working class.[11] A critical step in the emergence of the nonracialism movement was the formation of the Congress Alliance that comprised the Indian Congress, the Colored People's Congress, a small white congress organization, and the South African Congress of Trade Unions. The Alliance gave formal expression to an emerging unity across racial and class lines that was manifested in the Defiance Campaign and other means of protests of this period that also saw women's resistance take a more organized character with the formation of the Federation of South African Women.

The liberation movements moved from passive resistance to full armed struggle, when it became apparent that the Afrikaner government was not backing down on its oppressive laws. Nonwhites were required to carry passes whenever they were in areas designated for whites. A march to protest against the carrying of passes ended in bloodshed in Shapeville in the former Transvaal (now Gauteng Province) and Langa and Nyanga Townships in Cape Town. This led to the banning of all liberation movements, including the African National Congress and the Pan-African Congress (PAC) and their leaders were forced into exile or were arrested. Top leaders like Nelson Mandela, Walter Sisulu, and Kathrada who were still inside the country were arrested in 1963, and during the Rivonia trial, they were sentenced to life imprisonment. The 1960s was a decade of overwhelming repression and of relative political disarray among blacks in the country. Armed action from beyond the borders was effectively contained by the apartheid state. At the same time, South Africa became a republic and ended its membership of the British Commonwealth of nations.

If black resistance faltered in the 1960s, then it re-emerged in the 1970s with an irresistible determination. The 1970s saw the birth of the Black Consciousness Movement that sought to enhance a sense of pride and self-esteem among blacks. As capitalist economies sputtered with the oil crisis of the 1973, trade unions revived. A wave of strikes reflected a new militancy that involved better organization and was drawing new sectors, in particular, intellectuals and the student movement, into mass struggle and debates. This period also witnessed the mobilization of youth movements such as Pan-African Student Organization (PASO), and so on.

The 1976 school uprisings in Soweto changed the course of South African history. Black youths took to the streets to protest against the so-called Bantu education that was an inferior education system designed for the blacks. Youth protests were also directed against the imposition of Afrikaans as a medium of instruction in the black schools. This march ended in brutal suppression when the police opened fire, killing several students, including 13-year-old Hector Peterson. Following these killings, workers in Johannesburg, Cape Town, and the Eastern Cape went on strike, schools were burnt down, administration buildings were destroyed, and there were general uprisings in townships across the country. The 1976 uprisings in Soweto focused national and international attention on South Africa's political structures.[12] Internationally, South Africa was condemned and internally, a moderate consensus emerged that accepted the necessity for political reform.[13]

By the 1980s, black civil and military resistance intensified, as did international pressure in the form of boycotts and sanctions. The National Party government under P.W. Botha took steps to make apartheid work. Botha's elaborate scheme to rearrange apartheid was the introduction of a constitutional referendum that led to the enactment of a tricameral constitution. Accordingly, there would be a parliament with three houses (white, Indian, and colored), a central cabinet, a minister's council with the State president presiding over the parliament as the executive head. The African majority was excluded from political participation through this new constitutional arrangement. In effect, black South Africans remained under white minority dominion and the so-called black homelands were still retained. This was followed by years of civil and military resistance and international pressure. The 1980s were characterized by declarations of state of emergency, with the police and military joining forces to fight black opposition.

The 1990s witnessed a series of dramatic political changes after the address in parliament by the then president, FW de Klerk.[14] The ban on all liberation movements was lifted, political prisoners were freed and most forms of apartheid laws such as the Group Areas Act were abolished and completely taken off the statute book. The de Klerk government was clearly under a great deal of international pressure as sanctions were clearly biting harder. It was clear that Botha's strategy of reform initiatives combined with repression had failed to stabilize the internal situation. The government and the ANC met for their first round of talks at Groote Schuur. Both parties agreed on broad principles on the *modus operandi* of the formal negotiations. It was clear that both parties were committed to formal negotiations. The National Party government published its commitment to a free and democratic political order and two months later, the ANC produced its own commitment document that argued for a Bill of Rights, a constitutional court, and the official recognition of 11 national languages. Formal constitutional negotiations known as the Convention for a Democratic South Africa (CODESA) started on December 20, 1991.

The Transition from Apartheid to Democracy: The Negotiation Process

Although the 1990s are generally seen as the beginning of the transitional period from apartheid to democracy because of CODESA and the subsequent Kempton Park negotiations, the 1980s had equally witnessed increasingly intense negotiations among the National Party and the ANC and other parties from the resistance movement. In fact, the stage for the formal negotiations had already been set through a number of informal but well-calculated secret talks during the 1980s.

After a long history of struggle against the apartheid regime, the main protagonists finally agreed to come together, to negotiate steps toward a new South Africa. In December 1991, the main political parties, with the exception of the Pan African Congress (PAC) and the Conservative Party, gathered at Kempton Park to begin the constitutional negotiations, known as CODESA. All the parties present, except the Inkatha Freedom Party (IFP) and the Bophuthatswana government signed a declaration of intent, incorporating the guiding principles of a new democratic South Africa. The declaration was and remains an exceptionally important and historic document.[15] It was not only the first political agreement that was arrived at democratically and made a break from the racially divided past, but it also firmly committed all parties to the basic principles of genuine, nonracial, multiparty democracy where the constitution is supreme and regular elections are guaranteed.[16] Several working groups were set up in a committee-based negotiation process to negotiate the five sets of principles, that is, general constitutional principles, a constitution-making body or process, transitional arrangements or interim government, the constitutional future of homelands, and the role of the international community.[17]

By June 1993, 26 constitutional principles, later expanded to 34, were adopted as the building blocks for a new constitution. The constitutional principles would determine the shape of the new constitution and would also be the measure by which a proposed constitutional court would have to certify the constitution. It is important to note that the constitutional principles were valid only for a limited duration, that is, only after the final constitution was certified. Therefore, compliance or noncompliance could never be raised in any court of law after the coming into effect of the constitution. The principles, however, retain a very limited use in the sense that they may be consulted as guidelines for interpreting the constitution. By August 1993, several transitional bills were passed including the Transitional Executive Council Bill and the Independent Electoral Bill that allowed for the drafting of an Interim Constitution and the conducting of the first democratic elections.

The CODESA negotiations and the subsequent Kempton Park Multiparty negotiation process led to the adoption of the first Interim Constitution (IC) of the country. The Interim Constitution in turn provided for the establishment of the Constitutional Assembly (CA) that was entrusted with the task of drafting a new constitution for the Republic of South Africa.

This negotiation process was not without drama. It was further characterized by opportunistic violence from the right wing and its surrogates, and in some instances, sanctioned by elements of the state. After the collapse of the first talks, the political situation in the country deteriorated, 43 people in Boipatong (a township outside Johannesburg) were massacred, 28 people died in Bisho (the capital of the former Ciskei homeland) and the leader of the South African Communist Party (SACP), Chris Hani, was assassinated. The response of all political parties, particularly the ANC and its tripartite allies, reflected the political maturity of the leadership in the country across the political spectrum, and also clearly expressed the commitment of this leadership to negotiation and the desire for peace.[18]

This historic and unique process was further marked by constitutional compromises like the politics of the country had never witnessed before. The compelling political need to reach a compromise on the constitution meant that the framers had to avoid some hard questions on which consensus could not be reached. This resulted in a constitution with open-ended clauses that needed to be filled.

The 1993 Constitution

The transitional constitution was adopted in December 1993, but as it had not been a product of a democratic legislature, it was designed to serve for only two years.[19] It was a result of a lengthy and difficult process of negotiation between the representatives of the apartheid government and its opponents.[20] The main objective of the Interim Constitution (IC) was to lay down the procedures for the negotiation and drafting of a final constitution. But in spite of its transitional status, the IC was binding, supreme, and fully justiceable; for example, many judicial decisions handed down under the IC, remain authoritative and binding to this day. The IC was based on the fundamental constitutional principles of democracy, constitutionalism and the rule of law, constitutional supremacy, justiceability, accountability, separation of powers, checks and balances, and cooperative governance. According to De Wall,[21] the IC brought about three fundamental changes:

1. Franchise and political and social rights were accorded to all citizens irrespective of color or creed.
2. The Doctrine of Parliamentary Sovereignty was replaced by the Doctrine of Constitutional supremacy.
3. The past central government was replaced by a system of government with federal features where the central government shared powers equally with the provinces and local government. The IC provided for a Bill of Rights. In a country where the majority of the population had been denied the most basic human rights, it was inevitable that any new constitution would have to include a Bill of Rights in order to demonstrate that people's dignity could never be undermined again.[22]

The new South Africa illustrated a renewed faith in the judicial system by establishing a constitutional court as the highest legal authority in the country. While the adoption of a Bill of Rights may seem to be an obvious response to the gross violations of human rights that were the hallmark of the apartheid regime,[23] it does not explain the degree of faith in the judiciary implicit in the IC and the Final Constitution.[24] The Constitutional Court has jurisdiction over any dispute of a constitutional nature. It is tasked with an unprecedented task in the history of the country, that of certifying the text of the final constitution to be drafted by the Constitutional Assembly. The court had to test the compliance of the constitution with the agreed constitutional principles.

One of the interesting features of the transitional period was the Government of National Unity (GNU) that lasted for five years, between April 1994 and June 1999. It was a coalition administration in which the ANC shared cabinet positions with the National Party (NP) and the Inkatha Freedom Party (IFP). The spirit of the GNU was that of compromise across the political spectrum.

The Constitutional Assembly

The Constitutional Assembly (CA) was effectively the parliament that had been elected during the 1994 democratic elections, with a different name. The CA was tasked with the responsibility of drafting a legitimate, credible, and enduring constitution for the country, with the 34 constitutional principles as its guiding framework. It was legitimate because the members of the CA were democratically elected with a mandate and because of the inclusiveness of the process. It was credible because it represented the interests of all peoples, and enduring because it was designed to stand the test of time.[25]

The drafting of the final constitution had to be a people-driven process and therefore the CA made concerted efforts to involve the public in the constitution-making process. The other driving force behind public participation in the drafting of the constitution emanated from the history of the country. There was no way that the final constitution would have credibility and legitimacy had it not involved the broader South African citizenry. The constitution-making process revealed a unique South African characteristic: an obsession with consultation.[26] South Africans tend to be suspicious of any process about which they have not been consulted, and as a result, the process tends to be as important as the substance of the agreements.

The CA understood this phenomenon so well that it immediately established an administrative staff to put together publications, to liaise with the media, to foster public relations, and manage a large-scale advertisement campaign. The objective of this media strategy was to inform, educate, stimulate public interest, and create a forum for public participation. The broader South African public, especially the disadvantaged rural communities, had to be reached.

To further satisfy this principle of public participation, sector hearings and workshops were arranged in which interest groups could provide organized inputs to the constitution-making process. Constitutional education programs were coordinated in all nine provinces. More than 400 workshops were held in disadvantaged communities to prepare people to make meaningful submissions. When submissions were invited, almost two million letters and petitions were received. This could be attributed to the multimedia campaign that reached 75 percent of the South African population. It was rated one of the most successful government information efforts. In fact, no other country in Africa has equaled South Africa's participatory approach and use of new and creative mechanisms to reach the people, reach the outside world, and to bring the entire population into the constitution-making process.[27]

When the final constitution was adopted on May 8, 1996, the people of South Africa proclaimed the main purpose of the constitution, namely; to (1) heal the divisions of the past and establish a society based on democratic values, social justice, and fundamental rights; (2) lay the foundations for a democratic and open society in which government is based on the will of the people and every citizen is equally protected by law; (3) improve the quality of life of all citizens and free the potential of each person; and (4) build a united and democratic South Africa, able to take its rightful place as a sovereign state in the family of nations

The above signify the aspirations of all men and women of South Africa for a better country and a better future. These aspirations were born out of a long experience of oppression and exploitation under successive colonial regimes and the apartheid system, the long and painful struggle for freedom and dignity, and the determination that never again will the country be subjected to injustices, similar to those of the past.

The Constitution entrenches the value of human dignity, the achievement of equality, the advancement of human rights and freedoms, nonracialism, nonsexism and accountable, responsive, and open democracy, all of which forming the foundation of the new South African society.

The Main Features of the 1996 Constitution

The first and quite obvious feature of the 1996 Constitution is that South Africa now has a democratic political system, based on democratic values, social justice, and fundamental human rights.[28] From a constitutional perspective, the most significant feature of the constitution is that it is the supreme law of the country.[29] Any law or conduct inconsistent with it is invalid and the duties imposed by it must be performed.

A unique feature about the constitution is that it not only provides for the traditional liberal rights (i.e., civil and political rights), but also to the extent in which it provides for socioeconomic rights. It is worth noting that during the constitution-making process, there were serious debates about the constitutionalization of socioeconomic rights. There were constitutional and political fears that their constitutionalization would erode or undermine the constitutional principle of separation of powers, as the courts might have to interfere in the way in which the government distributes its resources.[30] Second, to effectively implement socioeconomic rights, it is often necessary to formulate policy and to create institutions to implement the policy. That role is out of line with the traditional role of the judiciary, which is to strike down unconstitutional legislation, rather than create new legislation. The third argument against the constitutionalization of these rights was that socioeconomic rights are nonjusticiable and judges do not have the necessary expertise to decide on policy matters.

The approach that was finally adopted saw the inclusion in the constitution of socioeconomic rights with special qualifiers or limitations or demarcations. As a result, the South African Bill of Rights does not distinguish between the justiceability and legality of socioeconomic rights. The constitution has adopted a progressive realization of these rights according to the availability of resources.

In addition to adherence to a system of separation of powers, the constitution further entrenches the three spheres of government through the principle of cooperative governance. The constitution further provides for the establishment of various institutions to support and promote constitutional democracy.[31] These institutions are independent, subject only to the constitution and the law. They are accountable to the national assembly that is in turn, accountable to the public through the parliament. These institutions include the South African Human Rights Commission, the Commission on Gender Equality, and the office of the Public Protector.

It should be noted that constitutionalism is not merely the establishment of the institutions, processes, and structures the constitution envisages, or the drafting and promulgation of legislation and the execution of duties and tasks that are laid down in the constitution. It is in performing these activities that the democratic fabric of society is strengthened. The adoption of the constitution was a very important step in the democratization process, but in reality, it is the manner, and decisiveness in which the constitution is given content to determine whether or not it is in fact a living document that makes a contribution to the development of society. As Laxmi M. Singhi mentioned, written constitutions do not create democracy; democracy is something that the political leaders of a nation decide to introduce and respect and this is done at the instance of the public and is enforced by the public.[32] Democracy could also be the extent to which basic needs that are provided for in the constitution are met through accessible socioeconomic upliftment programs.

The Truth and Reconciliation Commission (TRC)

The negotiation leading to the 1993 Transitional Constitution also wrestled with the question of how to deal with the human rights violations of the past. An Amnesty Clause was inserted in the Interim Constitution. A provisional National Unity and Reconciliation Act was passed, that established the TRC. The Act determined that the central objective of the TRC would be to overcome the injustices of the past by promoting national unity and reconciliation in a spirit of understanding that transcends the conflicts and divisions of the past. The TRC was seen as a pathway, the stepping stone toward the historic bridge whereby South Africa can move from the past of a deeply divided society characterized by strife, conflict, untold suffering, and injustice toward a future founded on the recognition of human rights and respect for all human life.[33]

The act recognized that the Commission could not deal with over 200 years of grievances or human rights violations committed by various administrations. Therefore, the Commission was only limited to gross violations of human rights from 1960 to 1993. In order to carry out its tasks, the Commission that operated for a period of two and half years, was divided into the following separate Committees:

- the Human Rights Violations Committee that investigated gross human rights violations, made findings on gross human rights violations and held public hearings
- the Amnesty Committee that dealt with applications for amnesty; and
- the Reparations and Rehabilitation Committee that helped to restore the dignity of victims of human rights violations and made recommendations on reparation and rehabilitation.

At the completion of its work, the TRC released its final report that aroused divergent views. To a certain extent, the TRC has succeeded in telling the story of human rights atrocities that took place between 1960 and 1993.

However, with regard to reparations, there are still very negative feelings because of the government's slow pace in finalizing its policy on reparations. Recently, we have witnessed lobbying groups steaming ahead with their efforts to have a large sector of the society compensated for their suffering. Some of the groups, like the Economic Alliance for Arms Reduction-South Africa (Ecaar-SA) have started proceedings in the United States' courts against governments and companies that defied the United Nations' arms embargo against apartheid South Africa. Ecaar–SA is seeking a minimum amount of R200 billion, for distribution as reparation to victims of apartheid, 21,000 of whom have been identified by the TRC. According to Ecaar-SA, because the current government has accepted liability for some of the crimes of the apartheid regime, it therefore will be liable to finance the reparation program. However, other commentators are of the opinion that the government should rather be instrumental in fashioning a legal framework to guide the process of reparations. It however remains to be seen how the government can tackle the issues without sending negative messages to would be-investors who were also exploiters of South Africa.

State of the Nation

With the adoption of the 1993 Constitution, a new chapter opened in the history of South Africa. This bold step laid the foundation for an entirely new constitutional framework intended to usher in a future founded on the recognition of human rights, democracy, and peaceful coexistence and development opportunities for all South Africans, irrespective of color, race, class, belief, or sexual orientation. In furtherance to this ideal, the final Constitution of South Africa was adopted, a milestone in the creation of a constitutional government, since the start of the multiparty negotiation process in the early 1990s.

Whether the various values and principles introduced by the constitutional resolution will one day characterize the fabric of South African society will certainly not depend on the constitution or its institutions alone. For that to happen, ordinary citizens of the country will have to reach at least a minimum consensus on how the values and principles of the constitutional dispensation inform the notion of being a citizen of a constitutional state. The same holds true for the incumbents of power. Although apartheid as a judicial system is gone, it still lives on as a socioeconomic structure, a security system, a lifestyle and, a mental legacy.[34]

Against this background, the question to be asked is whether South Africa's democracy is on course. It stands to reason that it takes time to reach a stage of mature constitutionalism and civility. But has the political climate developed enough to provide citizens with opportunities to participate in political decision making? All of the above will be discussed through an examination of a number of topics such as the national question, human rights, corruption, and so on.

The National Question in Postapartheid South Africa

In South Africa, like anywhere else in the world, fewer words generate as much controversy as the notion of the national question. This could be attributed to, among other things, all the compromises reached during the constitution-making process as a means of smoothing the transition. For example, the ANC had to accommodate the demands of the white right wing for an Afrikaner Volkstad. Conventionally understood, the national question concerns the oppression of one or a number of other people/s by a dominant colonial power.[35] Applied in South Africa today, the notion could relate to how people of different ethnic or racial groups live together and how all those identities work together within a single political order or how the question of politics, power, and territory are negotiated. The national question in South Africa also concerns how South Africans govern themselves and plan their economy without being unfair to other people. More specifically, it could refer to how South Africans would manage the transition from apartheid to democratic governance without killing one another.

Although racism is no longer institutionalized and South Africans have equal franchise, there can be no pretense that all South Africans share a common patriotism. There are still racist tendencies within the society, especially when one looks at the treatment of farm workers, who are mainly, poor uneducated blacks, and in the case of the Western *Cape, colored as well*. There are clear political and economic disparities in the country. The economic gaps between the rich and the poor are still quite visible.

In the new South Africa, the decision has been made to see multilingualism and national unity as being congruent and not contradictory.[36] South Africa has also accepted the now universal principle of equal status of all languages of the people in the country.[37] The constitution recognizes 11 official languages. But it also requires the respect and promotion of other ethnic groups living in South Africa such as the Khoi, Nama, Hindi, Portuguese, Arabic, and so on.[38]The government not only had to accommodate all linguistic, religious, and ethnic differences, but must by virtue of its design, create a space for each of the minorities of its population.[39] The government further adopted affirmative action policy to eradicate the systematic discrimination and denial of job opportunities for specific groups such as Africans, Indians, women, colored, and so on. Although the above groups have received affirmative action with open arms, it is still met with a lot of criticism from white South Africans, especially white males who see this as reverse discrimination.

Furthermore, the constitution established other institutions to promote conditions that are propitious to the enjoyment of rights, such as the Pan South African Language Board, the Human Rights Commission, and so forth. Parliament has passed a Bill that provides for the establishment of the Commission for the Promotion and Protection of the Rights of Cultural, Religious, and Linguistic Communities. According to the Minister of Provincial and Local Government, the necessity for the Bill derives from the fact that the "majority of our linguistic and religious groups were historically subjected to suppression and consigned to varying degrees of obscurity. Therefore, through this Bill, our common nationhood will express itself within the paradigm of a nation-state which is not of ethnic, religious and linguistic homogenous entity."[40]

While the Bill recognizes and celebrates the diversity in South Africa, it also seeks to create conditions to overcome the legacies of division and inequality among communities. The notion of the rainbow nation stems from this very history or legacy that South Africa is trying to overcome. The rainbow nation celebrates the numerous cultures, ethnicities, and religions of the people of South Africa. South Africa has embraced the notion of ubuntu, or humanity, to encourage nation building. The notion of ubuntu reminds us that we can only be fully human when we see and are seen by another human being as human beings. To appreciate our own humanity, we need to appreciate the humanity of others. The notion of ubuntu has brought with it a greater emphasis on the values, attitudes, skills, and knowledge needed by people to be able to function as part of a group or society.

Parallel to the debates on national question are issues of HIV/AIDS, land, unemployment, and so on. Some of the identities emerging in South Africa relate to some of those issues. For example, the question of land in contemporary black South Africa relates to issues of identity, recognition, subsistence, and freedom. HIV/AIDS is also linked to the national question debate in the sense that the most affected and infected are poor black Africans in rural areas. Being poor, they cannot afford expensive medication to sustain their lives, whereas their white counterparts, due to their privileged background, have access to medication. Education on HIV/AIDS or lack thereof, is also another contributing factor. While the majority of black South Africans lag behind in AIDS education, their white counterparts have access to all sorts of educational facilities. This unequal access reinforces the view that whites are still a superior race in South Africa as they still control the economy.

The State, Political Parties, and Opposition in South Africa

It is difficult to discuss governance without at least mentioning the state of political parties or opposition in South Africa. Political parties are an essential feature of the modern state and are critical forces in democratizing states.[41] Since 1994, South Africa's political landscape has changed dramatically. It is characterized by dominance of the ruling party, the African National Congress (ANC). Judging by the performance of the ANC during the 1999 and 2004 general elections, it is clear that it is unlikely to lose any electoral contest for national power in the foreseeable future. This, in turn, has aroused fears that the ANC might become increasingly unaccountable, and perhaps arrogant in its use of state machinery, because none of the political parties can mount any effective challenge against it. One political commentator has observed that getting into the hearts of the vast majority, that 80 percent black South Africans is proving to be a major stumbling block.[42] It will take some years and a much more change before real breakthrough occurs. White South Africans are decidedly divided. Many have become apathetic and feel exhausted. The rest are divided between the New National Party (NNP) and the Democratic Alliance (DA). On the other hand, the short-lived marriage between the NNP and the DA has presented new opportunities and possibilities for the ruling party. The NNP has now joined ranks with the ANC, that also promises jobs for the NNP at all three ties of government, including the national cabinet.

South Africa may be classified as a unique multiparty state with elements of a one-party state. As Dumisane Hlope writes, conventional wisdom suggests that South Africa is a multiparty democracy with one party dominating.[43] If multipartyism should reflect diversity on matters of policy, South Africa ceases to be a multiparty state. Crudely put, South Africa is a one-party state within a legal and constitutional framework for multipartyism, that is, a one party state within a multiparty system. Hlope goes on to indicate that the ANC has opted to co-opt other political parties and in the process has actively contributed to the current emergence of the one-party state scenario in the country.

The Democratic Alliance that is the only institutional guarantor of white privilege has failed to attract sizeable black support. The NNP, on the other hand, has been relegated to a regional party, the Western Cape

Province and its marriage to the ruling party, in fact, implies that the ANC is governing the Western Cape thorough the NNP.

KwaZulu-Natal, a strong Inkatha (IFP) stronghold, is the only province in the country not governed by the ANC. The ANC and the IFP entered into a coalition government in KwaZulu Natal only as a means of constructively managing the conflict between their supporters in the province. It was merely a way of creating and bringing peace to the conflict-ridden province. Although civil strife in the province was averted, the coalition's government did not succeed on any other front. It failed to create a climate for delivery, peaceful coexistence and, political maturity among senior politicians.[44] The situation in KwaZulu Natal could soon change with the new legislation on cross-carpeting. With the ANC's partnership with the NNP and the Minority Front, the ANC could easily grab KwaZulu Natal. Other minority parties like the Pan African Congress (PAC) and Azanian People's Organization (AZAPO) have revived plans for the formation of a patriotic front of black opposition parties, a sure sign of concern about their survival in a hostile political environment. However, the fact that AZAPO is part of government blunts the proposed front's ability to act as a watchdog of the ANC.

Considering all these developments that amount to a very heavy presence of the ANC in every political inch of the country, it might be true that South Africa is indeed descending into a one-party state democracy. This is a cause for concern as a one-party hegemony could be dangerous. There is no gainsaying that a strong, primarily black political front could be an important factor in preventing the ruling party from acting as if it is all too powerful, like other political parties in similar situations the world over. A well-organized political front could also prevent the ANC from becoming arrogant and dismissive of the imperative to be accountable to the electorate. On a positive note, this could actually make the ANC double its efforts to deliver to the masses.

Another intriguing development in the country on the state of political opposition is the new bill passed by parliament providing for public representatives at all three tiers of government to swap parties without losing their seats. The defection law, as it is popularly called, provides for a 15-day window period of free movement among parties. According to Paul Graham, the prime motive for floor crossing will be to join a party that can govern alone or in a coalition.[45] There have been some debates about the constitutionality of this defection legislation. At issue on whether the legislation is constitutional are two conflicting mandates: the constitutional provision that representation be in general and proportional, while the schedule to the constitution states that a specific law can be passed to regulate defection of public representatives. It is unclear whether this legislation is what the constitutional drafters meant by defection. Therefore, the matter has been brought before the Constitutional Court to decide whether the way in which the defection is conducted, undermines democracy in a fundamental way.

According to one political commentator, the legislation is opportunistic, illogical, and goes against the grain of the constitution.[46] The law negates the spirit in which millions of ordinary citizens, who have not been consulted properly, spend time on long lines to cast their vote for a political party. Until such time when voting in the country is not done on a constituency basis, floor crossing is illogical. The legislation would serve to undermine the ability of ordinary citizens to vote for their choice.

The fact that the legislation came into being at the same time as the cooperation agreement between the ANC and the NNP is another cause for concern. It appears as if the ANC is using the defection legislation to solve a political problem created a few years earlièr by an alliance between the NNP and the DA. It now appears as if the law is an attempt by the ruling party to save the political career of certain politicians by ensuring that they do not lose their seats in parliament. This is political opportunism, especially as it does not reflect any mandate that parties received through an election. The honorable thing to do is for representatives to go back to their electorate to get a fresh mandate if they decide to switch to other political parties. As it is, the matter is before the Constitutional Court to decide on its constitutionality. What is the value of the election if politicians are allowed to cross the floor as they wish? Crossing the floor should happen within an electoral system that allows for it. The current South African system does not.

According to two Markinor surveys on the voter approval of government, voters are not satisfied with the quality of opposition leadership.[47] The report goes on to say that the lack of trust in the current major opposition party's ability to lead other opposition political parties is most disconcerting and a strong indictment of political depth in the country. Another study conducted by the Human Science Research Council (HSRC) on Social Movement in South Africa suggests that between 1994 and 2000, political interest has declined and politics has become a less important part of everyday life.[48] The study further suggests that there is nothing wrong with this because South Africa, for many years, was highly politicized; but with the transition from apartheid to democracy, the political climate seems to have normalized. Another interesting dimension of the study is that it discovered that abstaining from voting was an expression of discontent with one's personal situation and the government. As such, it indicated political estrangement. This could explain the low turnout in the 1999 and 2004 elections, in which many people did not vote.

It is worth noting that in South Africa, political loyalties are, in large part, determined by race and ethnicity.[49] Blacks prefer black parties, whites prefer white parties and Coloreds and Indians are torn between the two. According to Eddie Maloka, white opposition parties are a threat to the consolidation of democracy in South Africa because of their continued reliance on race as a base of power.[50] Their failure to break into the African electorate is one factor that would continue to act as a check on their political strength. But it also goes without saying that no political party in South Africa can survive without winning over large numbers of black voters. To win such voters in the future means acting now to establish credibility based on constructive and effective contribution to the formation of the South African nation.[51] The overall impression is that our people want political parties that uphold ethical and moral standards, democratic values and that "walk the talk" and deliver.[52]

The State and Human Rights

Against the background of colonialism and apartheid, South Africa adopted a constitution with the most advanced Bill of Rights in the world. The cornerstone of South Africa's democracy,[53] it enshrined the rights of all people in South Africa and affirms the democratic values of human dignity, equality, and freedom.[54] The constitution further embodies an understanding that South Africans' democratic rights and freedoms encapsulated in the Bill of Rights can only gain true meaning as South Africa overcomes apartheid's legacies of poverty and injustice. However, a Bill of Rights should not be regarded as a panacea for all the ills of a country.

In discussing the state and human rights in South Africa, I would like to start from the premise that South Africa's transition is a work in progress. Realistically, we cannot expect more than 40 years of human rights atrocities to be overcome in 12 years. Therefore, in this discussion, I will try to focus on what I believe to be some of the achievements so far of the democratic process to bring about the promotion and protection of human rights. It should also be noted that South Africa inherited a state machinery designed to perpetuate human rights abuses. Recognizing that the protection and promotion of human rights cannot be left to individuals and the government, the constitution, in Chapter 9, provides for the establishment of national institutions to support constitutional democracy. One such institution is the South African Human Rights Commission (SAHRC), tasked with promoting respect for human rights and a culture of human rights, promoting the protection, development, and attainment of human rights, and monitoring and assessing the observance of human rights in the country.

Looking at the track record of the Commission and the country at large, one can say that the Commission is on the right track in terms of fulfilling its mandate. There are human rights educational programs conducted all over the country. It is a fact that people, especially previously disadvantaged rural communities, need more education on human rights and on how they can access some of their rights. Another interesting development in human rights education is its inclusion in the new 2005 school curriculum, according to which human rights will be integrated in all learning areas.

South Africa, through the SAHRC, has drafted a National Action Plan for the Protection and Promotion of Human Rights (NAP). Central to the NAP is the addressing of socioeconomic inequalities and structural disparities inherited from the past. Income distribution in South Africa still ranks among the most unequal in the world. Only a small share of the national income goes to the majority of the population. Black people are still at the bottom of the income levels and generally whites are on top. The NAP recognizes that the social and economic imbalances between black and white people do not only pertain to income distribution, but also to other socioeconomic factors like employment, housing, education, health, and so forth. These imbalances have deprived and continue to deprive many South Africans, especially black South Africans, of the full and equal enjoyment of their fundamental rights and freedoms. South Africa therefore needs to undergo deep and thorough structural transformation. It still needs to build a culture of human rights among its people. The two processes are inextricably linked. Without structural change, all talk of human rights is meaningless. But without entrenching a culture of human rights, structural transformations alone can become another form of unfair advantage and discrimination. South Africa still needs more concrete policy initiatives to ensure that this takes place.

The government has so far, legislated a number of policies to make human rights a reality. Some of these are the equality policies that are designed to prioritize the elimination of the legacy of systematic inequality, focusing on race, gender, economic status, and disability. The success of these legislations could perhaps explain the few cases concerning racial discrimination that have reached the courts recently. It is only in a few cases that people found it necessary to approach the courts for the enforcement of their equality rights on the basis of race.

Most discriminatory apartheid laws have been scrapped off the statute book. Equality rights were also pushed to the front, particularly in the case of gender issues. A Commission on Gender Equality (CGE) was established to specifically promote respect for gender equality and protection. Furthermore, the constitution provides for the establishment of a Commission for the Promotion and Protection of Cultural, Religious and Linguistic Communities that is tasked with among others, the promotion and development of peace, friendship, humanity, tolerance, and national unity among cultural, linguistic, and religious communities on the basis of equality, nondiscrimination, and free association. It should be taken into account that it is not only the responsibility of the government to promote and protect human rights. It is also the responsibility of the citizens through civil society movements, academics, media, and so on to consider ways in which they can contribute to the promotion and protection of human rights.

I agree with Rassie Malhebe that there is a need to educate people to accept human rights as the basis of the realization of the potential of all peoples and of the peaceful and harmonious coexistence of all segments of society.[55] Furthermore, we need to continuously research and study the way in which Western and African thoughts on human rights that coexist in South Africa can be brought together.

According to a study conducted by the SAHRC on public perceptions of the state of human rights in South Africa, particularly rights in the areas of environment, housing, health, food, water, social security, and education, the absence of a clear definition of rights and steps that the state must take to meet its constitutional obligations, make monitoring of the realization of those rights complicated.[56] Furthermore, it is difficult to distinguish between the realization of socioeconomic rights and the delivery of social services that are subject to parliamentary and public scrutiny and that does not impose any specific legal obligations on the state.

There is a widespread agreement with the proposition that criminals have too many rights. The police feels that its hands are tied in terms of law enforcement. Prison warders at most of the prisons feel that inmates are more protected by the law. The study further shows that general living conditions in South Africa are moderate. Expressions of satisfaction correlate strongly with levels of education and income. Jobs and unemployment were mentioned as the most important concerns that the government should address. Overall, jobs and housing are the biggest socioeconomic concerns that the government should also address to meet public demands. In approaching issues of housing and land reform, it must be recognized that large majorities across all groups support the notion that people who were forced off their land should get it back or receive compensation for it.

The framework for a progressive, equal and accessible healthcare system targeting those who need it most has been created over the past years. Difficulties in translating those intentions from policy to practice have been evident. For instance, the report has shown that the majority of Africans, especially in rural areas, still do not have potable water. The overall basic educational facilities exist in most places, but not enough. Of equal importance is the quality and value of education, which is determined more by the availability of educational resources in adequate quantities and the quality of service provided by them.

On the whole, it does appear that South Africa is on the right track with regard to the promotion and protection of rights. In addition to the above, the country has ratified a number of international conventions that oblige it to take certain steps for the promotion and protection of rights of its citizens. These include, *inter alia*, the United Nations' Convention on the Elimination of all Forms of Discrimination against Women, the African Charter on Human and People's Rights, International Covenant on Civil and Political Rights and International Covenant on Economic, Social and Cultural Rights. Despite its poor human rights record that it inherited from the apartheid regime, South Africa has made significant strides toward strengthening democracy and inculcating a human rights culture. Although compared with the past, South Africa has taken a giant leap forward, much has been done, but more needs to be done, as legacies of the past still remain. But as Hernie Kotze cautions, though nobody expected the postapartheid administration to be able to distribute the country's wealth overnight, 12 years is a long enough period and people may be beginning to wonder when the government would deliver on its promises and satisfy their needs.[57] Therefore, the state needs to expedite its process of ensuring that services are delivered and people's needs are met.

The State and Anti-Corruption Strategies

The term, corruption, is commonly used to describe a wide range of social conducts that are condemned and rejected by societies all over the world as dishonorable, harmful, and evil.[58] Corruption refers to irregularities, ranging from the granting of simple personal favors or lack of objectivity in the making of a decision, or simple cases of maladministration, to dangerous conspiracies that can sabotage the well-being of a nation.[59] Corruption is a societal problem; and it is not specific to the public sector and in particular the actions and attitudes of politicians and civil servants, but it has far wider reach and consequences, According to John Mbaku,[60] there are different strategies that state and corporations can employ to combat corruption. These include

- societal strategies, where the society itself decides which conduct is morally wrong
- legal strategies, where the courts define what is unacceptable behavior
- market strategies, based on the belief that there is a relationship between corruption and the market and
- political strategies, where the state creates alternative political motivation to make it difficult for people to engage in corruption.

The success of each of these strategies depends on a number of things, the judicial system, media, police, investigators, and so on. Of equal importance is that the success of any anti-corruption strategy should be coupled with good governance. South Africa, in its anti-corruption strategies, has employed all of those strategies. The 1996 Constitution committed South Africa to implementing an ethical, accountable, and democratic system of governance. In the past few years, the government has taken several significant steps not only to ensure a clean public administration system, but also to signal its intention to be responsive to local and international pressure and encouragement toward good governance and to promote greater openness, transparency, and accountability. The National Anti-Corruption Initiative was launched in 1999 following a number of landmark events like the Public Service Anti-corruption Conference, the National Anti-Corruption Summit, the Moral Summit, and so forth. The Public Service Commission was established to lead the national anti-corruption efforts. It has since convened a cross-sectional task team to manage the national program. Its mandate, among others, is to contribute toward the establishment of national consensus through the coordination of sectoral strategies against corruption. Other legislative and administrative measures employed include, *inter alia*, the following:

1. The establishment of constitutionally independent bodies like the Public Protector (National Parliamentary Ombudsman), the Auditor-General, and so on

2. The Special Investigative Unit
3. The Investigating Directorate on Corruption in the Office of the National Director of Public Prosecutions
4. The recent establishment of the Office of Inspector General within certain state departments including the military, the police, and intelligence services.

As far as civil society is concerned, several active and influential anti-corruption and nongovernmental organizations have adopted the South African NGO Coalition (SANGOCO) Code of Conduct aimed at enhancing their own internal ethical standards. The private sector is also engaged in a number of good governance initiatives. These include the implementation of the proposed business code. This initiative is to ensure that all sectors of the society are involved. Furthermore, the increased attention focused on corruption and the need to establish a process of good governance has necessitated the establishment of Transparency International–South Africa (TI-SA). This is an NGO that seeks to develop an annual profile on corruption and good governance in South Africa. The aim of the profile is to provide information and analyses on corruption and good governance as a first step toward developing comprehensive policy processes within and between different sectors of South African society. It is difficult to ascertain the precise extent of corruption in South Africa. However, the country is rallying to tackle corruption in all its forms through various means. There is therefore a reasonable chance that the efforts will pay off, be it in social, economic, or even political terms.

The State and the Economy

When the Government of National Unity (GNU) came into power, it faced, among other things, the challenge of transforming the economy of the country. It immediately implemented the Reconstruction and Development Program (RDP). The aim of the RDP was to lay the foundations for social and infrastructural development. The key areas to be achieved through the program included the economy, policing, housing, land, education, and health. The RDP hoped that people would be involved in regeneration programs at grassroots level. Building the economy had to focus on growth, development, reconstruction, redistribution and, reconciliation.[61] The key to that was an instrumental program providing effective services that will address basic needs, thereby liberating human capacity and increasing output.[62] The RDP has been further refined through the government's GEAR strategy that is aimed at operationalizing the RDP in the context of the global environment. Even though RPD's delivery has been slow, there are visible positive results; for example, more than a million homes have been supplied with electricity and land redistribution projects are under way.

However, since 1994, there has been a decline of 20 percent in per capita income and even greater deterioration in the overall quality of life. Unemployment has grown disastrously and much of the South Africa population is experiencing crushing poverty.[63] There has been a great decrease in economic and community efficiency and a growing menace of corruption.[64] Basic socioeconomic living conditions in South Africa are still very much unequal in racial terms. Wealth distribution is still racially defined. Black and Colored populations even now receive insufficient education and have high levels of unemployment. Although there is political liberation, economically, South Africa still has a long way to go. The economy is still firmly in the hands of whites. This is not withstanding the emergence of a strong black middle class, in the form of black business empowerment. The disparities are still clear, as the gap between rich and poor is noticeable. Admittedly the country cannot be changed overnight, but most South Africans do feel that the change has been happening at a very slow pace.

Most South Africans are questioning the priorities of the government. For example, the initial goal of the RDP was to provide a million houses in a period of five years from its inception. Delivery has unfortunately been disappointing with lengthy delays and overfinancing. In addition, the government decided to spend billions on the purchase of arms, when the most basic of needs such as housing, have not been met. Furthermore, the government's stance on HIV/AIDS has led the electorate to start questioning its commitment to improving the lives of the poorest of South Africans. The HIV/AIDS saga is one of the most contentious issues in South Africa today. The government's focus on philosophical debates on whether HIV causes AIDS, while crime and unemployment undermine South Africa's democracy, has led to widespread dissatisfaction in all sectors of society. This is especially true for the youth who are directly affected by the pandemic. There is a need for a new vision of the society, one that focuses on creating a new entrepreneurial class.[65] This is the only way to absorb the unemployed masses.

The State and the Environment

In South Africa, like the rest of the world, environmental rights were not taken seriously. Nation building was accorded a higher priority than matters of environmental degradation and pollution.[66] Since 1968, an increasing number of international declarations and statements have, with growing specificity, recognized the fundamental connection between environmental protection and the respect for human rights.[67] This is located in a multiple of multilateral and bilateral treaties among and between states as well as international declarations, programs of action, and resolutions relating to the protection and regulation of the environment.[68] These included the 1968 UN General Assembly Resolution identifying the relationship between the quality of the human environment and the enjoyments of rights, the 1972 Stockholm Declaration, the 1992 Rio Conference on Environment and Development.

The 1996 Constitution guarantees environmental rights by declaring in Section 24 that "everyone has the rights to an environment that is not harmful to their health or well-being and to have an environment that is protected for the benefit of the present and future generation" Like all other human rights, environmental rights touch upon all spheres of human activity, that is, land, water, air, plants, animals, social, economic, political, and cultural activities that form part of our everyday life. This protection is balanced against the constitution's portrayal[69] of a society with pressing social and economic needs.

Apart from protecting people from an unhealthy environment, Section 24 also places a specific duty on the state to take reasonable steps to protect the environment. It stipulates entitlement to an environment of a certain quality, that is not harmful to citizens' health or well-being. The term environment as interpreted in Section 24 of the 1996 Constitution, embraces "everything in man's living space that may possibly have an effect on man or that may be affected by man".[70] Section 24 also imposes duties on the state through legislative and other measures to see to the realization of the rights protected therein.

The government's National Environmental Policy recognizes that people must have access to information to enable them to protect the environment and to participate effectively in environmental governance.[71] One of the major goals of the policy is to develop and maintain mechanisms to increase access to information and ensure effective management of environmental information. The policy further recognizes that information on the state of the environment and activities with adverse or damaging effect on it is essential for effective environmental management, protection, and coordination.

The new policy on environmental management, developed through an exhaustive public participation process, further articulated its overarching goal to "move from a previous situation of unrestrained and environmentally insensitive development to sustainable development." Appropriate political commitment, policy frameworks, and legislation have largely been established to provide an architecture in which environmental protection can take place.

South Africa has fared much better compared with other parts of Africa, where political instability remains an obstacle to advancing the cause of the environment to the benefit of the people. Where there is instability, the environment is always at the bottom of the political agenda. Although South Africa has made significant strides in advancing the cause of the environment, especially in biodiversity, planning, coordination, and public awareness, environmental injustices are still among the biggest challenges facing the country.

South Africa's Continental Relations

Until 12 years ago, South Africa was an international pariah because of its racial segregation policies. Since its 1994 democratic elections, The country carries the hopes of millions of not only South Africans, but the whole continent at large. Its negotiated constitutional settlement, political, and economic stability (at least compared with most African states) and its vast mineral resources are an envy of most developing countries. It is true however that to be regarded as an African icon, South Africa still has a long way to go. It is noteworthy to mention the contribution that most African countries made to the struggle against apartheid in South Africa. Countries such as Tanzania, Nigeria, Zambia, and Botswana, to mention but a few, hosted most of the leaders of the liberation movements who now constitute the governing elite of South Africa. Other African countries such as Nigeria provided substantial funds to South African liberation movements. The discussions that follow will look at the role of South Africa in Africa through the eyes of the African Renaissance debate and the New Partnership for Africa's Development (NEPAD) and the African Union (AU).

The African Renaissance

The "African Renaissance" as a concept has captured the imagination of many South Africans.[72] It is not only a source of inspiration for the new South Africa, but it has also been elevated to a status that its mention or omission can render one either relevant or irrelevant.[73] To many South Africans, the "African renaissance" is a promise of a better life. When Thabo Mbeki, the then deputy president, unveiled the "African

Renaissance," he committed to democracy, development, and cooperative approaches to resolving emerging political challenges around the continent. The idea of the renaissance implies a conscious and determined decision to extricate society out of prolonged decay. But the idea of a renaissance was received with mixed reactions. Skeptics pointed to various flashpoints of political and economic problems like Angola, the DRC, Sierra Leone, and so on.

I agree with the Minister of Provincial and Local Government,[74] that as South Africa represents the hopes of Africans in the continent, it has the following responsibilities:

1. South Africa has to assume intellectual responsibility for ensuring that the "African Renaissance" represents indigenous progressive traditions on the basis of which the African continent shall organize itself into the future.

2. South Africa has to ensure that the vision is grounded on a sound appreciation of the empirical base of the contemporary world. Thus the need for us to subject the threats and opportunities facing our continent to scientific and intellectual analyses cannot be overemphasized.

3. There is a need to overcome the fragmentation of policymaking and intellectual resources that our continent is so well endowed with. All resources available must be mobilized and canalized toward the goal of setting our continent firmly on the path to sustainable development. The "African Renaissance" is not only concerned with political and economic advancement, but it is also about social and cultural renaissance.[75] South Africans see themselves as the part of the motive force for the victory of the "African Renaissance."[76]

The New Partnership for Africa's Development (NEPAD) and the African Union (AU)

It is difficult to separate the role that South Africa plays in NEPAD from its role in the African Union. The birth of the AU should be seen in conjunction with the launch of NEPAD because success in one area will be expected to reinforce success in the other. While upholding sovereignty, equality, and independence, the AU will, in the long term, lead African countries toward developing a common defense policy, a single currency, market synergies, uniform legislation, and the softening of borders.

NEPAD on the other hand, aims to eradicate poverty in Africa and to place African countries both individually and collectively on a path of sustainable growth and development. NEPAD might be regarded as the program of action of the AU. Put differently, the AU is an institutional framework for NEPAD. NEPAD as a mandated initiative of the AU will therefore establish linkages and synergies with all the other initiatives in the continent (especially adopted from the OAU and other regional bodies). South Africa has a prominent role to play in both processes. Its unique transitional process to democracy could serve as a model for democracy in Africa for the peer review process under NEPAD. A number of lessons could be drawn from South Africa's transition that could be applied to other African countries. It is one of the few countries in Africa where, among other positive developments, all political parties who lost electoral contests, nevertheless, accepted the election results. That is why South Africa has been called to play a leading role in resolving the problems in other parts of the continent, such as Burundi and Democratic Republic of the Congo (DRC). This role demands that South Africa be seen at all times to be upholding the principles of democracy and good governance. Just as Africa looks toward Amadou Toumani Toure of Mali for lessons on conflict management, Africa could look toward Thabo Mbeki for lessons on constitution-making processes and good governance. I also acknowledge that for any process to be successful, it has to be relevant to the context in which it is applied. So, instead of copying everything that South Africa did, other countries should only look at those lessons that are relevant to the kind of challenges they face.

Since 1997, South Africa has rekindled the debates on the "African Renaissance." Even though the debate is as old as the fight against colonialism in Africa, South Africa has given it a new meaning and impetus by locating it within the developmental framework of the African continent. It is true that the pillars on which the "African Renaissance" rests are the conceptualization of the AU and the bringing into life of NEPAD. Therefore, South Africa has a prominent role to play in contributing toward the realization of the African dream.

Finally, South Africa served as the Interim Chair of the AU for the first 12 months. That meant President Mbeki, who is a pivotal figure in the effort to get Africa back on its own feet to exercise self-determination, was placed at helm of African affairs. During his term in office, he brought a renewed spirit of rebirth, regional integration, flowering of cultural industries, and economic development to the continent. Furthermore, he helped to set up the structures of the AU within the newly developed work ethos. South Africa is also playing an important role in campaigning against the African debt, a mandate shared with Nigeria and Senegal.

Perspectives of the Youth, Women, and Activists

Having given such a broad background on issues, I would like to focus the discussion in the rest of the chapter on the perspectives of the young people, women, and civil society activists regarding the state in South Africa. It goes without saying that the democratic breakthrough would not have happened had it not been for the contributions made by all peoples in their varying sectors and strata. Key among those is of course the role played by the youth, women, and civil society. However, since the transition, there has been an overwhelming shift in ideologies in all sectors of society. This shift has subsequently led to a different youth, gender and, civil society sector from that obtained before the 1994 elections. The change is also influenced by the change in the nature of governance and politics in the country. So what do these sectors think of the state in South Africa?

State and the Youth in South Africa

As far back as the 1940s, the youth of South Africa have been fighting for recognition by the government. When the Government of National Unity came into being, President Mandela advocated the recognition of this sector of South African community: As he argued, "we must recognize the contribution that young people make to our society. We must build upon the imagination, energy, vibrancy and talents of this our precious national assets"[77] Mandela also observed that "the youth are the valued possession of the nation. Without them, there can be no future. Their needs are immense and urgent. They are the center of reconstruction and development."[78]

To satisfy this need to put youth issues on the national agenda, the GNU established a National Youth Commission. Its main objective was to provide the youth with an opportunity to place their concerns on the national agenda, and thus participate in political processes. The Commission was tasked with identifying youth issues and problems that specifically affect young people as opposed to societal problems. A National Youth Action Plan was then drawn to implement the objectives of the National Youth Policy. To further put youth issues on the national political agenda, the government ratified, without any reservations, the UN Convention on the Rights of the Child (CRC).

South Africa's Constitution is also one of the few in the world that has a "children's rights clause" that ensures socioeconomic rights to children; this is in addition to the other rights in the constitution.

According to a study conducted by the political wing of the ANC Youth League, the change in character, nature, and orientation of youth caused by political, social, and economic changes in South Africa may result in the youth becoming less political, opting for other activities rather than politics. It appears as if the youth cannot identify with the political vision of the government. There is a certain disaffection and disengagement of the youth toward politics. This could be attributed to, among others, the current contradictions blurred by the outstanding resolution of the national question. Issues of HIV/AIDS and unemployment are also high on the list of youth development. Therefore, attention must be paid to those issues to avert further crisis.

Since the 1994 elections, youth organizations have been trying to identify and define new modes of struggle after the collapse of apartheid. Political commentators argue that the current crop of youth leaders does not have clear political guidance.[79] Today's youth leaders, they maintain, display misguided adventurism and violent tendencies that belong to the period before the 1994 era. This was in response to the recent violent demonstrations at some institutions of higher learning. The new political climate has had an effect on the youth movement, reducing the level of youth activism in general. However, there is a different struggle that the youth are involved with, that is the economic struggle. Young people are aspiring business people. In rural areas, young people are leading their communities' reconstruction and development projects. According to *Business Map*'s Lucille Chawere, the youth are proving a safe investment for many businesses and have formed strategic partnerships with the government and the private sector on various developmental fronts. Other collaborations include the National Youth Parliament, under the auspices of the Office of the Presidency, motivated by the rationale that "democracy must be learned by all generations." Provincial legislators and other arms of provincial governments are working together to inculcate a culture of democracy in the youth. However, this is not withstanding the fact that unemployment and crime among the young generation continue to be a threat to the stability of the society.

The African youth are supportive of regional initiatives like NEPAD and AU and the role that South Africa is playing. They would also like to be involved in such initiatives if indeed they are meant to shape the future of the country in which they would be living. To facilitate greater youth involvement in regional initiatives like NEPAD, a youth chapter that would ensure that youth issues are placed on the regional agenda ought to be established. If the young people are going to take Africa through the twenty-first century, they need to be involved at the early stages of any developmental initiative. This will also enable them take ownership of the process.

Gender Perspective

South African women were involved in the struggle against apartheid. Women's sectors were organized within the liberation movements. Issues of gender equality were, however, subsumed under national liberation because at the time people responded to the more obvious source of oppression that was race rather than gender. At that time, women felt that progress would be best achieved by remaining in this political mainstream. There is, however, a growing lobby that argues that South Africa needs an independent women's movement. Debbie Bonin, Editor of the feminist journal, *AGENDA*, argues that there is an over reliance on women MPs and that women should form a national independent women's movement that will put the interests of women first as opposed to the interests of political parties, churches, or unions.

The South African Constitution allows for special measures to be designed and implemented as remedies against past gender discrimination and imbalances. To actualize this requirement, the government established the Gender Commission and the Office of the Status of Women to put the concerns of women on the national agenda. Furthermore, after 1994, the ruling party adopted a quota that led to the dramatic change in the representation of women in parliament. The policy of affirmative action also brought about changes in the representation of women in the employment market. This is notwithstanding the fact that women are still underrepresented in other areas of public life. The growing numbers of gender-based violence against women, unemployment, and poverty perpetuate the growing disillusionment within the gender sector. Most women still live in rural areas under patriarchal systems of traditional leadership.

South African women are still fighting to be accepted as equals and to be given the same opportunities as their male counterparts in the workplace. Discrimination continues to undermine the status of women, despite legislation and policy documents aimed at promoting gender equality. Ingrained attitudes toward women were identified in a recent employment equity plan conducted by the Gauteng Department of

Education as the key reason why many women were overlooked as managers at the secondary school level. But some comfort could be taken from the fact that in terms of policy, women's rights and the need to empower them are taken seriously by the government.

State and Civil Society in South Africa

Civil society groups, more than any other constituency, have played a central and critical role in the struggle to engage a rapacious state and set up new rules of politics.[80] Civil society is also seen as a way of securing substantive political rights and freedoms, essential for a functioning democracy in an arena outside state control.[81] In South Africa particularly, the civil society movement played a very important role, not only of creating links between South Africa and the world, but by also lobbying as pressure groups against the apartheid regime. If civil society had faltered, then the struggle to end apartheid would have faltered too.

The concept of participative governance is fairly new for civil society in South Africa. The challenge faced by civil society in South Africa is that the ANC-led government was in the forefront of the civil society movement. Former President Nelson Mandela alludes to this in his autobiography: "We were taken from the bush, or from underground outside the country or from prisons to come and take charge. We were suddenly thrown into this immense responsibility of running a highly developed country."[82] After decades of mobilization against the state, black civil society "became the state."[83] The liberation movement literally took office.[84] Civil society had to immediately adjust from being a liberation organization to a more service-orientated and professional movement. This has come at a time when around the world many NGOs were urged (not least by donor directives) to move from their more traditional roles (i.e., social activism and mobilization) to that of service providers and implementing agencies for governments and or international financial institutions.[85]

Civil society organizations also suffered their own hardships as they lost most of their prominent leaders to government positions. Not only did they lose key personnel to government and the private sector, but also witnessed the redirection of the largest proportion of foreign[86] funds to government. Civil society experienced organizational havoc and had to face the challenge of finding new ways to relate to government. In addition, these organizations increasingly found themselves excluded from the new developmental agenda. But depending on how this is viewed, it could work as an advantage in the sense that it could lead to a more active and participatory civil society that could urge the government to engage cooperatively with it.

The transformation of civil society also meant that it had to be willing to cooperate with the government, rather than work against it as in the previous dispensation. The movement had to form strategic partnerships with the government and the private sector to ensure that all sectors of the society are involved. This should however not be seen as compromising civil society's overall objective, that of addressing social injustice and standing for the truth. Its independence, freedom, and flexibility could not be compromised either.

A challenge facing both the government and the civil society movement is the fact that parliament is remote from the majority of the citizens. The policy making and law making processes are characteristically intimidating and inaccessible and ordinary people have limited experience of working cooperatively with the government. Ordinary citizens need to understand the link between service delivery and policy and law-making processes and because the lawmaking process is not common knowledge, communities are not motivated to participate in them. A paradigm shift is also needed so that civil society can move away from oppositional politics to embrace participative governance.

On the other hand, there appears to have been a demobilization of civil society following the achievement of representative democracy. According to Jeremy Seekings, the decline in mass direct action in civil society appears to be linked to the public confidence in political society, that is, in the political parties and elected councilors that provide a mechanism for local representation in representative democracy.[87] The crisis facing civic organizations is in large part one of adjustment, as they redefine their roles within the new institutional context, and accept that their roles will be more limited than in specific extraordinary periods in the past.

A wide gap still exists between intellectuals and common people regarding the understanding of sociopolitical issues. This has resulted in apathy in the people at the grassroots level, even in campaigns that would benefit the them. There is a problem of the politicization of the civil society. On the one hand, some civil society institutions seem to be failing to make a distinction between being political and being partisan. Nonpartisanship should be emphasized as a strategy toward maintaining the credibility of the civil society movement.

Recent reports in the media have indicated a drop in the membership of the ANC. According to the report, "the decline in party-activism can be seen as part of the normalization of South Africa's politics." However, it is reported that this could also be attributed to apathy among the middle class black people, together with some popular disillusionment with the government's economic policy, and the party's stance on HIV/AIDS.[88]

It has also been discovered that fewer people participate actively in political parties, and that political parties have become less central in the mediation between citizens and state. However, more people became actively involved in trade unions. Community Based Organizations (CBOs) and sociocultural organizations retained their position in multi-organizational civil society. Women's organization and educational organization particularly grew and became more significant as intermediaries.

Civil society also began playing another role, ensuring accountability on the part of the state, by creating links between the citizens and the state. It also needs to consistently advocate for government transparency and replace the culture of silence with speaking out against government corruption. The current political environment in South Africa is one with difficult challenges as well as exciting opportunities for civil society. In meeting those challenges, they must guard against posing simplistic wedges between the state and themselves and look at the possible avenues for collaboration between different social and political forces working for similar causes.[89] Advocates of participatory democracy and active involvement of civil society in the process of governance have not managed to counter the current emphasis on representative democracy and corporative arrangements.[90]

The experience of community participation in development project presents a mixed picture. The working mechanisms of local development forums, as well as extensive consultation of NGOs with stakeholders and submission made by civil society organizations to influence the policy process have revealed limited ability to make an impact on policy and development. The report also mentions that the channels for the involvement of civil society organizations have not been created, yet in most cases, and where they do exist, they are difficult to access and they yield uncertain results. The results indicate a degree of disillusionment with the feasibility of participatory democracy and people-driven development.

Conclusion

South Africa is unique in many ways: Its constitution-making process can be equaled to no other in the world; its peaceful transition to democracy which featured constitutional principles, the TRC process and the certification process, to mention a few, have no precedence anywhere else in the world; the adoption of the constitutional principles that were a framework for the certification of the process is just as unique; a civil society that has intriguing challenges; the rich diversity of the rainbow nation with its 11 official languages. So how does one even begin to compare this with any other democracy in the world? I think when analyzing the progress of democracy in South Africa, all its unique features with its unique challenges should be taken into account. At the same time, one has to acknowledge that analysis of social and political transformation in South Africa frequently suffers from insularity, for the very reason that we believe that what has happened here has no parallel anywhere in the world.

South Africa's exceptionalism has its advantages and disadvantages. But it is this exceptionalism that has made South Africa what it is today. It is clear that the country has made tremendous progress despite the horrendous legacies of apartheid. The honeymoon period is slowly disappearing in the minds of South Africans and reality is slowly sinking in. There is no need to blame the government for everything that did not go well. All sectors of the society need to take some responsibilities as well. As an example, with regard to the realization of socioeconomic rights, the constitution clearly stipulates that those can only be enjoyed subject to available resources. The government is bound by the constitution not to take retrogressive steps that would render enjoyment of those rights impossible. It is clear that the government has to expedite its processes of making those rights enjoyable. However, progress has been made in this regard.

Although the Reconstruction and Development Program was not very successful, it has nonetheless yielded some positive results. Not long ago in the Limpopo Province (formerly Northern Province), the government celebrated with the millionth recipient of tap water from its project on bringing water to the people. There has been a radical shift in the government's policy on HIV/AIDS (although with the help of the Constitutional Court and pressure groups like the Treatment Action Campaign). The government has agreed to provide the antiretroviral drug, neviropine, to all pregnant mothers. The state has to progressively facilitate the enjoyment of these rights by providing the drug according to the availability of its resources. This is also a case where the doctrine of separation of power could easily be eroded. Similar cases have been brought before the Constitutional Court, and the Court has been forced to provide relief, in most cases, having to direct the government to provide certain services. Is that not undermining the constitutional principle of separation of powers? At the same time, courts are there to ensure that rights are respected and to ensure that the state fulfills its constitutional mandate.

Considering that there are still tremendous challenges ahead, can we say South Africa has made a false start? I do not believe so. South Africa is a much better place compared to what it was 12 years ago. I believe South Africa has learned enough from the other countries in the region to allow its democratic dispensation to go down the drain. I agree with commentators who say that the political situation in the country is normalizing. Yes, the country is facing different challenges now that require different solutions. Therefore, we cannot for example, expect the youth to be just as politically aggressive and vigilant as was the case in the pre-1994 era. However, as it redefines its role, we expect to see a more matured and responsible youth sector that seeks ways of contributing positively to the development of the country.

The fact that South Africa is at the forefront of NEPAD and AU, places another exciting challenge, that of leading by example, on its shoulders. In trying to meet the demands of good governance, democracy and, respect for human rights, South Africa will be forced to put more effort in ensuring that the country is on course. This would, in turn, benefit the country, especially the poorest of the poor in rural communities. President Mbeki would have to adapt to the new circumstances that dictate that he, too, must, among others, allow effective and meaningful participation of the people on the ground.

Anticorruption strategies have yielded a lot of positive results. Recent reports in the media have shown that the courts deal with more cases of corruption. The anticorruption unit of the South African Police Services is hailed as one of the most successful units within the police service. The fact that the Unit has had to deal with corruption by high-level politicians and top civil servants, have restored some confidence in those who had lost faith in the judicial system. This has proved that the arm of the law knows no class or political distinction. Furthermore, crime is being dealt with. The Police Services has shifted its strategies from crime combating to crime prevention. This is also in furtherance of promoting a human rights culture within the Police Service. Turbulence, notwithstanding, democracy is on course in South Africa.

I will bring my conclusion to a close by quoting Pallo Jordan: "Comrade President Mandela has often remarked that we should not behave as if we are dealing with an enemy whom we have defeated on the battle field. Implicit in this warning is that the enemy is still strong and might have unexhausted reserves of power and energy that he could, marshal against us".[91] Therefore it is not enough to say we have the most progressive Bill of Rights in the world, we have done away with apartheid and all its inequalities, we are fighting corruption, and so on. There is still a lot to be done to make this democratic dispensation a reality. The government needs to prioritize its policies in terms of the immediate needs of the people. Eliminating these legacies of apartheid and transforming the entire nature of governance is an ongoing process and it is insufficient to believe that the establishment of a democratic order will and by itself successfully address nation building.

Notes

1. James A. Joseph, "South Africa and Year Three," Speech delivered at the Meridian House International, Washington DC, May 20, 1997, p. 1.
2. J. Kayode Fayemi, "Enforcement and Oversights Institutions in Africa: Current Challenges, Future Prospects," paper presented at the International Conference on Constitutionalism in Transition, Warsaw, Poland, May 17–20, 2001, p. 1.
3. Sebastiao Isata, *Good Governance: An Imperative for Africa in the Third Millennium* (Hout Bay: Gariep Publishing, 2000), p. 3
4. Ibid.
5. Ben Turok, *Beyond the Miracle: Development and Economy in South Africa: A Reader* (Cape Town: Fairshare, 1999), p. 2.
6. Ex parte Chairperson of the Constitutional Assembly: in re Certification of the Constitution of the Republic of South Africa 1996 (First Certification Judgment) 1996 (4) SA 744.
7. Mahomed DP, *Azapo v President of the Republic of South Africa, 1996 (4) SA 671 CC para 1. South African History in a Post card.*
8. Kristin Henrard, "Post-Apartheid South Africa's Democratic Transformation Process: Redress of the Past, Reconciliation and Unity in Diversity," The *Global Review of Ethnopolitics*, vol. 1, no. 3, 2002, pp.18–38.
9. D. Brown, "Speaking in Tongues: Apartheid and Language in South Africa," *Perspectives in Education*, 1988–1989, vol. 7, no. 2, 1989, pp. 33–34.
10. Heather Deegan, *The Politics of the New South Africa: Apartheid and After* (London: Longman, 2001), p. 28.
11. Ben Turok, *Revolutionary Thoughts in the 20th Century* (London: Zed Press, 1980), p. 147.
12. Phillip Frankel, *State, Resistance and Change in South Africa* (London: Croom Helm, 1988), p. 4.
13. Ibid.
14. Verbatim report of President FW de Klerk's speech on the occasion of the Opening of Parliament on February 2, 1990.

15. Hassen Ebrahim, *The Soul of a Nation: Constitution-making in South Africa* (Cape Town: Oxford University Press, 1999), p. 102.
16. Ibid.
17. Ibid.
18. Ibid., p. 153.
19. Deegan, *Politics of the New South Africa*, p. 89.
20. For a useful account of the Constitutional negotiations, see Ebrahim, *The Soul of Nation* (Cape Town: Oxford University Press, 1999).
21. Johan De Waal et al., *The Bill of Rights Handbook* (Cape Town: Juta and Co., Ltd., 2001), p. 2.
22. Deegan, *Politics of the New South Africa*, p. 91.
23. Albie Sachs, *Protecting Human Rights in a New South Africa* (Oxford: Oxford University Press, 1990), pp. 9–10.
24. Heinz Klug, *Constituting Democracy: Law, Globalisalism and South Africa's Political Restructuring* (New York: Cambridge University Press, 2000), p. 1.
25. Hassen Ebrahim, "The Constitutional Assembly Drafting South Africa's New Constitution," paper presented at the International Roundtable on Democratic Constitutional Development, held in Pretoria, South Africa, July 17–20, 1995, p. 22.
26. Ebrahim, *Soul of a Nation: Constitution-Making in South Africa*, p. 4.
27. Julius O Ihonvbere, *Towards a New Constitutionalism in Africa*, CDD Occasional Paper Series, no. 4 (London: Center for Democracy and Development, 2000), p. 58.
28. Preamble to the 1996 Constitution of the Republic of South Africa.
29. Rassie Malhebe, "A New Beginning: Introduction to South Africa's Constitution and Bill of Rights," *Netherlands Quarterly of Human Rights*, vol. 18, no. 1, 2000, p. 4.
30. Regarding the debate on socioeconomic rights in South Africa, see generally Ettienne Mureinid "Beyond a Charter of Luxuries: Economic Rights in the Constitution," *SALJHR*, vol. 8, 1992, p. 464; Betrus De Villiers "Direct Principles of State Policy and Fundamental Rights: The Indian Experience," SALJHR, vol. 8, 1992, p. 29; Dennis Davis "The Case Against Inclusion of Socio-economic Rights Except as Directive Principles," *SALJHR*, vol. 8, 1992, p. 429; Graig Scott and Patrick Macklem "Constitutional Ropes of Sand or Judicial Guarantees? Social Rights in a New South African Constitution," *Pennsylvania Law Review*, vol. 105, 1992, pp. 1–148.
31. Constitution of the Republic of South Africa, Chapter 9.
32. Laxmi M Singhi, *Roundtable on Democratic Constitutional Development*, p. 50.
33. Russell Ally, *The Truth and Reconciliation Commission: Legislation, Process and Evaluation of Impact*, The Center for Human Rights, University of Pretoria, occasional paper, no. 12 (Pretoria: The Center for Human Rights,1999), p. 5.
34. Thomas Ohlson, "South Africa: From Apartheid to Multi-Party Democracy," *SIPRI Yearbook* (Stockholm: SIPRI, 1995).

35. Pallo Jordan, The *National Question in Post-1994 South Africa*, a discussion paper in preparation for the ANC's 50th National Conference, held in Mafikeng , December 16, 1997, p. 4.

36. Neville Alexander, "Language and the National Question," in *Essays on Nation-Building in post-Apartheid South Africa: Between Unity and Diversity*, ed. Gitanjali Maharaj (Pretoria: Institute for Democracy in South Africa, 1999), p.22.

37. Ibid.

38. Section 6 of the 1996 Constitution.

39. Jyoti Mistry, "Conditions of Cultural Protection in post-Apartheid South Africa," *IWM Junior Visiting Fellows' Conference*, vol. 11, no. 8, 2001.

40. Parliamentary speech on the occasion of the signing of the Bill for the establishment of a Commission for the Promotion and Protection of the Rights of Cultural, Religious, and Linguistic Communities, available at http:// www.gov.za (accessed July 12, 2004).

41. Heather Deegan, *South Africa Reborn. Building a New Democracy* (London: Routledge, 1999), p. 37.

42. *Sunday Times*, July 7, 2002, p. 14.

43. *City Press*, June 9, 2002, p. 22.

44. *Sunday Times*, July 14, 2002, p.16.

45. *Mail and Guardian*, June 21–27, 2002, p. 6.

46. *City Press*, June 30, 2002, p. 18.

47. *Mail and Guardian*, April 5–11, 2002, p. 7.

48. The findings are published in an HSRC publication *State of the People: Citizens, Civil Society and Governance in South Africa*, ed. Bert Klandermans et al. (Pretoria: Human Sciences Research Council, 2001), p. 188

49. Robert Schrire, *The Realities of Opposition in South Africa: Legitimacy, Strategies and Consequences*, Konrad Audenuer Stiftung Seminar Report, no. 2 (Berlin: The Konrad Audeneur Foundation 2001), p. 7.

50. Eddie Maloka, *White Political Parties and Democratic Consolidation in South Africa*, Konrad Audenuer Stifung Seminar Report, no. 2., p. 100.

51. Sarakinsky, *Reflection on Politics of Minorities: Race and Opposition in Contemporary South Africa*, p. 197.

52. John Hunt and Reg Lascaris, *The South African Dream* (Pretoria: University of Pretoria Press, 1998), p. 126.

53. Constitution of the Republic of South Africa, 1996

54. D.V. Cowen, *The Foundations of Freedom: Law and Government in Southern Africa* (Cape Town: Oxford University Press, 1961).

55. Rassie Malhebe, "A New Beginning: Introducing South Africa's Bill of Rights," *Netherlands Quarterly of Human Rights*, vol. 18, no. 1, 2000, p. 12.

56. The Economic and Social Report of the SAHRC is available at http:// www.sahrc.org.za (accessed July 12, 2004).

57. Bert Klademans et al., *State of the People*, p. 137.

58. Andre Thomashausen, *Anti-Corruption Measures: A Comparative Survey of Selected National and International Programs*, Konrad Adenauer

Stiftung, occasional paper, (Berlin: Konrad Adenauer Stiftung Foundation, 2000), p. 5.

59. Ibid.

60. John Mbaku, "The State and Anti-Corruption in Africa," paper presented at the Conference on the African State: Beyond False Starts, held at the Grand Valley State University, Allendale, MI, April 11–12, 2002.

61. Heather Deegan, *Politics of the New South Africa*, p. 17.

62. Ben Turok, *Beyond the Miracle: Development and Economy in South Africa*, p. 42.

63. "New Agenda," *Journal of Social and Economic Policy*, vol. 4, no. 4, 2000, p. 104.

64. Ibid.

65. John Hunt and Reg Lascaris, *The South African Dream*, p. 56.

66. Pita Agbese, "The State and The Environment in Africa," paper presented at the International Conference on the African State: Beyond False Starts, held at the Grand Valley State University, Allendale, MI, April 11–12, 2002.

67. K. Bosselman, "Human Rights and the Environment: Redefining Fundamental Principles," paper presented at Conference on Environmental Justice, Melbourne, October 1–3, 1997.

68. Sandra Liebenberg, "Environment in Fundamental Laws in the Constitution," in *Fundamental Rights in the Constitution*, ed. D. Davis et al. (Cape Town: Juta, 1997), p. 256.

69. Rachel Wynberg, "Sustaining the Nation: Environment, Sustainability and Economic Development in a Democratic South Africa, in *Essays on Nation-Building*, ed. Maharaj.

70. Report of the Planning Committee of the Presidential Council on Priorities Between Conservation and Development, PC 5/1984, para. 3.1.

71. Department of Environment Affairs and Tourism, available at http://www.gov.za (accessed July 12, 2004).

72. Eddie Maloka and Elizabeth Le Roux, *Problematizing the African Renaissance* (Pretoria: African Institute of South Africa, 2000), p. 1.

73. Ibid.

74. Speech delivered at the African Renaissance KwaZulu Natal Festival held on March 20, 2002.

75. Thabo Mbeki, *1997 Speech at the Occasion of the Opening of Parliament*, p. 10.

76. Malegapuru Mokgoba, *African Renaissance* (Cape Town: Mafube, 1999), p. xxi.

77. South African National Youth Action Plan.

78. Ibid.

79. *Mail and Guardian*, June 14–20, 2002.

80. Julius O Ihonvbere, "Civil Society, the State and the New Politics in Africa," paper presented at the Conference on The African State: Beyond False Starts, held at the Grand Valley State University, Allendale, MI, April 11–12, 2002, p. 1.

81. D. Williams and T.Young , "Civil Society and Democratization," paper presented at the annual Conference of the British International Studies Association, 1993.

82. Anthony Sampson, *Mandela: The Authorized Autobiography* (New York: Vintage 1999), p. 495.

83. Klademans et al., *State of the People*, p. 133.

84. Kladermans, "A Movement Takes Office," *State of the People*, p. 133.

85. Hermien Kotze, "Swimming in a Wild Sea: The New Challenges Facing Civil Society," in *Essays on Nation-Building*, ed. Maharaj, p. 183.

86. Ibid., p. 172.

87. Jeremy Seekings, "Democratization and Urban Politics in South Africa," paper presented at the Urban Futures Conference, Johannesburg, July 2000, p. 1.

88. *Maila and Guardian*, March 15–21, 2002, p. 6.

89. Ran Greenstein et al., eds., *Civil Society and the State in South Africa: Past Legacies, Present Realities and Future Prospects* (Johannesburg and Cape Town: CASE, 1998).

90. Ibid.

91. Pallo Jordan, "The National Question."

PART III

Prospects for the Future

CHAPTER 9

State Renewal in Africa:
The Lessons

Pita Ogaba Agbese and George Klay Kieh, Jr.

Introduction

The various case studies in this volume on democratizing states in Africa have mapped out the travails of the difficult task of reconstituting the postcolonial state. Each of the case studies discusses the major short-comings of the particular postcolonial state, and the efforts by each of the countries to address these challenges through the state reconstitution project. Clearly, the countries examined in this volume have made laudable strides in addressing the plethora of cultural, economic, political, and social problems that have hamstrung the reconstitution of the post-colonial state. While they have made important strides in addressing their horrendous past records, they still have a long way to go. As crucial as the reforms undertaken in the past few years have been, they have fallen far short of meeting the expectations of the vast majority of the African people. As Adebayo Olukoshi aptly observes, "Of course, the reform process is itself incomplete in many respects, and there are still many important missing links that need to be in place. . . ."[1] In other words, irrespective of the level of progress made, all of the democratizing states addressed in this volume continue to face the enduring conundrum of reconstituting polities based on democratic processes. For state reconstitution to be judged a success, it must entail the following: (1) The democratic processes embedded in the reconstitution effort must be locally focused; (2) Politicoeconomic structures created in the wake of the reform must be democratic; (3) A major objective behind the reform must entail enhancing the ability of Africans to govern themselves, live together peacefully, and generate the wealth needed to confront poverty and deprivation; (4) State reconstitution will be meaningful only if the welfare of the people is the priority in public policymaking and implementation.[2]

Against this background, the purpose of this chapter is to decipher the lessons that can be drawn from the state reconstitution project in Africa, especially in the context of the experiences of Botswana, Cote d'Ivoire, Ghana, Kenya, Mauritius, Nigeria, and South Africa. In other words, what insights can we draw from the modalities that are being used by these polities to reconstitute their states?

The Lessons

Based on the experiences of the democratizing states addressed in this volume, we have identified several common issues as the bedrock of the lessons for state renewal. In this section of the chapter, we will address each of these issues.

The Nature of the Postcolonial State

The postcolonial state is a foreign construct. It was fashioned to reflect the interests and proclivities of the colonialists and imperialists. So, the postcolonial state does not reflect the objective conditions of African societies, including their cultures.

Against this backdrop, a sine qua non for successful state reconstitution is stripping the postcolonial state of its compositional core, its foreign-based orientation. This should be replaced by a new construct that reflects the values, beliefs, and norms of indigenous African cultures. Also, the reconstituting state should reflect the aspirations and interests of the African people rather than external interests.

The Character of the Postcolonial State

The character of the postcolonial state is a major hindrance to the democratic reconstitution of the state. It has been described variously in the scholarly literature as brutal, criminalized, negligent, neopatrimonial, oppressive, prebendal, predatory, privatized, rent-seeking, repressive, and suppressive. Accordingly, such a sordid character is antithetical to the democratic reconstitution of the state in Africa. As Julius Ihonvbere correctly observes, "the same repressive state that had shot at children, women, students and protesters yesterday, cannot be used to mobilize the people for justice, democracy, accountability, and development."[3]

Clearly, the reconstituted state must have a new character. At the core of the new character must be a consistent commitment to holistic democracy. That is, the reconstituted state must respect and promote the cultural, economic, environmental, religious, security, social, and political rights and freedoms of all of its citizens. It cannot be a state whose primary function is to enhance a minority class or group to use the instrumentality of governmental power for private appropriation of the commonwealth. So long as the state remains the exclusive preserve of particular groups or classes, so long will it be characterized by corruption, brutality, and repression.

Insights from the Traditional Systems

It is important that the state reconstitution project draws from the experiences of traditional African systems. This is because there is a wealth of knowledge that can be garnered in virtually every sphere: governance, the economy, and so on. For example, some of the precolonial state formations in Africa had political systems that fostered the tenets of political democracy. Also, there were various systems of state and multiple forms and types of governments. At the base of these various arrangements was a panoply of rules and norms covering a broad gamut of political issues, from routine administrative functions to the resolution of conflicts.

In the economic arena, precolonial African societies had a mode of production and its attendant relations of production that had, as their fulcrum, the promotion of the welfare of all the citizens. Similarly, the patterns of distribution of resources reflected the egalitarian ethos of these societies.

Socially, the various indigenous African societies stressed the importance of addressing the basic needs of the citizens, food, housing, education, and so forth. This orientation minimized poverty, deprivation, and inequalities. It also reduced the scope and intensity of conflicts.

So, rather than looking exclusively to Western countries for systemic models in the various spheres, African states can examine and learn from their own traditional systems. The purpose is not to recreate precolonial Africa; but, rather the idea is that the state reconstitution process must benefit from the consideration of a wide range of experiences, traditional African, Western, and so on. Ultimately, the specific contents of the reconstituted state must reflect the objective conditions of each African society.

The Exigency of a Developmental State

There is no doubt that a democratically reconstituted state can play a progressive role in helping to engender economic development. It can perform several critical roles. It can develop a national blueprint for development through consultation with the various stakeholders. The national blueprint would, inter alia, map out the totality of the development agenda, identify the modalities for implementation and the means to fund the various projects and programs.

Another crucial role would be the state's participation in the economy through its ownership and control of some of the major means of production. The purpose would be to provide various public goods to the citizens at reasonable cost, below what private enterprises would charge. This economic role of the state will enhance equitable distribution of public resources and will minimize greed and corruption. The current fashionable idea that the African state's economic role should be reduced to the barest minimum does not have historical validity in any part of the world. In the African case, given the ravages of colonialism and the depressing backlog of developmental activities that need to be urgently attended to, there is, as yet, no substitute for a robust, effective, and efficient state in the economic arena. Privatization and other forms of state withdrawal from the economy do not provide answers to what the continent needs for its accelerated growth and development.

Constitution and Constitutionalism

The reconstituted state must be governed by a compact embodied in a constitution. The constitution-making process must be process-led. That is, the drafting of the constitution must involve the participation of all citizens in the polity, not just the members of the political class or the literate few. Specifically, the drafting of the constitution must be based on extensive consultations, discussions, and debates at various levels of the society. The ostensible purpose is to help ensure that the views of all of the stakeholders are heard and taken into account. An open, inclusive, and consultative constitutional process helps to cement the idea that the constitution belongs to every citizen and not just the wealthy or the articulate few.

It is not however enough to invest ownership of the constitution on the people if their material interests, hopes, and aspirations are not reflected in the resultant document. Substantively, within a democratic framework, the constitution must address several critical issues such as citizenship, the obligations of the state to its citizens, the obligations of citizens to the state, the obligations of citizens to citizens, cultural, economic, security, political, religious, and social rights and responsibilities, the system of state, the system of government, the form of government, the distribution of power at the broader systemic and governmental levels, minority rights (for multiethnic and multiracial societies), group rights, and gender equality. In essence, while it is true that a constitution cannot possibly address all the issues confronting a polity, nevertheless, there are issues that are at the base of every democratic compact. And addressing these base issues is pivotal to the stability of the polity.

Clearly, it is not sufficient for a state to simply have a democratic constitution. More critical is the need to make the constitution a living document. In other words, the state functionaries and civil society groups must ensure compliance with the tenets of the constitution. This watchdog role devolves on every individual and group and institution. The practical application of the constitution is indispensable to the functioning and maintenance of a reconstituted democratic polity. In short, the constitutional order would be meaningless, if it is simply anchored on legalese devoid of praxis.

The Economy

Economically, the state must be what John Mukum Mbaku terms "protective."[4] That is, the state must provide an enabling environment for the creation of wealth needed to effectively confront poverty and deprivation.[5] The state can play this crucial role in many ways. The peripheral capitalist economic systems and their attendant pantomimes should be addressed. The kernel of the mode of production must shift from the exclusive reliance on monocrop or monomineral economies to diversification—agricultural, industrial, manufacturing, and service. The advantage is that sectoral diversification will help insulate the state and its citizens from the vicissitudes of the international capitalist order. Currently, because each African state relies either on an agricultural product or a mineral as the lifeblood of its economy, the decline in the prices of these agricultural products and minerals has devastating ramifications. For example, the decline in the prices of primary products means a corresponding reduction in an African state's export earnings. In turn, this negatively impacts the state's capacity to address the myriad social and economic problems.

Also, the wealth of the state must not be monopolized by, and used for the sole benefits of the members of the ruling class. The age-old practice in Africa has been, and continues to be the commandeering and use of the state resources for the benefit and comfort of the members of the ruling class, their families, and their coterie of supporters. Concurrently, the masses are marginalized and relegated to the periphery, where they wallow in abject poverty, mass misery, and socioeconomic malaise.

The reconstituted state should promulgate and enforce rules regarding all aspects of the economy—property rights, business and commercial rules, banking laws, insurance regulations, and so on. The purpose should not be the bureaucratization of the economy but rather an earnest effort to establish a stable economic architecture that minimizes arbitrariness and capriciousness. Undoubtedly, by basing the economy on well established institutions and clearly articulated rules, both consumers and producers would develop the confidence that is exigent for the promotion of economic exchanges.

A related issue is that the state must take steps to reduce the huge disparities in wealth between the compradorial and the subaltern classes. Specifically, this would require that the state formulates and implements policies that are designed to redistribute the national wealth.

Another critical issue is the provision of employment opportunities. The state should help create jobs in the private sector by helping with the establishment of nationalistic entrepreneurial classes. Through the provision of incentives such as tax holidays, duty free privileges for a period of time, and assistance with loans, the state can help the indigenous entrepreneurial classes to create jobs. Also, operating within a pro-people development framework, the state should encourage foreign investors to create jobs. Central to the exigency of employment opportunities is the development of a wage structure that enables African workers to have a decent standard of living. That is, based on the prevailing cost of living in each reconstituting African state, a wage structure should be developed that ensures that workers would earn salaries that can enable them to cover the basic necessities of life—shelter, food, and so on. In other words, it is imperative for the reconstituted African state to ensure that workers, both in the public and private sectors, earn living-wages. The current practice in which workers and pensioners are owed several months' salaries is detrimental to the well-being of workers and their families. It also portrays the state as an uncaring and insensitive institution.

The custodians of African states should develop modalities for minimizing and controlling corruption. Operationally, this could include the development and enforcement of a code of conduct for all public officials that includes the declaration of assets prior to the assumption of their offices, the making of regular annual disclosures of assets, and the issuance of final declarations on leaving their respective offices. A public commission devoid of political control should be established to enforce the code of conduct. Critically, the custodians of the state must have the political will to prosecute those who are engaged in corrupt practices.

Similarly, resources must be managed effectively and efficiently. The *modus operandi* should be that resources would be allocated prudently and steps would be taken to ensure the attainment of maximum public benefits. Embedded in the resource management culture should be the orientation toward the minimization of waste, especially the pervasiveness of conspicuous consumption in the public sector.

In addition, the custodians of the reconstituted state must reject the neoliberal *Weltanschauung* of the International Monetary Fund (IMF) and its associated asphyxiating Structural Adjustment Programs (SAPS). Clearly, as the repository of evidence shows, SAPS have promoted the interests of the suzerains of international finance capital but have wrecked the economies of African states and worsened social conditions. For example, the requirement that national currencies be devalued has made it virtually impossible for ordinary citizens to afford to meet their basic human needs. This is because as export enclaves, even the reconstituting African states remain reliant on imported goods. For example, the Cedi, the Ghanaian currency, is now virtually worthless. Similarly, the Nigerian currency, the Naira that in 1980 exchanged for $2 has been so devalued that by the end of 2005, 1 dollar exchanged for 145 Naira! While low exchange rates of African currencies benefit the ruling class, the resultant effect of a low exchange rate regime is the escalating cost of living for ordinary people. African states can impose their own regimes of financial discipline, through, *inter alia*, the prudent management of their resources. In other words, African states do not need IMF financial management tutelage. Instead, African states can develop their own modalities contingent upon the objective conditions prevailing in their respective countries.

Relatedly, African states should ensure that loans that are contracted from both domestic and international sources are invested in revenue-generating projects. These *revenue generating projects* would provide the capital for servicing the debts in the short time and ultimately paying them off. Conversely, the investment of loans in conspicuous consumption would not only increase the debt burden, but would also require the state to shift resources, especially from critical national needs such as education, health, housing, and so on to debt servicing.

African leaders must also disabuse their minds that the be-all and end-all of economic reform is the privatization of state-owned enterprises. Despite all the noise about the benefits of privatization, the reality is that the exercise has merely enabled the rich to continue to feed at the public trough without a corresponding advantage to the people.

Governance

One of the major lessons is that governance is critical to the state reconstitution project in Africa. But, in contradistinction to the chorus hailing "good governance" as the only appropriate genre, "democratic governance" is a better model. This is because democratic governance encapsulates and transcends the limited ambit of good governance—the efficient management of state resources—and includes the development of modalities that can address the epicenters of African states' cultural, economic, environmental, security, political, and social problems. While the "good governance model" is an important first step, it cannot be treated as the "only game in town." This is because the mere effective management of state resources, as important as it is, does not capture the totality of the "governance deficit" that has plagued African states. The point is that governance must be anchored on a more comprehensive multiplex that embodies the multidimensionality of the African crisis. Specifically, operating under the ambit of democratic governance, new pluralistic-centric institutions would be developed; new rules and processes would be formulated; and policies would be formulated and implemented to address issues such as abject poverty, hunger, access to health care, quality public education, and environmental degradation. Such a comprehensive approach to governance would help address the undercurrents of political instability much more than just the prudent management of public resources.

Importantly, in order to be successful, democratic governance must operate within the framework of democratic politics. That is, the efficient and effective management of state resources and the formulation and implementation of public policies to address the crises of underdevelopment must be conducted in an environment that promotes the free and frank exchange of ideas and views, including the tolerance for, and respect for dissenting views, the centrality of institutions and processes, the sanctity of the rule of law, accountability, and transparency. In essence, the issue of governance must be an essential part of the broader democratization project.

Significantly, the success or failure of the governance enterprise is dependent upon the quality of political leadership. Successful state reconstitution in Africa requires what Julius Ihonvbere calls a "new crop of highly motivated, committed, democratic, honest, and enlightened leadership—a leadership that appreciates the value of civil society, the rule of law, constitutions, and humanity, and in addition recognizes the meaning of pluralism, identity, nationality, and difference."[6] Undoubtedly, the perennial authoritarian leadership in African states is anathema to the reconstitution of the state; hence, it lacks both the will and the capacity to shepherd the state reconstitution project. Therefore, unless the old authoritarian regime is fundamentally transformed, that is, democratized, the state reconstitution project would essentially become an exercise in futility.

Political Parties

Undoubtedly, viable political parties are critical to the state reconstitution enterprise in Africa. This is because political parties are the primary vehicles through which the competition for the legitimate acquisition and control of state power occurs. Accordingly, the success or failure of the state reconstitution project is dependent upon the quality of leaders and programs that these political parties offer. In this vein, it is imperative that viable and vibrant political parties be established in Africa. Such political parties must transcend the realm of mere vehicles for electoral contests, and must remain visible and active in the political arena on a regular basis. Drawing from this, there are several critical steps that African political parties should take in order to make meaningful contributions to the reconstitution of the state and the broader democratization agenda. At the base, African political parties must be national in scope. That is, they must seek to recruit members and candidates from each state's various ethnic groups. Also, they must establish and maintain functional offices throughout the country, not just in the urban centers.

Another critical step is that political parties must be based on clearly articulated ideological frameworks. In turn, these ideological prisms must set the parameters for formulation and promotion of competing national agendas to help present the electorate and the citizenry at large with clear leadership choices.

In addition, African political parties should design and implement various plans with the primary objective of developing a viable economic base. Having a viable economic base is critical to each political party's ability to promote its programs and compete effectively in the electoral arena. It is also essential to the ability of the parties to maintain their independence.

Civil Society Organizations

Civil society organizations have two broad sets of critical functions in the promotion of democratic state reconstitution in Africa. They should serve as effective checks on the custodians of state power. However, in order to adequately perform this function, civil society organizations must develop competencies and constituencies. In other words, they should develop expertise in the area or areas of their operational scope. Armed with the requisite expertise, they can evaluate the state's performance in these particular areas and offer alternatives.

The second broad function is to provide information to the general public. Civil society organizations can serve as vehicles for educating the citizenry about the policies and performance of the state. Clearly, this would require a balanced and objective assessment rather than partisan-based criticisms.

Political and Civil Liberties

One of the major hallmarks of a reconstituted state is the government's demonstration, through concrete actions, that the polity is committed to the promotion and protection of fundamental political and civil liberties—freedoms of association, speech, press, thought, movement, and so forth. Of the country case studies in this volume, only two—Botswana and Mauritius—have long records in the state's promotion and protection of political and civil liberties. In contradistinction, in the case of Nigeria, for example, the country has been a cesspool of authoritarianism, particularly of the military variety.[7] Therefore, the state reconstitution project in Nigeria is quite nascent: It began in 1999, following the end of military rule and the commencement of the transition to democratization. Almost seven years after the return of the military to the barracks, there are still indications of the deep entrenchment of the authoritarian reflex. For example, the forced resignation of Audu Ogbeh as the National Chairman of the ruling People's Democratic Party (PDP) because of his criticisms of the policies of President Olusegun Obasanjo, is a vivid reminder that the state reconstitution project in Nigeria will be long and arduous, especially the transformation of what we term the "militaristic presidency." Because Nigeria was under military rule for 30 of its 44 years of independence, the military culture has conditioned the country's presidency and created a "militaristic presidency." For example, under the "militaristic presidency," the incumbent perceives himself as a military general and the society as an amalgam of subordinate officers and enlisted men and women. Hence, President Obasanjo expects and requires that his views, edicts, and orders would not be challenged, but simply obeyed and scrupulously implemented. What makes the matter even more problematic is that President Obasanjo fancies himself as a messiah who would single-handedly resolve all the country's ills and crises. A pliant legislature and a timid judiciary have allowed President Obasanjo to run the country according to his own whims and caprices. Ahmadu Ali, a retired Army Colonel whom Obasanjo handpicked to succeed the ousted Audu Ogbeh as PDP chairman, recently articulated the militarized nature of politics in Nigeria. When Chairman Ali was asked about an orchestrated attempt to have Governor Ladoja of Oyo State impeached, he argued that Ibadan, the state capital, was a like a military garrison and that Adedibu, Ladoja's erstwhile godfather, was the garrison commander who must be obeyed by Ladoja!

In Kenya, the authoritarian state took roots at independence, and kept its stranglehold on the polity until 2003, when the ruling Kenyan African Union (KANU) was ousted from power in the country's first democratic elections. The new government led by President Mwai Kibaki has outlined and is endeavoring to execute the state reconstitution project. But, as in Nigeria, the vestiges of authoritarianism have mounted a campaign of resistance that is designed to undermine the democratic reconstitution of the Kenyan State. As in Nigeria, corruption has become so entrenched that Kibaki who ran as an anticorruption candidate, has not been able to make much headway against it.

Basic Human Needs

The state reconstitution project must be designed to address the basic needs—food, education, healthcare, and shelter—of the people. Addressing the basic needs of the citizens is indispensable to the success of the state reconstitution enterprise. This is because the other aspects of the reconstitution agenda would be meaningless, if the "bread and butter" issues of the people are not met. In the area of food, the state should formulate and implement agricultural policies that would guide food production. For example, the state needs to work with the farmers in helping the latter in a variety of ways, training, and so on to produce enough food to feed the population.

In the area of education, the state must take steps to provide free and compulsory education from the primary to the secondary levels and subsidized education at tertiary public institutions. The loci of the educational enterprise should be developing the skills and competencies of the workers. This would serve as the motor to drive forward national development and nurture informed citizens.

With population on the increase throughout Africa, the state reconstitution project must make the implementation of a national housing program one of its priorities. The purpose would be to provide decent housing, especially for low income earners. In order to succeed, the housing scheme must transcend the boundaries of the urban centers and include the rural areas, and must benefit the intended targets, the low wage earners and the poor.

Security

Central to the process of state reconstitution should be the rethinking of security. This is because the traditional view of security in Africa has been, and is the protection of the incumbent regime or head of state from popular uprisings, military putsches, and hijacked democratic struggles by warlords and armed bandits.[8] In a reconstituted state, on the contrary, the focus of security should be on the provision of the basic needs of the citizens, the protection of their persons from physical harm and the safeguarding of their properties from thievery and illegal destruction. This shift is critical because addressing the human security conundrum is important for the maintenance of domestic peace and tranquility. Undoubtedly, if the needs of the citizens are not addressed by the state, despair would set in. In turn, this would provide fertile grounds for activities that would then adversely affect stability. As the repository of evidence shows, whatever be the resources a regime devotes to its own protection, such a measure ultimately would not succeed if the needs of its citizens are not met. So, there is no doubt that while traditional security is important it must be only secondary to human security.

Gender Equality

The state reconstitution project will not succeed, if it is primarily a male-driven, male-centric, and male-dominated enterprise. The success of the state reconstitution and the larger democratization project would depend upon the forging of a partnership based on gender equality and mutual respect between the male and female citizens of the polity. As Patricia Williams correctly observes, "Women are critical to the democratization and development enterprise in Africa."[9]

Specifically, the agenda to promote gender equality involves four critical issues. First, women must participate meaningfully at all levels—national and local—of the decision-making process. Women should be involved in discussing and debating various issues and policy options and their views should be accorded serious consideration. This is important because the mere demonstration of tokenism would not help to foster the gender equality agenda.

Second, the state must give attention to the education of women. It is quite common in Africa for men to be given priority in education. Women, especially the traditional and rural ones, generally do not have access to educational opportunities. Instead, they are usually relegated to the role of producing and raising children, caring for their respective homes, and assisting on the family farm.

Third, priority must be given to the health issues of women. This means that the state must allocate significant portions of the national health budget to the meeting of the health needs of women, including rural women. Generally, rural women have limited access to health services; therefore, particular attention must be paid to their health needs.

Fourth, the state must formulate and implement laws that are designed to protect women from violence. This would entail, among other things, the designing and enforcement of laws dealing with spousal abuse and rape. This would help to minimize the capricious beating of women by their husbands, boyfriends, and other males. In addition, effective enforcement of laws against violence on women will help arrest the increasing incidence of the sexual exploitation of underaged girls by men.

Ethnic Pluralism

Since the postindependence era in Africa, ethnic privileging has become an albatross around the democratization project is neck in many states. Even the custodians of the state have become ethnic entrepreneurs, who have used ethnic diversity for the purposes of "divide and rule." Given the fact that many African regimes lack broad-based national support, it is fashionable for the custodians of the state to pit one ethnic group against another or others. The ostensible goal is to divert the attention of the citizenry away from the crises of the state. Too many Africans have been killed in senseless violence because of the political manipulation of ethnic identities.

Against this background, as part of the state reconstitution project, various steps must be taken to promote peaceful coexistence in multi-ethnic societies. At the core of the enterprise must be the promotion of the value of respect for ethnic diversity. That is, each ethnic group should have the right to take pride in its culture, while simultaneously respecting other groups' cultures. Additionally, the reconstituted state must promote the idea of an "ethnic mosaic": The reconstituted state should promote the idea that all its ethnic groups are integral parts of a larger national tapestry. Also, as John Mukum Mbaku notes, "The [reconstituted] African state should provide mechanisms that do not place any individual or group at a competitive disadvantage or advantage in the competition for resources on the basis of ethnicity."[10]

Religious Pluralism

Like ethnicity, religion has become a potent weapon in the hands of the advocates of intolerance and self-righteousness. For example, in a reconstituting state like Nigeria, religious conflicts are on the increase, especially the resort to violence. These religious conflicts have primarily been between Christian and Islamic groups. Beneath these conflicts are deep-seated ethnic and regional antagonisms. In many cases, the so-called religious conflicts have very little to do with competing theological dogmas. Such conflicts have led to the deaths of scores of people, including the innocent and the destruction of both public and private properties.

The state reconstitution project throughout Africa can learn several major lessons from the travails of religious intolerance. The base lesson is that the state should be secular. That is, the reconstituting state cannot be subservient to any religion in the formulation and implementation of public policies and the overall treatment of citizens. In other words, the state must be religiously neutral. Religion must be an individual matter, not a prerogative of the state. The other related lesson is that all religions including traditional African religions, should have equal recognition, access, and treatment under the law. No matter how religiously pious, an African political leader is, or pretends to be, it must be made clear that such a person was elected as a political leader and not as a spiritual leader. The current practice in Nigeria in which President Obasanjo sees himself as a "born-again" Christian and as the commander-in-chief of the faithful is as phony as it is dangerous. Finally, the state should promote the idea of tolerance and mutual respect among its various religious groups.

Conclusion

The chapter has attempted to draw the lessons that are common to the state reconstitution projects in Botswana, Cote d'Ivoire, Ghana, Kenya, Mauritius, Nigeria, and South Africa. The base lesson is that the success of the state reconstitution project is dependent upon the degree to which the postcolonial state is deconstructed and democratically reconstructed. Specifically, the nature and the character of the postcolonial state must be changed. There is agreement that the character of the postcolonial state is the embodiment of the values, norms, and interests of external powers. Thus, the state reconstitution project should give importance to the development of a new character of the state that reflects the features of the cultures of the various African states. As for the nature of the state, there is the need to strip it of its anti-people and anti-democratic core. The reconstituted state should have in fact, a pro-people, pro-development and pro-democracy character.

Specific lessons were then drawn from a compendium of issues. One of the major issues is the need to establish a developmental state in Africa: The reconstituting state needs to play an active role in the promotion of democratic development that focuses, *inter alia*, on addressing the needs of the citizens. Also, insights need to be drawn from the experiences of traditional African systems of governance coupled with democratic governance, a people-centered economic agenda, the promotion of respect for political and civil rights, ethnic and religious pluralism, addressing the basic human needs of the citizens, and a rethinking of security that would involve an emphasis on human security.

Finally, the state reconstitution project must be an integral part of the larger project of holistic democratization—empowering the citizenry and addressing their cultural, economic, political, security, social, and religious needs. Confronted with the multidimensional crises of the African state, the state reconstitution project has no choice but to take cognizance of the criticality of addressing the broad gamut of social pantomimes, as the *sine qua non* for the success of the enterprise.

Notes

1. Adebayo Olukoshi, "State, Conflict and Democracy in Africa: The Complex Process of Renewal," in *State, Conflict and Democracy in Africa*, ed. Richard Joseph (Boulder, CO: Lynne Rienner Publishers, 1999), p. 451.
2. See Julius O. Ihonvbere and John Mukum Mbaku, "Introduction: Establishing Generalities and Specificities in Africa's Struggle for Democracy and Development," in their edited volume *Political Liberalization and Democratization in Africa: Lessons From Country Experiences* (Westport, CT: Praeger, 2003), p. 3.
3. Julius Ihonvbere, "Africa in the Twenty-First Century: The Challenges and Opportunities," in *Preparing Africa for the Twenty-First Century*, ed. John Mukum Mbaku (Aldershot, UK: Ashgate Publishing Co., 1999), p. 53.

4. See John Mukum Mbaku, "Making The State Relevant in African Societies," in his edited volume, *Preparing Africa for The Twenty-First Century*, p. 317.

5. Ibid.

6. Ihonvbere, "Africa in the Twenty-First Century," p. 54.

7. For an assessment of Nigeria's record on political and civil liberties, see Freedom House, Freedom in the Country Ratings, 1972–1973 to 2001–2002, available at www.freedomhouse.com (accessed August 22, 2005).

8. See George Klay Kieh, Jr., "Regional Security and Sustainable Development in Africa," in *Sustainable Development in Africa*, ed. Okechukwu Ukaga and Osita Afoaku, . (Trenton, NJ: Africa World Press, 2004), p. 169.

9. Patricia Williams, "Women: The Other Variable in Africa's Development Struggle," in *Preparing Africa for the Twenty-First Century*, ed. John Mbaku, p. 293.

10. John Mukum Mbaku, "Ethnicity, Constitutionalism and Governance in Africa," in *Ethnicity and Governance in the Third World*, ed. John Mabaku, Pita Ogaba Agbese, and Mwangi S. Kimenyi (Aldershot, UK: Ashgate Publishing, 2001), p. 95.

Index

Aba mu awie, 105, 107
Abacha, Sani, 13
Abdul-Rasheem, Tajudeen, 20–21
Abiola, Moshood, 209
Abubakar, Atiku, 14, 15
Acheanpong, General Ignatius Kutu
    execution of, 121n.2
    NRC regime, 105
Addo-Kufuor, Kwame, 111
Affirmative action, 248
Africa and the Curse of the Nation-State, 80
Africa
    colonial era, 8–9, 12
    Constitutional Politics Model, 17–19
    economic privatization, 16t
    Institutional Reform Model, 14–16
    multiparty states, 19
    needs of, 27–28
    political developments, 19–20
    Power-Sharing Model, 16
    precolonial social contract, 18
    reconstitution thresholds, 23–24
    state legitimacy, 181–182
    State Deconstruction Model, 19
Africa Competitiveness Report, on
    Mauritius, 199
Africa Growth and Opportunity Act
    (AGOA), Mauritius, 198
African Charter on Human and People's
    Rights, 255
African National Congress (ANC)
    Afrikaner Volkstad, 247
    banning of, 237
    CODESA talks, 239–240

    dominance of, 249–251
    formation of, 236–237
    in GNU, 242
    negotiations with government, 239
    victory of, 28
African National Congress (ANC)
    Youth League, 264
African People's Party (APP), Kenya,
    138
"African Renaissance," 260–261, 262
African state. *See also* Postcolonial state
    analysis of, 11–12
    failure of, 3–5, 11, 12, 75
    lessons learned, 280–292
    and political class, 234
    and popular sovereignty, 10
    postcolonial expectations, 8, 9
    reconstitution criteria, 279–280
    theoretical considerations of,
        77–81
    view of, 136–137, 172
*African State at a Critical Juncture,
    The*, 80
African Union (AU), 235, 261–263,
    270
Afrikaner nationalism, 236, 247
Afrique Occidentale Française, 84
Agbese, Pita Ogaba
    lessons learned, 27
    on the Nigerian state, 212
    on state reconstitution, 23
Age-set system, Kenyan, 128
Agenda for Positive Change, An, 108,
    113, 114, 115

296 • Index

Agricultural Development Policy,
    Botswana, 62
Agricultural Development Program
    (ADP), Bakolori project, 221–222
Agricultural Finance Corporation
    (AFC), 149–150
Ajayi, Ade, 218–219
Ake, Claude, 217
Alamieyesigh, Diepreye, 223
Ali, Ahmadu, 289
All Workers Conference (AGO),
    Mauritius, 198
Alubo, Sylvester Ogoh, 26
Amnesty Committee, South Africa, 245
Amondji, Marcel, 93
Anangwe, Amukowa, 135
Angola, 15t
Angoulvant, Governor Gabriel, 83
Apartheid
    replacement of, 26
    in South Africa, 235–239
arap Moi, Daniel
    economic development, 134
    human rights violations, 153,
        154–155
    Kalenjin favoritism, 141, 142
    multiparty system, 139
    state reconstitution, 25, 165–166
Aseka, Eric, 134, 152
Atger, Paul, 82
Aura Poukou, Queen of Sakasso, 82
Awolowo, Obafemi, 209
Ayyiteh, George, 82
Azanian People's Organization
    (AZAPO), 250
Azapo v. President of South Africa, 235

Babangida, General Ibrahim
    "ethnicization" of, 209
    military coup, 215
    SAPs, 216–217
Badru, P., 211
Bakalanga people, 48, 64
Bakassi Boys, 220
Bakolori Massacre, 221–222

Bank of Botswana, 42, 44
Banking industry, Nigeria, 213
Bantu people, Kenya, 127, 129
Basadi, Emang, 55, 56–57
Basarwa people. *See* San groups
Battersby Report, on Mauritius,
    199–200
Beckman, B., 222
Bedié, President Henri Konan
    deposition of, 85
    mismanagement of, 86, 95
    relationship with France, 93
Bello, Walden, 218
Benedict, B., 186
Benin, 17t
Berlin Conference, Cote d'Ivoire, 83–84
"Berlin Conference/OAU framework," 80
Berlinguer, Giovanni, 217
Berman, Bruce, 147
"Best loser" system, Mauritius, 26, 83,
    187
Bheenick, R., 189
Bill of Rights
    Kenyan constitution, 154
    South Africa, 241, 244, 252
Black Consciousness Movement,
    237–238
Black Man's Burden, The, 80
"Blow to the state," 76, 86
Bologun, Tafa, 21
Bondoukou, Kingdom of, 82
Bonin, Debbie, 265
Botha, P. W., 238, 239
Botswana
    as accountable state, 22
    civil society, 51–52, 60–65
    colonial era, 34–35, 46, 66
    discussions of, 33
    economic development, 35–44,
        67–70
    evaluation of, 65–72
    modernization agenda, 36, 40–41
    political/civil liberties, 288
    political interest groups, 45–47
    as single party state, 47, 71

and South Africa, 260
state reconstitution, 22, 24
Botswana Democratic Party
early role, 46–47
plural politics, 55–60
single party state, 47, 49–55
Botswana Development Corporation,
39, 69
Botswana Housing Corporation, 58
Botswana Meat Commission, 37
Botswana National Front (BNF), 54
Botswana People's Party (BPP), 53–54
British colonial empire
Kenyan Protectorate, 130–131
Mauritius, 184
Nigeria, 206–207
Buhari, General Muhammadaud, 215
Bunwaree, Sheila, 25–26
Burkina Faso
job losses, 17t
separation from Cote d'Ivoire, 88
Burundi, 5t
Bushmen. *See* San groups
Business, in Ghana, 108, 116, 117

Cantons, 84
Cattle-beef industry, Botswana, 36, 37,
39
Center of Human Rights and
Democracy (CHRD), 156
Cercles, 84
Chad, 4
Chama Cha Umma (CCU), 140
Chang, Ha Joon, 191
Chawere, Lucille, 264
Chef de cantons, 84, 88
Chieftainship Act, 64
Chinese Mauritians, 185
Christians, in Nigeria, 209
Chunga, Bernard, 169
Citizenship
Botswana, 60–61
Nigeria, 226
Civil service, Nigeria, 215
Civil society

in Botswana, 51–52
in Nigeria, 227
in the postcolonial state, 288
in South Africa, 263, 266–268
Civilian control, 110–113
Class, state failure, 78
Climate, Botswana, 40
Colonial era
Africa, 8–9, 18
Botswana, 34–35
British Kenya, 130–133, 147–148
Cote d'Ivoire, 82, 83–84
Mauritius, 184–186
Nigeria, 206, 208–209
Comite National de Salut Public
(CNSP), 85
Commercial triangle, 211
Commercialization, Nigeria, 215
Commission on Gender Equality, South
Africa, 244, 254, 265
Commission for the Promotion and
Protection of the Rights of
Cultural, Religious and Linguistic
Communities, 248, 254
Committee on the Elimination of Racial
Discrimination, recommendations
of, 64–65
Community Based Natural Resources
Management Programs, 62
Community Based Organizations
(CBOs), South Africa, 268
Compaore, Blaise
destabilization of Ghana, 25
and Kufour administration, 114, 115,
121
Congress Alliance, 237
Conservative Party, 239
Constitution
Botswana, 37–38, 71–72
Cote d'Ivoire, 85, 87
Interim South African, 241–242, 245
Kenyan, 154, 167
Nigeria, 227
South Africa, 17, 234, 236, 243–246,
259, 264

Constitutional Assembly (CA), South Africa, 240, 242–243
Constitutional Politics Model, 17–19
Constitutionalism, postcolonial state, 282–283
Convention for a Democratic South Africa (CODESA), 239–240
Convention on the Elimination of all Forms of Discrimination against Women, 255
Convention Peoples' Party (CPP), 120
Convention on the Rights of the Child (CRC), 263
"Cooperants," 92
Corporatist state, 91
Corruption
    in Botswana, 44
    in the Cote d'Ivoire, 91, 92
    in Ghana, 108, 116–117, 118
    in Kenya, 147–153, 169–170
    Kibaki government, 20–21, 165, 289
    Obasanjo government, 21–22
    in the postcolonial state, 284–285
    in South Africa, 235, 255–257, 270
    and state power, 12–13
    TI rankings, 152
Cote d'Ivoire
    colonial era, 82, 83–84
    economic privatization, 15t
    and France, 78–79, 92–93
    Gbagbo regime, 96
    Houphouet-Boigny regime, 89–93, 99
    human rights violations, 7
    independence, 85
    military coup, 24, 76, 85–87, 95
    peacekeeping operations, 5t
    precolonial era, 82
    recommendations, 96–98
    refugees in, 4
    state failure, 76, 77–79
    state reconstitution, 22, 23, 24
    unraveling of regime, 94–95
Credit Guarantee Scheme, 43
Creoles, 182, 185, 186, 190, 196, 201

Crime, state failure, 3
"Cultural capital," 201
Currency depreciation/devaluation
    in Ghana, 117, 117t, 285
    in Nigeria, 215, 219
Cushites, 127, 129

Dachala, Marcelo Moses, 115
Davidson, Basil, 80, 81, 97
de Klerk, F. W., 238–239
Debt. See Foreign debt
Defection law, 250–251
Defiance Campaign, 237
Deforestation, ECA report, 162–163
Democracy
    in Mauritius, 188–190
    in the postcolonial state, 286–287, 293
    in South Africa, 244–245
Democratic Alliance (DA), South Africa, 249, 251
"Democratic corporatism," 192
"Democratic game," 17
Democratic Party (DP), Kenya, 139, 140
Democratic Republic of the Congo
    human rights violations, 7
    peacekeeping operations, 5t
    refugees in, 4
"Democratization," 26, 221
Developmental state, 191–192
"Dialogue," 89, 94
Diamonds, Botswana, 38, 40, 41, 42, 44, 67–68
Discrimination
    in Botswana, 55
    in Kenya, 142
    San groups, 61
    in South Africa, 247–248, 265–266
District Commissioners (DC's), 130
District Officers (DO's), 130
Doe, Samuel, 208
Dommen, E., 194
Donatus state, 207
Doornbos, Martin, 135–136

East African Protectorate, 130

Economic Alliance for Arms Reduction-South Africa (Ecaar-SA), 246
Economic Commission for Africa (ECA), 3, 162
Economic Community of West African States (ECOWAS), 208
Economic and Financial Crime Commission (EFCC), 21
Education
   Kenya, 158, 161
   Mauritius, 183, 188, 189, 192, 199
   Nigeria, 215, 219
   postcolonial state, 289–290
   state failure, 3, 7–8
Egwu, Sam, 209
Eigen, Peter, 152
Elaigwu, Isawa, 229
Elections
   Ghana, 107, 119, 120
   Mauritius, 185, 189
   South Africa, 234–235
Electoral system
   Botswana, 52–53
   Mauritius, 186–188
Employment
   Ghana, 117
   Institutional Reform Model, 16, 17t
   Kenya, 159
   postcolonial state, 284
Englebert, Pierre, 80, 81
Environment
   Botswana, 39–40
   Kenya, 161–164
   South Africa, 235, 258–260
   state failure, 3
Ergas, Zaki, 79
Eritrea, 5t, 17
"Errand boy," 26
Esman, M., 200
Ethiopia, 5t, 16, 17
Ethnic conflict
   Mauritius, 186
   Nigeria, 223–225
"Ethnic mosaic," 292
Ethnic nationalism, 16

Ethnic pluralism, 291–292
Ethnicity
   African state failure, 79
   Botswana, 48–49, 60–65
   British Kenya, 131
   Cote d'Ivoire, 92, 97
   Ghana, 109–110
   Kenyan, 127, 128, 137, 141–147
   Mauritius, 184–185, 187, 195
   Nigeria, 209–210
   South Africa, 252
Evans, P., 191
Ewurade kasa (Speak O Lord), 105
Export industry, Ghana, 119
Export-Processing Zones (EPZs), 193, 195–196
Eyadema, Gnassingbe, 25, 114, 121

Fatton, Robert, 78, 79
Fauré, Yves, 90
Federalism, Nigeria, 227
Federation of South African Women, 237
First Decade of Development, 36, 66
Ford Asili (Ford-A), 139
Ford Kenya (Ford-K), 139, 140
Ford People, 140
Foreign aid
   Kenya, 136, 153
   Mauritius, 198–199
Foreign debt
   Ghana, 117
   Nigeria, 205, 215
Foreign investment
   postcolonial state, 285
   Nigeria, 213–214
"Forum for National Reconciliation," 86
"Forum for Political Reform," 226
Forum for Restoration of Democracy (FORD), 176n.53
France, and Cote d'Ivoire, 78–79, 92–93
Freedom Charter, ANC, 237
French colonial empire
   Cote d'Ivoire, 82, 83–84
   Mauritius, 184

"French connection," 78
French East India Company, 184
French-Mauritians, 185, 186
Front Populaire Ivoirien (PFI), 87, 95–96

Gabon, 162
Galla pastoralists, 129
Gandhi, Indira, 189
Gbagbo, Laurent
    civil war, 96
    election of, 23, 24, 95–96
    repressive regime, 86–87
Gender inequality. *See* Women
Ghana
    constitutionalism, 17
    currency devaluation, 117, 117t, 285
    current status, 120–121
    democratic transition, 105–106
    economic policies, 115–119
    economic privatization, 15t, 17t
    foreign policy, 113–115
    military's role, 109–113
    refugees in, 4
    state reconstitution, 22, 23, 24–25,
        119–120
Githongo, John, 20
Good, Kenneth, 49, 55, 59
Government of National Unity (GNU),
    242, 257
Gowon, Yakubu, 211
Graham, Paul, 250
Grand morcellement, 192
Gray, J., 200
Group Areas Act, 236, 238
Guardian, The, 21–22
Guei, General Robert
    military coup, 23, 85, 86
    "self-succession scheme," 95–96
Guinea, 4, 15t
Gulhati, R., 190
Gun control, 113, 123n.26

Hani, Chris, 240
"Haouphouet Phenomenon," 24, 96

Healthcare
    Kenya, 159–160, 161
    Mauritius, 183, 188
    postcolonial state, 291
    state failure, 3, 7–8
Hindus, Mauritius, 185–186
HIV/AIDS
    economic impact, 118
    Kenya, 160
    South Africa, 248–249, 258, 269
Hlope, Dumisane, 249
Holm, J.D., 48
"Holy War," 106
"Home-grown alternative," 215
Houphouet-Boigny, Felix
    French colonial era, 84, 88
    regime of, 89–93, 99
    relationship with France, 87–89, 92
    state failure, 79
    as "strongman," 78
    unraveling of state, 93–95
House Cleaning Exercise (HCE), 106
House of Chiefs, 50, 63, 64
Housing, postcolonial state, 290
Human Development Index,
    194–195
Human rights
    Botswana media criticism, 58
    Kenyan violations, 153–158
    in South Africa, 235, 252–255
Human rights violations, 6
Human Rights Commission, 248
Human Rights Violation
    Committee, 245
Human Rights Watch
    African conditions, 6–7
    on Zaki Biam massacre, 224
Human Science Research Council
    (HSRC), 251
Huxtable, Phillip, 80, 81

"Imagined communities," 185
Indenié, Kingdom of, 82
Industrialization, Botswana, 39, 67

Inflation
    Ghana, 118, 118t, 119, 285
    Nigeria, 220
Information and Communication
        Technology (ICT), 218, 219–220
Infrastructure
    Botswana, 40–41, 70
    Kenya, 167
    Nigeria, 220
    state failure, 3, 7–8
Inkatha Freedom Party (IFP)
    absence from CODESA talks, 239
    GNU, 242
    KwaZulu-Natal dominance, 250
Institutional Reform Model, 14–16
International Covenant on Civil and
        Political Rights, 255
International Covenant on Economic,
        Social and Cultural Rights, 255
International Monetary Fund (IMF)
    Botswana, 36–37
    postcolonial state, 285
    role of, 10
Isong, Clement, 211
Issah, Mallam Yusuf, 116–117
"*Ivoirité*," 24, 87, 98
Iyayi, Festus, 212

Jackson, Robert, 91
Japan, 191
Johannesburg World Summit on
        Sustainable Development, 164
Jordan, Pallo, 270–271
Joseph, James A., 234
Judicial Service Committee (JDC),
        168–169
Judiciary (Botswana)
    citizen activism, 60
    ethnic discrimination, 63
    gender equality, 58
Judiciary (Kenya)
    corrupt practices, 150, 151
    state reconstruction, 167–169
Judiciary (Nigeria), 289

Kaba, Ahmed Tejan, 208
Kalenjin people
    ethnic conflicts, 143
    resource allocations, 141, 142
Katende, João, 115
Katzenstein, P., 192
Kempton Park Multiparty negotiations,
        239–240
Kenya
    African socialism, 133–135
    colonial state, 130–133, 147–148, 172
    democratization of, 13–14
    economic development, 135–137
    economic privatization, 15t
    economic reforms, 166–167
    ethnic allocations, 141–142
    ethnic conflict, 142–147, 170
    ethnic diversity, 127, 128, 129
    gender issues, 158–161
    human rights violations, 153–158
    independence, 133, 140, 172
    Kibaki government, 20–21
    multiparty system, 138–139
    political/civil liberties, 289
    precolonial society, 128–130
    security sector investment, 170–171
    single party rule/state, 10, 138
    state reconstitution, 22, 25, 157–158,
        160–161, 165–173
Kenya African Democratic Union
        (KADU), 137, 138
Kenya African National Union (KANU)
    defeat of, 20, 138, 164, 289
    ethnic politics, 137, 138
    formation of, 13, 127–138
    multiparty elections, 140
Kenya People's Union (KPU), 138
Kenya Seed Company (KSC),
        149, 150
Kenyatta, Jomo
    economic development, 134–135
    Kikuyu favoritism, 141, 142
    on opposition politics, 10
    state reconstruction, 25, 165–166

Kenyatta, Uhuru, 139
Kgalagadi people, 48–49, 64
Khama, Seretse, 52
Kibaki, Mwai
    election of, 164–165
    governance of, 20–21
    on Kenya, 13–14
    NARC candidate, 140
    plans of, 289
    state reconstitution, 25, 165
Kibera incident, 146
Kieh, George Klay, Jr.
    lessons learned, 27
    state reconstitution, 23
Kikuyu people
    ethnic conflicts, 143, 144
    resource allocations,
        141, 142
Kong, Kingdom of, 82
Korea, 191
Krindjabo, Kingdom of, 82
Kufour, John Agyekum
    economic policies, 115–119
    election of, 105, 107
    evaluation of, 120–121
    foreign policy, 113–115
    governance of, 24–25, 110
    military's role, 109–113
Kulah, Matthew, 207
Kuria, Gibson Kamau, 155
KwaZulu-Natal, IFP dominance, 250
Kwesi-Aning, Emmanuel, 24–25

La Baule Doctrine, 93
Laakso, L., 217
Land, Botswana, 36, 37–38, 50
Language
    Kenyan diversity, 129
    Mauritian Creole, 184
    South Africa, 247
Le repli tactique (tactical retreat), 87, 91
Leadership
    failure of, 5–6
    single party rule, 10
    state failure, 77–78

Leftwich, A., 191
"Legitimacy deficit," 81
Liberal Democratic Party (LDP), 139, 140
Liberia, 4, 5t
Limann, Hilla, 106, 122n.6
Local Native Councils (LNCs), 130,
    131–132
LOME Convention, 197
Lonsdale, John, 129
Lost Decade of Development, 42

Maasai pastoralists, 129, 143, 144
Macmillan, Harold, 210
Mahama, Alhaji Aliu, 118
Makoba, Wagona, 172
Malaise creole, 196, 197, 200–201
Malawi, 17
Malhebe, Rassie, 254
Malinke Empire, 82
Maloka, Eddie, 252
Maloka, Victoria, 26–27
Mamdani, Mahmood, 50
Mandel, Nelson, 28, 237, 263, 266
Mantu, Ibrahim, 227–228
Marx, Karl, 79–80, 207
Mascarene group, 184
Masire, Ketumile, 52
Master Plan of Education, 199
Matiba, Kenneth, 155
Mauritian Labor Party (MLP), 189, 193
Mauritius
    colonial era, 184–186
    democratization of, 183–184, 188–190
    developmental state, 183, 193
    economic challenges, 183, 197–200
    independence, 186–190
    political/civil liberties, 288
    postcolonial period, 182
    social inequality, 194–197
    state reconstitution, 22, 25–26,
        200–201
Mauritius Export Processing Zones
    Association (MEPZA), 198
Maxon, Robert, 133, 147
Mbaku, John Mukum, 256, 283, 292

Mbeki, Thabo
  "African Renaissance," 260–261
  international relations, 262
  political change, 270
Meade Report, 193, 194
Médard, Jean François, 77, 90
Media(Botswana), government critic,
    58–59
Migrant labor, 35, 39, 72n.7
"Militaristic presidency," 288–289
Military coups
  Cote d'Ivoire, 24, 76, 85–87, 95
  Ghana, 105, 106
  Nigeria, 215
Military, Ghana, 109–111
Mkandawire, T., 182
Modernization agenda
  Botswana, 40–41
  Western role, 35–36
Moi, Daniel arap. See arap Moi, Daniel
Mombasa, 145–146, 157
Moral Summit, 256
Mouvement Militant Mauricien
    (MMM) Party, 188, 189
Mozambique, 15t
Muite, Paul, 155
Multifibre Agreement (MFA), 197
Muslims
  Mauritius, 185
  Nigeria, 209

N'Diaye, Boubacar, 24
Nabudere, Dan, 221
Nairobi, 146, 156–157
Nakuru District, 143
Nalhari, R., 190
Nandi pastoralists, 129
Nangulu-Ayuku, Ann, 25
Narok District, 143
Nation-state, postcolonial, 80
National Action Plan for the Protection
    and Promotion of Human Rights
    (NAP), 253
National Alliance (Party) of Kenya
    (NAK), 139

National Anti-Corruption Initiative, 256
National Cereals and Produce Board
    (NCPB), 149, 150
"National conference" movement, 96
National Democratic Convention
    (NDC) party
  defeat of, 23
  formation of, 107
  recent elections, 119, 120
National Development Bank
    (Botswana), 39, 58
National Development Party (NDP),
    139
National Environmental Policy, 259
National Independent Electoral
    Commission, 115
National Micro-Credit Scheme,
    Botswana, 43
National Party
  apartheid policies, 236, 238
  CODESA talks, 239
  GNU, 242
  talks with ANC, 239
National question, 235, 247–249
National Rainbow Coalition (NARC),
    139–140, 164–165
National Redemption Council (NRC),
    105, 121n.2
National Unity and Reconciliation Act,
    245
National Youth Action Plan, 263
National Youth Commission, 263
National Youth Parliament, 264
Native Hut and Poll Tax Ordinance,
    131
Ndikumana, Leonce, 14
New African Initiative, 3
New KANU, 139
New National Party (NNP), 249–250,
    251
New Partnership for African
    Development (NEPAD)
  Nigeria, 220
  South Africa, 235, 261–262,
    264–265, 270

New Patriotic Party (NPP)
  economic policies, 116–117
  foreign policy, 114
  governing party, 108–109
  recent elections, 119, 120
  slogan, 108
  victory of, 105–106
"New World Order," 217
Ng'ethe, Njuguma, 78
Nigeria
  call for power-sharing, 16
  colonial era, 206, 208–209
  corruption, 13
  currency devaluation, 285
  economic management, 205–206
  economic privatization, 14–15,
    15t–16t
  foreign policy, 208, 213–214
  globalization era, 206, 217–221
  "militaristic presidency," 288–289
  Obasanjo government, 20, 21–22,
    209–210
  oil boom era, 206, 211–214
  oil bust era, 206, 214–217
  oil legacy, 207–210
  postcolonial era, 206, 210–211
  refugees in, 4
  and South Africa, 260
  state characteristics, 207–208
  state reconstitution, 22–23, 26
  state reconstitution tasks, 226–228
Nigerian Labor Congress (NLC), 222
Nilote people, 127, 129
Non-Communist Manifesto, 36
Nyachae, Simeon, 152–153
Nyanza Provinces, 142–143
Nyerere, Julius, 6

O'Brien, Donald Cruise, 78, 94
Obasanjo, Olusegun
  Abacha family deal, 212
  "born-again" Christian, 292
  governance of, 21
  Ikeja Cantonment visit, 225
  impeachment proceedings, 209–210
  at Kufour inauguration, 114
  messiah, 289
  "militaristic presidency," 288
  NEPAD, 220
  Nigeria as trading post, 211
  Zaki Biam massacre, 224
Ochieng', William, 127, 128
Odi Massacre, 221, 223, 225
Odua People's Congress, 220
Office of the Status of Women, 265
Ogbeh, Audu, 288, 289
Oil
  Kenya's consumption, 135
  Nigerian boom, 206, 211–214
  Nigerian bust, 206, 214–217
  and Nigerian state, 207–208
Okiek people, 127
Olukoshi, Adebayo, 217, 279
Osafo-Maafo, Yaw, 117
Othman, S., 212
Ouattara, Alassane Dramane, 87, 95
Ouattara Dynasty, 82
Ouko, Robert, 154–155

"Pacification," 83–84
Pan African Congress (PAC)
  absence fromCODESA talks, 239
  banning of, 237
  black opposition party, 250
Pan South African Language Board, 248
Pan-African Student Organization
    (PASO), 238
*Parti Democratic de Cote d'Ivoire-
    Rassemblement Democratique
    Africain* (PDCI-RDA), 84, 88, 90
Parti mauricien social democrate
    (PMSD), 189
Patrimonial state, 79
Patrimony, 207, 208
Pensions, 199–200
People's Democratic Party (PDP), 288
People's National Convention (PNC), 120
People's National Party (PNP), 106
Peterson, Hector, 238
Picard, L., 49

Police force (Kenya)
corrupt practices, 150–151
human rights violations, 155, 156
reconstitution of, 170–171
"Politics of the belly," 79
"Polygamous existence," 127
Popular sovereignty, 10
Postcolonial state
African traditions, 281
basic human needs, 289–290
character of, 280–281
and civil society, 288
constitutionalism, 282–283
economic development, 282
economic role, 283–286
ethnic pluralism, 291–292
expectations of, 8, 9
gender equality, 290–291
governance deficit, 286–287
as nation-state, 80
nature of, 280
political/civil liberties, 288
political parties, 287
religious pluralism, 292
security, 290
Poverty, 201
Power-Sharing Model, 16
Prebendalism, 207–208
Private ownership, 134
Privatization
Botswana, 43–44, 68–69
economic, 14–15, 15t–16t
Kenya, 136, 137
Nigeria, 215
postcolonial state, 286
public places, 163–164
Produce Marketing Boards, 209
Progress Party, 105
Prostitution, 195
Protectorate, 34, 39
Provisional Commissioners (PC's), 130
Provisional National Defense Council
(PNDC), 105, 107
Public Order Act (1971), 188–189
Public Protector, 244, 256

Public Service Anti-corruption
Conference, 256
Public Service Commission, 256
Purges, "1963 events," 91

Racial segregation, 236. *See also*
Discrimination
Rainbow Coalition, 139. *See also* National
Rainbow Coalition (NARC)
Rawlings, Jerry John
end of rule, 23
executions of, 121n.2
military council, 112n.5
military coups, 106
political activity, 122n.6
transition, 24–25
Reconstruction and Development
Program (RDP), 257–258, 269
Refugees, 3–4
Religious pluralism, 292
Remote Area Dwellers strategy, 41
Rent seeking, 207
Reparations and Rehabilitation
Committee, 245
Representation, 61, 63
Republic of Botswana, 45. *See also*
Botswana
Reunion, Mascarene group, 184
Rift valley, ethnic conflicts, 142–143,
144, 146
Rio Conference on Environment and
Development, 259
Rodrigues, Mascarene group, 184
Rosberg, Carl, 91
Rostow, W. W., 36
Roy, S., 36, 37, 67
Rubia, Charles, 155
Rwanda, 4

Saitoti, George, 139
Sakasso, Kingdom of, 82
San groups
development strategy, 41, 61–63
media attention, 58–59
SAP rebellion, 221, 222

Savimbi, Jonas, 115, 124–125n.35
Second Independence Movement, 13
Security
   Nigeria, 220
   postcolonial state, 290
"Security family," 111
"Security sector," 110, 111–113
Seekings, Jeremy, 267
Selolwane, Onalenna, 24
Selormey, Victor, 116
Sen, Amartya, 196
Sharia, Nigeria, 209
Sierra Leone, 4, 5t
Singer, H., 36, 37, 67
Singhi, Laxmi, 244
Sisulu, Walter, 237
Skocpol, Theda, 191
Slavery, 184
Small Business Council, 43
Small, Medium, and Micro-Enterprises
   (SMME) policy, 43
Social contract, 216–217
Social Democratic Party (SDP), 139,
   140
"Social dialogue," 193
Sokoto Caliphate, 206
Soludo, C., 182
Solway, J., 48–49
Somalia, 11
South Africa
   anti-corruption strategies, 235,
      255–257, 270
   apartheid era, 234, 235–239
   and Botswana, 34, 35
   constitutional dispensation, 233
   constitutionalism, 17, 234, 236,
      241–246, 259, 264
   continental relations, 260–263
   economic policies, 235, 257–258
   environmental policies, 235,
      258–260
   exceptionalism, 269
   GNU, 242, 257, 263
   human rights, 235, 252–255
   inherited government, 234–239
   political parties, 234–235, 249–251
   state reconstitution, 22, 26–27
South African Communist Party
   (SACP), 237, 240
South African Congress of Trade
   Unions, 237
South African Human Rights
   Commission (SAHRC), 244, 253,
   254–255
South African Native National
   Congress. *See* African National
   Congress (ANC)
South African NGO Coalition
   (SANGOCO), 257
Soweto uprising, 238
State, definition of, 77
"State bourgeoisie," 90
"State in a Changing World, The," 181
State Deconstruction Model, 19
*State Legitimacy and Development in
   Africa*, 80
Stockholm Declaration, 259
Stockwell, Graham, 169
"Stolen verdict," 107
"Strongman," 78
Structural Adjustment Program (SAP)
   as human experiment, 217
   Nigeria, 208, 216–217
   Mauritius, 183, 189
   postcolonial state, 285
   state legitimacy, 181–182
Subdivisions, 84
Sudan, 4
Sugar industry, 184
Sugar tax, 193–194
Supreme Military Council (SMC) II, 106
Swahili city states, 129
Switzerland, 13
Syndicat Agricole Africain (SAA), 88

Taiwan, 191
Tanzania
   economic privatization, 15t

refugees in, 4
and South Africa, 260
Taxation
colonial Kenya, 130–131, 133
Nigeria, 208
Textiles, 197
Third colonial occupation, 221
"Third Wave of Democratization," 13, 17
Tignor, Robert, 147
Togo, 17t, 114–115
Torture, 155
Toungara, Jeanne, 97
Toure, Amadou Toumani, 262
Touré, Samory, 83
Trade liberalization, 215, 219
Transparency International (TI)
on Kenyan corruption, 150–152
on Nigerian corruption, 21
Transparency International–South
Africa (TI-SA), 257
Tribal Grazing Land Policy (TGLP), 62
Tribal Police, 132
Tribal Territories Act, 64
Truth and Reconciliation Commission
(TRC), 245–246
Tswana people, 48, 58–59, 63, 64, 65
Turkana pastoralists, 127, 129, 143–144
Turner, Teresa, 211

Ubuntu (humanity), 248
Uganda, 4, 17
*União Naçional para a Indepêndencia
Total de Angola* (UNITA), 115
United Democratic Movement (UDM),
140
United Nations
Botswana ethnic discrimination, 64–65
First Development Decade, 36
human rights conventions, 255, 263
peacekeeping operations, 4, 5t
United Nations Population Fund
(UNFPA), 159
United States, modernization agenda,
35–36

"Velvet revolution," 107
Villalon, Leonardo, 80, 81
"Virtual deification," 89
Vision 2020 Report, 188, 195

Wamwere, Koigi wa, 155
Wanga, Kingdom of, 128
Wayei of Ngamiland, 63–64
"We Want the Bodies," 121–122n.2
Weber, Max
African state failure, 79–81
definition of the state, 77
"Welfare state," 26
West Africa, 4, 208
Western Provinces, 142
Williams, Gavin, 208–209
Women
Botswana political mobilization, 55–60
Kenyan gender inequality, 158–161
Kenyan state reconstruction, 167
Mauritian inequality, 182, 183, 190,
193, 201
Mauritian labor force, 195–196
Mauritian prostitution, 193
postcolonial state, 290–291
in South Africa, 263, 265–266
Women in Law and Development in
Africa (WILDAF), 198
Women's Association, Botswana,
55, 56
Woods, Dwayne, 91
World Bank
ADP, 221–222
Botswana, 36–37
role of, 10, 218, 219
and state failure, 38
World Development Report
on the Mauritian electoral system, 187
on the state, 181
World Investment Bank, 199
World Trade Organization, 197

Yacé, Philippe, 90
Yan banga, 220

Young, Crawford, 80–81, 83, 85
Youth, South African, 238, 263

Zaki Biam Massacre, 221, 223–224,
225

Zambia
economic privatization, 15t, 17t
and South Africa, 260
Zartman, I. William, 75
Zolberg, Aristide, 89, 97